THE COLLEGE GUIDEBOOK: MECHANICAL ENGINEERING

University Profiles & Admissions Information on the Top University Programs

Rachel A. Winston, Ph.D.

Lizard Publishing is not sponsored by any college. While data was derived by school, state, or nationally published sources, some statistics may be out of date as published sources vary widely based upon the date of submission and currency of numbers. Attempts were made to obtain the best information during the writing of this book from, NCES, U.S. Census Bureau, U.S. Department of Education, Common Data Set, College Board, U.S. News & World Report, college, and organizational sites. Descriptions of colleges are a compilation of college website information as well as student, faculty, and staff interviews with individuals and often from unique experiences and impressions. Attempts were made to triangulate multiple points of light. If you would like to share program information, data, or an impression of a specific college, please write to Lizard Publishing at the address below or at the e-mail address: *collegeguide@yahoo.com*

ISBN 978-1958558089 (hardback); 978-1958558096 (paperback); 978-1958558201 (e-book)

LCCN: 2023906816

© Copyright 2023 Lizard Publishing. All rights reserved.

All rights reserved. No part of this work may be reproduced or transmitted in any form or by any means, including, but not limited to, photocopying, recording, image capture, electronic, mechanical or any other information storage and retrieval systems, without the express written permission from Lizard Publishing.

Lizard Publishing, 7700 Irvine Center Drive, Suite 800, Irvine, CA 92618 *www.lizard-publishing.com*

Lizard Publishing creates, designs, produces, and distributes books and resources to provide academic, admissions, and career information. Our mental process is fueled by three tenets:

- Ignite the hunger to learn and the passion to make a difference
- Illuminate the expanse of knowledge by sharing cutting edge thinking
- Innovate to create a world that makes the transition from dreams to reality

We work with academic leaders who transform the educational landscape to publish relevant content and advise students of their educational and professional options, with the aim of developing 21st-century learners and leaders. We also work with students to publish their books and present widely diverse ideas to the college/graduate school-bound community. With headquarters in Irvine, California, Lizard Publishing works virtually with authors to edit, publish, and distribute both hard copy and paperback books.

This book was published in the U.S.A. Lizard Publishing is a premium quality provider of educational reference, career guidance, and motivational publications/merchandise for global learners, educators, and stakeholders in education.

Book design by Michelle Tahan *www.michelletahan.com*

Book formatting by Obinna Chinemerem Ozuo

Book website: *www.collegelizard.com*

LIZARD PUBLISHING

This book is dedicated to John Smart who never stopped innovating, imagining, and inventing a better future for society.

ACKNOWLEDGMENTS

There is never enough room to acknowledge every person. Numerous people contributed to my perspective about design and engineering. Students, faculty, counselors, and researchers assisted in enhancing my knowledge base or taught me indelible lessons. Over a lifetime of experiences working with students, I am wiser and more worldly.

I gratefully acknowledge Michelle Tahan, Jasmine Jhunjhnuwala, E. Liz Kim, Jacqueline Xu, and Chenoa Robbins as well as my family, friends, colleagues, and professors. With profound gratitude, I also acknowledge those I have known in the universes of design and engineering.

As a faculty member in the UCLA College Counseling Certificate Program, I met many dedicated counselors who spend their life serving and supporting students. Meaningful contributions to the book have been made indirectly by admissions representatives, college counselors, and faculty members who took a special interest in this book's success.

> *"If I see so far, it is because I stand on the shoulders of giants."*
> — Isaac Newton

I would also like to thank the thousands of students I have taught, counseled, or supported in my nearly four decades of service.

Isaac Newton once said, "If I see so far, it is because I stand on the shoulders of giants." A few of those giants whose broad shoulders lifted me higher and helped teach invaluable lessons include Courtney Crisp, Bob Denton, Arman Ramezani, Fred Feldon, Mark Harbison, Gail Nichols, Karyn Holtzman, Rachel Sobel, Andrew Hunter, Ed Goul, JT Geehr, Barbara Pasalis, Shan Schumacher, Eric Hanzich, and Joe DeBilio.

Finally, there would be no book on university's for mechanical engineering and no career in college admissions counseling without the support of Robert Helmer, whose tireless efforts support me every single day.

ABOUT THE AUTHOR

Dr. Rachel A. Winston is a tireless student advocate. She has served the educational community as a university professor, college advisor, statistician, researcher, author, cryptanalyst, motivational speaker, publishing executive, and lifelong student. As one of the leading experts in college counseling and an award-winning faculty member, Dr. Winston has spent her lifetime learning, teaching, mentoring, and coaching students. Her counseling practice centers around college admissions, college essays, portfolios, and intellectual conversations about life and career pursuits.

She started college at thirteen and graduated from college majoring in such widely ranging disciplines as chemistry, mathematics, computers, liberal arts, international relations, negotiation, conflict resolution, peacebuilding, business administration, higher education leadership, interpreting, college counseling, and publishing. Throughout her education, she attended and graduated from Harvard, University of Chicago, University of Texas, GWU, UCLA, Syracuse, CSUF, CSUDH, Pepperdine, Claremont Graduate University, and Gallaudet University.

Her position working in Washington, D.C. on Capitol Hill and with the White House in the 1980s took her to approximately a hundred universities training campaign managers at colleges from Colorado to California, thoroughly dotting the western states. Later, she led college tours with students and their families on road trips throughout the United States. She has taught or counseled thousands of students over her career and speaks at conferences and academic programs throughout the world.

As a professor and avid writer for numerous publications, she won the 2012 McFarland Literary Achievement Award, Bletchley Park Cryptanalyst Award, and numerous other awards, including Faculty Member of the Year, Leadership Tomorrow Leader of the Year, and college service and leadership awards. While studying Human Capital at Claremont Graduate University, she was a scholarship recipient at the Drucker School of Management. She was also elected to the statewide Board of Governors for the Faculty Association for California Community Colleges, where she served on the executive committee.

She also served as a faculty member for the UCLA College Counselor Certificate Program and the Director of Mathematics at Brandman University. She taught at Embry Riddle Aeronautical University, Chapman University, Cal State Fullerton, and a handful of California Community Colleges, including Cerro Coso College where she represented the entire faculty as the Academic Senate President and retired in 2016. Over her career, she taught mathematics on television, in small and large lecture halls, online, and via live interactive satellite and telecourses.

AUTHOR'S NOTE

You are reading this book because you are considering admission to colleges where you open the doors to the world of design, engineering, and creativity. Whatever route you took to get to this point, you are in the right place. Right now, you need to gather information to make informed decisions.

While many people offer advice, suggestions differ. Friends will tell you the 'right' way or the way their neighbor was accepted. Graciously accept this anecdotal information, pursuing projects, analytics, and imaginative artistry with your heart and mind as you commit to learning more.

Dig deeper to consider both expert and current information from counselors who have worked with hundreds of students. Changes in programs, curricula, requirements, and links happen each year.

Doublecheck each program's specifics yourself. Most of the profiles are current as of March 2023. However, since researching this book, changes may have taken place. There are other college guidebooks written by talented and experienced counselors, though none are like this book on college programs for mechanical engineering. Nevertheless, I admire and cheer on their efforts.

> *"We are what we think. All that we are arises with our thoughts. With our thoughts, we make the world."*
> *— Buddha*

This book, providing lists of colleges and admissions information is different in that it also offers unique tidbits. I hope you find the information valuable. Your job is to begin early by assembling lists of possible schools to consider. Create a road map and set yourself on a clear path.

If you see an error in this book or even a suggestion for a future edition, please write to Dr. Rachel Winston at collegeguide@yahoo.com. We will fix the entry with the next printed version. All of that said, this book was written with you in mind.

This book contains a wealth of information. Meanwhile, there are also Internet sites that contain free downloads, FAQs, testimonials, and offers to help you with your applications. Some of these advisors are knowledgeable and provide valuable assistance. Unfortunately, students and parents hunt around the web, searching for a tremendous number of hours to seek the information they need. This book aims to resolve this problem with college admissions data and profiles to make your search easier.

For now, though, I will assume you want to attend college to study mechanical engineering and are exploring this book to find a program that will get you on your way toward your goal. You are undoubtedly a talented candidate who is willing to work very hard. In these programs, you will explore your creative mental capabilities while collaborating in hands-on lab projects. To begin, mastery of physics, chemistry, and technology are requirements for success.

As you investigate colleges, you will find differences in programs, equipment, methods, priorities, or first-year requirements. At some schools, you will not declare an engineering discipline until your second year. Either way, this book will help you reach your goal. Applying to and writing essays for each application will require research. Discover why each program you are considering may be right for you and determine the specific reasons why you are a good fit.

While you might believe that engineering schools are relatively similar, each program's nuances make them unique. These small differences may seem confusing. My goal is to demystify the information and process.

CONTENTS

Chapter 1: Mechanical Engineering – Past, Present, & Future   1

Chapter 2: Expectations & Training: Engineering High-Tech, Environmentally Conscious Systems   11

Chapter 3: Academic Preparation & Career Options: Opportunities for Mechanical Engineers   23

Chapter 4: Summer Programs & Internships for High School & College Students   33

Chapter 5: University Options: College Programs for Engineering   57

Chapter 6: College Degrees: Timing, Location, Costs, & Earning Power   65

Chapter 7: College Admissions: Terms, Data, Applications, Tests, Essays, Recommendations, & Resume   75

Chapter 8: Financial Aid and Scholarships: Finding Money To Pay for College   99

Chapter 9: Post Pandemic Employment Outlook: Statistics and Economic Projections   109

Chapter 10: Next Steps: Preparation and Real-World Skills   119

Chapter 11: Region One - Northeast   132

Chapter 12: Region Two - Midwest	164
Chapter 13: Region Three - South	184
Chapter 14: Region Four - West	204
Chapter 15: Top 12 Mechanical Engineering Programs	224
Chapter 16: Top Mechanical Engineering Schools – Alphabetical by State	226
Chapter 17: Top Mechanical Engineering Schools by Admit Rate and Undergraduate Enrollment	230
Chapter 18: Abet Accredited Mechanical Engineering Programs	236
Chapter 19: Top Programs for Aerospace Engineering	248
Chapter 20: Top Programs for Chemical, Petroleum, & Nuclear Engineering	252
Index	264

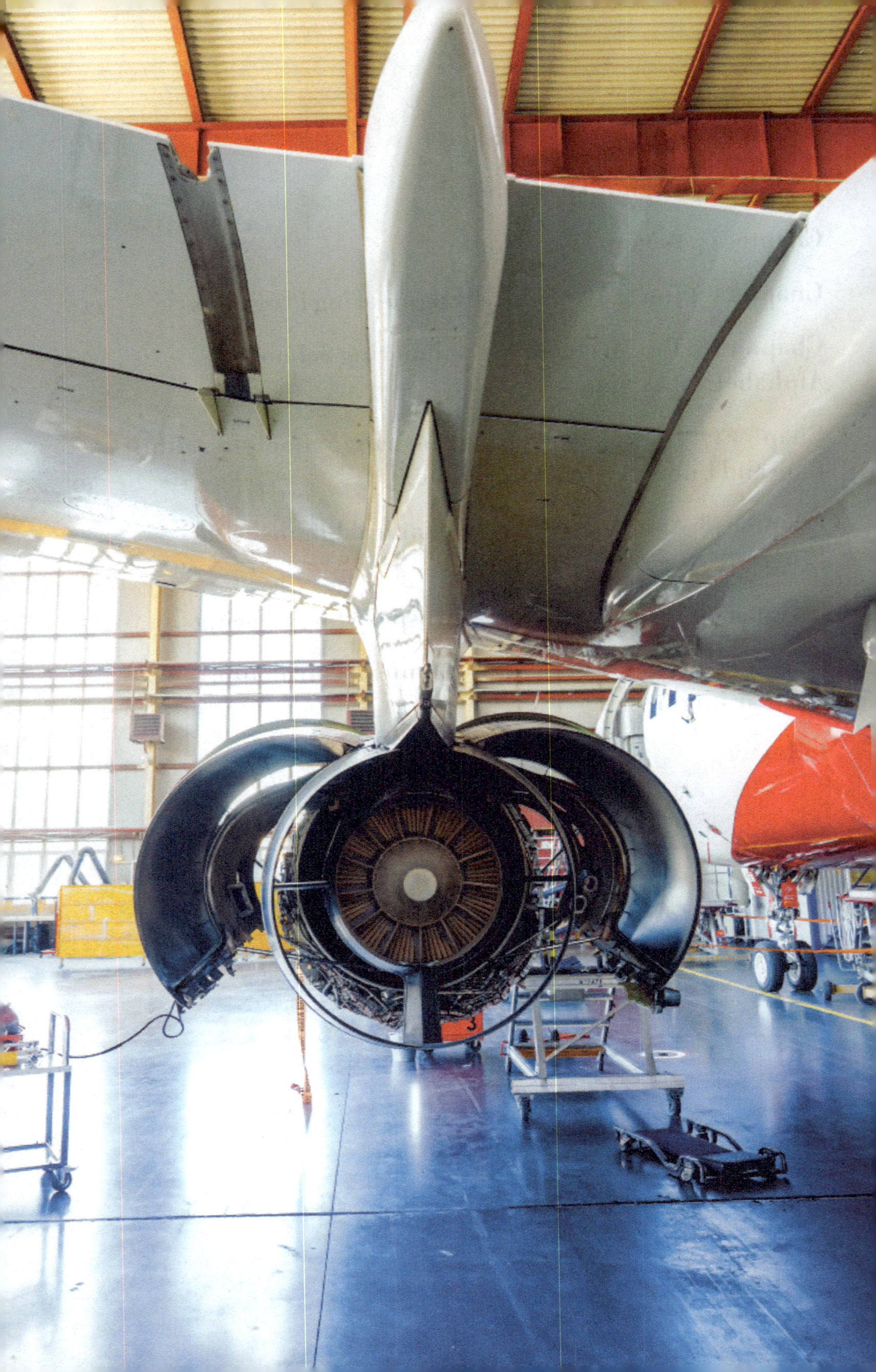

CHAPTER 1

MECHANICAL ENGINEERING – PAST, PRESENT, & FUTURE

"Scientists dream about doing great things. Engineers do them."

— **James A. Michener**

Mechanical engineers improve the way we live and work by automating society, creating 'green' vehicles, developing biomechanical devices, researching nanotechnology/microscale processes, and making robots more human. Mechanical engineers are at the forefront of transportation development – bikes, boats, cars, conveyors, drones, elevators, escalators, planes, robots, trains, and wheelchairs. Career and research opportunities include the improvement of suspension, transmission, aerodynamics, and power.

Problems that confound society can be resolved with improved sensing devices, touch displays, heat/cooling mechanisms, and vision capabilities. The bodies of water that divide us can bring us together through a mutual commitment to collaborate resolve challenges and make this world better than ever before. Mechanical engineers improve our interconnected relationship between work, transportation, family, and fun. With numerous avenues you can pursue, mechanical engineering is one of the most versatile degrees you can obtain.

I am impressed with the urgency of doing.
Knowing is not enough; we must apply.
Being willing is not enough; we must do.

- Leonardo da Vinci

CAREER OPTIONS WITH A MECHANICAL ENGINEERING DEGREE

- Aerospace
- Automotive
- Biomechanics
- Biotechnology
- Chemical
- Computer Technology
- Construction
- Defense
- Electronics
- Engineering Design
- Entrepreneurship
- Fuels & Energy
- Intellectual Property
- Car Manufacturing
- Materials and Metals
- Patent Law
- Pharmaceuticals
- Production/Process Control
- Project Management
- Quality Control
- Research and Development
- Robotics
- Sales
- Surgical Robotics/Instrumentation
- Transportation Technology
- Thermal Process/Thermodynamics
- Virtual Reality, Metaverse

ORIGINS OF MECHANICAL ENGINEERING

From apes to Neanderthals to Homo Sapiens, the legacy of mechanical engineering began with cutting and molding to create cooking and hunting tools. 'Designed', 'redesigned', and reimagined over the next few millennia, early humans began to hunt, cook, and eat, using materials and equipment developed with the 'high technology' of the day. Albeit, primitive compared to today's high-tech industrialization, put yourself in their shoes; they did the best they could living in the jungle with only stones, wood, mud, leaves, twine, vines, fruit, and animals.

Living in caves or huts, they began their journey into fabrication and molding. They soon transformed hides, furs, and leaves into rudimentary clothing. Artisans used form, shape, and function to crafted bowls, vessels, and tools. Skillbuilding led to crafts, which in turn led to trades. A few thousand years ago there were specialists in stone toolmaking, hide production, ornamental design, pottery craftsmanship, fire building, wood carving, hunting tools, and epicurean treats.

Mechanical engineering's emergence 4,000 to 6,000 years ago mirrored humankind's development as needs arose with transportation, buildings, water, and resources. As people left their temporary cave dwellings, abandoned their nomadic lifestyle, and sought permanent shelter, mechanical engineering deepened its roots. In Egypt, Mesopotamia, and the Indus Valley crossing a river by laying tree trunks was replaced with cutting tools that sliced wood and vines that strapped them together to make rafts.

Inclined planes aided material transport while the wheel and axle originated in Mesopotamia in 5200–4700 BC. The lever, invented in 5,000 BC and found in Egypt in 4,400 BC, helped lift massive and heavy objects like stones and obelisks.

Metalworkers came next as did shipbuilders. Okay, maybe they started with wooden rafts, but navigating a river, lake, or sea was very important for transportation. Experimenting with lightweight materials, buoyancy, and binding options, they conducted 'research'. Every new product developed a few millennia ago needed to be tested, remodeled, and retested. Horses offered excellent transportation and cows were strong enough to plow fields.

In 250 BC, Archimedes' writings speak about mechanical objects, planes, cranes, and levers. The Archimedes screw, a hollow cylinder with a spiral inside, invented around 250 BC, served as an important tool to draw water from wells. This positive displacement pump traps fluid. Then, by twisting, the water continually moves up to where it is retrieved.

Give me a lever long enough and a fulcrum on which to place it, and I shall move the world.

- Archimedes

The Egyptian pyramids represent one of the greatest engineering feats of all time. More than 100 pyramids remain in Egypt today. The oldest pyramid was constructed more than 4,000 years ago. The lack of water in the Egyptian desert demanded innovative engineering design for discovery, drilling, and storage. In ancient Mesopotamia, water channels called Qanats, built 3,000 years ago transported water from wells and aquifers for agriculture and human consumption.

The engineer has been, and is, a maker of history.
— **James Kip Finch**

The Persian Empire in the 4th-century BC brought water wheels and watermills while steam-powered devices were developed in ancient Rome. The Chinese developed gears for vehicles and chain drives.

Thatched-roofed buildings were commonplace, as were methods for primitive airflow, heating, cooling, water, food, and lifestyle. Over time, cities became enclaves for craftspeople who produced a variety of goods. The Renaissance transformed medicine, politics, art, and life. *The Book of Ingenious Devices*, written by Al-Jazari in 1206, gives a testament to inventions and engineering marvels.

One of the most significant developments was the printing press, which allowed for the transmission of information as scientific progress and communication technologies gained steam - literally. In 1657, Christiaan Huygens invented the pendulum clock while Isaac Newton developed his Laws of Motion. Both Isaac Newton in England and Gottfried Wilhelm Leibniz in Germany simultaneously developed the calculus, though their notations differ and the symbols Leibniz developed are commonly used today.

Steel and steam transformed society into the burgeoning industrial revolution. Manufacturing innovations led to automation and mass-production. With these changes, industrialization took off, harnessing mechanization, labor, cost reductions, and rapid production. Efficiencies allowed for the quick construction and assembly of furniture, musical instruments, and household items. Millions of people were able to access goods never before available to the average family.

With the Industrial Revolution, mechanical engineering took off as a field. Machine tools and mechanized devices were needed and developed. One of the key inventions was the engine. In 1791, John Barber patented a gas turbine, Meanwhile, Thomas Mead patented a gas engine; Robert Street patented an internal-combustion engine three years later. Patent applications for the inventions of bikes, boats, and other vehicles came soon afterward. Many of these names you know today - Nicolaus Otto, Gottlieb Daimler, Rudolf Diesel, Karl Benz, Robert Goddard, Heinkel He, and Felix Wankel.

The first formal group of mechanical engineers, the Institution of Mechanical Engineers, was gathered in 1847. The American Society of Mechanical Engineers (ASME) was formed in 1880. The formalization of the field continued with the development of the Accreditation Board for Engineering and Technology (ABET), which was founded in 1932 as the Engineers' Council for Professional Development (ECPD) to certify, approve, and oversee engineering departments and degrees. Presently, there are approximately 4,307 accredited programs in 846 institutions and 41 countries.

FIRST COLLEGES TEACHING MECHANICAL ENGINEERING

The first colleges to teach mechanical engineering began in France and Germany, though England soon began teaching this discipline. In 1802, the U.S. Military Academy at West Point was established. In 1817, the Academy created a program to teach students engineering. Norwich University, founded in 1819, created an engineering program. However, the first degree in engineering in the U.S. was conferred in 1835 at Rensselaer Polytechnic University. James Watt (1736 – 1819) who graduated from the University of Glasgow is considered the 'Father of Mechanical Engineering'. As a Scottish inventor, he improved the steam engine, creating the Watt steam engine in 1776.

MECHANICAL ENGINEERING'S FUTURE BEGINS TODAY

Committed to solving complex engineering challenges, mechanical engineers invent the future. Mechanical engineers can savor a job well-done while individuals go about their daily business. With innovations in technology, energy, and communication, people will no longer make calls on a land telephone line or drive a gasoline-fueled car in much the same way as they no longer type on a typewriter.

Our walls will become massive computer monitors, bathroom mirrors will have embedded televisions, and building materials will be stronger, thinner, and more durable than ever. Solar, self-driving cars, geolocated on kinetic roads and powered by not-yet-invented wireless technologies will transform the future. Drones will construct buildings, deliver mail, and transport people. This moment is exciting. Technological innovation is disrupting every facet of life. Thus, we live in a time when rapid change will require that we think differently.

The future of humanity depends on engineering. You live at a critical juncture where 5G, 6G, and 7G will mesh with digital currencies and Metaverse spaces. We will barely recognize our current existence by 2050. Much of that transformation will happen as a function of mechanical engineers who will design tomorrow's transportation, robots, machinery, and renewable energy processes.

Innovation is the solution to today's challenges. Mechanical engineers, on the cutting edge of material science, automated drone construction, autonomous solar-powered vehicles, and augmented reality. These innovations were developed with the foresight and power to transform 21st-century society to improve and simplify our lifestyle. With efficient transportation, manufacturing, and automation, this live-learn-work-evolve environment awaits.

USING ENGINEERING METHODS TO AWE AND INSPIRE

A city's twinkling lights, dimmed after a long bustling day of work, retain their magic in a process that takes place around the dials of a timepiece. Like clockwork, urban centers electrify. The energy of people rushing to and fro may be hushed for now but will awaken soon enough. This process begins and ends in our living spaces where we, too, dim the lights in the evening and wipe our eyes in the morning, refreshed from our necessary moments of rest.

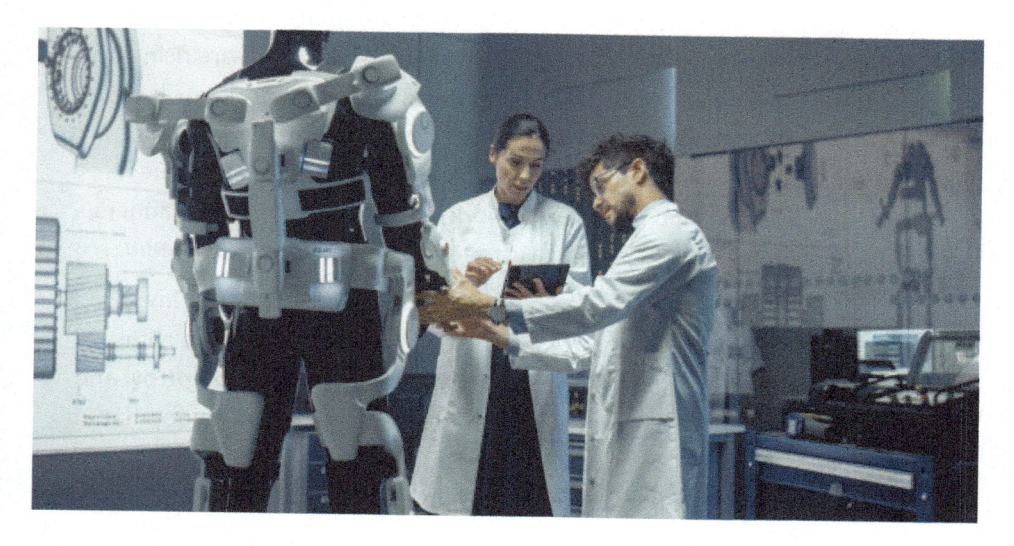

In workshops and studios, creativity is unleashed. Mechanical engineers, inspired to invent the future, blend vision and wonder with the nuts and bolts of CAD development, fabrication, and digitization. Students studying mechanical engineering are invited to set free the barriers of their mind's-eye and imagine what has yet to be considered. Mechanical engineers will overcome today's transportation, manufacturing, and appliance challenges and invent the future.

TRIFECTA OF SOCIOCULTURAL & TRANSFORMATIONAL CHANGE

The tsunami of uncertainty can be summed up in the trifecta of sociocultural and transformational change.
1. Climate Change
2. Political Strife
3. Engineering Innovation

Overwhelming evidence portends dynamic change on the horizon. Sea levels are rising. Social tensions rage in cities and countries. A wave of engineering advances are rapidly percolating in university and industrial research labs. You sit at this most exciting, yet harrowing juncture. You can make a difference. Your role is to envision and create tomorrow today.

CHALLENGES AHEAD

Climate change is one of the most significant challenges facing mechanical engineers today, particularly regarding infrastructure damage. According to the Environmental Protection Agency (EPA), while absolute sea levels are rising 0.12 – 0.14 inches per year, relative sea levels are not uniform. New York City has 578 miles of shoreline with most of its inhabitants within a mile of its waterfront. Planning agencies in New York are mitigating for "managed retreat". While sandbags, berms, dams, and barriers will work in the short term, city planners, architects, and engineers are working with agencies to mollify this problem.

The National Oceanic and Atmospheric Administration (NOAA) estimates the prognosis for Miami is worse. So, how can engineers help to create entirely new cities in the wake of unprecedented flooding? In envisioning tomorrow and rebuilding today's cities, engineers must prepare for climate change, population growth, delivery disruptions, and environmental challenges with new fuels, efficient energy, and faster processing to support people's lives and livelihoods.

Furthermore, today's unsustainable waste practices must shift toward repurpose and reuse options which pose opportunities and challenges for engineers. Also, for many people, security is paramount in their living and working spaces. As a result, college academic programs offer a myriad of ways to view today's safety and protection, while designing next-gen possibilities to invent a new tomorrow.

A FEW FACTS TO CONSIDER

- Poverty, inflation, war, and disease increased global food insecurity.
- Africa's population is expected to double by 2050.
- Supply chains, transportation mechanisms, and limiting factors of nonrenewable resources will threaten populations.
- Oceans are dying due to overfishing, pollution, and environmental change.
- Many islands and some U.S. cities are likely to be partially underwater by 2050. According to NOAA, Miami's sea level is 8 inches higher now than in 1950.
- Global angst, propaganda mechanisms, and philosophical divisions threaten to widen the fissure between people.

HOPE AND PRAGMATISM

An engineer's work exists at the intersection of hope and pragmatism. While resolving transportation and mechanization problems, engineers will develop stronger, lighter, and more efficient materials, functionality, processes, tools, and design. The possibilities are limitless. Mechanical engineers build the systems and tools for civilization's future. Begin this journey by stepping into the possibilities of today and developing the augmented realities of tomorrow.

There are numerous directions you can take with an educational foundation in engineering. The mechanical engineering programs available at the universities profiled in this book offer varied paths to licensure, design, planning, business development, and management.

The future is yours. Choose the path that makes sense for your life goals. The information contained within this book will lead you on your way and, hopefully, inspire you as a leader to empower others along their educational pathway.

The ideal engineer is a composite ... He is not a scientist,
he is not a mathematician, he is not a sociologist or a writer;
but he may use the knowledge and techniques of any or all of these disciplines
in solving engineering problems.

— **Nathan W. Dougherty**

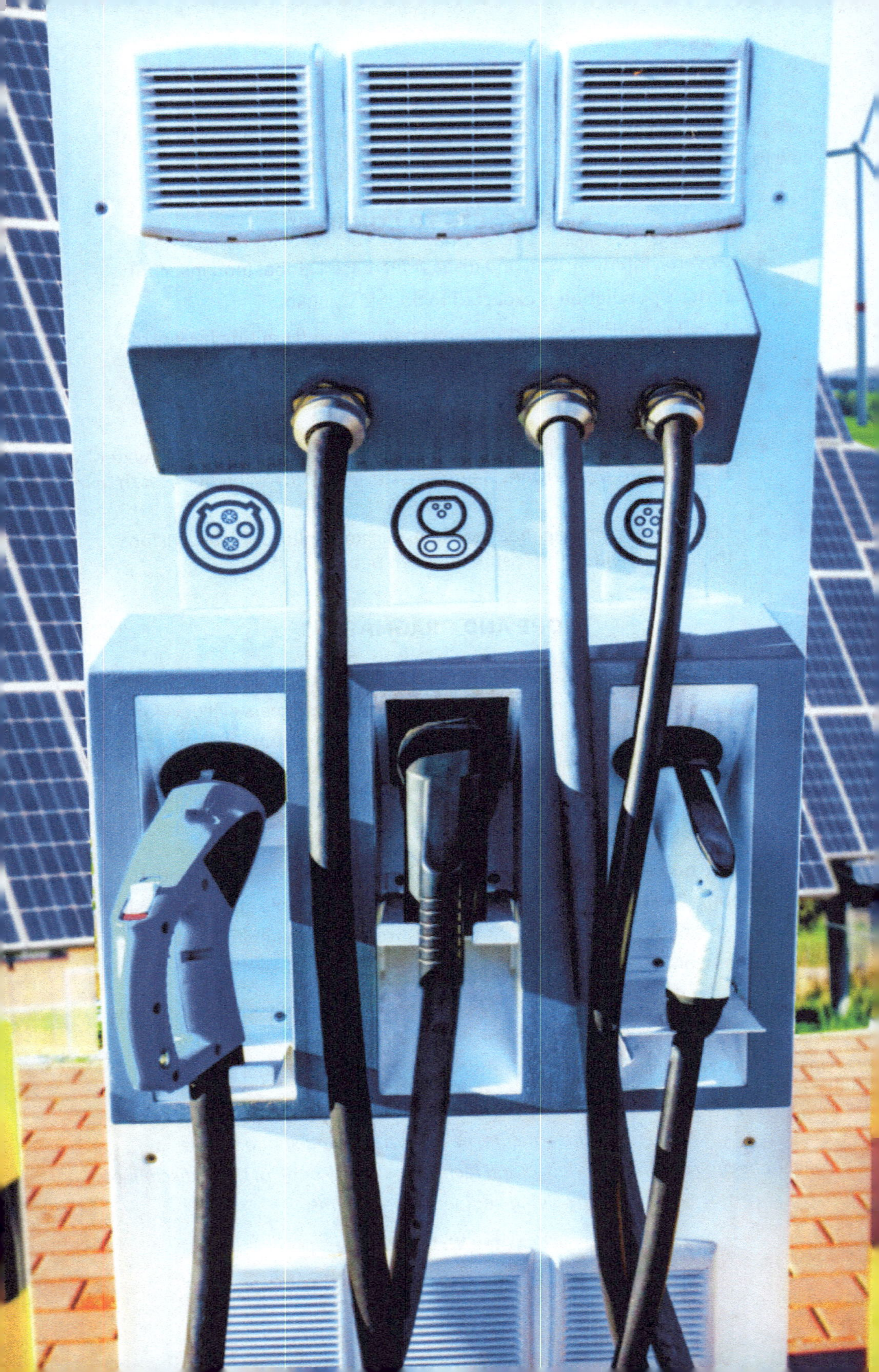

CHAPTER 2

EXPECTATIONS & TRAINING: ENGINEERING HIGH-TECH, ENVIRONMENTALLY CONSCIOUS SYSTEMS

"Failure does not exist. Once you hit the construction zone roadblocks, follow the detour signs to get back to your original path."

— **Behdad Sami**

Mechanical engineering covers the broadest set of analytical, problem-solving, and applications-oriented skills. From the manufacture of household products and medical devices to the design of generators and the development of turbines, mechanical engineers oversee processes and production.

Mechanical engineers consider factors like safety, functionality, sustainability, efficiency, and viability. Mechanical engineering requires the knowledge of material science, computer-aided design, chemistry, and physics, along with project design, programming, management, construction, analysis, and evaluation. The combination of these complex topics adds to the challenge and intrigue of this career path.

One focal point of mechanical engineering is the construction of power-generating devices which harness wind energy, along with solar, nuclear, chemical, geothermal, and hydroelectric power. With the increased demand to use renewable energy, new energy-producing methods will continue to percolate to the top of national priorities. Note that while nuclear power is not renewable, it is efficient.

Additionally, there is an increased demand for automated devices in homes, businesses, and manufacturing. Mechanical engineers are integral in the design of home and industrial robots, refrigeration and air-conditioning systems, conveyor belts for manufacturing, and elevators and escalators for transportation within buildings. Solar and electric vehicles are also hot areas where college researchers and innovative startups are taking their skills.

Computer-aided design and cutting-edge software skills are critically important for communication, simulations, analysis, and project management. Mechanical engineers rely on computers to crunch data, sense anomalies, and control processes. Finally, computers allow for efficient prototype design, system updates, and operational oversight.

ACADEMIC ROAD TO LICENSURE

Mechanical engineering applies mathematics and science to the creative exploration of solutions to real-world problems. Bridging physics, chemistry, and environmental science with technological challenges, mechanical engineers apply their knowledge as idea-generators and inquisitive problem solvers. Advanced topics in mathematics and physics provide the foundation for future coursework.

Bachelor's-level university engineering training programs require a minimum of 45 engineering-focused semester hours. The master's level requires one to two years. With the need to master concepts across a broad set of subjects, expanded due to technology innovation and regulations, engineers must develop numerous proficiencies. Starting with theoretical underpinnings, students go on to consider the external structure and material possibilities as well as internal mechanics, power, plumbing, and spatial dynamics. Workshops and tool rooms offer the environment to imagine and invent unique designs.

After gaining experience working on the job, mechanical engineers can apply for the Professional Engineering (PE) license. Only licensed engineers can take on higher roles in many areas of project management. With this licensure, professional engineers may also gain credentials and certifications in a variety of specialty areas to enhance their abilities, work on more complex projects, and take senior-level positions.

Thus, mechanical engineers must balance multiple, conflicting objectives. Safety, budget, and policy knowledge are required to determine the feasibility of overall plans. Taking the lead on projects, mechanical engineers are responsible for technical knowledge, troubleshooting, and contingency planning. Working in industry, consulting, and the private sector, engineers are part of a larger group of design and development experts.

Project management is another focal point of a mechanical engineer's work. On the job, bottlenecks occur due to worker, supply chain, or manufacturing challenges that may impact a coordinated plan. Since mechanical engineers sign off on projects, they must be organized, while also monitoring manufacturing, evaluating procedures, and ensuring compliance.

Furthermore, mechanical engineers often coordinate complex sets of activities for multiple projects at the same time. Thus, mechanical engineers must be able to simultaneously multitask with several teams as problem-solvers and decision-makers.

Effective communication is a foundational requirement for the job. Translating complicated scientific information to individuals with a wide range of literacy and technical expertise on all levels of projects is essential. Thus, written and oral communication skills must include the ability to modulate appropriate language for those who operate machinery, managers, clients, and engineering team members.

ENGINEERING PROGRAM LEARNING OBJECTIVES

Communication – Mechanical engineers must present clear, engaging writing and speaking that transmits information appropriately and effectively to those with no technical or scientific background. However, effectively translating complex scientific topics into written text is not as easy as it sounds. Listening is equally important since team members may offer valuable suggestions to complete tasks. College engineering programs train students in how to communicate with a wide range of audiences through group presentations, poster sessions, and research outcome delivery.

Teamwork - Engineering projects not only provide for group communication, but also the necessary skill of team membership, leadership, and inclusivity. As such, students get to know each other's strengths and weaknesses while establishing group goals, dividing tasks, and creating a plan for the delivery of performance outcomes.

Creativity – Engineers need to think differently. In the development of new products, creativity is essential to envision new and better options. Often, mechanical engineers must rely on workarounds using existing equipment. Ingenuity stimulates ideas, offering new avenues to accomplish the same task.

Problem Solving – Students identify problems in society that need to be resolved. With a solutions-oriented approach, mechanical engineers formulate best-fit alternatives by applying lessons learned in math, science, and engineering classes. Furthermore, there are often multiple options to achieve an optimal solution given the project's specifications and critical variables.

Analysis – Students are taught design thinking for functionality, feasibility, and aesthetics while also ensuring factors like health, safety, environment, and costs. Engineers rely on holistic analysis, experimentation, and testing. To improve judgment, engineers must understand, harness, and apply statistical analysis and data-informed decision-making.

Ethics – Engineers have an ethical responsibility to society and professional responsibility to clients. Thus, mechanical engineers must use good judgment and transparent communication, while also considering political, societal, and environmental consequences.

Lifelong Learning – Students soon discover that knowledge and skills are quickly outdated. From the moment a student begins college to the moment they leave, technological transformations take place that require information renewal like learning new software and using state-of-the-art materials. Furthermore, like a time warp, some antiquated projects or processes may use decades-old equipment.

DESIGN SCIENCE OF MECHANICAL ENGINEERING

As a mechanical engineering student who will play a role in inventing the future, you should expect to spend long hours developing your projects. The synergy and energy of collaboration can be electrifying as projects take shape and masterful designs propel ideas to a whole new level. However, there is much to learn by widening your scope regarding society, innovation, and trends.

Despite the structure of science, creativity is fundamental to the work. Ultimately, the jigsaw puzzle of mechanical elements, magnificently blending art and science, will seamlessly fit together, connecting its moving parts. Yet, with a limited timeframe and compact lab space, clarity and design have their bounds.

You will learn how to manage time and quickly evaluate the status of your projects. Collaboration can be both challenging and exhilarating at the same time. Each member must listen attentively and conceptualize options in 2-D and 3-D space while proposing ideas, accepting alternative viewpoints, and creating a clear line of communication. By discussing opportunities for improvement, pitfalls in design elements, and financial and spatial limitations, the team can efficiently and effectively cooperate to craft the best representation of the design.

Within the engineering design process, students devise systems, components, or processes given a specified set of constraints. Realizing that customers provide terms and conditions that need to be fulfilled, mechanical engineers must efficiently budget time, costs, and materials as required. Mechanical engineering, thus, is both a creative and analytical process. Coursework leads students from the basic sciences to the solutions-oriented development and implementation of engineering design.

Students learn to spot opportunities where problems need to be overcome. Then, by exploring alternatives and evaluating multiple solutions, students identify the optimum plan to remedy the problem. The process requires considering risk-reward trade-offs. Some considerations might include LEED (Leadership in Energy and Environmental Design) rating requirements and the ability to accomplish the specified objective within the legal requirements of regulation, functionality, and accessibility.

LEED (LEADERSHIP IN ENERGY AND ENVIRONMENTAL DESIGN) RATINGS: CERTIFIED (40-49 POINTS); SILVER (50-59 POINTS); GOLD (60-79 POINTS); AND PLATINUM (80+ POINTS)

As students infuse environmental consciousness into society and research centers develop stronger and more durable materials, mechanical engineers will inject noticeable improvements in design, efficiency, and sustainability. LEED projects undergo a systematic verification and review process through a 'green' rating system, awarding points corresponding to a LEED certification level. Mechanical engineers may become involved with one or more of the seven LEED areas of concentration: Sustainable Sites, Water Efficiency, Energy and Atmosphere, Materials and Resources, Indoor Environmental Quality, Innovation in Design Process and Regional Priority.

MATERIALS SCIENCE

Chemistry may seem dry, pardon the pun, but there is an immense amount of research transforming tomorrow's materials into those that are lighter, thinner, stronger, conductive, and absorbent. Carbon is one of the most intriguing elements in the research sphere today. When graphene grabbed people's attention, researchers clamored to discover its many uses.

Graphene is a one-atom-thick sheet of carbon that conducts heat and electricity along its plane, absorbs light of all visible wavelengths, is 100 times stronger than the strongest steel, and nearly transparent. The possibilities for graphene are endless, including building materials, electronics, medicine, transportation, and military uses. Companies have already begun using offshoots to construct buildings' foundations and computer screens that lay flat like wallpaper on your wall. You could be part of some very big and potentially profitable innovations.

In mechanical engineering, one way graphene is being used is in concrete additives. Graphene increases strength, reduces the carbon footprint, and increases the longevity of the finished product. With graphene's strength and ability to decrease a structure's permeability, completely new fabrications can be made. Graphene acts as a mechanical support and a catalyst surface for initial hydration reaction, better bonding, and nanoscale support for durability and corrosion resistance.

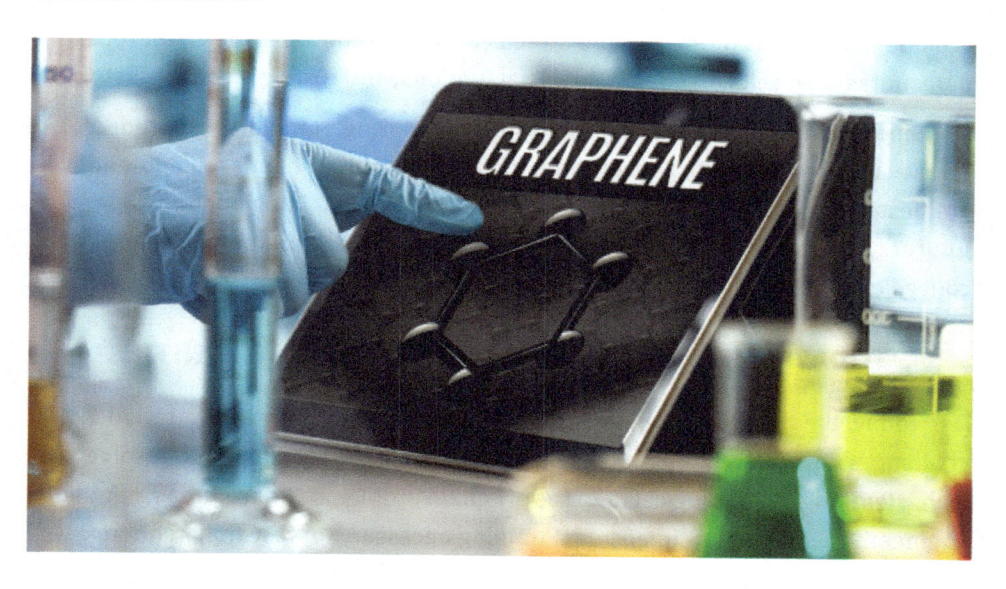

In 2010, two Russian scientists were awarded the Nobel Prize in Physics for their discovery and groundbreaking research in graphene. This nanomaterial offers high tensile strength, electrical conductivity, and transparency. Earlier, in 1996, two Americans and one British researcher won the Nobel Prize in Chemistry for their discoveries regarding another carbon-based molecule, fullerene.

Fullerene, C_{60}, a hollow cage of atoms or cylindrical mesh with similarly fascinating properties with a tremendous number of possible uses for nanotubes, nanorods, and other nanotechnologies like tumor therapy. Presently researchers believe that C_{60} is not only an antioxidant, but the molecule has healing properties that may slow down aging, boost immunity, increase energy, reduce wrinkles, inhibit fat cell production, and provide stronger mental capacity.[1]

Meanwhile, new synthetic leathers may improve clothing, footwear, steering wheel covers, seats, bags, furnishings, sports, and electronics. Liquid and spray camouflage coatings may have utility for some defense, aircraft, and wearable products. Aspheric lenses, low in cost and high in performance, offer high-end optical solutions with sharper images and reduced optical imperfections for cameras, camera phones, CD players, and reading glasses.

With concerns for safety, flame retardant coatings are critically important. A wonder material more flexible than nylon and thinner than human hair is spider silk. Spider silk can be used for medical purposes as well as for bulletproof vests since it can absorb three times more energy than Kevlar. However, since spider silk is biodegradable, its properties are more eco-friendly and can be used for ropes, parachutes, seatbelts, bandages, artificial tendons, and rust-free boat accessories.

Since there are quite literally thousands of amazing materials and products on the cutting edge of idea generation, the future is in your hands. The potential is limitless to reduce, reuse, recycle, and create. How do you imagine the future? I hope this chapter got you thinking as you embark on your dynamic college experiences. You might even change your major to materials science.

TODAY'S MECHANICAL ENGINEERING OPPORTUNITIES

Today, the world faces significant spatial, electronic, and transportation challenges. Intelligent, human-centered design thinking is essential to resolve living, learning, technological, and supply chain problems. Smart, broad-minded engineers gain the multidimensional training necessary for research, rendering, and fabrication. In turn, they will produce, test, and present solutions.

Remember that everything in our sphere exists in a system. Interfaces and functionality must make sense within the environment. Thus, mechanical engineers must be aware of people's surroundings and what might support or interfere with functionality. For example, while drones may eventually repair supply chain issues, software glitches, delivery errors, and nefarious instigators must also be considered. Nanomaterial medical technologies may save a person's

---

[1] Rebecca Suhrawardi. "This Nobel Prize-Winning Molecule Could Be the Best Thing For Anti-Aging." Forbes, April 30, 2021. https://www.forbes.com/sites/rebeccasuhrawardi/2021/04/30/this-nobel-prize-winning-moleculecould-be-the-best-thing-for-anti-aging/?sh=2d7fa2ca6ada

life, but will the materials be rejected by or interfere with natural human body processes?

Additionally, what solutions will make industrial work safer, cleaner, healthier, and more productive? And, considering sustainability, are the newly-developed products environmentally friendly? In metal fabrication workshops, you will mold, laser-cut, and weld material after rapid prototyping. In a modeling shop, you will experiment with foam, plastic, and wood. A woodshop assignment may require you to reinvent an ergonomic massage chair, creating code that includes safety specifications, while adding upholstery and backings that fit your design concept.

When working on a transportation engineering project, you will use design software to convert sketches and orthographic drawings into renderings. You may create innovative motion-sensored toys for children, delivering your vision and prototype in a presentation. You might even translate your ideas into the next nifty and popular toy.

From your first-year experiences to sponsored workshops, labs are abuzz with activity. You will survey consumer needs, translating proposals from concepts to physical products using aesthetic appeal and engineering design. There are no limits to what you can imagine. For your senior project/capstone, you might choose to create game consoles, phones, cars, tools, computers, or healthcare items.

You may train in auxiliary skills like interaction or entertainment design, mass production, or manufacturing. Avoid the steep learning curves by taking design courses from the moment you think you might be interested in this pursuit.

You will also need to know the law. While patenting your inventions, you must be extremely detailed, while also mastering the nuances of intellectual property. College classes will push you into the deep end, but you will learn how to swim using your instincts and problem-solving skills to make products more functional and attractive. Ultimately, you will produce your unique vision and improve society.

Emerging technologies, UX design, and software adaptations will force you to swim faster to say ahead of the next wave of new tools coming your way. Virtual Reality (VR), Augmented Reality (AR), Artificial Intelligence (AI), and machine learning opportunities are here and they are taking society by storm. Research and development in next-gen uses captivate the minds and attentions of students, faculty, and independent researchers. Full force innovation and implementation are right around the corner.

NEVER-ENDING FASCINATION

You will study history, social structures, and computer science while building eco-friendly tools, machinery, energy products, and vehicles. By learning variations in local, state, national, and international policy, you will discover that every region holds its unique opportunities and challenges. Furthermore, restrictions can be a big factor in the success of a project. Securing materials, mitigating obstacles, and obtaining permits can be impediments or open doors to new possibilities.

The journey you are taking will have its ups and downs, but you will have stories to tell for the rest of your life. Your education may also include unpredictable events. Pitfalls may lay in your path. Since you have endured a pandemic and the repercussions of a war, you are imbued with a few doses of resilience.

Even so, you will be tested in your mechanical engineering program as there is much to learn and a short amount of time. You are embarking on a thrilling, demanding, and disciplined pursuit. You will work with extremely skilled and brilliant students who participated in summer programs since elementary school and also took courses in programming, engineering, and technical drawing each year.

Some classmates have interned in engineering firms and will blow you away with their abilities. However, rarely are there engineering students equally skilled in all areas. Some of your work will be a team effort where everyone will contribute what they know. You will too. Some students will be amazingly talented. Do not let their abilities bring you down or make you feel as if you are not good enough.

You will add your element and learn more during college. Besides, your enthusiasm for engineering will show through in your work and effort. Recognizing your potential, commitment, and attitude, people will be awed at your creations as you also step back to appreciate your work.

21

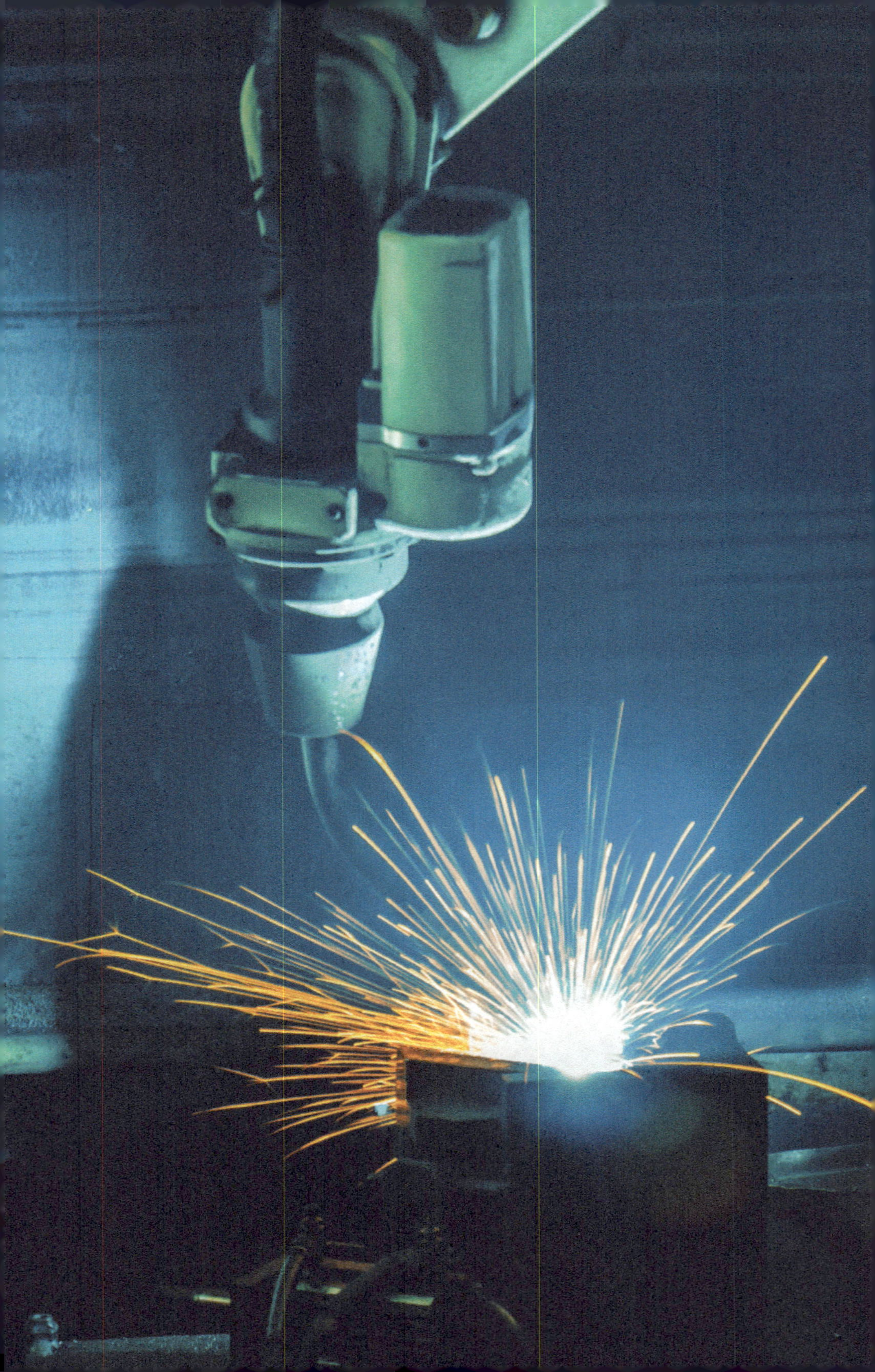

CHAPTER 3

ACADEMIC PREPARATION & CAREER OPTIONS: OPPORTUNITIES FOR MECHANICAL ENGINEERS

"Therefore, O students, study mathematics and do not build without foundations."

– Leonardo da Vinci

COLLEGE EXPERIENCES IN MECHANICAL ENGINEERING

Studying mechanical engineering will challenge you in multiple ways. You will never be bored. You will use design software and prepare models using prototyping machinery. You will work together with others. You will also spend long hours working alone. If you like drawing, modeling, building, repairing, and solving problems, you will get plenty of practice.

EXPECT TO PULL A FEW ALL-NIGHTERS

You will not be alone resolving problems related to projects on the nights before they are due. Collaboration is at the core of mechanical engineering. You will not only work on projects with people in your major, but you are likely to consult with students in civil engineering, electrical engineering, industrial engineering, and materials science. You will also need to be practically obsessed with inspecting fine details since the smallest crack, melted sheath, or defective metal piece will hang your project out to dry. Plan ahead!

If you fail to plan, you are planning to fail.

- Benjamin Franklin

ACADEMIC PREPARATION

The moment is now. You are full STEAM ahead on a course toward engineering mastery. To gain admission you must be smart in science, analytical in math, and talented in design. Even if the admission requirements do not demand that you have experience in robotics, machinery, building construction, or engineering design, you should prepare with summer activities or school year projects since many of your future classmates will have dabbled in engineering.

Students should develop preliminary skills before applying. Admissions committees may find it difficult to justify selecting an applicant without research experience or a tech background. Often, applicants took two years of coding, interned with an engineering firm, participated in an engineering magnet program, worked in a lab, participated in engineering contests, and/or competed in hackathons. While engineering may sound fun and offer a high income, it takes real work.

Plan for your future now. Some applicants have competed in bridge-building, egg drops, paper skyscraper constructions, robotics clubs, concrete canoe events, solar oven competitions, rope and wood bridge contests, engine design, automobile construction, solar car racing, or water balloon challenges.

TALENT IS ONLY THE BEGINNING

High school students must build solid computational and critical thinking skills in science and math. AP Physics, AP Chemistry, and AP Calculus are almost always a prerequisite. More is better. However, you must also be a talented and creative thinker.

HARDWARE AND SOFTWARE SKILLS

You will spend much of your time on laptop computers and digitized machinery. The more you know, the better prepared you will be. Computer science classes in high school, community college, or summer programs are extremely valuable. Hardware and machinery classes are a definite plus.

You would benefit from classes in graphic design or robotics. You are walking into a future where virtual reality, augmented reality, and machine learning will require greater technology skills than applicants even ten years ago when most engineers created 2-D renderings that were often difficult to visualize. Yet, as you enter college, technology's rapid advancements will transform from primarily 2-D drawings to primarily 3-D virtual reality graphics.

VISUALIZE, COMMUNICATE, EXECUTE

The excitement and promise of 5G, 6G, and 7G will advance engineering in revolutionary rather than evolutionary ways. Computing power, many times faster than today, will allow for quick permutations of design options and animations never before possible. Teams will collaborate on holograms of mechanical systems designed together in a shared space with members who need not be physically present.

Clearly visualized 3-D animations of designs using virtual reality will allow customers and patrons to walk through a manufacturing facility, power plant, or a machine not yet fully created. Augmented reality will add to this experience by providing the viewer a user experience, possibly, one day, in the Metaverse.

These environments can be constructed and fully automated with computer design and programming tools. Group members will adapt designs in quick iterations, allowing for a near-real visualization of the physical model as each person analyzes the form and function of each piece of equipment.

Translation and implementation of the construction design can be witnessed and managed since every built part will be computerized and visualized without the necessity of manual paper and audio call updates. Automated processes will be more efficient without the necessity of frequent site visits.

A 3-D PRINTER IN EVERY SCHOOL

While 3-D printing machines were initially developed in the 1980s for rapid prototyping, a decade ago, the broader public got a glimpse of a desktop model by MakerBot, a company, that envisioned a 3-D printer in every home. More than a hundred thousand guests at the 2012 Consumer Electronics Show (CES) witnessed the creation of plastic parts printed for the first time. CES will be held in Las Vegas again in January next year. I highly recommend going to CES.

The show is three days of tantalizing inspiration for the maker in you. Nevertheless, what started as an expensive novelty machine changed its market focus when the company, Stratasys, purchased MakerBot and realigned its sales and distribution strategy toward the technology and education markets.

By 2023, almost every engineering school had 3-D printers in their fabrication. At one point or another, while studying engineering, 3-D printing will come into play. Projects are likely to include fabricating vehicle parts, improving automated heating and cooling systems, and developing robotic arms for surgeons to conduct hands-free surgery.

You may also be asked to design machinery using filament in a wide variety of colors with matte, silk, shiny, or transparent and finishes resembling wood, cardboard, and an assortment of metals. Some filaments even glow in the dark while others change color based on temperature. Imagine the extraordinary possibilities.

COMPELLING REASONS TO STUDY MECHANICAL ENGINEERING

1. Freedom of creative expression and scientific investigation
2. Mind explosion of possibilities for research and development
3. Desire to experiment and bring cutting edge ideas to fruition
4. Keen understanding of science and math, undaunted by tough questions
5. Love for problem-solving in a fast-paced, dynamic environment
6. Interest in learning new technologies and computer software
7. Desire to work with groups toward a common goal
8. Inquisitive hunger to test, shape, mold, and adapt materials
9. Emotional feeling that beckons you toward engineering design
10. Opportunity to turn your passion for engineering into a lifetime career

In this constantly changing profession, continually upgrading and evolving, mechanical engineers must keep pace with rapid technology advancements. Today, new materials and power sources are rapidly reinventing what remained constant for many decades. As a result, the ever-conscious, forward-thinking engineer will need to think five paces ahead.

Amazing college professors who are successful outside of academia will suggest ways for you to find your niche in mechanical engineering. A few faculty members whose experiences an knowledge are outdated, may not use the latest equipment or software since technology changes so rapidly.

You might get frustrated with their lack of knowledge. Don't. The fundamental principles of engineering will not change. Some college professors may even link you to their contacts for internships and jobs. Throughout college, you will discover your brand of professionalism along with a calling card of experiences that allow others to understand what you offer.

GAINING VALUABLE EXPERIENCES

Train now in the application of 3-D printing, holograms, virtual reality, and augmented reality spaces. Anything you learn now will help you be better prepared to immerse yourself in power generation, vehicle development, CAD, and computer science. Find avenues where you can experiment with these new technologies or volunteer in any way at a mechanical engineering firm. Even if all you do is get coffee for people during your volunteer service, you will gain invaluable lessons as you watch how companies tick.

While engineering classes may not be offered at your school, summer camps, short-term programs, online training, maker clubs, and college classes will help you immensely along the way. Additional science classes would not hurt you either. Knowledge of chemistry and physics is imperative. The more you understand analytical tools, computational methods, and design options, the more you will be able to access the information necessary to be an engineering guru.

Additionally, there is no way to understate the value of basic understanding of robotics. Building, programming, and working with robots in high school will help you while you are in college. Join or create a robotics team. See if there is a regional robotics club or league. If neither of these is available, find an avid robotics student and have them help you start from scratch..

Enjoy the experience.

Don't judge each day by the harvest you reap but by the seeds that you plant.

- Robert Louis Stevenson

"THERE IS NO ROYAL ROAD TO GEOMETRY" - EUCLID

When a student asked Euclid if there was an easier way to learn geometry, he cautioned that discipline and persistence are essential. Hard work is absolutely necessary. Additionally, there is no one way to succeed, just as there is no one way to enter the fields of engineering design and manufacturing.

You may choose to produce new technologies for a company, test devices, or work on large integrated team-based projects. Either way, engineering design is a versatile skill. Related professional options with your skills include engineering management, entertainment, education, and much more. You could manage an engineering firm or create an innovative start-up with some friends. You might enjoy consulting or helping engineers market their services.

TEACHING, EDUCATION, AND TRAINING

Kids clamor to create. Their imaginations run wild with ideas. Self-expression and exploration through design and engineering offer people young and old the chance to put their ideas onto a paper, computer, or still/moving medium. Lego projects, robotics, and scientific experiments offer limitless possibilities for the STEAM (Science, Technology, Engineering, Art, and Math) student. As a result, there are numerous jobs in private and public education.

Schools everywhere employ science teachers. Additionally, families hire science, engineering, and robotics coaches. Private studios conduct workshops and training. College professors can make more than $100,000/year teaching students while continuing to conduct research, publish, and travel to conferences.

Of course, you would need to attend graduate school, but a master's degree in Civil Engineering, Industrial Engineering, or Business would also take you to the next level of your profession. Furthermore, a doctorate opens new doors if you choose the research route. There is so much to innovate that you will always stay engaged.

In 2021, there were approximately 130,000 public and private K-12 schools in the U.S. according to the National Center for Educational Statistics (NCES). During the 2020-2021 school year, there were 10,545 K-12 public schools and another 1,296 charter schools in California alone.[1] On the college level, during the 2019-2020 school year, there were 3,982 degree-granting higher education.

---

[1] California Department of Education, "Fingertip Facts on Education in California," 2020-2021, https://www.cde.ca.gov/ds/ad/ceffingertipfacts.asp

A FINAL NOTE

Finally, William James Durant and his wife, Ariel, wrote a nearly 11,000-page tome called "The Story of Civilization" in which they broke down history into events that captured the ideas and philosophy of the time. One of his sayings was, "Science is organized knowledge. Wisdom is organized life." You will efficiently and effectively collect massive amounts of knowledge and invent your future with wisdom and passion.

Science unveils the mystery of the universe. Everything contained within can be explained by its principles. Thus, as you embark on your journey, learn as much as you can about science and mathematics, remembering that making a game plan now and challenging yourself to learn new and often difficult subjects is the first step along that journey.

Mathematics is the language in which God has written the universe.

- Galileo

"Philosophy is written in that great book which ever lies before our eyes — I mean the universe — but we cannot understand it if we do not first learn the language and grasp the symbols, in which it is written. This book is written in the mathematical language, and the symbols are triangles, circles, and other geometrical figures, without whose help it is impossible to comprehend a single word of it; without which one wanders in vain through a dark labyrinth."

- Galileo – The Assayer (1623), translated by Thomas Salusbury (1661)

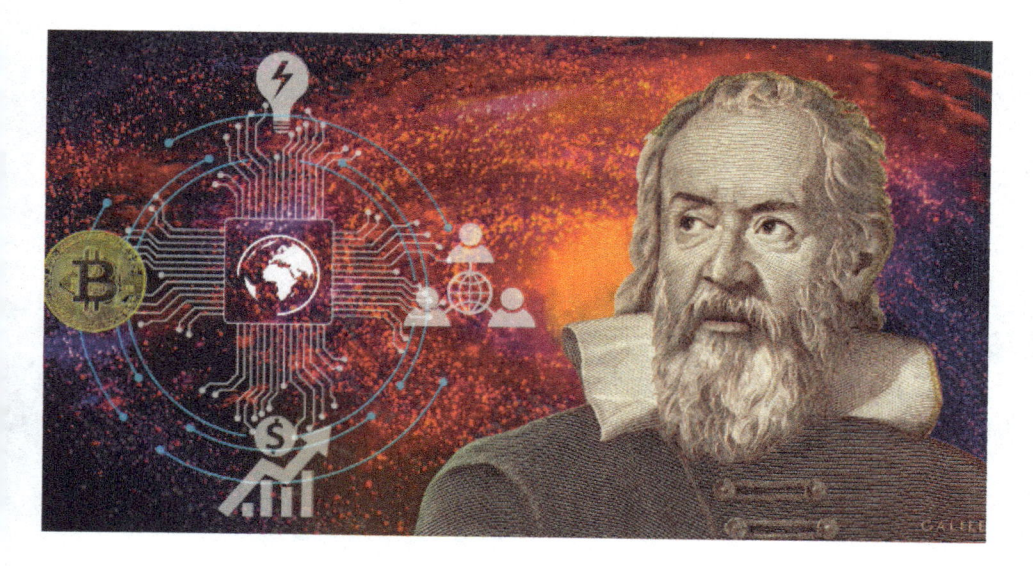

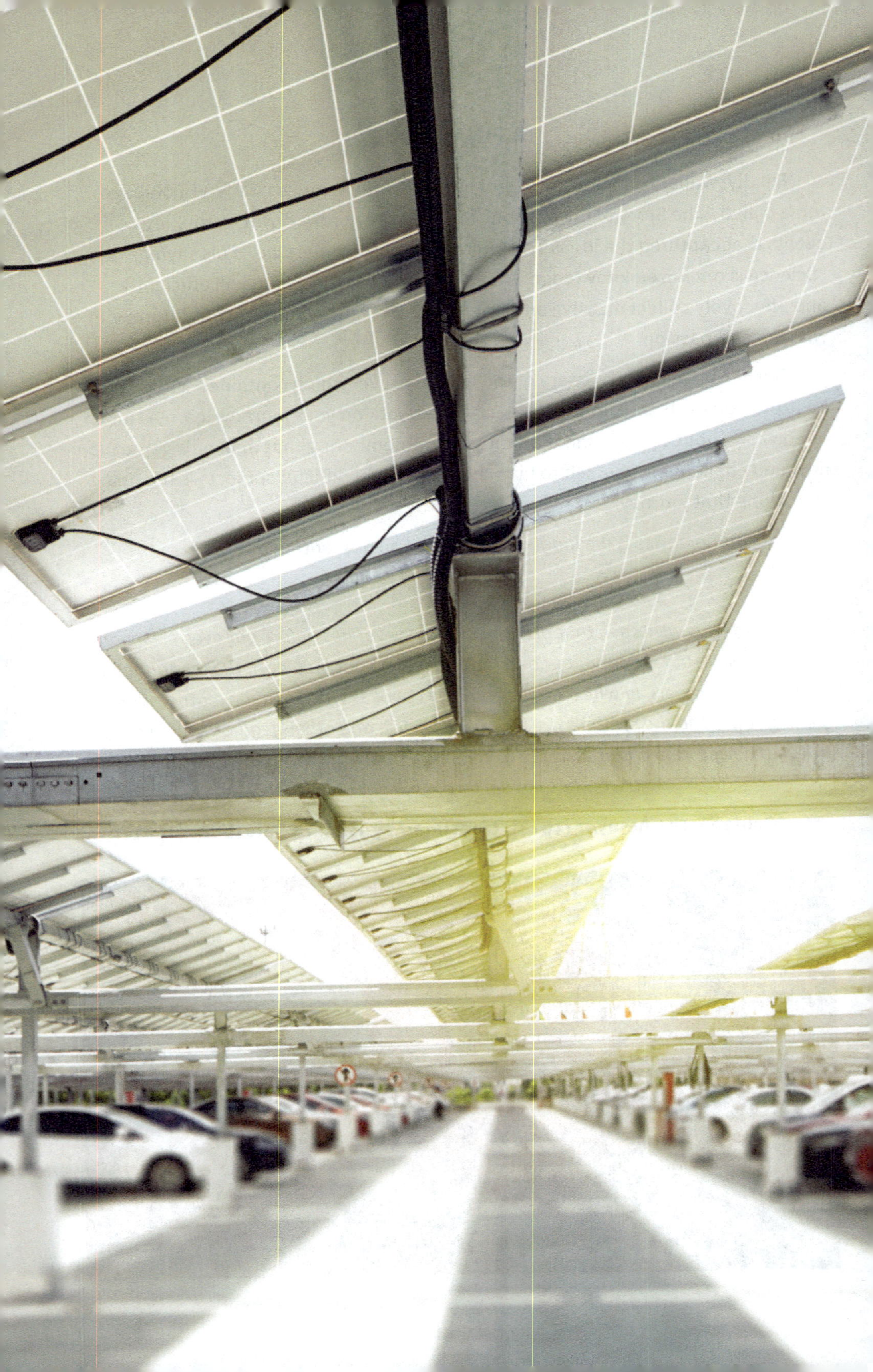

CHAPTER 4
SUMMER PROGRAMS & INTERNSHIPS FOR HIGH SCHOOL & COLLEGE STUDENTS

"Create with the heart; build with the mind."

– **Criss Jami**

Start early to gain software, design, and engineering experiences. Internships and summer programs are as important in your educational pathway as coursework. The lessons you learn from working collaboratively and collegially with design-focused mentors is equally important. Historian and scholar, W.E.B. DuBois (1868-1963), a founding member of the NAACP and the first Black American to earn a Ph.D. at Harvard said, "Education must not simply teach work - it must teach life." Your college, experiential, and life education go hand-in-hand, driven by purpose and foresight since life truly is a journey, not a destination.

WHY PARTICIPATE IN SUMMER PROGRAMS/INTERNSHIPS?

Summer programs and internships lay a foundation. providing a context for your science education. While some students and parents chose summer opportunities to look good or show dedication, the real reason you should participate is to develop skills, accept critique, and gain feedback from specialists in the field. Others who came before you can shine light on the many directions you can take as an engineer.

Discussions, seminars, studio work, and portfolio development are immensely valuable for your future pursuits. However, merely living on a campus and getting a feel for what college would be like cannot be understated.

Note: The following list of summer programs and internships is not exhaustive, and it is not an endorsement of any program. Dates, camps, internships, program descriptions, and program length may change from year to year.

SUMMER CAMPS & PROGRAMS FOR ART, DESIGN, FILM, PHOTOGRAPHY, ARCHITECTURE, AND ENGINEERING

Alabama

Auburn University – Architecture Camp – Creative Writing – Industrial Design

One week – Three Session Options – Full Scholarships Available (apply by April 1) Students produce designs while working directly with professors.
Camp counselors support students with 24/7 questions, safety, and supervision.

Tuskegee University Taylor School of Architecture & Construction Science

Virtual Preview of Architecture and Construction at Tuskegee (V-PACT), 3-hour Virtual Program. Preview Architecture & Construction Science 2-Week Program

Arizona

Arcosanti – Re-Imagined Urbanism – 6-week discussion-based classes - AZ

Combining architecture and ecology (arcology), you can learn in the World's First Prototype Arcology.

(1) Frugality and Resourcefulness, (2) Ecological Accountability, (3) Experiential Learning, and (4) Leaving a Limited Footprint, Arcosanti is juxtaposed to mass consumerism, urban sprawl, unchecked consumption, and social isolation.

Arizona State - SCience and ENgineering Experience (SCENE)

HS Students - Work in labs on original resesearch in Biodesign, Medicine, Molecular Sciences, Physics. Solid State Science, and Sustainable Engineering.

Arizona State Univ. Cronkite School Summer Journalism Institute - June (App due in April)

On-campus (one-week) - HS Students - writing, photography, pitching, storytelling, editing, video editing, reporting, script development, AR/VR media

National Institute of Health – 8-week Research Program – Phoenix, AZ

Research biomedical internship for students 17 years or older by June 15th.

Science and Engineering Apprenticeship Program (SEAP) – US Navy - Flagstaff

8-weeks, 300 openings, 30 labs, $4,000-$4,500 science/engineering research. HS students must be 16+ years old. Apps available in the previous August

Arkansas

University of Arkansas – In Person & Virtual Design Camp – Fayetteville, AK

In-Person Grades 9-12 - design projects, studio groups, tours, & meetings with local designers. No fee; completely remote; design camp lessons embedded; students are paired with a faculty member in a studio group.

Advanced Design Camp: students entering Grades 11-12, 2 weeks in Fayetteville

California

Aviation Career Education (ACE) – Sponsored by the Federal Aviation Admin.

Summer aviation education programs for elementary, middle, & high school students.
Victorville, CA - https://obap.org/ace/highdesert/ June - 13-18 yrs
West Los Angeles College - https://obap.org/ace/losangeles/ July - 13-18 yrs
Los Angeles International Airport (LAX) - June - https://www.lawa.org/ace - 13-18 years

Boeing Summer Internship – High School & College – Seal Beach & Palmdale, CA

Hands-on Industry Experience - Aviation and Engineering Internships

California State Summer School of the Arts (CSSSA) – Sacramento, CA

Rigorous 4-week, pre-professional visual and performing arts 2D and 3D training program in painting, printmaking, sculpture, ceramics, digital media, and photography; scholarship possibility for CA residents. Grades 9 – 12.

Cal Poly SLO EPIC - Engineering Possibilities in College - 5-day Residential Program

6th - 8th & 9th - 12th grades - Engineering Speakers, Panels, and Projects

Canon Insights Summer Internship – Canon USA – Irvine, CA

Computer Science Major – 2nd or 3rd year; Position: Computer Vision Tech; Assist with Quality Assurance Engineers; Digital Imaging Solution Division

COPE Scholars Program – Healthcare Internship – 280 Training/Experience Hrs

Locations: Anaheim/Orange, Bakersfield, Covina/Glendora, Hanford, Irvine, L.A., Mendocino County, Mission Viejo, Newport Beach, Oxnard, Riverside, Simi Valley, Tulare, and Woodland Hills

Health Scholars must be 18+. Students assist w/basic healthcare for medical or nursing school, etc. Certificate of Completion - Keck Graduate Institute.

COSMOS – California State Summer School for Math & Science – 4 weeks; UC Campuses - Locations Change Each Year - CA HS Students Pursuing STEM

Students live on campus and work with UC researchers. Application opens in January and closes in Feb. Topics from biomedical to space science.

Edwards Lifesciences Summer Internship Program – BS, MS, Ph.D., MBA - Irvine, CA

Currently Enrolled in College - Interested in Healthcare Related Programs Proficient in Engineering Drafting Software, Writing, or Business/Leadership

Getty Museum – Paid Student Gallery Guide – Los Angeles, CA

Paid summer internship for teens ($2,400 in 2022). Learn the fundamentals of museums and public speaking while leading visitors around the grounds.

Also available – Open Call for teen photographers to share images, 8-week paid STEAM internship, and Summer Latin Academy at the Getty Villa to learn Latin.

Laguna College of Art & Design Pre-College Program – Laguna Beach, CA

Animation, Sculpture, Drawing Fundamentals, Figure Drawing, Graphic Design

NASA Jet Propulsion Laboratory – Pasadena, CA (Apply by March 31)

Paid Internship - Must be in an undergraduate in a STEM subject

Otis College of Art and Design Summer of Art – Los Angeles, CA

Intensive 4-week program for students 15+ for portfolio and studio training in architecture, conceptual art, digital media, graphic design, and printmaking, with lectures and critiques. Merit and need-based scholarships are available.

Parker Hannifin Corporation – Paid Summer Internship – Irvine, CA

Mechanical or Industrial Engineering Major – Flight Control, Aircraft Systems

Santa Clara University Summer Engineering Seminar (SES) – 10th and 11th Grade

4-day program introduces students to engineering practice, research, and education

School of Creative & Performing Arts (SOCAPA) – Occidental College (13-18-year-olds)

2-week, 3-week - learn Filmmaking, Screenwriting, Dance, Music, Photography

SCI-Arc (Southern California Institute of Architecture) Immersive 4-week Summer Program (Design Immersion Days) – Los Angeles

Introduction to the academic and professional world of architecture – Grades 9-12

Science and Engineering Apprenticeship Program (SEAP) – US Navy Camp Pendleton, Port Hueneme, Pt. Mugu, San Diego, Monterey, and Corona

8-weeks, 300 openings, 30 labs, $4,000-$4,500 science/engineering research. HS students must be 16+ years old. Apps available in the previous August

SpaceX – Summer Eng/Co-op Prog – Hawthorne, Irvine, & Vandenberg AFB
Paid Engineeing Internship - Must be in an undergraduate in a STEM subject

Stanford Programs - SUMaC – Stanford University Mathematics Camp; Humanities Institute; Stanford Institutes of Medicine Research Program
10th and 11th Grade – Highly competitive 3-week programs for exceptional students with proven subject mastery; Application Deadline: March 15.

Stanford Univ– RISE Internship, SYIP Intensive, Earth Investigations, Arts Inst. 8-Week Summer Courses and 3-Week Arts Institute
Architecture, Art, Drawing, Dance, Creative Writing, Music, and Photoghy; Engineering, STEM, Science Research Internship, Intensives, Hands-on Projects

Stanford University - Reischauer Scholars Prog - Research & Peer Reviewed Paper
Academically Rigorous Fellowship - 25-30 students selected to study Japan Stanford CSP credit & SPICE Certificate of Completion

Tesla Internships – Ave. $33/hour – Full-Time Paid Positions Throughout CA
Automotive Design, Engineering Tech, Vehicle Service, Research/Training

UCLA Applications of Nanoscience Summer Institute - July, In-Person 10th - 12th
Propose and conduct your experimental research project. Live on-campus.

UCLA Summer Jumpstart Summer Art Institute, Digital Media Arts Institute, Digital Filmmaking Institute, and Game Lab Institute
2-week program - Portfolio development– college credit available
Drawing, Painting, Photography, Sculpture, Video Art, Animation, & Game Design

University of San Diego - TryEngineering Summer Camp - 11 days, 13-17 year olds
Institute of Electrical & Electronics Engineers (IEEE) Camp for future engineers
Civil, Electrical, Mechanical, and Aerospace Engineering

USC Summer Film, Writing, and Architecture Programs – Los Angeles
2-4-week program, "Creative Writing Workshop", "Comedy Performance", "Exploration into Architecture"

Colorado

National Security Agency (NSA) – Paid Computer Internship – Aurora
Students must be at least a junior in high school with interest in business, engineering, or computer science. Apply between September 1 and October 31.

Connecticut

Science and Engineering Apprenticeship Program (SEAP) – US Navy – Groton
8-weeks, 300 openings, 30 labs, $4,000-$4,500 science/engineering research. HS students must be 16+ years old. Apps available in the previous August

Summer Studio: Discovering Graphic Design (AIGA) – Bridgeport, CT

Free 4-week hands-on program for Bridgeport rising juniors and seniors
Week 1 – Music Festival Poster, Week 2 – Digital Media Poster
Week 3 – Animating Your Ideas, Week 4 – Portfolio Art for College Applications

Yale Young Global Scholars (YYGS) 13-days - Four programs on-campus

Yale dorms, professors, seminars, capstone project; Innovation in Science & Technology, Literature, Philosophy, & Culture, Solving Global Challenges

District of Columbia

American University - Discover the World of Communication - HS Students - 9-day

June on-campus - Newswriting & Investigative Reporting; Broadcast Journalism; visits to newsrooms, National Press Club, CNN, C-Span, ESPN, NBC, Post

Catholic University School of Architecture and Planning

Summer High School Program - 2-week Residential (Two Session Options)

George Washington University Digital Storytelling Pre-College Program – July

Produce stories with smartphones, learn storyboarding, and broadcast through social media; craft ideas, capture images, & create compelling content.

Georgetown University – 1-week – Creative Writing – Publishing

Fiction, Short Story, Poetry, and Professional Writing; visit literary hubs

Georgetown University Medical Center – 1, 2, & 3-week Summer HS Academies

Hands-on lectures & activities focused on medicine, healthcare, and science

National Air and Space Museum in Washington, D.C. – HS/College Students
The Explainers Program offers a $15 hr, year-round paid position for students to help visitors understand the Museum, artifacts and exhibitions.

Florida

Florida Atlantic University – Boca Raton, FL and Ft. Lauderdale, FL
School of Architecture – July (Three Session Options)

July 3-week program for rising sophomores, juniors, seniors, and students in their first 2 years of college - Portfolio development, fabrication, architectural education, portfolio display, critique

Certificate of Completion Awarded – Enrollment on a first-come, first-served basis

Ringling College of Art and Design – Sarasota, FL
Intensive 4-week program focused on art and design including computer animation, creative writing, digital sculpting, entertainment design, fabrication, film directing/production, game art, game design, illustration, painting, photography, storyboarding, and virtual reality development

Science and Engineering Apprenticeship Program (SEAP) – US Navy
Patrick SFB, Jacksonville, Orlando, Panama City
8-weeks, 300 openings, 30 labs, $4,000-$4,500 science/engineering research. HS students must be 16+ years old. Apps available in the previous August

SpaceX – Summer Engineering/Co-op Program – Cape Canaveral, FL
Paid Internship - Must be an undergraduate in a STEM subject

University of Florida Design Exploration Program (DEP)
3-week Residential Immersion into architectural studios. Construction of studio design projects, teamwork, seminars, field trips, architectural theory

University of Miami Summer Scholars, Architecture & Design– Coral Gables
3-week Residential program; 6 college credits; Design, Graphics, and Theory. Architecture, Landscape Architecture, Historic Preservation; Urban Planning. Studio experience with drawing, model making, drafting, CAD, visual analysis

Georgia

Emory University – Atlanta, GA – 2-, 4-, 6-Week Writing Programs
Journalism, Dramatic Writing, Media & Politics, Psychology & Fiction

Georgia Institute of Technology Pre-College Design Program – Atlanta, GA
2-week Residential program – College of Design – Grades 11 & 12 (Two Session Options); Architecture, Building Construction, Industrial Design, Music Tech

Georgia Tech Research Inst.- 5-Week Paid Engineering Internship for HS Students
Rapid Prototyping, Robotics, Drone Tech, Physics of Radar, Night Vision

National Security Agency (NSA) – Paid Computer Internship – Augusta
Students must be at least a junior in high school with interest in business, engineering, or computer science. Apply between September 1 and October 31.

Savannah College of Art & Design – Savannah, 5-wk Rising Star & SCAD Courses
2-week College of Design Residential program –– Grades 11 & 12 - Courses include Advertising, Animation, Virtual Reality, Illustration, Storyboarding, Photography, Painting, Fashion, Digital Film, Graphic Design, and Industrial Design

Hawaii

COPE Scholars Program – Healthcare Internship – 280 Hrs Training - Kailua
Health Scholars must be 18+. Students assist w/basic healthcare for medical or nursing school, etc. Certificate of Completion - Keck Graduate Institute.

National Security Agency (NSA) – Paid Computer Internship – Oahu
Students must be at least a junior in high school with interest in business, engineering, or computer science. Apply between September 1 and October 31.

Science and Engineering Apprenticeship Program (SEAP) – US Navy – Honolulu
8-weeks, 300 openings, 30 labs, $4,000-$4,500 science/engineering research. HS students must be 16+ years old. Apps available in the previous August

Pacific Discovery - Hawaii Mid-Teen Summer Program - Big Island
21-day Sustainability, Conservation, Environmental Science Program

Hawaiian Electric Summer Internship Program - College
Paid full-time electrical engineering opportunity - May-August

Idaho

Idaho National Laboratory Internships - 16+ Years Old - Paid Internship - Idaho Falls
Projects in Nuclear Energy, Renewable Energy, National Security - 6 weeks

Illinois

Illinois Institute of Technology Summer Introduction to Architecture
2-week Experiment in Architecture for HS students – Comprehensive overview 1-week Exploration in Architecture for middle school students – studio-based, firm visits, field trips, projects.

Northwestern University – National High School Institute
5-week Film & Video, Music, Speech & Debate, Theatre

School of the Art Institute of Chicago – Early College Program for HS Students
1-, 2-, 4-week Residential programs in Painting, Drawing, Animation, Comics/Graphic Novels, and Fashion Design. Portfolio development programs; earn college credit. Full-tuition scholarships are available.

Southern Illinois University Carbondale – Kid Architecture
1-week Elementary Grades, Middle School & High School Architecture Camp

University of Chicago - RIBS (Bioscience Lab Exp) & Creative Writing Immersion
Research in the Biological Sciences - Intensive hands-on lab experience in biology "Collegiate Writing: Awakening Into Consciousness" & "Creative Writing: Fiction"

University of Illinois Urbana-Champaign - Exploring Your Options - 1 week
HS Juniors & Seniors - interact with UIUC engineering faculty and students

University of Illinois at Chicago Architecture - HiArch Summer High School Program
1, 2-week (July) - Study the culture of architecture, design, thinking, & making

Indiana

Purdue University - HS/College Residential and Virtual Programs
Pre-Vet/Animal Medical, Engineering, Global Challenges, Mgm, Civil Eng. Tomorrow's Infrastructure Prog, Women in Business, plus 650 courses

Rose-Hulman Institute of Technology - Summer Engineering Programs
Rose Power - 9th grade girls; Program Select - 9th, 10th STEM-based; Operation Catapult - 10th, 11th - 12-day project-based

Science and Engineering Apprenticeship Program (SEAP) – US Navy – Crane
8-weeks, 300 openings, 30 labs, $4,000-$4,500 science/engineering research. HS students must be 16+ years old. Apps available in the previous August

University of Notre Dame Summer Scholars Program - 2-weeks - HS Students
Film, Photography, Performing Arts - studios, seminars, and field trips
Introduction to Engineering Program - Aero, Mech, Civil, Computer, ChemE

Iowa

Iowa State University – College of Design - High School Design Camps - 1 week
Architecture, Studio/Fine Arts, Graphic, Interior, & Industrial Design

Louisiana

Louisiana Wildlife & Fisheries - Paid Internship
Wildlife, natural resource protection, fishery support

Science & Engineering Apprenticeship Program (SEAP) US Navy – New Orleans
8-weeks, 300 openings, 30 labs, $4,000-$4,500 science/engineering research. HS students must be 16+ years old. Apps available in the previous August

Maryland

Goddard Space Flight Center (NASA) - High School & College - Greenbelt
Summer Internship - Greenbelt, MD
Research, Mentorship, Experiential Learning Opportunities

Johns Hopkins University - Online/ and In-Person, Hands-On Engineering
Tracks: Engineering Innovation, Biomedical Engineering, or Sustainable Engineering

Lockheed Martin STEM Internships - Multiple Locations
Data Analytics, Computer Science, Business, Intern Academy

Maryland Institute College of Art (MICA) – Baltimore
2-, 3-, 5-week HS Students – Live instruction, studio time, workshops, artist talks, collaboration, feedback, critique, evaluation

National Institute of Health – 8-week – Bethesda
Research biomedical internship for students 17 years or older by June 15th.

National Security Agency (NSA) – Paid Computer Internship – Ft. Meade
Students must be at least a junior in high school with interest in business, engineering, or computer science. Apply between September 1 and October 31.

Science and Engineering Apprenticeship Program (SEAP) – US Navy – Bethesda, Patuxent River, Silver Spring, Indian Head, and Annapolis
8-weeks, 300 openings, 30 labs, $4,000-$4,500 science/engineering research. HS students must be 16+ years old. Apps available in the previous August

University of Maryland – 4-week ESTEEM/SER-Quest Summer Program
Rising seniors undertake engineering-focused projects while conducting research

US Naval Academy Summer STEM Program - Annapolis, MD - 5-day
Engineering, Comp Sci, Design, Robotics, and Motor Engines

Massachusetts

Boston College - Boston, MA – Creative Writing Seminar Program
3-week (July) Residential Program – HS Students – nonfiction, fiction, poetry Create & edit the class literary journal and present writings at a public reading

Boston University Math, Engineering, Technology, Media, and Journalism
AMP - Academy of Media Production – Cinematic/journalistic in visual storytelling (Grades 10 – 12)
Code Breakers – 10th and 11th Grade Females - Cybersecurity, Cryptography, Programming (Free)
GirlsGetMath@BU – 5-day Non-residential summer program for enthusiastic 10th – 11th graders
Journalism Academy – 2-week Training in Writing, Photography, Reporting (students 14-18)
PROMYS – Program in Mathematics for Young Scientists – 6 weeks 80 high school students 14+ years old (scholarships available); seminars in number theory, cryptography, linear algebra, matroids, graphs, and data visualization.
RISE – Research in Science & Engineering - 6-week Research in Science & Engineering program in astronomy, chemistry, neuroscience, and medicine. Engineering Research Options: Biomedical, Computer, Electrical, Mechanical
U-Design – 2-week Engineering Design Program – hands-on build workshop (Grades 6 – 10)

Harvard University GSD Design Discovery – Cambridge, MA

3-week Residential Program – Architecture, Landscape, Urban Planning & Design Physical modeling, fabrication, assembly (Ages 18-mid-career professionals)

Harvard Summer Program for High School Students - Transferable College Classes

3.5 and 7-week college credit program (live in campus dorms)

Credit classes include: Physics, Chemistry, OChem, Biology, Creating Comics & Graphic Novels; Drawing & the Digital Age; Advertising, Landscape, & Visual Imagery; Creative Writing

Massachusetts College of Art & Design – 4-Week Art Immersion Program

Students take 3 foundation courses; final art show at closing exhibition

Massachusetts Institute of Technology – HS Students – Cambridge

Urbanframe Summer Design - Build Project CAD, drafting, sketching, mapping and context study, historical research, carpentry & construction

MITES – Minority Introduction to Engineering and Science – Intensive 6-week residential program for 80 high school juniors who intend to enter STEM programs, especially from underrepresented groups. The program is free.

RSI – Research Science Institute – Intensive 6-week program for 70 high school juniors who study advanced theory/research in math, science, and engineering. The program is free. Extremely competitive; start the application early!

WTP – Women's Technology Program – 4-week engineering program focused on Electrical Engineering, Mechanical Engineering, or Computer Science.

SSP – Summer Science Program – Research program on Astrophysics or Biochemistry. This 6-week research program is located in Colorado, New Mexico, and Indiana.

Beaver Works Summer Institute – 4-week intensive program for first-generation high school juniors. Programs include Autonomous Underwater Vehicles to Quantum Software and to Serious Game Design with AI

LLRise (Lincoln Laboratory Radar) - 2 weeks - HS radar-building program

National Geographic Explorers-Seminars/experiments/capstone AI, Robots, Tech

Inspirit AI Scholars Program - 2-week Project-based comp sci, AI, genomics

Additional MIT Hosted Programs: LaunchX, OSC, iD Tech Camps

National Institute of Health – 8-week – Framingham

Research biomedical internship for students 17 years or older by June 15th.

Tufts University - Pre-College - 2-week - HS School Students

Engineering Design Lab, Engineering Investigations (Residential & Commuter)

Tufts University – 6-Week Writing Intensive

Writing exercises, evaluation from professors, revise, develop papers that build on a theme

University of Massachusetts Amherst Pre-College – Amherst, MA
1-, 2-, 3-week Residential Intensives Grades 10-12; 3-D Design, 3-D Animation, Building & Construction Technology; Combatting the Climate Crisis Summer Engineering Institute, Design Academy, Programming for Aspiring Scientists

Wellesley College – Wellesley, MA - 2-week Residential Program - EXPLO
Pre-College + Career for Grades 10-12 Three session; Topics include – AI, Entrepreneurship, Engineering, Medicine, Law, CSI

Youth Design Boston (AIGA) – Boston, MA
Summer Graphic Design Internship & Mentoring Program

Michigan

Andrews University School of Architecture & Interior Design - Renaissance Kids – Berrien Springs, MI
Virtual Studio Projects; lecture; community build projects

Interlochen Center for the Arts – Summer Arts Camp – 1-6 Weeks
Creative Writing, Dance, Art, Motion Picture, Music, Theatre, Visual Arts

Michigan State University - High School Engineering Institute (HSEI)
2 Sessions - June & July - Mechanical, Biosystems, Computer Science, Electrical, Computer, Civil, and Environmental Engineering; Vex Robotics challenge.

Michigan Technological University Summer Youth Program (SYP) Grades 6 - 11
1,000 students attend MTU each summer - On-Campus College Experience Women in Eng, Geospatial Eng, Railroad Eng, Automotive Eng, Comp Sci

National Institute of Health – 8-week – Detroit
Research biomedical internship for students 17 years or older by June 15th.

University of Michigan – Stamps School of Art & Design – BFA Preview
3-week (June/July)– HS Students – Creative retreat with state-of-the-art facilities & museum excursions

University of Michigan – Summer Engineering Exploration Camp (SEE)
1-week, co-ed, residential program resolving engineering design challenges Apply Jan-Feb – Grades 10-12

Mississippi

Science and Engineering Apprenticeship Program (SEAP) – US Navy – Stennis
8-weeks, 300 openings, 30 labs, $4,000-$4,500 science/engineering research. HS students must be 16+ years old. Apps available in the previous August

Missouri

Washington University in St. Louis – 2-week Creative Writing Institute and HS Summer Scholars Program - 5-8 week Arts/Journalism Program

Writing Workshop - Fiction, nonfiction, and poetry; editing and sharing work Arts - Dance, Journalism, Photography, Music, Drama, Photojournalism

University of Missouri Kansas City – Architecture, Urban Planning & Design

Design Discovery Program – Architecture, Interior Design, Landscape Architecture 3-day (July) Non-Residential Program – HS Students/Current College Students

Nebraska

University of Nebraska College of Architecture – Grades 11 & 12 - Lincoln, NE

6-day (June) Residential Program – Studio; architectural design; scholarships

New Jersey

New Jersey Institute of Technology – Hillier College of Architecture & Design

1-week (July) Residential Program – HS Students – Architecture, Interior Design, Industrial Design, Digital Design-2 Start Dates

Princeton's Laboratory Learning Prog. - 5-6 Weeks - HS Engineering/STEM Research

Free - Mentored by Princeton Faculty - Apply Feb/March - Competitive

Rutgers University - Engineering Summer Academy - Ages 16 - 18 - July 9 - 15

Aerospace, Biochemical, Biomedical, Chemical, Civil, Computer, Electrical, Environmental, Forensic, Industrial, Materials Science, Mechanical, & Systems Eng

Science and Engineering Apprenticeship Program (SEAP) – US Navy – Lakehurst

8-weeks, 300 openings, 30 labs, $4,000-$4,500 science/engineering research. HS students must be 16+ years old. Apps available in the previous August

New York

AIA New York – Center for Architecture

Grades 3-12 - Architectural Design Studio, Drawing Architecture, Rooftop Dwelling, Dream House, Treehouses, Skyscrapers, Green Island Home, Subway Architecture, Waterfront City, Parks & Playground Design, Neighborhood Design

Canon Insights Summer Internship – Canon USA – PR/Marketing - Huntington, NY

Public Relations & Marketing Majors – 10 Week Paid Position

Columbia University - New York, NY – Summer Arts Immersion

3-week July-August Residential Program – Architecture, Creative Writing, Drawing, Filmmaking, Photography, Theater, or Visual Arts

Columbia University SHAPE - Summer HS Academic Program for Engineers
Selective 3-week pre-college program for rising soph, jr, senior, & entering freshmen; comp sci, electrical, robotics, innovation

Cooper Union - New York, NY – Summer Art Intensive - 4-week on campus
Portfolio Development, Exhibition, Anthology Publication; Animation, Creative Writing, Photography, Drawing, Graphic Design, & Stop Animation

Cornell University – Ithaca, NY – Precollege Studies & 3-Week Transmedia: Image, Sound, Motion - 3-, 6-, 9-week June-August Residential Program
Drawing and New Media (collage, drawing, digital photography, screen printing, & video) Architecture: Science & Technology Design Studio, Culture, & Society

Cornell University – CURIE Academy for females going into 11th and 12th
Students who excel in math and science *break the rules* to make new discoveries.

Corning Summer Internships for College Students – Corning, NY
Advanced Optics, Gorilla Glass, Emerging Innovations, Life Sciences, Pharmaceuticals Internships Offered in Engineering, Science, and Business

Goddard Institute for Space Studies Summer Internship - High School & College
Research, Mentorship, and Experiential Learning Opportunities

Jacobs Institute 8-week Paid Biomedical Internship (Apply Nov.-Jan.)
HS Jr/Sr or Enrolled College Student – Gates Vascular Institute, Buffalo Niagara Medical Campus; Lunch & Learn, Weekly Grand Rounds, Research, Presentations

Lockheed Martin STEM Internships - Oswego & Liverpool
Intern Academy, Testing, Quality, Systems, Data Analytics, Electronics, Cybersecurity, Manufacturing, Supply Chain

New York University Summer Art Intensive
4-week Immersive program in Digital & Video, Sculpture, or Visual Arts

New York University Applied Research in Science and Engineering (ARISE)
ARISE is a Free 7-week STEM program focused on Biomedical, Chemical Civil, Computer, Electrical, Mechanical, and Aerospace Engineering

Parsons School of Design – New York and Paris - 4-week - 3rd to 12th grade
NYC - Portfolio building in 3-credit immersive Design, Studio Art, Photography, Illustration, Game Design

Paris – Design & Management, Explorations in Drawing & Painting, Fashion Design

Rensselaer Polytechnic University – Troy, NY
Architecture Career Discovery Program

School of Creative & Performing Arts (SOCAPA) – New York (13-18-year-olds)
2-, 3-week - Learn Filmmaking, Screenwriting, Dance, Music, Photography

Sotheby's Summer Institute – Pre-College, Undergrad, Graduate, and Professional
New York, London, and Virtual Programs; Intensives in Painting & Drawing, Curating, Luxury Marketing, Art Crime/Art Law, Fashion, and Art Business

Spotify – Summer Internship w/Gimlet & The Wall Street Journal – New York
Research, Writing, News Stories, Podcast Work

Syracuse University – Syracuse – On-Campus/Online Programs for HS Students
2-, 3-, 6-week programs 3-D Studio Art; Sculpture; Architecture; Design Studies; Writing Immersion

University of Rochester - Biomedical Engineering - 2 & 4-week - 13+
Solving the Body's Challenges with Technology - Online Course

Vaughn College of Aeronautics & Technology, NYC, TryEngineering Summer
Institute of Electrical & Electronics Engineers Camp for future engineers - 11 days Civil, Electrical, Mechanical, and Aerospace Engineering - 13-17 year olds

North Carolina

Corning Summer Internships for College Students – Charlotte, NC
Advanced Optics, Gorilla Glass, Emerging Innovations, Life Sciences, Pharmaceuticals Internships Offered in Engineering, Science, and Business

Duke Talent Identification Program (TIP)
Pre-College Program for 6th - 11th Grade Students

National Institute of Health – 8-week – Research Triangle Park
Research biomedical internship for students 17 years or older by June 15th.

North Carolina State University - Numerous Summer HS Programs in Engineering, TV, Broadcasting, and Design

Communication - TV, Broadcasting, Camers, Audio Boards Pre-Vet, Agriculture, Horticulture, Poultry, and Livestock Engineering, SATELLITE, Polymers, and Nuclear Engineering

Science and Engineering Apprenticeship Program (SEAP) – US Navy – Cherry Point

8-weeks, 300 openings, 30 labs, $4,000-$4,500 science/engineering research. HS students must be 16+ years old. Apps available in the previous August

Ohio

Ohio State Univ - 1-week Hands-On   STEM/Engineering Summer Camp - Marion

6th - 8th grade - Middle School Engineering & Career Pathway Program; 9th - 12th grade STEM Program & 11th - 12th grade Project-Based

Science and Engineering Apprenticeship Program (SEAP) – US Navy – Dayton

8-weeks, 300 openings, 30 labs, $4,000-$4,500 science/engineering research. HS students must be 16+ years old. Apps available in the previous August

Oklahoma

University of Oklahoma Architecture Summer Academy - 1-week (June) Campus

HS Students – Architecture, Interior Design, Construction Science Design in Action: Creativity, Innovation, and Sustainability Shaping the Built Environment

Pennsylvania

Bucknell Engineering Camp - BASE (Summer Experience) - HS Students

Academically challenging hands-on introduction to engineering

Carnegie Mellon University Pre-College Art Program - Pittsburgh, PA

3-, 4-, 6-week (July-August) Residential Program – Intensive Studio Studies Portfolio development in Drawing, Sculpture, Animation, and Concept Studio Art Chestnut Hill College Global Solutions Lab

Carnegie Mellon SAI Academy, Computer Science Academy, Electrifying Africa

Project-Based Camp - Comp Sci/Engineering Progs for HS Students in Electrical Engineering, Software, Technology, Machine Learning & AI National High School Game Academy - Visual Arts, Music & Audio Game Design & Software Devlpt

Summer Academy for Math & Science - STEM opportunity for underrep students to explore science w/hands-on projects and class instruction. Free.

SEE: Summer Engineering Experience - grades 8 - 11 - Hands-on - 1 week

SEE: Biomedical Engineering - grades 10 & 11 - July 24-28 - Presentations/projects in biomechanics, stem cell, tissue engineering, robotics, circuits, 3D bioprinti

Drexel University College of Media Arts & Design – Summer Architecture
2-week Residential Program – HS Students – Intensive Studio Architecture Program Visit prominent architectural, multi-disciplinary design offices; meet architects

Maywood University Pre-College Summer Workshop School of Architecture
2-week (July) Residential Program – HS Students – Design Your Future Architecture Program

Pennsylvania State University Architecture & Landscape Architecture Summer Camp
1-week (July) – HS Students – Architecture, Graphics, Design, and the Built Environment Program

Science & Engineering Apprenticeship Program (SEAP) US Navy – Philadelphia
8-weeks, 300 openings, 30 labs, $4,000-$4,500 science/engineering research. HS students must be 16+ years old. Apps available in the previous August.

Temple University Tyler School of Art and Architecture Pre-College Program
2-week (July-August) Residential Program – HS Students – Studio Architecture

University of Pennsylvania - 9th - 11th - STEM Academies and Tech Business
Summer Research - Biomedical, Chemical, Experimental Physics, Mathematics, Neuroscience, Coding. Also, Social Justice, Global Cultures, & Media

University of Pennsylvania, TryEngineering Summer Camp - 11 days - 13-17 year olds
Institute of Electrical & Electronics Engineers (IEEE) Camp for future engineers Civil, Electrical, Mechanical, and Aerospace Engineering

Rhode Island

Brown University – 1-4 Weeks – Art Themed Courses
Creative Writing, Music, Studio Art, Art History

Rhode Island School of Design Pre-College School of Design – Providence, RI
6-week (June-July) Residential Program – HS Students – Foundational Art & Design Studies - Figure drawing, projects, trips, exhibitions

Roger Williams University High School Summer Academy in Architecture
4-week (July-August) Residential Program – Grades 11 & 12 – Explore Studio Architecture - Seminars, fieldwork, studio, portfolio development

South Carolina

Clemson University Pre-College School of Architecture Program
1-week (July-August) Residential Program – Grades 7-12 - Engineering Design, Mechanical/Civil Engineering, Intelligent Vehicles, Materials Engineering

Science and Engineering Apprenticeship Program – US Navy – Charleston
8-weeks, 300 openings, 30 labs, $4,000-$4,500 science/engineering research. HS students must be 16+ years old. Apps available in the previous August

Tennessee

University of Memphis Discovering Architecture + Design - 1-day – HS Students
Design programs on architecture, interior design, and the built environment

University of Tennessee, Knoxville College of Architecture + Design
1-week UT Summer Design Camp (July) Residential – HS Students
Immersive architecture, graphic design, and professional practice program

Vanderbilt Summer Academy – Nashville, TN – 3-Week Program
"Digital Storytelling", "Writing Fantasy Fiction", "Math & Music", "Writing Short Stories"

Texas

Boeing Summer Internship – HS & College – Lewisville and San Antonio
Hands-on Industry Experience - Aviation and Engineering Internships

Corning Summer Internships for College Students – Keller, TX
Advanced Optics, Gorilla Glass, Emerging Innovations, Life Sciences, Pharmaceuticals Internships Offered in Engineering, Science, and Business

Jacobs Engineering Internship – Summer Internship (College) - Dallas
Civil, Electrical, Environmental, Geotechnical, & Transportation Engineering; Sustainability, Cybersecurity, Mobility, and R&D with worldwide projects

Lockheed Martin STEM Internships - Multiple Locations
Intern Academy, Industrial Engineering, Project Mgmt, Data Analytics, Aerospace, Manufacturing, Quality, Testing, Software, and Mechanical Engineering

National Security Agency (NSA) – Paid Computer Internship – San Antonio
Students must be at least a junior in high school with interest in business, engineering, or computer science. Apply between September 1 and October 31.

Rice Univ, Houston, Try Engineering Summer Camp - 11 days - 13-17 year olds
Institute of Electrical & Electronics Engineers (IEEE) Camp for future engineers Civil, Electrical, Mechanical, and Aerospace Engineering

SpaceX – Summer Engineering/Co-op Program – Brownsville and McGregor, TX
Paid Internship - Must be in an undergraduate in a STEM subject

Tesla Internships – Ave. $33/hour – Full-Time Automotive Design/Engineering
Austin – Manufacturing Engineering; Waco - People Analytics - Vehicle Service Research/Training

Texas Tech Anson L Clark Scholars Program – Research Areas: Advertising, Architecture, Art, Dance, Engineering, or Theatre
7-week – Grades 11 & 12 – Residential Program (must be 17 by start date) -Intensive research-based program; $500 meal card; $750 tax-free stipend

University of Texas at Austin - My Introduction to Engineering (MITE)
5-day camp for 11th grade students to work on team-based engineering projects

University of Houston & Wonderworks Pre-College Summer Discovery Program
Hines College of Architecture & Design – Introduction to Architecture

6-week – HS Students – Design programs with hands-on studio, field trips, and portfolio workshop

University of Texas at Austin Summer Design Camps -1 week – HS Students
2-D Game Design, 3-D Game Design, 3-D Animation/Motion - School of Design & Creative Technologies - portfolio development and design

University of Texas Moody College of Communication - Sports Journalism Camp
Hands-on weekend - Mock Press Conf - Learn Print, Television, Online Platforms

University of Texas - Longhorn Engineering Summer Camp (LESC) - Houston, San Antonio, Austin - 5-day, free camp for students in 8th & 9th & MITE for 11th
LESC - Interactive, mixing art, sports, medicine, sustainability, and engineering

My Introduction to Engineering (MITE) - 5-day camp for 11th grade students work on team-based engineering projects

Utah

BYU - Youth Cybersecurity Camps - July (1-week) Free 13-18 year olds
Cyber projects, Security Awareness, AI, Hands-On Projects
Intergallactic Coding Camp and Girls' Coding Camp

Edwards Lifesciences Summer Internship Program – Draper, Utah
Currently Enrolled in College - Interested in Healthcare Related Programs
Proficient in Engineering Draft ing Soft ware, Writing, or Business/Leadership

Vermont

School of Creative & Performing Arts (SOCAPA) – Burlington, VT (13-18-year-olds)
2-week, 3-week - learn Filmmaking, Screenwriting, Dance, Music, Photography

Virginia

Liberty University - CyberPatriot Cybersecurity Safety/Career Camp for HS Students
National Cyber Defense Competition - cyber ethics/threats, virtual machines

NASA's Langley Research Center - Hampton, VA - Paid Internship for HS Students
Space Hardware Design, Mars Surface Habitat, Aerial Robotics/Dynamics/Control

NASA's Wallops Flight Facility Summer Internship - High School & College
Research, Mentorship, and Experiential Learning Opportunities

Northrop Grumman – Engineering Intern– Space Systems R & D Team
Graduating HS Seniors – Join an engineering team to design, develop and test space systems and satellites; R & D - land, sea, air, space, and cyberspace.

Science and Engineering Apprenticeship Program (SEAP) – US Navy Hampton Roads and Dahlgren
8-weeks, 300 openings, 30 labs, $4,000-$4,500 science/engineering research. HS students must be 16+ years old. Apps available in the previous August

University of Virginia - UVA Advance - 4-week Program for HS Juniors & Seniors
Residential program for highly motivated students - take 2 undergrad classes
Options include: Space, Oceans, IR, Humanities, Writing, Art, Culture, Africa

Virginia Commonwealth Univ (VCUArts) Pre-College - 3-Week, On-Campus
2D Portfolio Dev., Photography; Clay: More Than Just Mud, Sketchbook to Controller, Animation Workshop, Sculptural Forms, Jewelry Making, Fashion Design, Stage Combat, Musical Theatre, Acting From Page to Stage

Virginia Tech Inside Architecture + Design
1-week – HS Students – Hands-on design studio architecture program

Washington

COPE Scholars Program – Healthcare Internship – 280 Hours Training Locations in Puyallup, Seattle, Spokane, and Tacoma

Health Scholars must be 18+. Students assist w/basic healthcare for medical or nursing school, etc. Certificate of Completion - Keck Graduate Institute.

DigiPen Academy – K-12 Animation, Film, Music, Game Design Summer Programs – Redmond, WA

1-week and 2-week programs, including Teen Art & Animation; Film Scoring Music & Sound Design; Video Game Development; Animation Masterclass

Eastern Washington University - HS CyberPatriot Cybersecurity Safety/Career Camp

National Cyber Defense Competition, cyber ethics/threats, virtual machines

Science and Engineering Apprenticeship Program (SEAP) – US Navy – 2 WA Locations

8-weeks, 300 openings, 30 laboratories nationwide, $4,000-$4,500 science and engineering research. High school students must be 16 years old or older. Apply starting in August for following summer.

University of Washington – Seattle, WA – Middle and HS Students

1-Week - Neurotechnology Young Scholars Program, DawgBytes Computer Science Camp, Material Science Camp, and Summer Session Art Classes

West Virginia

NASA Independent Verification and Validation Facility, Fairmont, WV

Internship - Research, Mentorship, and Experiential Learning Opportunities

Wisconsin

The University of Wisconsin Milwaukee School of Architecture & Urban Planning

1-week – HS Students – Design program on architecture, interior design, and the built environment

TAKE ADVANTAGE OF THIS TIME TO EXPLORE

During high school and college, you have the opportunity to explore your interests through summer programs, skill-building camps, and internships. Try out different fields you might not have considered before. You never really have the same chance to consider alternatives in quite the same way.

Learn something new. There are hundreds of career areas you may never have considered. Meanwhile, meet new people and have some fun while you are at it!

Everything has its beauty, but not everyone sees it.

– Andy Warhol

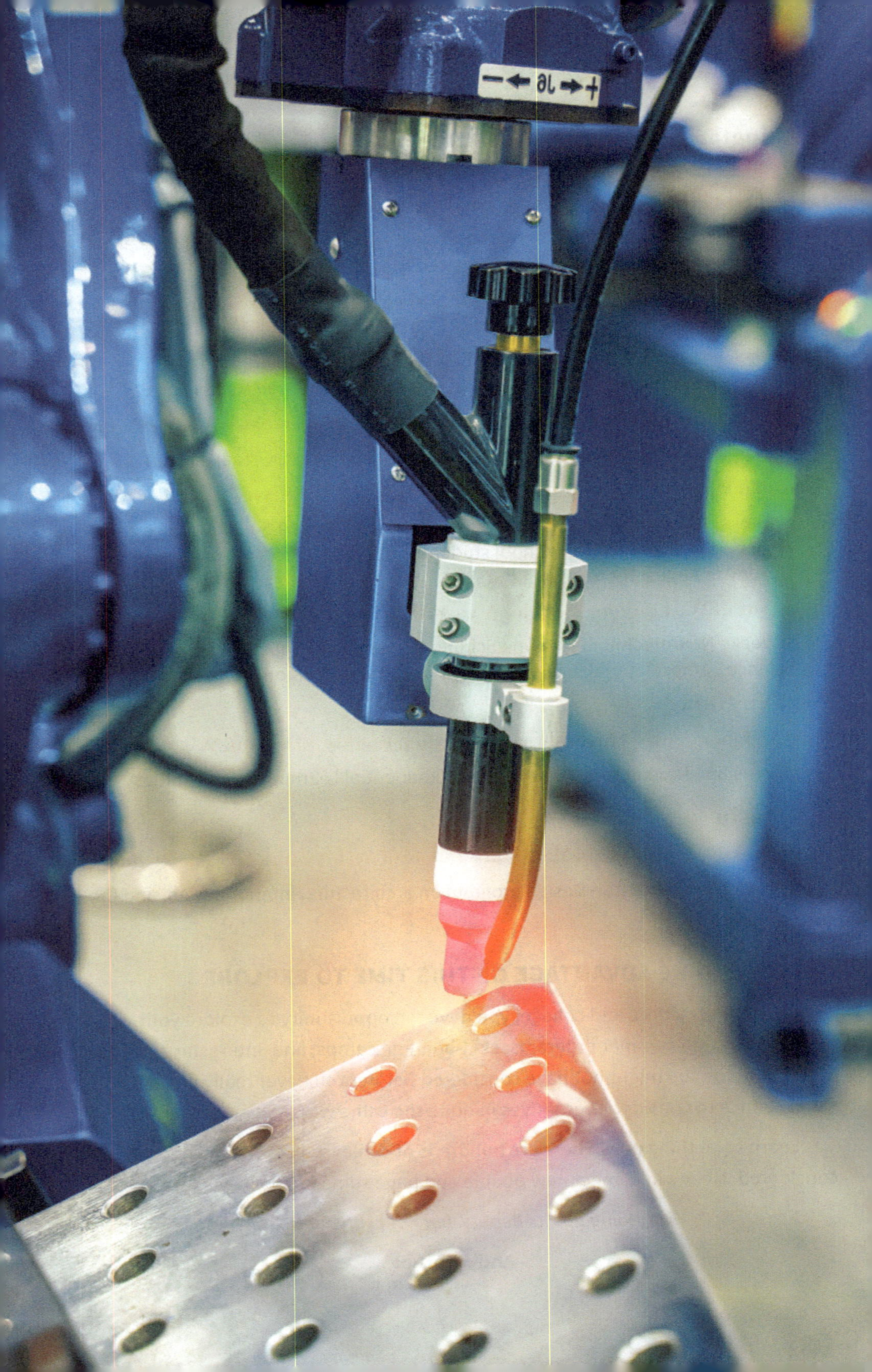

CHAPTER 5
UNIVERSITY OPTIONS: COLLEGE PROGRAMS FOR ENGINEERING

"Take the best that exists and make it better."

– **Henry Royce**

The Accrediting Board for Engineering and Technology (ABET) is the body that approves engineering programs. To be licensed, you should attend an ABET-accredited school. Though accreditation is voluntary, colleges use ABET accreditation to ensure the legitimacy of their programs to outside parties.

As of May 2022, there were 4,361 ABET-accredited programs at 850 colleges and universities in 41 countries. Moreover, approximately 175,000 students graduate from ABET-accredited programs each year. To date, there are millions of graduates from ABET-accredited programs. Employment is rising for engineers after a drop during the pandemic. The need for engineers in all areas of expertise is high.

By the numbers, here are some big picture data for 2022.

- 19.6 million U.S. College Students
- 14.5 million attending public colleges
- 5.14 million attending private colleges
- 2,679 4-year colleges
- 1,303 2-year colleges

Another interesting statistic is that undergraduate enrollment dropped more than 4% from fall 2019 to fall 2020 and another 3.5% from fall 2020 to fall 2021, representing approximately a 1,500,000 loss of students during the pandemic. However, with test-optional admissions opening the door to more students without test scores or who test poorly, more students applied to the top schools.

In 2022, there were 485 accredited mechanical engineering programs offering bachelor's degrees worldwide. Just within the United States, there are 392 ABET-accredited mechanical engineering programs.[1] There are two schools that offer ABET-accredited master's programs in mechanical engineering.

US NEWS & WORLD REPORT
2022 Mechanical Engineering Rankings (Top 12)

1. Massachusetts Inst. of Tech
2. Georgia Institute of Technology
3. Stanford University
4. University of California—Berkeley
5. California Inst. of Technology
6. University of Michigan--Ann Arbor
7. University of Illinois--Urbana-Champaign
8. Purdue University
9. Carnegie Mellon University
10. Cornell University
11. University of Texas--Austin
12. Texas A&M University

---

1   ABET.org. Accredited Programs. https://amspub.abet.org/aps/category-search?disciplines=15&degreeLevels=B&countries=US

TOP COLLEGES WORLDWIDE IN MECHANICAL ENGINEERING

(QS Top 50 Universities – Titles Abbreviated)

1. Massachusetts Institute of Tech. (MIT)
2. Stanford University (US)
3. University of Cambridge (UK)
4. Harvard University (US)
5. Delft Univ. of Tech. (Netherlands)
6. University of California, Berkeley (US)
7. Nanyang Technological Univ. (Singapore)
8. ETH Zurich – Swiss Federal Inst. of Tech.
9. National Univ. of Singapore (NUS)
10. Imperial College London (UK)
11. Univ. of Michigan, Ann Arbor (US)
12. University of Oxford (UK)
13. Politecnico de Milano (Italy)
14. Georgia Tech (US)
15. California Institute of Tech. (US)
16. EPFL (Switzerland)
17. Purdue University (US)
18. Tsinghua University (China)
19. RWTH Aachen University (Germany)
20. University of Tokyo (Japan)
21. Technical Univ. of Munich (Germany)
22. KAIST – Korea Adv. Inst. of Sci. & Tech.
23. Univ. of Manchester (UK)
24. Univ. of Illinois at U-C (US)
25. Seoul National University (Korea)
26. KTH Royal Inst. of Tech. (Sweden)
27. Cranfield University (UK)
28. Pennsylvania State Univ. (US)
29. Univ. of California, Los Angeles (US)
30. Univ. of Texas at Austin (US)
31. Politecnico de Torino (Italy)
32. Shanghai Jiao Tong Univ. (China)
33. Univ. of Toronto (Canada)
34. Peking University (China)
35. Northwestern University (US)
36. Eindhoven Univ. of Tech. (Netherlands)
37. Princeton University (US)
38. KU Leuven (Belgium)
39. KIT Karlsruhe Inst. of Tech. (Germany)
40. Institut Polytechnique de Paris (France)
41. McGill University (Canada)
42. Hong Kong Univ. of Science & Tech.
43. Tokyo Inst. of Technology (Japan)
44. Technical Univ. of Denmark
45. Cornell University (US)
46. Texas A&M (US)
47. Universitat Stuttgart (Germany)
48. Technische Universitat (Germany)
49. University of Waterloo (Canada)
50. Univ. of New South Wales (Australia)

AMERICAN SOCIETY OF MECHANICAL ENGINEERS

The American Society of Mechanical Engineers (ASME) includes more than 600 student chapters in 40 countries with more than 20,000 student members.

The American Society of Mechanical Engineers (ASME) has over 110,000 members in 150 countries. Student chapters offer opportunities for training, competitions, and leadership. Membership is free for freshmen and $25 per year afterward. Students receive the *Mechanical Engineering Magazine, R&D Pulse* quarterly access, *Codes & Standards*, mentoring, webinars, career center, book/car/technology discounts, and more. Members can obtain certifications in specific areas.

ASME ENGINEERING FESTIVALS (E-FESTS)

ASME engages young people and inspires them to pursue engineering through three-day flagship E-Fest mechanical engineering events, allowing engineering undergraduate students worldwide to learn, innovate, and expand their skillsets. ASME EFx offers a college campus version with the support of ASME staff. ASME FutureME is a community of early-career engineers to gain new technical and professional tools. ASME Contests include

- Extended Reality Challenge: Autonomous Racing 2022
- Environmental Systems Engineering Division Competition
- Human Powered Vehicle Challenge (e-HPVC), sponsored by Altair
- Student Design Competition (SDC), sponsored by Boeing
- Innovative Additive Manufacturing 3D Challenge (IAM3D™)
- Elevator Pitch Competition, sponsored by the ASME Old Guard
- Oral Competition, sponsored by the ASME Old Guard
- Technical Digital Poster Competition, sponsored by the ASME Old Guard

ADMISSIONS DATA TO CONSIDER

The following chart presents data (in white) for the Ivy League class of 2026. The data in yellow is for the class of 2025.

University	Total # Applied	Total Admit Rate	# Applied Regular Decision	# of Admits Regular	Reg. Dec. Admit Rate	Applied ED/SEA	Accepted Early Dec or SEA	ED/SEA Admit Rate
Brown	50,649	5.03%	44,503	1,651	3.71%	6,146	896	14.58%
Columbia	60,377	3.73%	54,072	1,603	2.96%	6,305	650	10.31%
Cornell	71,000	10.3%	61,500	3,922	6.7%	9,500	1,930	21.4%
Dartmouth	28,336	6.2%	25,703	1,237	4.81%	2,633	530	20.13%
Harvard	61,220	3.19%	51,814	1,214	2.34%	9,406	740	7.87%
Penn	55,000	4.4%	47,205	2,008	4.2%	7,795	1,218	15.63%
Princeton		3.98%	Princeton did not publish data for 2025 & will not publish data for 2026					
Yale	50,015	4.46%	42,727	1,434	3.36%	7,288	800	10.98%

Additional Schools Note: - yellow areas - data unavailable or from the class of 2025.

University	Total # Applied	Total Admit Rate	Applied ED/Early Action	Accepted ED/Early Action	ED/EA Admit Rate
Boston College	40,477	16.5%	4,443	1,250	28.13%
Boston U	80,792	14.15%	6,311	1,640	25.99%
Duke	50,002	6.17%	4,015	855	21.3%
Emory	33,559	10.66%	2,127	672	31.59%
Georgetown	26,670	12.11%	8,832	881	9.98%
GWU	27,301	49%	1051	681	65%
Georgia Tech	50,601	17.14%	6,100	2,399	39.33%
Harvey Mudd	4,440	12.97%	Unavailable		
Johns Hopkins	37,100	6.49%	2,500	520	20.8%
MIT	33,976	3.94%	14,781	697	4.72%
NYU	105,000	12.2%	19,000	7,220	38%
Northeastern ED	91,100	6.7%	2,700	880	32.59%
Northeastern EA			50,000	3,000	6%
Northwestern	51,554	7.0%	26,506	1,675	12.87%
Notre Dame	26,506	12.87%	9,683	1,675	17.30%
Rice	31,424	8.56%	2,700	650	24.07%
Tufts	34,880	9.0%	Unavailable		
Tulane	42,000	10.0%	26,483	4,588	17.32%
USC	69,000	11.88%	USC does not have EA, ED, or REA		
Vanderbilt	46,717	6.13%	2,700	650	24.07%
Villanova	23,813	23.%	2025 – EA - 25.2%, ED – 58%		
Wash U St. L.	35,980	10.0%	Unavailable		17.6%
Wesleyan	14,521	13.86%	2026 – EDI - 44%, EDII – 31%		

UNIVERSITY OF CALIFORNIA

The 2022 University of California Fact Sheet data below from UC Admissions, says, "Data are Subject to Change". Nonetheless, here is a comparison between admissions to the class of 2024 and admission to the class of 2026.[2]

University of California Campus	Residency of Applicants	Class of 2024	Class of 2026	Class of 2027
Berkeley	California	50,223	72,417	72,656
	Out-of-State	20,659	32,580	31,309
	International	17,114	23,195	21,909
	Total	**88,026**	**128,192**	**125,874**
Davis	California	54,570	65,367	65,109
	Out-of-State	6,505	10,748	11,402
	International	15,798	18,610	18,098
	Total	**76,873**	**94,725**	**94,609**
Irvine	California	72,391	84,743	86,409
	Out-of-State	8,000	14,309	15,410
	International	17,525	20,113	19,255
	Total	**97,916**	**119,165**	**121.074**
Los Angeles	California	67,877	91,544	90,747
	Out-of-State	23,016	34,627	33,066
	International	17,944	23,608	22,069
	Total	**108,837**	**149,779**	**145,882**
Merced	California	22,244	22,516	21,854
	Out-of-State	598	1,319	1,271
	International	1,534	2,208	2,605
	Total	**24,376**	**26,043**	**25,730**
Riverside	California	43,151	46,456	47,823
	Out-of-State	1,473	2,492	2,807
	International	4,628	5,417	5,832
	Total	**49,252**	**54,365**	**56,462**
San Diego	California	66,350	84,326	84,910
	Out-of-State	14,364	23,778	23.951
	International	19,320	23,112	21,969
	Total	**100,034**	**131,226**	**130,830**
Santa Barbara	California	63,269	73,575	74.902
	Out-of-State	10,988	18,432	18,390
	International	16,690	18,984	17,569
	Total	**90,947**	**110,991**	**110,861**
Santa Cruz	California	43,893	53,051	54,846
	Out-of-State	3,897	6,878	7,382
	International	7,213	5,937	6,592
	Total	**55,003**	**65,886**	**68,820**

---

2   University of California. 2022. "Table 1.1: University of California FRESHMAN Applications by Campus and Residency Fall 2020, 2021, and 2022. https://www.ucop.edu/institutional-research-academic-planning/_files/factsheets/2022/table-1.1-freshman-applications-by-campus-and-residency.pdf

THE MANY ROADS TO ENGINEERING SUCCESS

There are numerous ways you can navigate your personal success strategy by applying your knowledge of mechanical engineering. You might focus on fuels, mechanics, or smart technologies as artificial intelligence and robotics transform society. Applications to LED/light sensors, climate control, navigation technologies, smart sound, roadway kinetics, and energy efficiency offer novel opportunities in your future as the Internet of Things (IoT) connect devices in the seamless, voice activated, and wireless future.

Imagine telling your personal robot to repair your engine or change a tire. Consider how geolocation technologies can sense nearby drones, find open landing pads, or avoid collisions. You might even choose to pursue the policy-making route to devise next-generation rules of the air, land, and sea.

The training you get in college can be immensely valuable, particularly while being surrounded by highly skilled practitioners. There is no one road to get to your goal, just as there is not one goal you may want to achieve. Skills in engineering design and manufacturing offer numerous pathways and byways.

Some successful engineers attended smaller college programs where they first gained a broader or more extensive hands-on and personalized education. Exposure to the many different possibilities of engineering with students who have diverse interests cannot be understated.

Whichever road you take, enjoy the journey.

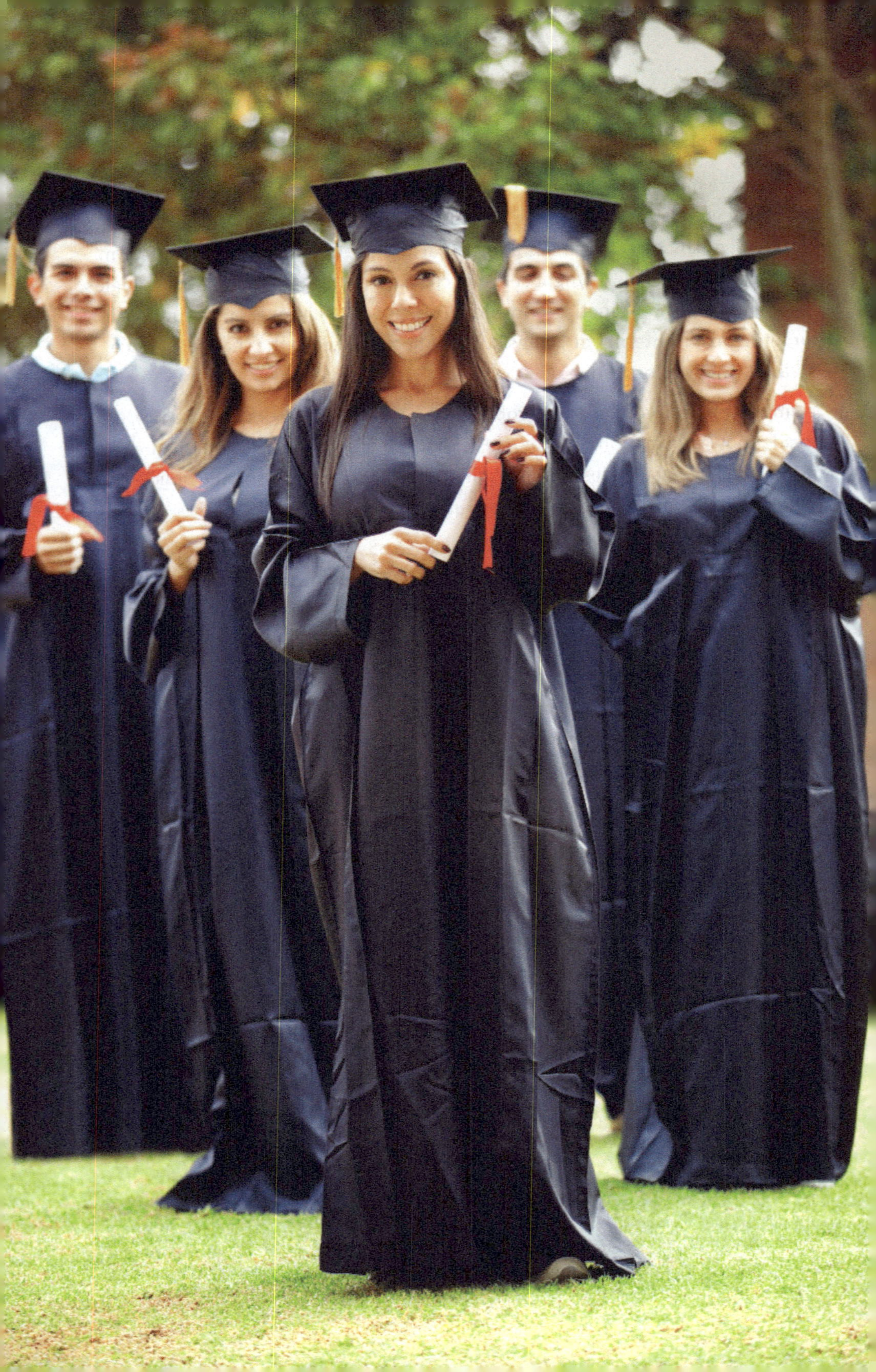

CHAPTER 6

COLLEGE DEGREES: TIMING, LOCATION, COSTS, & EARNING POWER

"We are all the construction of a story and it is only at the end that we can assess the value of the plot."

– **Anonymous**

UNDERGRADUATE AND GRADUATE DEGREES

AA – Associate of Arts: 2-year degree

AS – Associate of Science: 2-year degree

BA – Bachelor of Arts: 4-year degree

BArch – Bachelor of Architecture: 5-year professional credential program

BDes – Bachelor of Design: 4-year degree with classes focused on design

BEd – Bachelor of Education: 4-year program focused on teaching & learning

BEng – Bachelor of Engineering: 4-5-year engineering-focused program

BESc – Bachelor of Engineering Science: 4-year science & engineering program

BFA – Bachelor of Fine Arts: 4-year degree with classes focused on art/design

BID – Bachelor of Industrial Design: 4-year Industrial Design-focused degree

BS – Bachelor of Science: 4-year STEM-focused degree

BSCE – Bachelor of Science in Civil Engineering

BS Chem E – Bachelor of Science in Chemical Engineering

BS Comp Sci – Bachelor of Science in Computer Science

BSEE – Bachelor of Science in Electrical Engineering

BSIE – Bachelor of Science in Industrial Engineering

BSME – Bachelor of Science in Mechanical Engineering

EdD – Doctor of Education: 3-5-year program focused on teaching & learning

MA – Master of Arts: 1-2-year specialized degree

MArch – Master of Architecture: 1-3-year professional credential program

MDes – Master of Design: 1-2-year design-focused specialized

MEd – Master of Education: 1-2-year education-focused program

MEng – Master of Engineering: 1-2-year engineering program

MFA – Master of Fine Arts: 1-2-year degree earned after the BA, BS, or BFA

MID – Master of Industrial Design: 1-2-year Industrial Design-focused degree

Minor – Students take 6 to 10 additional classes in an interest area

MS – Master of Science: 1-2-year STEM-focused

MSID – Master of Science in Industrial Design: science-focused Industrial Design

Ph.D. – Doctor of Philosophy: doctorates in any field (typically 3 – 8 years)

AA (ASSOCIATE OF ARTS) & AS (ASSOCIATE OF SCIENCE)

The AA or AS degree is typically a 2-year general studies degree offered online or in-person through a community college. However, some universities offer AA or AS degrees as well. Often, the Associate of Arts degree, while focused on the liberal arts, has no barrier to entry, meaning that students can enter most AA programs with a high school diploma or the equivalent.

The AS degree frequently emphasizes science and math and often has additional requirements. Some students take more or less time to complete the AA based upon their skills upon entering the program, certainty of their direction, and the transfer requirements. For example, students majoring in engineering have additional science and math requirements and need to create an academic plan early in their program to finish in two years.

BA (BACHELOR OF ARTS) & BS (BACHELOR OF SCIENCE)

The BA and BS degrees are 4- or 5-year undergraduate degrees that typically offer a liberal arts foundation along with a major or concentration in a specific subject. The BA and BS degrees frequently require students to take lower-division (first and second-year) liberal arts courses before taking specialized courses focused around a major or concentration in their third and fourth years.

For accredited engineering programs, there is typically a fifth year due to the additional experiential requirements. Classes may be taught online or in person. Some students complete their BS in fewer years depending upon AP/IB credit, dual enrollment, and summer/intersession classes.

A BFA is considered a professional arts-focused degree with fewer courses in English, science, math, social science, and the humanities. Thus, the BFA, BDes, BID, BArch are specialist qualifications. The BEng focuses on STEM subjects, while

BEd focuses on education. The BA and BS degrees include significantly more liberal arts classes and thus are more general degrees.

The intention of the BFA, BDes, BID, BArch degrees is for students to pursue a focused curriculum with uniquely tailored courses. Finally, a BA or BS are often interchangeable. Thus, a BFA may be seen as different since there is typically more coursework focused on a specific pursuit with limited broad knowledge and more of a concentration on technical, profession-oriented experiences.

MASTER'S DEGREES & DOCTORAL DEGREES

Both the master's degree and doctorate are specialized, graduate degree programs for students who have completed their bachelor's degree. These degrees can take between one and eight years depending upon coursework, research, practicum, capstone, thesis, qualifying exams, and experiential requirements. Students focus on their field of interest and immerse themselves to gain in-depth practical, coursework, and research training.

I have more than ten graduate degrees so far; each set of requirements is distinct. Their programs and processes are designed differently as well. Do not expect standardization. However, one consistency is that with a master's degree or doctorate you graduate with a much deeper knowledge of the specialty. While admission into these programs is generally selective, planning, preparation, and a good resume of experiences are required. Search for a program that fits your needs. There are numerous options for you to pursue your interests.

THE SEVEN MAJOR DIFFERENCES BETWEEN THE ASSOCIATE, BACHELORS, AND MASTER'S DEGREES

1. Starting Point
2. Academic Discipline
3. Time to Completion
4. Location of the Education
5. Educational Costs
6. Earning Power
7. Professional Opportunities

STARTING POINT

Most students who begin with an Associate of Arts (AA) or Associate of Science (AS) have no college credits. Starting from scratch with their college education, students accumulate 60+ units beginning with community college as a starting point. While most students earn AA or AS degrees at a community college, some earn this degree at a 4-year college or university.

The AA or AS is either a terminal degree, meaning that the student will not continue on with their bachelor's degree or just a steppingstone to their BA, BS, or BFA. The difference between associate's and bachelor's degrees is just the starting point. Meanwhile, the starting point for the master's degree (MA, MS, or MFA) begins after obtaining a bachelor's degree.

ACADEMIC DISCIPLINE

Every degree encompasses different requirements. Requirements for the AA differ from an AS. Similarly, the requirements for the BA, BS, and BFA also differ. With two additional years of coursework, the BA, BS, and BFA are more thorough. The MA, MS, and MFA build upon the bachelor's degree and even deeper. Students studying civil engineering will not take the same classes as those pursuing mechanical engineering, though some may overlap. While both are essential to engineering, the necessary skills for each career area are distinct. Thus, the course requirements are also unique.

Furthermore, with the myriad of combinations, it is rare that any two undergraduate students take the same exact classes in the same exact order. For example, since the requirements for a physics degree are not the same as for mechanical engineering, the various degrees not only include a different number of credits but different types of classes and program specifications.

TIME TO COMPLETION

Associate of Arts (AA) and Associate of Science (AS) degrees typically take two years, while most BA, BS, and BFA degrees are 4- or 5-year programs, depending upon full-time or part-time status. Students who transfer in credits or earn credits through CLEP or testing out can reduce their time to completion.

The time required to earn a bachelor's degree depends upon each student's skills and advanced credit. Still, some students change their chosen major which can add more time. According to the National Center for Educational Statistics, college advisors aid students in finishing "on time" though less than half of all students in the United States who start a bachelor's degree do not finish their degree in four years.[1]

Time in college can be reduced. Some students enter bachelor's degree programs with college credits because they were either dual-enrolled or they took college classes outside of school. Some students who earn qualifying scores on AP/IB tests from advanced classes taken in high school are granted credits by the college or university. Policies regarding AP/IB credit vary widely. Look on each college's website.

Other ways students can enter at a different starting point are with credit-by-exam, CLEP tests, experiential credits, and units granted in the military. Colleges and universities are keenly aware of the challenges students face today with work, illness, and family responsibilities. Thus, many schools of higher education offer flexible enrollment with opportunities for part-time, evening, weekend, and online classes.

LOCATION OF THE EDUCATION

The AA and AS are earned at colleges that grant 2-year degrees. The location may be at a local community college or a university. BA, BS, and BFA programs are offered at a 4-year college or university. However, with online classes, students have the flexibility to take classes from colleges farther away as well.

---

1   IEC NCES, "Digest of Education Statistics, Table 326.10," IES NCES, n.d., https://nces.ed.gov/programs/digest/d20/tables/dt20_326.10.asp?referer=raceindica.asp

Thus, the location in which a typical student studies is not as set as it once was. Nevertheless, the in-person internships are often situated in corporate hubs and thus require grounding in a specific location.

EDUCATIONAL COSTS

Since the AA or AS requires a shorter amount of time and is typically completed at a lower-cost community college, the cost of an associate's degree is typically less than a bachelor's degree. Master's degree programs cost more per credit but take less time than a bachelor's degree. Graduate students tuition is often waived for those who are teaching or research assistants.

Many students also obtain grants, loans, and both merit and need-based scholarships. This financial aid can pay for school and reduce debt after college.

> *We must be willing to let go of the life we planned to have the life that is waiting for us.*
>
> **- Joseph Campbell**

EARNING POWER

Students with more education can earn more. According to the 2019 National Center for Educational Statistics (NCES) data for the median person is as follows.[2]

- Master's Degree or Higher - $70,000
- Bachelor's Degree - $55,700
- Associate's Degree - $43,300
- High School - $35,000

Of course, there is a wide range in salaries from those who have consistent contracts and are paid six-digit or seven-digit salaries to those who earn less than $20,000. Thus, the average salary may seem low since the variation is huge.

PROFESSIONAL OPPORTUNITIES

Earning a BA, BS, BEng opens more doors than an AA or AS. Similarly, an MA, MS, or MFA typically opens more doors than a BA, BS, or BEng. Master's degrees require more training. You can also obtain some skills through workshops, symposia, and

---

2 IES NCES, "Annual Earnings by Educational Attainment," IEC NCES, May 2021, https://nces.ed.gov/programs/coe/indicator/cba

conferences, but with a scholarship to pay for college, you might find that the training and opportunities are worth your time. Besides, you will gain additional skills that could prove valuable in your future.

The beautiful thing about learning is that no one can take it from you.

- B.B. King

Professional opportunities depend upon your specific interest and country. Many engineering and manufacturing companies are also moving into AR, VR, and Machine Learning. However, some focus on prototyping, testing, and manufacturing. Scroll through the firms that hire engineers in your specific specialty or interest to get a sense of the hundreds of professional options available to you.

Company size may also be a factor in your decision-making. While large firms may have more diversity of function and upward mobility, you might also be tasked with a specialized or limited role. On the other hand, a smaller firm may give you the chance to multitask on a wide range of projects and have a greater stake in the big picture of the operation. Whatever you decide, by taking internships in firms, large and small, you will discover your preferences and, at a minimum, know the questions to ask during interviews.

Internet of Things (IoT) design combines hardware and software in an integrated system that allows computers to monitor tasks, collect data, relay information, and revise processes. This specialization transforms product ideas into comprehensive strategies into networks to embed, sense, and track, providing more ubiquitous flow into consumer and cloud-based interactions. In addition, individuals and companies will readily 3D print parts for quick repair.

Law school might be another direction you could take your education. One of the biggest challenges facing engineers is the control of their intellectual property. While filing for a patent is not terribly difficult, maintaining control of that property is much more challenging. In our copycat world, globalization delivers products worldwide to places that do not conform to international law. Products are taken apart, reconfigured or modified, and put back onto the market. Some firms focus on protecting intellectual property by seeking out and prosecuting violators.

Jump at chances to gain real-world experiences. You may be in the workforce for fifty years. That is a really long time if you do not feel fulfilled. Sure, internships may mean sacrificing a summer holiday for a month somewhere, but it could make a significant difference in your future.

Engineering is the art of modeling materials we do not wholly understand, into shapes we cannot precisely analyze so as to withstand forces we cannot properly assess, in such a way that the public has no reason to suspect the extent of our ignorance.

- Dr. A.R. Dykes

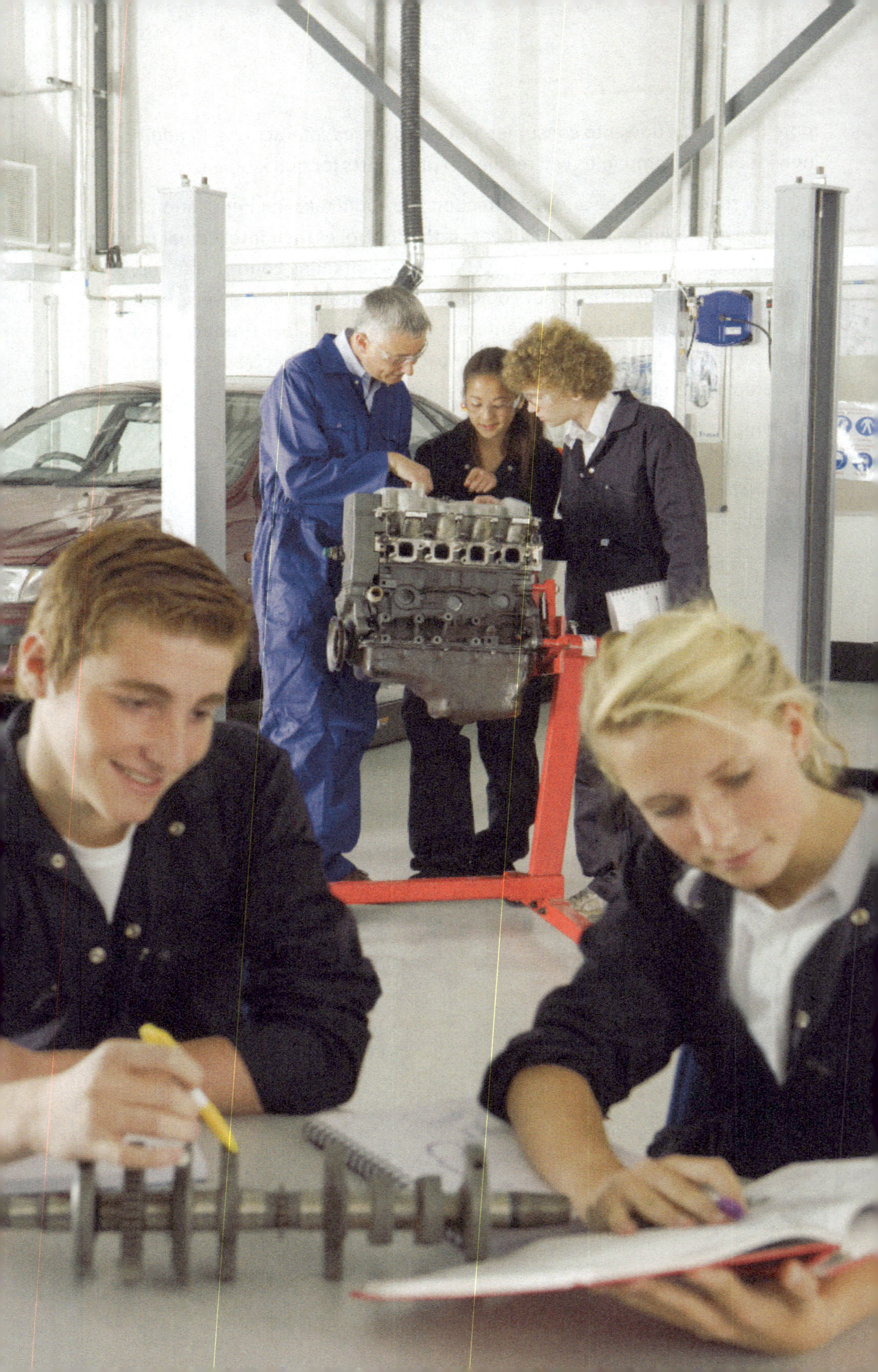

CHAPTER 7
COLLEGE ADMISSIONS: TERMS, DATA, APPLICATIONS, TESTS, ESSAYS, RECOMMENDATIONS, & RESUME

"Science is about knowing; engineering is about doing"

— **Henry Petroski**

Apply to colleges with the curriculum, clubs, activities, and opportunities that best fit your interests. MIT, Georgia Tech, Stanford, UC Berkeley, CalTech, Carnegie Mellon, USC, and the University of Michigan are eight colleges that stand out for mechanical engineering with amazing faculty, excellent facilities, and relatively easy access to job opportunities.

While most students consider college where internships abound like New York City, Los Angeles, Chicago, and San Francisco, they should not discount other areas ,that are meccas for research, design and manufacturing. You cannot go wrong with the UIUC, Texas A&M, UT Austin, Purdue, and the University of Florida for a deep dive into the world of mechanical engineering. These colleges offer rigorous courses of study and socially responsible projects on the cutting edge of innovation, design, engineering, and forward-thinking optimism.

However, planning is required before you apply. Let's look at a few terms you should know, then move on to community service, connecting with the colleges, and whether or not you should take standardized tests. Then, I offer some data, a checklist, and some tips for applying to and succeeding in college. Best wishes on your journey!!!

ADMISSIONS TERMS TO KNOW

Admissions Tests – These are standardized exams like SAT, ACT, GMAT, GRE, MCAT, etc. that universities use to compare student's aptitude in basic academic skill areas.

Admit Rate – The percent of applicants who are admitted.

Articulation Agreement – This is the agreement between 2-year and 4-year colleges that determines whether credits transfer from one institution to another.

Candidate Reply Date – For freshman admissions, students must reply back to colleges by May 1 with their choice of college or university they will attend from those in which they were accepted.

Class Rank – Most high schools no longer rank students. However, a few still do. This ranking puts students in order of weighted GPA or a combined set of criteria. Some schools rank in percentiles or deciles.

Coalition Application – This application can can be sent to multiple schools within its network of approximately 150 colleges. Many of the affiliated college also require supplemental applications with additional essays and requirements.

College Credit – Most colleges require 120 – 130 semester credits to graduate with a bachelor's degree. Students earn credits upon successful completion of classes. Colleges may also award college credit for qualifying AP/IB scores, CLEP exams, and military training courses.

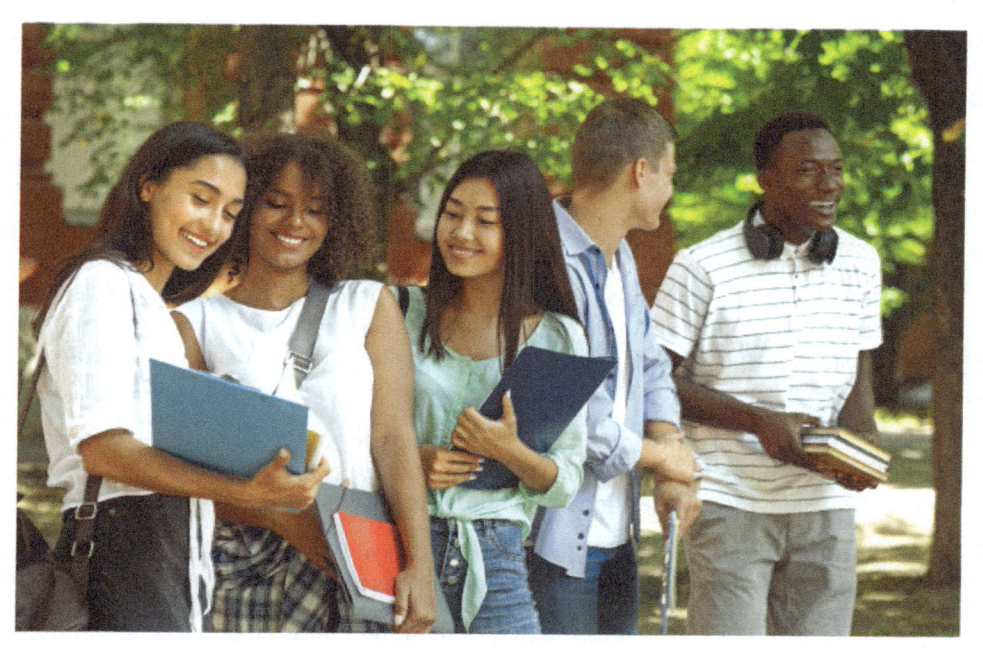

Common Application – This standardized digital application can be sent to multiple schools within its network of approximately 900 colleges. Most colleges also require supplemental applications with additional questions, essays, and requirements.

Deferred Admission – After the EA/ED admissions cycle, students are accepted, denied, or deferred to regular decision. Typically, the chances of being accepted during the regular admissions cycle after being deferred is 5–10%.

Deferred Enrollment – Colleges allow a student to postpone their attendance for up to one year. Note: Not all colleges allow students to defer.

Domestic Student – U.S. citizens or permanent residents at the time of admission are considered domestic students irrespective of the country in which they reside.

Early Action (EA) – EA is an early application submission in which a student also finds out their admission status before regular decisions students. Early action is typically not binding, meaning that students do not need to enroll if accepted. Most EA application due dates are between October 15th and November 15th. Almost all EA decisions come back between December 1st and February 1st with most responses between December 10th – 20th.

Early Decision (ED) – A few colleges have ED whereby a student commits to a specified school should they be accepted. Students agree to attend when they apply, and they can only apply to one ED school. If admitted, students pay the deposit and withdraw their applications from other schools. ED applications are typically due November 1 and decisions typically come back in mid-December.

Financial Aid – This award is money offered to students to help pay for school. The amount may be composed of scholarships, grants, loans, and work-study. Financial aid may be granted from the government, college, or private organizations.

First-Generation – Students are 'first-gen' if neither of their parents has a four-year college degree. Some colleges specify that that the parents also never attended college.

High School GPA – This number is considered or recalculated differently by each college depending upon whether they include 9th – 11th, summers, middle school, AP/IB/Honors credit, and courses like health, computer applications, leadership, sports, etc. Some colleges like the University of California cap their weighted GPA for admissions purposes with only 8 semesters of 'honors' points. No more than 4 of these can be from 10th grade.

In-State – Students are 'in-state' if they have residency in the state with evidence like a driver's license, taxes, bills, school attendance, etc. no matter where they physically reside. Rules regarding DACA students differ.

International – International applicants are those who are not U.S. citizens or permanent residents. This designation can vary based upon college/state rules.

Legacy – A close relative, generally a parent or grandparent, of one who graduated from a given college. Some colleges give preference to legacy applicants.

Lower Division – These are courses typically taken during the first two years of college. Most community college classes are lower division. At a university, lower division courses for a BA or BS degree are primarily liberal arts classes.

Need-Aware Admissions – The policy where admissions teams consider financial circumstances in the admissions process.

Need-Blind Admissions – The policy where admissions teams do not consider financial circumstances in the admissions process.

Open Admissions – A college opens enrollment to all students until the seats are filled without consideration of past academic performance or just minimum requirements.

Placement Tests – Most colleges require certain levels of mastery before entering a class. Upon enrolling in a college, students take placement tests to determine the level in which they are placed. Since information recall may not be strong from a class taken years before, review the material before taking the test. Otherwise, you may need to take one or more remedial classes which may prolong graduation.

Portal – This is the online center where you to connect with each individual college. You will login regularly to this website portal after you submit your application to find out what the college may be requesting or missing like transcripts, test scores, portfolio pieces, or recommendation letters. The site may offer you opportunities to submit a resume, abstract, or artistic material. When available, you will find your admissions status, financial aid, scholarships, housing assignment, and roommate.

Registrar's Office – This is the office of college officials who are responsible for your student records - recording grades, certifying completion, and sending transcripts.

Residency – This is the determination of state residency, non-resident U.S., or international.

Rolling Admission – This is the college policy to accept students as the applications are received rather than waiting for a specific date. Many colleges with rolling admissions deliver admissions decisions within a month of receipt of a students application materials.

Summer Melt – The phenomenon whereby students submit an intent to enroll at a college after being admitted, pay the deposit, and decide not to attend during the summer. While this situation may have increased during the pandemic, the phenomenon has recurred for decades. The primary reasons for summer melt include the inability to pay, illness, family matter, change of heart, acceptance of a job, or getting off the waitlist at another college.

Transfer Student – A student who has taken college classes after completing high school and applies to a 4-year university. Typically, if college classes are taken during high school students are still considered for freshman admissions.

Upper Division – These are courses typically taken in your second two years of college. At a university, upper division courses for a BA or BS degree are primarily major-specific classes.

Waitlist – Admissions offices accept, deny, or waitlist students. Those students on a waitlist must wait until a spot opens. If there is a vacancy, the student may be taken off of the waitlist on a priority basis, ranking system, or admissions review.

Yield – This is the percent of admitted students who pay the deposit with the intent to enroll (enrolled/admitted x 100).

PRESIDENT'S VOLUNTEER SERVICE AWARD

Many students support their communities through service opportunities. These include volunteering in homeless shelters, soup kitchens, schools, sports camps, research, nursing homes, Special Olympics, Adopt-a-Family, Habitat for Humanity, Youth Action Teams, political campaigns, docent work at theaters, charity 5Ks, concerts, parades, international projects, medical missions, church-sponsored service work, and forest, park, beach, and wetlands cleanups. Some students are recognized for their volunteer contributions with certificates while others serve with no recognition in order to help society. Either way, by accumulating hours, you can earn one of these Presidential Volunteer Service Awards.

Hours Required to Earn Awards in Each Age Group				
Age Group	Bronze	Silver	Gold	Lifetime Achievement Award
Kids (5–10 years old)	26–49 hours	50–74 hours	75+ hours	4,000+ hours
Teens (11–15)	50–74 hours	75–99 hours	100+ hours	4,000+ hours
Young Adults (16–25)	100–174 hours	175–249 hours	250+ hours	4,000+ hours
Adults (26+)	100–249 hours	250–499 hours	500+ hours	4,000+ hours

COLLEGE ADMISSIONS:

Success in the Face of Uncertainty

There are no guarantees in college admissions. However, planning is essential for success. The most beneficial advice is to pursue your passions with gusto, train to be the best you can be, take advantage of internships and experiences, and meet lots of people along the way.

Remember, "life is a journey, not a destination." Often the journey is more exciting, leading to lessons, friendships, and unforgettable moments. However, the fact is, in the end, if college is your goal, then you need to remember a few action items to achieve success.

Should you worry about grades in high school? Of course. You should also take classes that will challenge you. Colleges pick the best candidates from those who apply. Students should be academically prepared, socially conscious, and talented in areas in which they are passionate (engineering design, graphic arts, musical instruments, theatre, debate, public speaking, leadership, athletics, community service, computer coding, robotics, construction, etc.).

The college selection process is not that much different than companies picking employees. While colleges are more or less competitive, companies may have only one job, and a hundred resumes. Discover the unique drive and internal motivations within you that make you the very best you can be. Be exceptional at what you choose to do academically, personally, and professionally.

Most of all, You Do You!

TALENT FOCUSED

Not all schools require high grades and test scores. Many are simply interested in selecting students who are the most talented, most driven, and the most willing to be team players on the college campus. Thus, you should take a solid set of courses and fulfill the standard requirements.

According to the National Student Clearinghouse Research Center, an estimated 18 million students enrolled in U.S. undergraduate or graduate courses in 2023. Of those students, millions attended college with high school GPAs between 2.0 and 3.5. Furthermore, more than ten million college students never took standardized tests.

On the other hand, if you are applying to highly competitive schools, you should take the test. However, there were hundreds of colleges that did not require test scores in 2023 and probably never will in the future.

In a comprehensive April 22, 2022, report,[1] Melanie Hanson of the Education Data Initiative did a fabulous job presenting copious educational data. I pulled some that you may find informative.

In 2020, total college enrollment was approximately 19 million, dropping by two million from its high in 2010 with 3.1 million in graduate school. Approximately one-third (66.2%) of high school students continued for post-secondary study. California has the most college students with 2.72 million; 89.5% attend public institutions; 11.6% leave the state to attend college; 35.8% of full-time college students are female.

---

1 Melanie Hanson. "College Enrollment & Student Demographic Statistics" EducationData.org, April 22, 2022, https://educationdata.org/college-enrollment-statistics

In approximate numbers, here is some college student data.

DEMOGRAPHIC CHARACTERISTICS

Caucasian – 54.3%
LatinX - 19.3%
Black or African American - 12.6%
Asian or Asian American – 6.8%
American Indian/Alaska Native – 0.66%%
Pacific Islander – 0.26%

Foreign-born – 12%
Women - 55.5%
15 years old or younger – 0.7%
Under 24 years old – 92%
45 years old or older – 1.5%

DEGREES AND MAJORS

4.43 million students graduated from college in 2021

* 24.6% received associate's degrees
* 49.9% received bachelor's degrees
* 20.8% earned master's degrees
* 4.7% earned doctorates/professional degrees

Majors – 58% of all bachelor's degrees are in five areas of study

* 19.1% in business
* 11.9% in health-related professions
* 8% social sciences and history
* 5.9% in psychology
* 5.9% in biological and biomedical sciences

COLLEGE ENROLLMENT (EDUCATIONDATA.ORG)

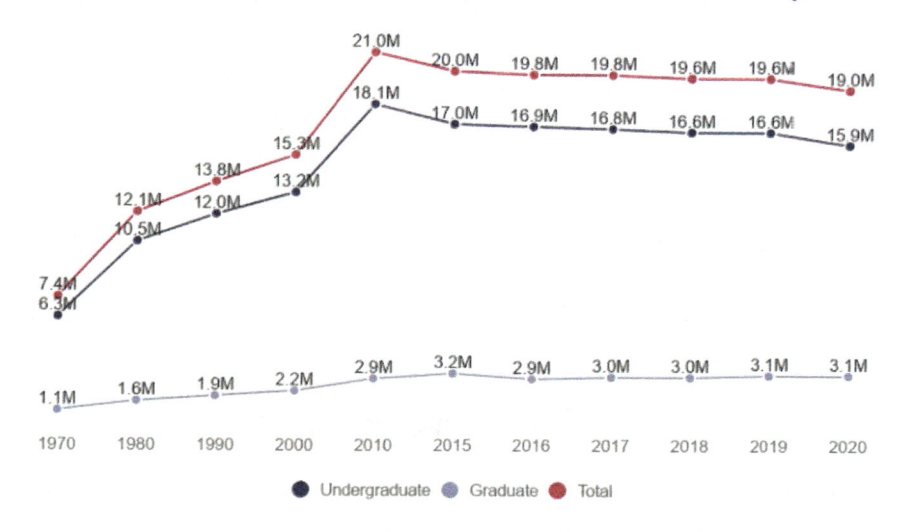

Chart showing undergraduate, graduate, and total college enrollment from 1970 to 2020:

Year	Undergraduate	Graduate	Total
1970	6.3M	1.1M	7.4M
1980	10.5M	1.6M	12.1M
1990	12.0M	1.9M	13.8M
2000	13.2M	2.2M	15.3M
2010	18.1M	2.9M	21.0M
2015	17.0M	3.2M	20.0M
2016	16.9M	2.9M	19.8M
2017	16.8M	3.0M	19.8M
2018	16.6M	3.0M	19.6M
2019	16.6M	3.1M	19.6M
2020	15.9M	3.1M	19.0M

COMPETITIVE COLLEGE ADMISSIONS

A few highly selective colleges seek extraordinary talent over academics, but most zero in on a student's challenging courses and high grades. To gain admission into the most highly selective academic colleges, you must take the most challenging course load you can balance and ace. Highly selective colleges want disciplined scholars AND remarkably talented students.

Determine what you can handle, knowing that some colleges with extremely competitive admission will only take students who have completed more than ten AP, IB, or honors classes over the four years.

Why would the most competitive colleges require classes like AP Calculus or Physics for an art program? However daunting these classes may seem, remember, the top colleges have lots of applicants, and they need to draw the line somewhere. UCLA had 149,779 applicants for fall 2022; UC Berkeley had 128,192 applicants. The numbers are truly staggering since neither first-year class will have no have more than 7,000 students starting in the fall.

College admissions can feel like a rollercoaster of energy and emotion. Creating a portfolio of talent, training, and experience is just the beginning. Meanwhile, some colleges want to see standardized test scores aided by practice. Applications and essays may seem easy at first, but managing the various requirements and deadlines can be difficult. Therefore, this moment is a good time to get a calendar and organize your tasks.

REQUEST INFORMATION

Almost every college has a location, a link, or a contact us page where you can request information from the school. If you are considering a school, request information from them. In this way, they may send you updates, scholarship opportunities, an application fee waiver, special invites, and other information that could be valuable in the process. Of course, you may not need one more e-mail, and you may be receiving e-mails from the school anyway. Still, I recommend that you fill out their form. Then, since you are likely to be inundated with e-mails, make a file folder in your e-mail for all colleges you are considering. Then, when you get an e-mail from one of those schools, file it away.

STANDARDIZED TESTING

A few schools still require standardized testing. Check first. Many colleges remain test-optional. This means that you are not required to take the SAT or ACT. However, if you have a good score, it may make all the difference in gaining admission. College admissions offices are studying this topic and considering their future policies. Much of their concern began with worldwide test cancellations due to the pandemic.

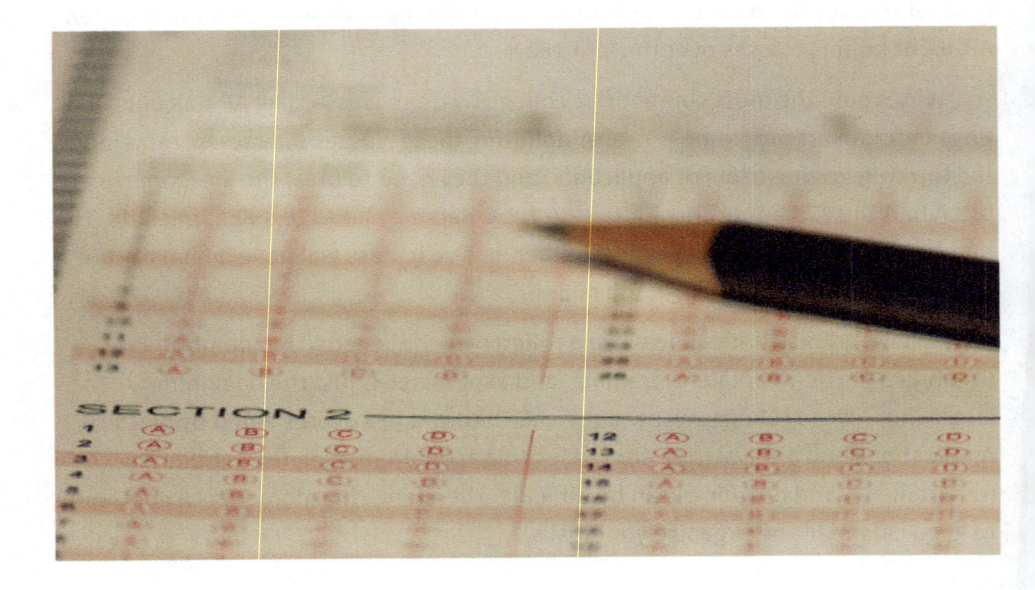

Schools did not want to let students onto their campus to take the test who may be infected, nor were they able to ensure safety. In addition, social distancing requirements limited the number of students who could take a test at any given site. Yet, for decades, college admissions decisions centered around grades and test scores. This change in the landscape of decision-making has rattled admissions departments.

Meanwhile, some colleges proclaim that test-optional truly means that the test is not required. Yet, evidence proves otherwise. Thus, many students are still taking the test and working around test preparation and test site hurdles amid the confusion. Competition continues to drive students to present evidence to show that they are the most worthy candidates. In the end, colleges need to make a final decision between excellent candidates. If one student has a high score, that student may have a higher likelihood of admission depending upon the admissions committee's decision-making process.

Data show that students who submitted scores within the college's range or higher were accepted at a higher rate than those without a score. Some schools claim to be test blind and not consider scores, yet few of these colleges still provide a place to input scores. Thus, some college are not truly blind. Nevertheless, the decision regarding whether to take the test or submit a score is yours. If the school does not require an admissions test, you can choose not to take the test or decide to submit a score as you like. If your academics are solid and you are willing to prepare for the test, you should take the test.

APPLYING EARLY
Early Action (EA), Restricted Early Action (REA), and Early Decision (ED)

With low acceptance rates, students clamor to apply early to schools. Also, additional scholarship money is often available to early applicants. With the chaos surrounding test cancellations and changes in AP, IB, SAT, and ACT testing, students' anxieties increased. In addition, applications to the top schools surged during the pandemic, resulting in colleges needing to make difficult admissions decisions in their quest to build a diverse, talented, and engaged class of students. This confluence sent students in droves to apply early. This trend is likely to continue.

In Early Action (EA), Restricted Early Action (REA), and Early Decision (ED), students apply to college in late summer or early fall and generally find out around winter break, though some decisions come out earlier and a few arrive later. This advantage not only gives students a chance for more scholarship money in some cases but the benefit of finding out early reduces the tension of the long waiting period until regular decision determinations arrive.

Early Action (EA) and Restricted Early Action (REA) are different. In restricted early action, a limitation is placed on either how many or what colleges you can apply to simultaneously. Many REA schools do not allow students to apply to other early action schools, though some will allow students to apply early to public colleges. Check each college website to be sure. In addition, some schools like Georgetown will allow students to apply EA elsewhere but not apply to a binding Early Decision (ED) program where the student commits to attending if they are accepted. However, most EA schools do not have these restrictions, and some students apply to a handful of EA schools during the admissions process.

Early Decision (ED) is a binding agreement between the student and college with signatures from student, the student's parents, and the high school counselor/advisor ensuring that the student is committed to the first-choice ED school and will attend if accepted. Each of these parties acknowledges and agrees that, if granted admission, the student will fulfill their agreement. There are caveats to this requirement, though you should fully apply fully committed to your ED school.

There are incentives to applying ED. Frequently, acceptance rates are higher. At some colleges, a large percentage of the incoming class includes students who profess their unequivocal love for their dream school. Students who know they have a top choice school, fulfilled the necessary admissions prerequisites, and are committed to accepting the binding agreement to attend, should apply ED.

COMMON APPLICATION, COALITION APPLICATION, OR COLLEGE-SPECIFIC APPLICATION

Every college's process is unique. However, there are a few commonalities. In 2022, approximately 900 colleges used the Common App; about 150 colleges used the Coalition Application. A few used both. The University of California system has its own application as do the California State Universities and the Texas schools.

The Common App and Coalition App may be started early. In your junior year, consider getting a head start on reviewing what is required. The college-specific questions may change each year. However, the basic application is generally the same and can be created ahead of time. At the end of July, make a copy of everything you have completed just in case.

Some schools admit on a rolling basis. 'Rolling' means that periodically, after all of the materials are received, the admissions committee determines who they will accept, and they send the notification right away. Some students are accepted as early as August. The thrill of acceptance cannot be overstated.

ESSAYS

The Common Application and Coalition Application essays are often posted months ahead of time. Since this main essay is required or recommended for nearly all Common Application and Coalition Application schools, this is an excellent place to start thinking about what you might want to say to colleges.

In addition to the main essay on the Common Application and Coalition Application, about three-fours of the colleges have their own specific questions or essays. In August, most admissions applications are open and ready for you to dive into the college-specific questions, though many of the essay topics are available earlier, and some schools hold out until later for their big essay reveal.

These can be prepared ahead of time too. One popular question is, "What activity is most important to you and why?" Another is "Why did you choose your major?" A third common question is, "Why do you want to attend our school?" Others you should prepare or at least consider the topics of diversity, adversity, and challenges since these topics have become increasingly important in the admissions process. Everyone has a challenge they needed to overcome. What did you learn from that experience?

Complete the application fully. Think carefully about optional sections. Typically, universities offer you the chance to provide the school with just the right cherry on top of the sundae, allowing you to share something unique about you. If you have absolutely nothing to say, leave it blank. There is also an additional information section on the main Common App, Coalition Application, and University of California application. This location is not a place to write another essay, but you can include information that cannot be adequately explained in the rest of the application.

There are also schools that include scholarship essays within the supplement part of the application. Start early.

LETTERS OF RECOMMENDATION

Most applications, though not all, request letters of recommendation from a counselor and one or more teachers. Engineering programs may want teachers in mathematics, science, or the humanities. Plan for this. Occasionally, colleges provide section for optional recommendations. You might ask a summer program leader, research director, internship supervisor, employer, or member of the clergy. A quarter of the applications allow you to include a letter from a coach. Finally, if there is a supplemental application where you can showcase your talent, projects, writing, or art, like SlideRoom, you may need additional and separate recommendations to be reviewed by the specific program.

COLLEGE APPLICATION CHECKLIST

- [ ] **Calendar** - Keep a calendar of due dates for summer program applications, contests, AP tests, SAT/ACT, applications, scholarships, and financial aid.

- [ ] **Career Interest Survey** - Take a career interest/aptitude test. Learn more about the majors and career options that best fit your interests and abilities

- [ ] **Consider College Majors** – What classes are offered in the curriculum? Many students who dislike math are surprised to learn that most business degrees require both calculus and statistics while incorporating math in nearly every class. It pays to research the subjects now.

- [ ] **Investigate Colleges** – Consider possible schools based on the programs they offer, research opportunities, internships, clubs, activities, sports, and personal interests - visit if possible.

- [ ] **National College Fair** – In the spring, colleges send representatives to a couple of dozen cities where you can meet with their admissions staff. These are good to walk around and learn more about the colleges and ask questions.

- [ ] **Request Information** – Fill out the request for information for each college you are considering so that they keep you informed of opportunities you may not have considered. They may send you a fee waiver or streamlined application.

- [ ] **Summer Programs** – Summer camps, skill-building, tours, research, internships, and college programs often have deadlines. Apply and consider your options.

- [ ] **Narrow Choices** – Narrow down your choices in the summer before your senior year so that you have an equal number of target, reach, and safeties.

- [ ] **Communicate With Your Counselor** – Your counselor is your guide who not only helps you with your course selection but also advocates for you in the admissions process through their recommendation and sometimes with admissions. Get to know them.

- [ ] **SAT/ACT** – Decide if there is a benefit of taking these tests for the colleges you are considering.

- [ ] **Extended Time** – Determine if you qualify for extended time on tests.

- [ ] **Fee Waivers** – Ask your counselor if you qualify for fee waivers for the SAT/ACT, CSS Profile, or application fees.

- [ ] **Resume** – Create a resume whether or not the college requests one – some do. First, you may need one for a job. However, even if not required or submitted, a resume allows you to gather your activities and accomplishments in one place for you to see what you want to present to a school.

- [ ] **Essays and Short Answer Questions** – Determine aspects of your life that stand out. Give colleges the best impression of your interests, inspirations, commitment, and life journey.

- ☐ **Counselor Recommendation Form** – Determine if your school requires a special form to obtain a counselor recommendation.
- ☐ **Recommendations** – Ask your teachers in the spring of your junior year or when school starts in your senior year.
- ☐ **Early Action/Early Decision** – These applications are due first, typically between October 15th and November 15th.
- ☐ **Regional Representative** – Some colleges have a regional representative. If you have any specifications, contact them to have them answer questions you cannot find the answers to on the website.
- ☐ **Transcripts** – Order transcripts to be sent to colleges from your high school (s) and any colleges you have attended. Note: Some colleges like the University of California do not want transcripts sent until you are admitted.
- ☐ **Deadlines** – Keep your eye on the deadlines.
- ☐ **Portals** – You must log into your portal after you submit your application and then every couple of weeks afterward to see if the college is missing something from your file. Some colleges will close your application if you do not log in or will move your early application to regular decision.
- ☐ **Scholarships** – Scholarships vary in due dates. Some begin the process of considering students in the spring of your junior year. The Coca-Cola Scholarship is due October 31st. However, due dates continue throughout most of your senior year. Scan www.fastweb.com and www.bigfuture.collegeboard.org/scholarship-search.
- ☐ **Regular Decision** – Regular decision applications for public colleges vary, but many are right after Thanksgiving. Regular decision application deadlines for most private schools are the first two weeks of January.
- ☐ **FAFSA** – Apply for federal financial aid (grants, work study, and loans).
- ☐ **CSS Profile** – About 300 colleges require this form to obtain financial aid.
- ☐ **Student Aid Report (SAR)** – Approximately 4 weeks after completing your FAFSA you should receive your SAR. Follow the instructions to complete updates or add schools.
- ☐ **Update Colleges** – Make sure you update colleges with your continued interest.
- ☐ **Keep Copies** – Keep copies of your application materials in a folder.
- ☐ **Visit Colleges** – If possible, visit colleges to which you were accepted. Since you are going to live there for four years, you should get a feel for the campus and not just judge a school by its rankings. Take notes, especially contact names.
- ☐ **Communicate With Students** – Find students who currently attend the university who are willing to answer a few questions. How hard is it to change your major? Are students friendly? What do students do on the weekends? As your counselor, teachers, or the admissions office if they can refer you to a student who currently attends or just graduated.

- ☐ **Waitlisted Schools** – Most schools will allow you to write a letter updating them on your accomplishments during your senior year and your continued interest. Read the instructions since every school has a different format and set of requirements. Demonstrate your commitment.
- ☐ **Candidate Reply Date** – By May 1st you must choose one school and place a deposit.
- ☐ **Senior Year Grades** – Colleges rescind admissions offers for students who do poorly in their senior year. Do not slack off. You will regret it.

DECISIONS, DECISIONS: WAITING FOR A RESPONSE

The period between submitting your application and receiving admissions results may not require a tremendous effort. However, waiting requires extraordinary patience and often follow-up requirements. Many schools send a portal link to check admissions decisions, though the most important reason for frequent checking is to ensure that the college is not missing something or offered you the chance to apply for a scholarship or some other opportunity

Check each portal regularly. Additionally, read the college's correspondence sent through your e-mail. Waiting from November to April is agonizing. Students clamor to know the results since their future is on the line. However, colleges typically notify students of the date they will send admissions results on the portal. Some college advisors aggregate the information and post decision notification dates too. You will find out soon.

THICK OR THIN ENVELOPE

Students eagerly check for notifications each day as winter turns to spring, waiting to hear via e-mail, the college portal, or snail mail for a cheery welcome or denial. As spring arrives, regular decision admissions results steadily roll in one at a time. In March, every day seems to last 26 hours, two extra for the period that lingers until that day's announcement. With each school announcing on a different day, the slow drip torture waiting to find out is exacerbated by the uncanny way each college picks a different day in March or April to announce their decision.

At some point you will know. That statement offers little solace in the middle of the fray. You have until May 1 to make a decision. Yet, with limited available housing and a first-come, first-served basis of selection, the pressure is on to choose. Even so, visiting the college is vital, despite the fact that AP tests and finals are just around the corner and there seems like there is no time. Yet, this decision determines where you will live, eat, study, make friends, take classes, and get involved for four years. If you do not consider your options, you are basing your decision on a few college-selected pictures and the tweets or feeds of other people.

There are many variables to consider in the end. This is why forward thinking at the beginning of the application process is valuable and even necessary to seek scholarships, merit money, or opportunities for financial aid. This proactive planning is especially needed with the spike in college applications at selective schools and the ever-changing landscape of test-optional admissions. MIT, for example, resumed its test requirement.

Plan ahead. The college application process is not a good time to procrastinate. The fall of your senior year is tough, often with a demanding course load. It is even tougher for athletes who compete in a fall sport However, throughout your life you will need to work on time management, organization, and goal setting. This is a good time to start so you do not miss thousands of dollars in financial aid. Time management challenged students who adjusted their lifestyles due the self-paced and online classes and assignments during the pandemic.

CELEBRATING ACCEPTANCES AND DEALING WITH REJECTION

Acceptance is not guaranteed. Colleges seek students who are wholly committed to their education, talents, and learning experiences. Unfortunately, even for dedicated students, the probability of acceptance is low at the most highly selective schools. Solid academics, work ethic, and planning makes the outcome sweeter when you are accepted and celebrate the next step along your way.

Congratulations! The colleges in which you gain admission go on your list of options. Check your financial aid and scholarship packages too. Money is often an important factor in making your final decision. Consider visiting the school. Many students apply to college merely by someone's recommendation, *U.S. News and World Report* ranking, reviewing campus photos on Google, or researching profiles posted on a website or in a book.

There is nothing that replaces the actual campus visit. After all, you will be spending a few years there. While you may not be accepted everywhere you apply, you may decide when you visit that the college is high on your list or that you do not want to apply after all. Understandably, the pandemic's uncertainty added more question marks to an already complicated set of admissions processes.

The buzzword for 2020-2030 is resilience. It is never easy to be rejected. However, rejection happens, and you will survive this. Note that many colleges still accept applications in April, May, and June long after most school's applications are closed. If you did not get accepted, look up colleges that still have openings just in case schools you have not considered might be good options for you. In April and May, Google "College Openings Update". You will be surprised to see the colleges that show up on the list that still have open spots.

WAITLISTS: THE ART OF WAITING

Immediately confirm if you are given a waitlist spot and still want to attend. There is often a deadline. You do not want to miss this. If you are no longer interested or have selected another school, go into the portal and turn down the offer. Someone else is bound to be thrilled by your anonymous gift.

If you are still interested, find the location on the portal or site designated by the college to update them on what you have done – accomplishments, awards, extra class, honors, art, shows, or films. You only want to add what they have not yet seen, but if you have taken the initiative to do something more than what you originally stated on the application, by all means, tell them.

You could just wait for their decision, but you are better off being proactive and demonstrating that you really want to be at their school. A few students do get off waitlists at most schools. How much do you want to attend? Meanwhile, you will have to deposit somewhere else before the May 1st deadline. Stay hopeful. This next year will be a significant step along your journey. Relax!

ACCEPTANCE IS JUST THE BEGINNING

Once you are accepted to college, you begin your journey toward your future. They call graduation "commencement" because this is your beginning. Start your trek on your own path. The decisions you make now are primarily yours with significantly less input from your parents. For better or worse, your parents taught you lessons that you will keep or discard. Going forward, your behaviors, attitudes, internships, study abroad, and career choices will determine what you become.

Warning ahead of time…the path is rarely straight and there are pitfalls along the way. Much like Monopoly, you will roll the dice and move ahead a few squares, but you will go back a few spaces as well. You might buy a house or save money. However, you might lose a property or investment too. You might get accepted to your dream school and succeed in tough classes; might do poorly in a few too. Life is full of lessons. Successful adults sometimes forget about wrong turns. Although they sting at the time, and then they are often dismissed over the years as lessons.

I have literally attended college for fifty years and have degrees that span a multitude of disciplines. I have also taught chemistry, mathematics, engineering, counseling, public relations, and politics. Here are 21 tips as you go forward.

1. Attend class even when other students don't. Surprisingly, many lecture halls are half empty when there isn't a test. Go anyway. Most college professors know if you attend.
2. Buy your books and start reading before the semester starts. When classes begin, you live in a blizzard of activities, opportunities, and assignments. Again, surprisingly, most students do not complete their assigned readings.

Some get by without reading but getting As that way is tough.Some get by without reading but getting As that way is tough.

3. Work ahead. Finish your paper or project first, then go out and celebrate your friend's birthday, sports team win, or friend-group's successes. Not only can you be more relaxed, but you might even improve on your work later when you come up with a new idea.

4. Most colleges offer free tutoring. Tutors often read over your papers or assignments and almost always give you valuable assistance that you would never have considered. Return to #3. To get help, you must complete your assignments ahead of time.

5. Have a backup plan or two. Murphy's Law says: (1) anything that can go wrong will, (2) nothing is as easy as it looks, (3) everything takes longer than you think it will.

6. Save your digital documents – often. The worst nightmare is when you lose an entire assignment, your computer turns off, or malware attacks your files. Google Drive and the iCloud are fine, but there are pitfalls.

7. Develop solid notetaking and reminder systems that work for you. You will need these for the rest of your life. Small things slip through the cracks. Checklists are extremely helpful.

8. There is never enough time. Bring enough clothes so you do not need to wash them as often. When you do wash them, take them out when they are done or else someone else will and you may never find them again.

9. Register for classes the minute registration opens up for you. Trust me on this one. Otherwise, you get a bad professor at a horrible time that conflict with your commitments. You might not even get into critical prerequisites which may extend your time in college a semester or a year.

10. Petition to get into a class. Send a note to your professor before classes begin. Begging is fine. The professor can say no, but at least you tried.

11. If you have an academic problem, serious illness, critical family matter, or emergency, let your professors know immediately. Most will not help you later if you wait a month thinking you can handle it on your own.

12. Make a calendar and keep track of what you need to accomplish

13. Teamwork is a mantra in college. You will work on teams. A few members are likely to be unmotivated slackers or talented, but extreme procrastinators. Determine this ahead of time and set intermediate goals. Remember, your grade is on the line. It's not fair but go back to #5. In the end, finish the project anyway. The unmotivated slacker will also get an A, which may thoroughly frustrate you, but you will earn an A too.

14. Book prices vary widely. The university bookstore prices are often high but the location is convenient. I have friends who swear by certain online stores where they always buy textbooks, get coupons, and then buy more books. One advantage of buying books in digital format is that you can often use 'Control F' to find on demand information you need. Sometimes

you can also take digital notes, which is impossible with a physical copy. I prefer physical books, but you choose. Also, renting books is okay unless you forget to send the book back.

15. Get involved as soon as you can. Meet students who have similar interests. Join clubs, learn about the school's traditions, try activities you always wanted to learn, ask professors about volunteering on research projects, and get involved with intramural sports.

16. Don't bring a car. A car sounds wonderful, offering you freedom, until your vehicle is broken into, the gas runs out, the car breaks down before a test, or you get a half dozen parking tickets. You never realized how much trouble a car could be on campus, particularly when there is limited and expensive parking.

17. Communicate with your professors and TAs. Most of them have office hours. Well, they probably all have office hours, but sometimes professors or teaching assistants are absent. Either drop by during scheduled times or make an appointment. Especially if you have a question or a problem, speak to them. A professor rarely helps a student after they turn in grades but may have excellent advice during the term if they are struggling. Surprisingly, the answer key is occasionally wrong. Sometimes professors are intimidating, standoffish, or mean-spirited. Fortunately, there are only a few bad ones, and even these professors teach important lessons.

18. Don't get so excited about credit cards. Credit card companies will continually hound you to sign up with tempting offers. College students are prime targets because they do not yet really understand the challenge of paying monthly bills when there is little time and numerous items to purchase. You will probably have to learn the hard way, but credit cards are not the savior they purport to be. Furthermore, you will likely spend more than you imagined, and the interest payments will dig into your pocketbook with a deep hole.

19. Drinking and drugs are around you 24/7. It does not matter what school you attend. Rarely is a campus void of alcohol or drugs. However, some colleges have more – much more. Some students will even sell illegal drugs in the dorm. You need to use your own judgment. Be careful. Students consume more than they realize, make judgment errors, get seriously injured, die of overdoses, and spread STDs. This item was not written to scare you but to make you aware of the life-changing realities.

20. During Christmas break starting your first year, apply for internships, training opportunities, co-ops, or jobs for the summer. Create a resume. Getting experience cannot be understated if you want to jump on the job market and get real-world experience. Career fairs are extremely helpful so you can see what kind of job you might want. Every college has a career center. Get to know the people there.

21. Go boldly into this world and try new things. Thomas Edison once said, "I have not failed. I've just found 10,000 ways that won't work."

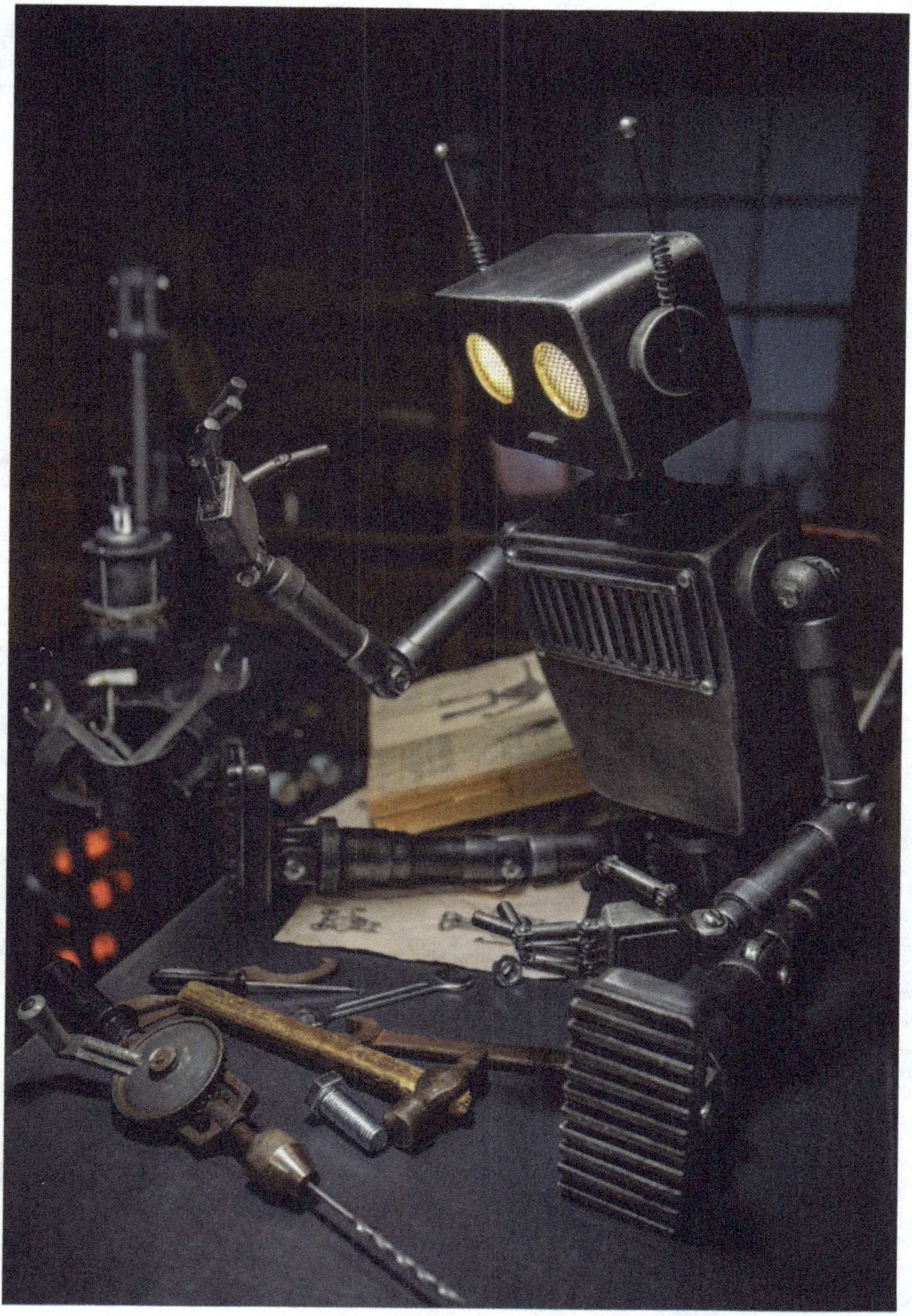

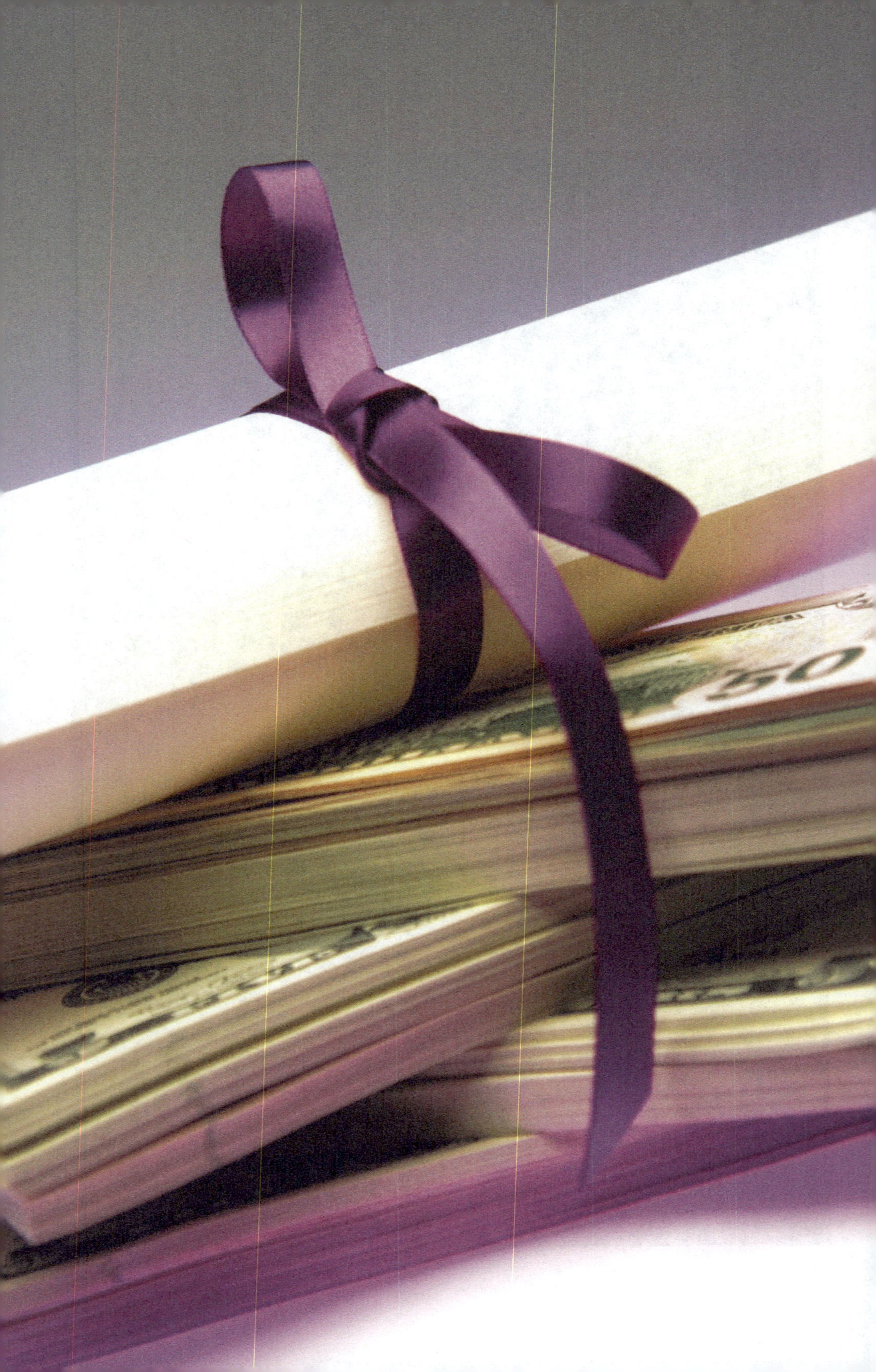

CHAPTER 8
FINANCIAL AID AND SCHOLARSHIPS: FINDING MONEY TO PAY FOR COLLEGE

"Science can amuse and fascinate us all, but it is engineering that changes the world."

— Isaac Asimov

Nearly every university in the United States offers money for college. These funds come in the form of grants or scholarships that do not need to be paid back, loans that must be repaid, and 'work study', where students are paid to work at a job associated with the college or university. The grants or scholarships are either need-based or merit-based.

Need-based means that the college or government determines that, based on your income, you will be unable to attend without additional resources. Merit-based means that the college or university offers money based on some combination of talent, skills, background, experiences, or academic achievement.

NEED-BASED FINANCIAL AID

To obtain need-based financial aid, most colleges require students to submit the Free Application for Federal Student Aid (FAFSA) found at www.studentaid.gov. Some colleges also require the College Scholarship Service (CSS) Profile which is available on the College Board website at www.collegeboard.org.

Both the FAFSA and CSS Profile require you to submit of family income based upon the tax returns you and/or your family file with the U.S. federal government.

If your answer is yes to any of the following you do not need to declare your parent's income when filing your FAFSA form. There are nuances to this for students who are verifiably independent, ex-pats that have a unique situation, and parents who are unavailable for a variety of reasons. The federal government offers free advice to families if students have a unique case.

1. Will you be 24 or older by Jan. 1 of the school year for which you are applying for financial aid? For example, if you plan to start school in August 2022 for the 2022–23 school year, will you be 24 by Jan. 1, 2022 (i.e., were you born before Jan. 1, 1999)?
2. Are you married or separated but not divorced?
3. Will you be working toward a master's or doctorate degree (such as MA, MBA, MD, JD, Ph.D., Ed.D., etc.)?
4. Do you have children who receive more than half of their support from you?
5. Do you have dependents (other than children or a spouse) who live with you and receive more than half of their support from you?
6. Are you currently serving on active duty in the U.S. armed forces for purposes other than training?
7. Are you a veteran of the U.S. armed forces?
8. At any time since you turned age 13, were both of your parents deceased, were you in foster care, or were you a ward or dependent of the court?
9. Are you an emancipated minor or are you in a legal guardianship as determined by a court?
10. Are you an unaccompanied youth who is homeless or self-supporting and at risk of being homeless?

Most people will be able to download the tax information directly into the FAFSA form using the Data Retrieval Tool (DRT). This automatic process not only saves time, but the DRT also ensures that the correct information goes into the right locations on the form. Check anyway afterward since there could be an error. If your family has not filed a tax return yet, you may estimate the amounts. However, all income and other financial information will eventually need to be verified for you to receive need-based aid.

SCHOLARSHIPS

Merit scholarships are offered through a college/university, private donors, or corporations. These are based upon academic success, talent, background, or life experiences. Scholarships may require additional forms, essays, recommendations, or proof of academic success. Note: A few universities, particularly the highest-ranked schools, do not offer any merit scholarships, though most colleges do.

Merit scholarships based upon talent typically require a portfolio, performance, audition, or some other demonstration of your skills. Check your art, dance, music, writing, debate, theatre, research, robotics, engineering, or program to see what the college requires. Each college or university has a different set of rules for what and how you submit your art, video, writing samples, or other demonstration of mastery.

Please check out the profile section at the back of this book for scholarships and requirements. Additionally, look up the college website for their financial aid process. To help you get a sense of available scholarships, I selected four schools from the colleges listed in the profile section.

GEORGIA TECH

While finding out how much Georgia Tech offers is not as easy as other schools, one thing is certain, the price tag is lower. The cost for tuition, room, board, and books for 2022-2023 is $28,166 for in-state students and $49,278 for out-of-state students. With a lower average educational cost that is less than private universities, this should remind families that the net cost is a key figure. Like other schools, Georgia Tech refers students to outside scholarships. However, Georgia Tech does offer a full-ride Stamps President's Scholarship to the top 1% of first-year students. Additionally, Tech's Provost Scholarship is awarded to 40 first-year, non-resident students which gives these students an out-of-state tuition waiver for eight semesters. That reduces tuition, room, board, and books for out-of-state students to slightly over $100,000 for four years.

NORTHWESTERN

Northwestern awarded $200 million to undergraduate students in 2020-21 with half of the students receiving a scholarship. Northwestern provides a chart with the average total aid packages offered to students. More than 90% of students whose families have incomes below $120,000 receive above $50,000 per year in financial aid to attend. Students from lower-income families receive up to $74,000 per year. Northwestern also participates in the Questbridge College Match Program. Additional scholarships include those for Chicago-area residents as well as the Northwestern Endowed Scholarship, Founders Scholarship, and Karr Achievement Scholarship. The McCormick School of Engineering website also provides a list of outside scholarships, fellowships, and competitions.

SYRACUSE UNIVERSITY

Syracuse University students received more than $400 million in financial aid. Syracuse offers internal merit-based scholarships and supports students in finding external funds as well. Merit-based funding is offered to more than 35% of the incoming class. Approximately 80% of SU's incoming students received some type of financial support. Syracuse University offers a financial aid package to incoming students that meet full need. The College of Engineering and Computer Science (ECS) offers additional specific scholarship opportunities.

The ECS Leadership Scholars and ECS Ambassadors Scholars, provide significant resources to support exceptional students, including a significant merit scholarship that is renewable for four years. In addition, the College of Engineering and Computer Science offers ten renewable scholarships to students who participated in *FIRST* programs in high school and ten renewable scholarships to students who have taken at least two Project Lead The Way courses in high school. Additional scholarships are available for ECS students who participate in the ACE Mentor Program. To be eligible for the *FIRST,* Project Lead The Way, or ACE Mentor scholarships, students must complete the scholarship form on the SU website.

THE UNIVERSITY OF TEXAS AT AUSTIN

The University of Texas covers full tuition for any student whose family income totals $65,000 or less. Additionally, UT Austin also offers full-ride Forty Acres scholarships as well as scholarships from alumni and chapters of Texas Exes (award amounts and deadlines vary). UT offers 3,000 scholarships to students as well as financial aid to pay for undergraduate education. In addition to federal aid, Texas students can get special grants. Finally, students in ROTC and class valedictorians are eligible for exemptions and waivers from tuition.

In UT Austin's Cockrell School of Engineering alone, undergraduates received more than $5.6 million in merit awards. To earn one of these scholarships, students must complete the Engineering Honors Program application by December 1.

PRIVATE SCHOLARSHIPS FOR MECHANICAL ENGINEERING

Allen Rhodes Memorial Scholarships

This scholarship is for college student members of the American Society of Mechanical Engineers (ASME) who are interested in pursuing careers in the oil and gas industry. Applications are due in February.

American Electric Power Scholarship ($4,000) & ASME Power Division Scholarship ($3,000)

These scholarships are granted to college student members of ASME whose goal is to pursue a career in power engineering. Applications are due in February.

Dan & Vicky Hancock Scholarship for Mechanical Engineering Excellence

One $5,500 scholarship is awarded yearly to applicants pursuing mechanical engineering. Students submit an application, FAFSA form, two letters of recommendation, and demonstrated leadership. Applications are due in March.

Frank & Dorothy Miller Scholarship (2 - $2,000); F.W. "Beich" Beichley Scholarship (1 - $3,000); Garland Duncan Scholarship (2 - $5,000), Irma and Robert Bennett Scholarship (2 - $3,000); John & Else Gracik Scholarships (5 - $5,000); Allen J. Baldwin Scholarship (2 - $3,000); Berna Lou Cartwright Scholarship (2 - $3,000); Sylvia W. Farny Scholarship (2 - $3,000); Agnes Malakate Kezios Scholarship (2 - $3,000); Charles B. Scharp Scholarship (1 - $3,000), Kenneth Andrew Roe Scholarship (1 - $13,000); Melvin R. Green Scholarship (1 - $8,000)

Up to 23 awards are given yearly to college student members of ASME. Considerations include integrity, leadership, academics, and potential to contribute the mechanical engineering profession. Applications are due in February.

John Rice Memorial Scholarship

This $3,000 scholarship is for students who attend one of nine New York City area colleges. Students will be judged based on their transcript, leadership, integrity, and potential to contribute to the mechanical engineering profession. Applications are due in February.

Ralph K. Hillquist Honorary SAE Scholarship

This $1,000 award offered every other year at the SAE Noise & Vibration Conference is for junior mechanical engineering majors who are interested in noise, vibration, statics, dynamics, and physics. Applications are due in March.

Stephen T. Kugle Scholarship

This $3,000 scholarship is for an active ASME student member who attends college in AZ, AK, CO, LA, NM, OK, TX, UT, or WY. Applications are due in February.

William J. & Marijane E. Adams, Jr. Scholarship

This $3,000 scholarship is for one mechanical engineering student ASME member from CA, HI, or NV with a special interest in product design and development. Applications are due in February.

PRIVATE SCHOLARSHIPS

Some scholarship money does not come directly from the college. Private individuals, corporations, and endowments offer outside scholarships for students who apply. Some of these scholarships are significant. A few offer full tuition. Here are a few of the thousands to consider.

AQHA and AQHF – $25,000 - $35,000 (Dec 1) Quarter Horse Members

A few scholarships for journalism, communications, agricultural studies, and equine research.

Boren Scholarships ($8,000 - $25,000) and Boren Fellowships ($12,000 -30,000) – Foreign Language Study

The National Security Education Program (NSEP) awards funding for students to study one of about 65 languages the U.S. deems necessary for national security through a study abroad program. Applications open from mid-August to early February. Approximately 300 student selected.

Brower Youth Awards

Environmental activism awards are granted to 6 winners; each receives $3,000.

Coca Cola Scholarship

1,400 students are selected to receive scholarships. The total amount awarded annually is approximately $3,550,000. 150 students receive $20,000 scholarship each.

Comcast NBCUniversal Leaders and Achievers Scholarship

More than 800 high school student winners each year win a $2,500 scholarship.

Dell Scholars Program – 500 students selected – $20,000 - First-Generation
This scholarship is awarded to students who exhibit grit, potential, and ambition.

Distinguished Scholars Awards, Art Contest Scholarships
There are numerous scholarships that fall into these categories.

Gates Millennium Scholarship
Scholarships covering the full cost of attendance not already covered by other aid and expected family contributions are granted to 300 African American, American Indian/Alaska Native, Asian Pacific Islander, or Hispanic American student leaders.

GE-Reagan Foundation Scholarship Program $40,000 (10 students)
Another $50,000 is awarded in the Great Communicator Debate Series.

Gloria Barron Prize for Young Heroes
25 students each year ages 8 – 18 receive $10,000 for community service projects.

Hispanic Scholarship Fund
Approximately 10,000 winners - $30,000,000 awarded annually.

K-12 Educator Scholarship
This scholarship is for children with parents who teach in the K-12 system.

NAACP – National Association for the Advancement of Colored People
African Americans - about 170 students receive awards of $3,000 to $15,000.

NASSP – National Association of Secondary School Principals

600 NHS Scholarships awarded per year, 1 national winner ($25,000 scholarship). 24 national finalists ($5,625 each), 575 national semifinalists ($3,200 each). Apply between October 1 and December 1.

Parent Employment

Many companies offer scholarships for their employees and their children.

Prudential Spirit of Community Award (Prudential Emerging Visionaries)

25 students in grades 5 to 12 are granted a $1,000 - $5,000 award for community service.

Questbridge Scholarship

$200,000 is granted to each of 1,464 students to be used over 4 years.

ROTC

These military scholarships are not given to everyone in ROTC. A select group of outstanding candidates is given tuition, fees, textbooks, plus a monthly stipend.

Scholastic Art and Writing Competition

Herblock Award - $1,000 scholarships for editorial cartoons

New York Life Award - $1,000 writing award about personal grief and loss

One Earth Award - $1,000 scholarship for writing about human-caused climate change

Portfolio Scholarships – Up to $10,000 granted for top portfolios

Civic Expression Award - $1,000 scholarships for writing on political and social issues

Best-In-Grade – Juror favorite awards receive $500 scholarships

College Tuition & Summer Scholarships - https://www.artandwriting.org/scholarships/

Service/Leadership/Focused Organization Scholarship

Lions Club, Moose Club, Elks Club, Rotary Club, Soroptimists Club, Mensa

Target Scholarship

HBCU Design Challenge for African Americans – Students submit designs for Black History Month.

Target Scholars Program – 1,000 students get $5,000 each.

Thurgood Marshall College Fund

African Americans – approximately 500 scholarships per year (average award - $6,200 per year).

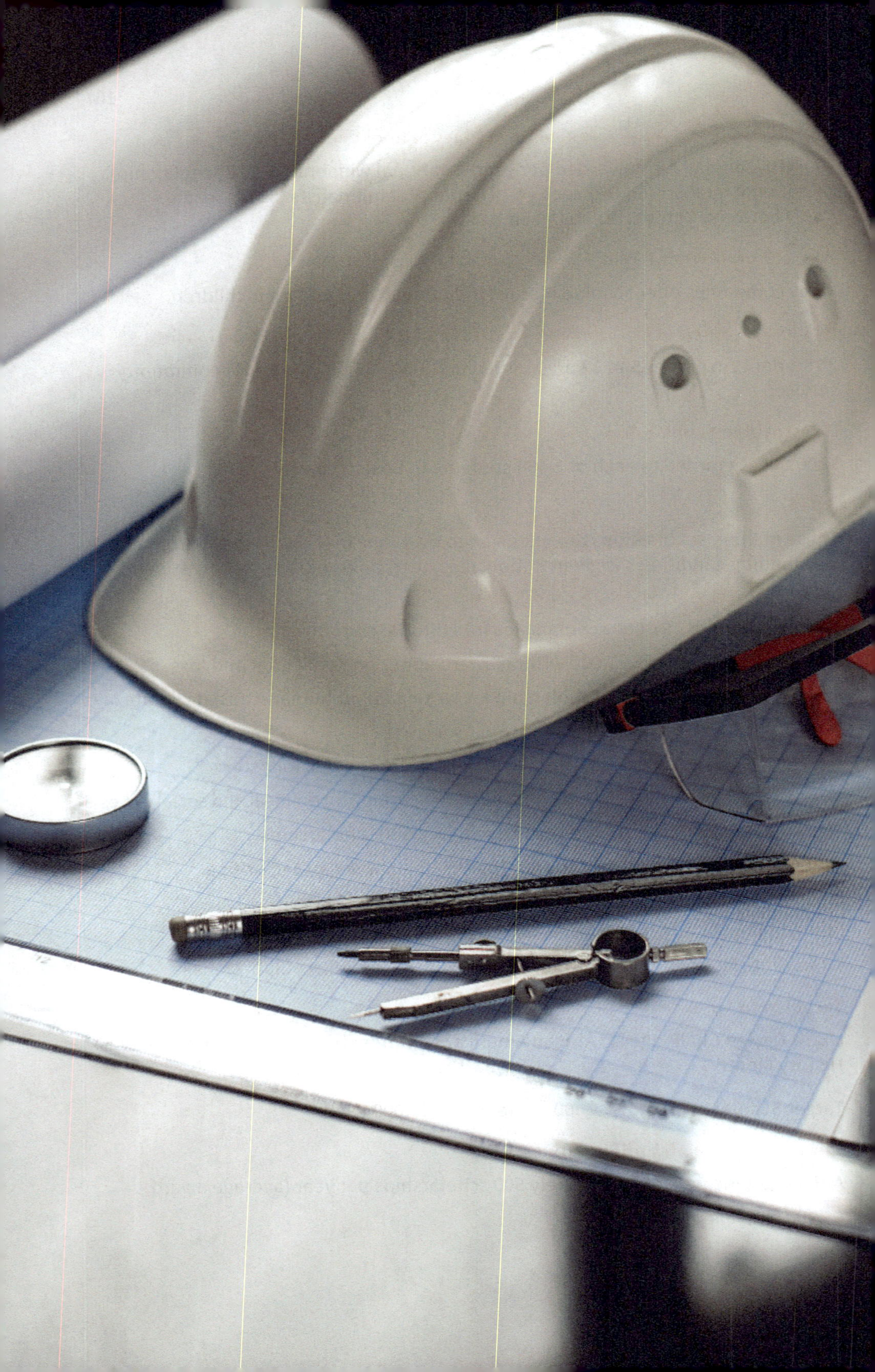

CHAPTER 9
POST PANDEMIC EMPLOYMENT OUTLOOK: STATISTICS AND ECONOMIC PROJECTIONS

"The scientist discovers a new type of material or energy and the engineer discovers a new use for it."

– Gordon Lindsay Glegg

Mechanical engineers play essential roles in society. Working in offices, they research, design, develop, build, test, and manufacture mechanical devices and systems. According to the *Occupational Outlook Handbook*, employment opportunities in mechanical engineering are slated to grow 7% from 2020 to 2030 with approximately 146,000 new jobs expected.

With the demand for high-tech equipment, vehicles, and automated processes along with computerized tools, machinery, phones, and robots, mechanical engineers will continue to be in high demand. The median annual wage $95,300. Furthermore, since innovations are rapidly being developed in many sectors of society, mechanical engineering wages are likely to increase.

Licensure is necessary in order to offer services to the public. Leadership positions in mechanical engineering typically require a graduate degree in mechanical engineering, industrial engineering, architecture, or business administration.

According to the May 2022 Bureau of Labor Statistics data,[1]

OCCUPATION	JOB SUMMARY	Entry-Level Education	2022 ANNUAL PAY
Aerospace Engineering & Operations Technologists & Technicians	Aerospace engineering and operations technologists and technicians run and maintain equipment used to develop, test, produce, and sustain aircraft and spacecraft.	Associate's Degree	$75,690
Aerospace Engineers	Aerospace engineers design primarily aircraft, spacecraft, satellites, and missiles.	Bachelor's Degree	$122,970
Agricultural Engineers	Agricultural engineers solve problems concerning power supplies, machine efficiency, the use of structures and facilities, pollution and environmental issues, and the storage and processing of agricultural products.	Bachelor's Degree	$96,310
Architects	Architects plan and design houses, factories, office buildings, and other structures.	Bachelor's Degree	$107,490
Bioengineers & Biomedical Engineers	Bioengineers and biomedical engineers combine engineering principles with sciences to design and create equipment, devices, computer systems, and software.	Bachelor's Degree	$101,020

OCCUPATION	JOB SUMMARY	Entry-Level Education	2022 ANNUAL PAY
Cartographers & Photogrammetrists	Cartographers and photogrammetrists collect, measure, and interpret geographic information in order to create and update maps and charts for regional planning, education, and other purposes.	Bachelor's Degree	$70,590
Chemical Engineers	Chemical engineers apply the principles of chemistry, biology, physics, and math to solve problems that involve the use of fuel, drugs, food, and many other products.	Bachelor's Degree	$121,840
Civil Engineering Technologists & Technicians	Civil engineering technologists and technicians help civil engineers plan, design, and build infrastructure and development projects.	Associate's Degree	$61,510
Civil Engineers	Civil engineers design, build, and supervise infrastructure projects and systems.	Bachelor's Degree	$91,050
Computer Hardware Engineers	Computer hardware engineers research, design, develop, and test computer systems and components.	Bachelor's Degree	$136,230
Drafters	Drafters use software to convert the designs of engineers and architects into technical drawings.	Associate's Degree	$63,410
Electrical & Electronic Engineering Technologists & Technicians	Electrical and electronic engineering technologists and technicians help engineers design and develop equipment that is powered by electricity or electric current.	Associate's Degree	$66,420
Electrical & Electronics Engineers	Electrical engineers design, develop, test, and supervise the manufacture of electrical equipment.	Bachelor's Degree	$111,290
Electro-mechanical & Mechatronics Technologists & Technicians	Electro-mechanical and mechatronics technologists and technicians operate, test, and maintain electromechanical or robotic equipment.	Associate's Degree	$63,640
Environmental Engineering Technologists & Technicians	Environmental engineering technologists and technicians implement the plans that environmental engineers develop.	Associate's Degree	$52,610
Environmental Engineers	Environmental engineers use the principles of engineering, soil science, biology, and chemistry to develop solutions to environmental problems.	Bachelor's Degree	$100,320
Health & Safety Engineers	Health and safety engineers combine knowledge of engineering and of health and safety to develop procedures and design systems to protect people from illness and injury and property from damage.	Bachelor's Degree	$103,160

OCCUPATION	JOB SUMMARY	Entry-Level Education	2022 ANNUAL PAY
Industrial Engineering Technologists & Technicians	Industrial engineering technologists and technicians help engineers solve problems affecting manufacturing layout or production.	Associate's Degree	$63,110
Industrial Engineers	Industrial engineers devise efficient systems that integrate workers, machines, materials, information, and energy to make a product or provide a service.	Bachelor's Degree	$99,500
Landscape Architects	Landscape architects design parks and other outdoor spaces.	Bachelor's Degree	$69,140
Marine Engineers & Naval Architects	Marine engineers and naval architects design, build, and maintain ships, from aircraft carriers to submarines and from sailboats to tankers.	Bachelor's Degree	$95,690
Materials Engineers	Materials engineers develop, process, and test materials used to create a wide range of products.	Bachelor's Degree	$105,420
Mechanical Engineering Technologists & Technicians	Mechanical engineering technologists and technicians help mechanical engineers design, develop, test, and manufacture machines and other devices.	Associate's Degree	$62,690
Mechanical Engineers	Mechanical engineers design, develop, build, and test mechanical and thermal sensors and devices.	Bachelor's Degree	$101,400
Mining & Geological Engineers	Mining and geological engineers design mines to safely and efficiently remove minerals for use in manufacturing and utilities.	Bachelor's Degree	$100,150
Nuclear Engineers	Nuclear engineers research and develop the processes, instruments, and systems used to derive benefits from nuclear energy and radiation.	Bachelor's Degree	$124,540
Petroleum Engineers	Petroleum engineers design and develop methods for extracting oil and gas from deposits below the Earth's surface.	Bachelor's Degree	$145,720
Surveying & Mapping Technicians	Surveying and mapping technicians collect data and make maps of the Earth's surface.	High School Diploma or Equivalent	$48,670
Surveyors	Surveyors make precise measurements to determine property boundaries.	Bachelor's Degree	$62,680

We know what we are but know not what we may be.

– **William Shakespeare**

Mechanical engineers typically earn a bachelor's degree from an ABET (Accreditation Board for Engineering and Technology) program, though many go on to earn an M.S. or MBA. The ABET is required to earn the PE (Professional Engineer) license. The knowledge civil engineering student gain in school include computer-aided design and drafting (CADD) and project management software.

Beginning with coursework focused on math, statistics, chemistry, and physics, they move on to advanced classes in mechanical systems, fluid dynamics, and hands-on project development. Many programs are five years and incorporate a co-op program where they work for a firm gaining on-the-job training. On the job, mechanical engineers research and develop mechanical systems, often with engineers having different backgrounds.

To achieve state licensure, mechanical engineers must pass the FE (Fundamentals of Engineering) exam, after which they are considered EITs (Engineers in Training) or EIs (Engineer Interns). Afterward, they must complete a specified number of years of work experience (varies by state) with a licensed engineer and a passing score on the PE (Principles and Practice of Engineering) exam.

Mechanical engineers can gain specialist certifications from the American Society of Mechanical Engineers (ASME) in the following areas.
- Bioprocessing Equipment Certificate
- Boiler/Pressure Vessel Certification
- Nuclear Component Certification

- Nuclear Material Org Certification
- Nuclear Quality Assurance Certification
- Personal Certification
- Reinforced Thermoset Plastic (RTP) Certification

To earn these certifications, mechanical engineers must have their PE license, master's degree, and post-licensure progressive engineering experience.

Mechanical engineers work in offices and then research and test projects on teams in consultation with other engineers. Some spend most of their time on construction sites where they oversee projects. Approximately 21% of all mechanical engineers work in architectural, engineering, and related services, while 14% work in machinery manufacturing, 12% in transportation equipment manufacturing, 8% in computer and electronic product manufacturing, and 5% in scientific research and development services.[2] The rest hold a variety of different positions.

Some mechanical engineers work on large engineering projects abroad. Thus, although difficult to fit travel experiences into a student's packed academic schedule, a semester or summer abroad learning another language or working in a co-op engineering program in another country is helpful.

The employment prospects for mechanical engineers are positive with approximately 299,200 individuals who noted this field of employment in 2021.

ROAD TO LICENSURE

The road to licensure is typically four years. This should not be discouraging. There are a few steps to take along the way and possibly some certifications that elevate your career and offer you new possibilities. Even so, achieving the goal is rewarding. Encourage those around you. If mechanical engineering is the field you want to pursue, pave the road in front of you and drive. Summer internships or apprenticeships each year will only help you in your pursuit of a position at a good firm.

Although some internships are unpaid, you will find that most students will have completed one or more before they graduate. Some internships pay fairly well. If you are serious, you will make a fantastic career out of your pursuit.

---

2 Bureau of Labor Statistics, U.S. Department of Labor, *Occupational Outlook Handbook*, Mechanical Engineers, at https://www.bls.gov/ooh/architecture-and-engineering/mechanical-engineers.htm

Initiative-taking persistence, talent, creativity, and moxie can get you into your desired college program and career. You may have to start at the very bottom of the ladder, but you can climb the rungs methodically one by one.

Companies want to know the work ethic, personality, and professionalism of the employees they hire. An internship allows you to get to know their corporate climate better and allows them to get to know you better too. Thus, many companies hire the interns they feel are the best fit rather than choosing candidates from the piles of resumes that have been submitted from candidates they barely know.

Education unlocks doors no matter which direction your career takes you. Whatever avenue you pursue, if you lay a foundation, undaunted by the competition, and are unafraid of starting at the bottom, you will do fine. Hard work and creativity go a long way in this industry. Start by getting a solid education.

IMPACT OF COVID-19

The pandemic slowed education and learning with online classes, reduced access to faculty/advising, limited access to labs, inability to attend workshops, retail closures, and fewer conferences, meetings, and trade shows. Health concerns rose to the top of importance as did financial stress, job uncertainty, and social consciousness.

COVID-19 impacted the number of internships and jobs people could get in mechanical engineering. A significant drop in opportunities led many mechanical engineering students to the Internet to post their availability, create models, and produce independent work for freelancing. The dynamic changed as Pinterest, Instagram, and Facebook became inundated with images and ideas. While the field is growing with more entrants presenting what they created, practice and training continue to be essential, and techniques can always be improved.

During the pandemic, many students accepted internships for work experience or started virtual stores to gain financial resources or professional qualifications when they could not access community service or continue with their sport, instrument, or hobbies. Nevertheless, with the changes in lifestyle and fears about health, safety, and wellness, many bright and talented students developed a fearless sense of autonomy and independence. For many students, necessary practical skills, ordinarily developed in school laboratories were fraught with limitations.

MANAGEMENT AND EMPLOYEE RETENTION

Skills to Know: Management, Human Resources, Social Consciousness, Ethics

One of the most significant challenges facing employers in the years from 2022 - 2030 will be locating and retaining talent. Finding talent within the changing hiring atmosphere will require new skills to retain staff. Employees are increasingly looking elsewhere for a better opportunity. This development will require managers to earn and harness employee trust and loyalty.

The digital workforce has also placed demands on human resources. While many companies want their employees to work in-person, the convenience of working at home and the drudgery of commuting to work have created an environment where employees seek greater flexibility. Changes are coming. The employee talent challenge is likely to create a more global workforce where companies look for less expensive online talent from a pool of eager workers in other countries.

Companies are back to hiring now and good jobs are available in mechanical engineering. There is no doubt that the skills you learn in college will be tremendously valuable in the pursuit of your ultimate goals.

117

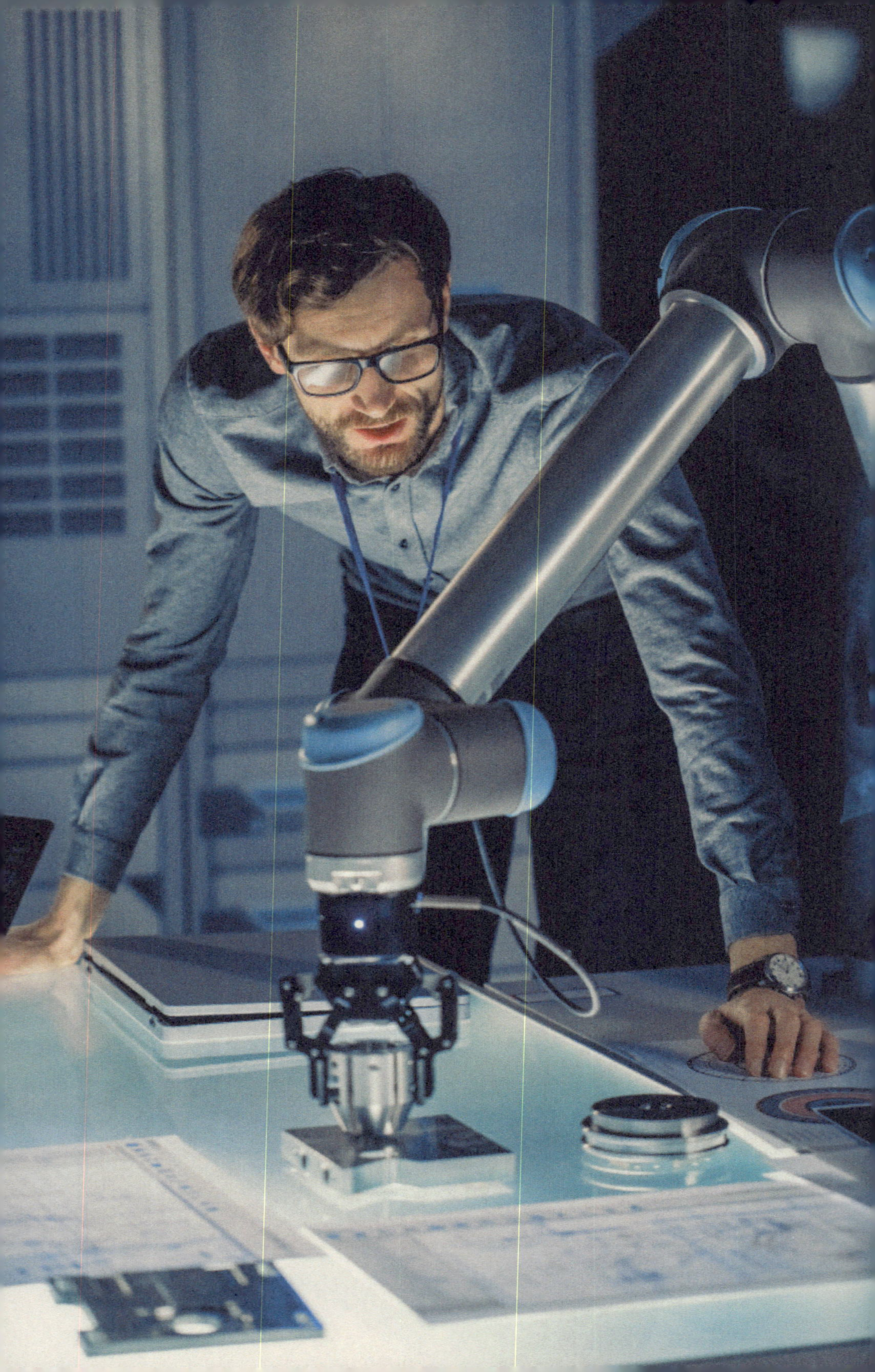

CHAPTER 10

NEXT STEPS: PREPARATION AND REAL-WORLD SKILLS

"This job is a great scientific adventure. But it's also a great human adventure."

— **Fabiola Gianotti**

College offers you the freedom to express yourself openly, dynamically, and interactively. As you explore the nuances of mechanical engineering, you will engage the adventurous spirit within you, hungry to emerge. The next step is for you to choose a college where your personality fits into the makeup of the environment. In college labs, you will receive personalized, interactive training, immersed in the inspiration of fellow classmates. Each model you construct will leave a lasting impression.

Through social media, instantaneously, you can share your inspirations, designs, and projects with millions of people in a matter of moments. The possibilities are limitless. In school or out of school, you may want to take a few classes on social media dynamics and website editing. Furthermore, on the leading edge of the Metaverse, you might possibly invent mechanical tools, vehicles, or processes that were never before possible. It's unbelievably thrilling.

Mechanical engineering is a dynamic, multidimensional field where you will contribute to the ongoing innovations that will transform thermodynamic, structural, and mechanical systems. In some careers, repetitive tasks and uninspiring projects lead employees to loathe their jobs and tick off minutes until their day is done. Yet, your life will undoubtedly be different and ever-changing since the world around you will evolve from moment to moment. Over time, whichever area of mechanical engineering becomes your focus, you will earn your way to a career of endless possibilities.

If you want to find the secrets of the universe,

think in terms of energy, frequency, and vibration.

Nicola Tesla (1856 – 1943)

German engineer, Rudolph Diesel (1858 – 1913), who designed the diesel engine said, "The automobile engine will come, and then I will consider my life's work complete." What big ideas do you have that you want to see come to fruition in your lifetime? Teleportation? Completely wireless carbon-neutral electric power? Nanomaterials that reduce the size of computers to the size of a credit card? Natural computer language processing? Quantum computing? A world free of paper currency?

Spend time envisioning new possibilities, even though time sometimes seems short. You may feel as if time slips through your fingers like sand in an hourglass. Resist the temptation to upload your breakthroughs before contemplating what you want to express. With your electrified ideas and commitment to school, you can turn your brainstorms into reality.

While social media opens doors to locations where you can share your creations, truly magical works are created when time stands still, and you immerse yourself in a creative state. Today is a precious moment. As you contemplate college choices and tomorrow's future, you will explore your passions. Open doors you never expected and walk inside to discover opportunities that will tantalize and challenge you along the way. As such, you will capture a new, exciting, and eclectic way of life.

Attending a respected school can help you get noticed, though motivation is the key factor. Your next steps will be aided by connections offered by professors, classmates, and alumni. Networking events are also excellent ways to discover opportunities. Conferences, displays, and contests in school, out of school, in the summer, or through social media can help you get noticed. Bring people into your world. Allow them to consider your innovations in their own unique way.

Throughout your varied experiences, you will meet other engineers who may recommend you to employers or inform you about open positions or contract opportunities, even some that are not publicly announced. In addition, many schools have a culminating event where you can put your best foot forward and showcase your work.

Exposure to industry professionals will open new doors. Also, by interacting with people online or in person you can maintain those connections. The autonomy and freedom to choose freelance jobs by venturing out on your own may seem alluring, but this independence may result in uncertainty or even career limitations. Without a clear track record, those who may hire you may choose another individual or company with a solid reputation.

Companies often choose seasoned professionals with work experience in other firms. However, there are ways to mitigate against the lean times of solo work. A few options include demonstrating mastery, producing amazing work, designing something innovative, resolving client problems, aligning ideologies, and initially charging less. Despite challenges, put yourself out there.

You could wait for the phone to ring to be discovered. However, you should post ideas, articles, or availability regularly to professional sites. To be seen, you need to be out and about. Some individuals pine away by sending in resumes with the hopes of being selected and then deciding which organization would be a perfect fit. Others decide that they only want to work at a specific firm or location. Still others determine that they will work for themselves and be their own boss. Yet, sometimes taking any position at the start is a steppingstone to your dream life, commitment to service, and opportunity to put your unique mark on society.

BOLD NETWORKING

Networking takes social skills and a bit of moxie. From elevator speeches and professional encounters to interviews and masterclasses, your job is to find a way to get your talent and abilities in front of people and have employers discover your knowledge of mechanical engineering, leadership potential, and willingness to contribute. You have something special and fresh ideas.

Finally, there are professional entities that will welcome your style, ingenuity, discipline, and impact. How can you be recognized? Meet people. Hand out your resume, give them your business card, ask for their business card, and follow up.

Ask if you can call or meet them. Sometimes approaching these professionals may seem uncomfortable. Stay in touch with those you meet, even if it is just happenstance or serendipity. Keep a log of each individual's phone, e-mail, and identifying information. Track both the date and location where you met. You never know when you will need it.

If you meet people professionally at a workshop, leadership event, or industry conference, even if you do not exchange information, you will recognize them at a later date. They may recognize you at a future event too. Keep training. You should always seek ways to improve, irrespective of your experience. Lifelong learning improves your ability to maintain up-to-date skills and transition to new ventures. Furthermore, the outside world's perspective changes more quickly with social media's instant influences.

You should not register for workshops just for the sake of meeting people. Plan to learn something new. When you do attend, be present and contribute, lead, and serve. If your focus is not on your learning or professional development, you may appear insincere in your intentions. However, workshops, conferences, and meetings can allow others to see your purpose, vision, and talent.

Big-ticket training does not always mean better trainers or opportunities. Find time to research companies, survey your industry surroundings, and notice cultural changes that may determine what people want or need. While gathering new thoughts, remember that humility and open-mindedness go a long way. Defer to the wise and listen. There is much you can learn.

STAY IN TOUCH

Do not annoy busy people, but you can keep in touch every couple of months. Communicating more frequently is overwhelming. However, life is long. People who grow with their craft transition fluidly through life's career phases. In engineering, contacts are essential in all phases of your career. Also, do not be surprised. Many go-getters seeking to gain a coveted contract do the following:

1. Speak at Chamber of Commerce meetings.
2. Attend industry trade shows.
3. Gain a following and post ideas on Instagram, Facebook, and Pinterest.
4. Write a newsletter and publish it on LinkedIn and other sources.
5. Link your high school and college projects to social media.
6. Enter engineering design, solar, drone, satellite, and innovation contests.

7. Join professional associations.
8. Attend social gatherings of potential customers.
9. Keep in touch with your professors.
10. Stay involved with your alumni associations.

Friendships matter. Become lifelong colleagues by finding friends who share mutual interests and offer a sounding board or connections to new opportunities. People tend to stay in touch with "important" people. Note to self: Your contemporaries or peers are important people...although possibly not yet. As you form lists of contacts, you are likely to know these people throughout your career.

Be audacious while also being authentic. Networking can sometimes appear fake or forced as if you are going out on a hunt to find people for your own benefit. Worse, the act of networking can appear like stalking for those who incessantly attempt to connect. The mental image of this type of 'networking' conjures the vision of people congregating at meetings.

Friendships and the mutual support of allies can be enormously helpful, though 20,000 or even 200,000 followers on your website do not mean you are popular. However, you can have unexpected meaningful exchanges if you get out, meet people, and live life. There are times when deeply moving, casual conversations in non-professional settings could also turn into connections.

Do not lose touch with people or burn bridges along the way. This industry is not that big, especially in whatever subspecialty you choose. You will continually see extraordinary talent. You never know. They may contact you to collaborate one day or meet for coffee at an event.

COLLEGE AND CAREER CENTERS

Although engineering departments frequently have internal connections to help you secure an internship or job, you might also speak to someone at your campus career center. They often have interesting and possibly different prospects you might not get elsewhere. In addition, there may be a specific career liaison for their engineering programs. Connect with them for help in your search process. Besides, you might want a related job that utilizes your creative, design, problem-solving, and presentation skills.

Career center coordinators often have excellent ideas of alternative options you may have never considered. Furthermore, they can assist you with creating a professional resume and cover letters for specific industries that are different from the ones you have for engineering, especially if you are considering MBA, law school, or Ph.D. programs.

They may also connect you with past graduates in the industry who make excellent connections. Some of them may have been in your program and have been through the ropes, know a few people, and may be able to get you an interview or invite you to an industry event. Any contact may help you get your foot in the door or find a job to make money in the meantime.

LINKEDIN

LinkedIn is especially helpful for career searches. You can find numerous influential contacts on LinkedIn. After interviews or events, connect with each person you met on LinkedIn. Keep a contact list of individuals you get to know in your area of interest. Do not constantly try to connect with people you do not really know. However, if you have made the connection, occasionally keep in touch.

While some LinkedIn message boxes may be full and you may not get a reply, you can try. Some people have tens of thousands of LinkedIn followers. I have more than 20,000 LinkedIn 'connections', which does not necessitate that I am important. It just means that I have connected with 20,000 people. Remember that a big paycheck or lots of friends does not make you more worthy or successful. Worth and value emanate from your heart. You have the power to improve your life in any way you choose.

Occasionally on LinkedIn, you hit on a lucky break with a new customer, communicate with a client, or make a close friend. Some professionals prefer

LinkedIn to other methods of communication. While that may seem odd, a few people I have known for decades only communicate with me through LinkedIn. Lastly, I do not have time to communicate with everyone. However, I have connected with some of my most inspiring authors, advisors, and intellectual leaders through the LinkedIn platform.

FINALLY

Most people are willing to help you. Five percent will not. Thus, you have a 19 out of 20 chance of interacting with decent people who have the time and are willing to give you advice. Don't lose faith in humanity just because you run into a few people who are too busy to stop for you or are too self-absorbed that they cannot answer your question. They may be consumed with problems of their own that they cannot yet resolve.

Remember that talent is only the beginning. You need to sell yourself. As you organize your goals and responsibilities, remember to think one step ahead of where you want to be by making a game plan. Since actions speak louder than words, take action without complaining and spread kindness along the way. Burned bridges are tough to reconstruct.

Honesty and trustworthiness are worth more than any physical object. Earn this by working hard, being efficient, and telling the truth. In your work, imagine you are the manager, what would you do in difficult situations? One day, you may just be a manager and be on the opposite side making decisions.

Professionalism in your words and deeds is essential. Be productive. Put away all distractions and focus on your tasks. Texts and social media take a surprising amount of time. Get the job done. When you are finished, ask for another project. Do this not because you are brownnosing, but because you should want your company to be successful. Discipline is achieved by creating a goal and making it happen.

A nice note, card, or gift reminds people you are thinking about them, even when you are incredibly busy. Good friends who have your best interest may know doors that are not yet open for you. Keep in touch with them. Every action you take is a steppingstone to your future.

So, go on a walk, meet people, and live fully. Serendipity happens when you live life. However, your education is immensely valuable. The adage goes - success happens when preparation meets opportunity. Thus, preparation is the best way to generate luck. Finally, even the most disciplined person can be lazy or inefficient. Fight this. Stay active. Make your life happen for you.

Here are a few things to remember as you go out to pursue your dreams.

- Work ethic is everything.
- Excellence is expected.
- Learn what you do not know on your own time.
- Come to work prepared.
- Take constructive criticism well.
- Be respectful and courteous.
- Keep your cool under pressure.
- Avoid being timid.
- Stay on task.
- Come early.
- Stay late.
- Take your work seriously.
- Do more than expected.
- Be thoughtful and respectful.
- Read your e-mail/texts after hours in case something is important.
- Ask questions. No question is too stupid.
- Maintain a clean workspace.
- Dress and act professionally.
- Don't gossip or complain.
- Play when you are done.
- Avoid frustrating your phenomenally busy supervisor.
- Be straightforward, and don't beat around the bush.

You've Got This!

Be yourself; everyone else is already taken.

- Oscar Wilde

4 Regions

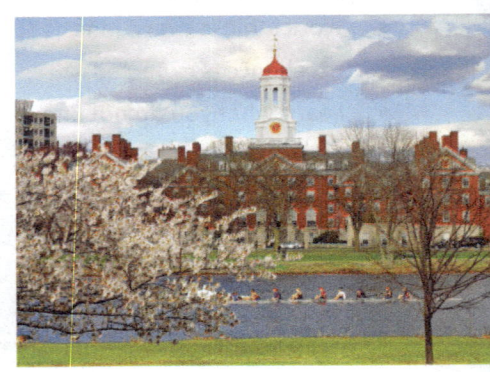

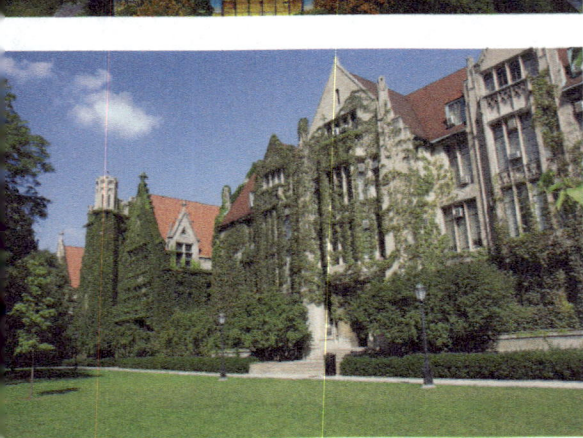

65 Programs

COLLEGE PROFILES AND REQUIREMENTS

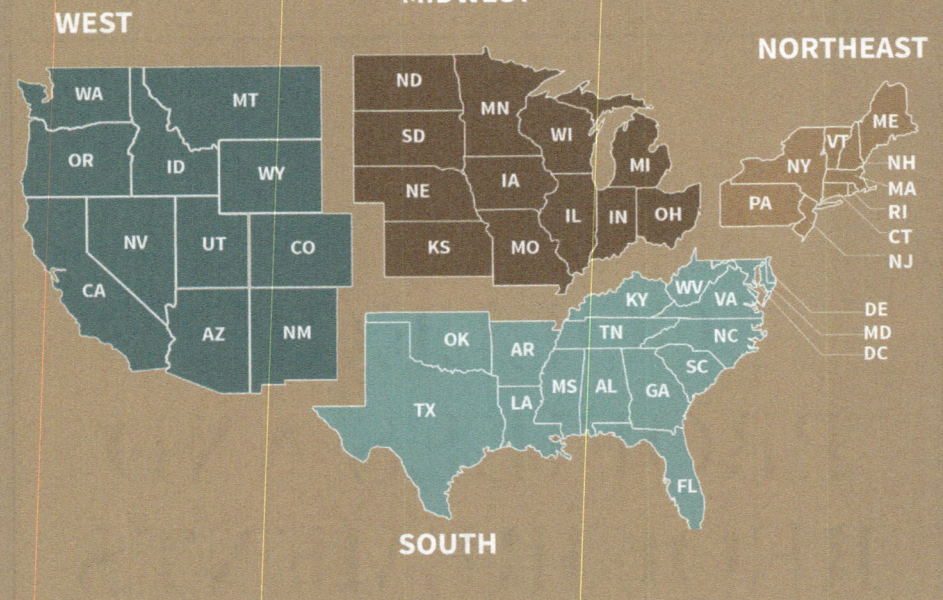

PROGRAMS BY REGION
U.S. CENSUS BUREAU CLASSIFICATIONS

REGION 1 – NORTHEAST

Connecticut, Maine, Massachusetts, New Hampshire, New Jersey, New York, Pennsylvania, Rhode Island, and Vermont

REGION 2 – MIDWEST

Illinois, Indiana, Iowa, Kansas, Michigan, Minnesota, Missouri, Nebraska, North Dakota, Ohio, South Dakota, and Wisconsin

REGION 3 – SOUTH

Alabama, Arkansas, Delaware, District of Columbia, Florida, Georgia, Kentucky, Louisiana, Maryland, Mississippi, North Carolina, Oklahoma, South Carolina, Tennessee, Texas, Virginia, and West Virginia

REGION 4 – WEST

Alaska, Arizona, California, Colorado, Hawaii, Idaho, Montana, Nevada, New Mexico, Oregon, Utah, Washington, and Wyoming

PROFILES OF SELECTED MECHANICAL ENGINEERING PROGRAMS

The 65 undergraduate programs listed in the following pages include the top mechanical engineering programs as of March 2023 along with a few additional college programs that offer closely related degrees. Many students interested in studying mechanical engineering also interested in aerospace and civil engineering. Those schools are profiled in other books, though some lists are provided in the back.

Majoring in mechanical engineering is not for everyone. Success requires passion, interest, and initiative. Along with having a creative instinct, students must also be academically talented in math and science. In college, students discover their priorities, commitments, and perseverance. A few students change their major and choose an alternative path. Keep your options open.

Thus, this book provides you with lists of other programs so you can also explore those options. Keep the book handy. Even after you begin college you may find the summer internships and alternative college programs helpful.

Creating lists is often tedious and cumbersome. These lists were gathered to help you with this task. Descriptions of the college programs, opportunities, tuition, requirements, and deadlines are given as of March 2023.

However, the requirements may have changed by the time you purchase this book. Nevertheless, this information is a great place to start!

Note: To simplify the text and fit information into the charts and profiles, abbreviations were used as well as shortened sentences and acronyms. For example, eng = engineering, ctr = center, sys = systems, appl = applied, dev = development, res = research or resources, soc = society, and Amer = American.

CONNECTICUT
MAINE
MASSACHUSETTS
NEW HAMPSHIRE
NEW JERSEY
NEW YORK
PENNSYLVANIA
RHODE ISLAND
VERMONT

CHAPTER 11
REGION ONE
NORTHEAST

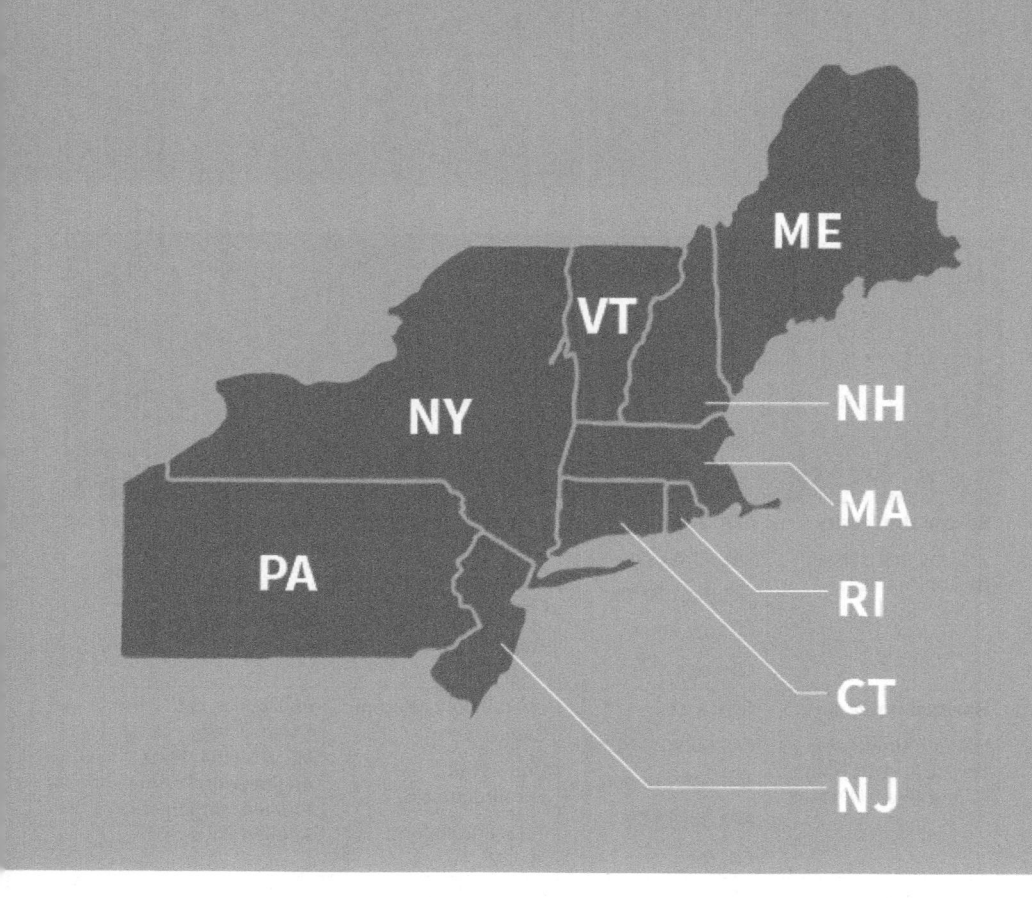

24 Programs | 9 States

1. MA - Boston University
2. MA - Harvard University
3. MA - Massachusetts Institute of Technology (MIT)
4. MA - Northeastern University
5. MA - Olin College of Engineering
6. MA - Tufts University
7. MA - Worcester Polytechnic Institute (WPI)
8. NJ - Princeton University
9. NJ - Stevens Institute of Technology
10. NY - Columbia University
11. NY - Cooper Union for the Advancement of Science and Arts
12. NY - Cornell University
13. NY - Rensselaer Polytechnic Institute (RPI)
14. NY - Syracuse University
15. NY - University of Rochester
16. PA - Bucknell University
17. PA - Carnegie Mellon University
18. PA - Drexel University
19. PA - Lafayette College
20. PA - Lehigh University
21. PA - Pennsylvania State University
22. PA - University of Pennsylvania
23. PA - Villanova University
24. RI - Brown University

MECHANICAL ENGINEERING PROGRAMS

School	Avg. GPA, SAT Evidence-Based Reading Writing (ERW), SAT Math (M), and ACT Composite (C) Early Decision (ED): Yes/No	Admission Statistics	Selected Program(s)
Boston University 233 Bay State Road, Boston, MA 02215	GPA: 3.76 SAT (ERW): 640-720 SAT (M): 670-780 ACT (C): 30-34 ED: Yes	Overall College Admit Rate: 20% Undergrad Enrollment: 16,872 Total Enrollment: 32,718	BS, MS, Ph.D. Mechanical Engineering, Conc in Aerospace Eng, Energy Tech MS Robotics & Autonomous Systems
Harvard University Harvard University, Massachusetts Hall, Cambridge, MA 02138	GPA: 4.22 SAT (ERW): 720-780 SAT (M): 740-800 ACT (C): 33-35 ED: Yes	Overall College Admit Rate: 5% Undergrad Enrollment: 8,527 Total Enrollment: 30,391	AB Mechanical Engineering MS, MS/MBA, Ph.D. Engineering Science, Applied Mathematics, Applied Physics
Massachusetts Institute of Technology (MIT) 77 Massachusetts Ave, Cambridge, MA 02139	GPA: N/A SAT (ERW): 730-780 SAT (M): 780-800 ACT (C): 34-36 ED: No	Overall College Admit Rate: 7% Undergrad Enrollment: 4,361 Total Enrollment: 11,254	SB, SM, ScD, Ph.D. Mechanical Engineering ScD, Ph.D. Transportation Engineering
Northeastern University 360 Huntington Ave, Boston, MA 02115	GPA: N/A SAT (ERW): 690-750 SAT (M): 720-790 ACT (C): 34-36 ED: Yes	Overall College Admit Rate: 20% Undergrad Enrollment: 15,156 Total Enrollment: 22,905	BS, BS/MS, MS, Ph.D. Mechanical Engineering, Industrial Engineering MS Applied Physics & Eng, Adv & Intelligent Manufacturing
Olin College of Engineering 1000 Olin Way, Needham, MA 02492	GPA: N/A SAT (ERW): 730-780 SAT (M): 760-800 ACT (C): 34-35 ED: No	Overall College Admit Rate: 18% Undergrad Enrollment: 382 Total Enrollment: 382	BS Bioengineering, Eng Computing, Eng Design, Engineering Robotics, Engineering Sustainability, Electrical Engineering, Mechanical Engineering

MECHANICAL ENGINEERING PROGRAMS

School	Avg. GPA, SAT Evidence-Based Reading Writing (ERW), SAT Math (M), and ACT Composite (C) Early Decision (ED): Yes/No	Admission Statistics	Selected Program(s)
Tufts University 419 Boston Ave, Medford, MA 02155	GPA: N/A SAT (ERW): 710-760 SAT (M): 730-790 ACT (C): 33-35 *Test-optional ED: No	Overall College Admit Rate: 11% Undergrad Enrollment: 6,676 Total Enrollment: 13,293	BS, MS, Ph.D. Mechanical Eng BS, MS Human-Factors Eng; MS Human-Robot Interaction Jt Ph.D. Mech Eng, Mech Eng w/ Human-Robot Interaction
Worcester Polytechnic Institute 100 Institute Road, Worcester, MA 01609	GPA: 3.85 SAT (ERW): 630-710 SAT (M): 670-760 ACT (C): 29-33 *Test-optional ED: Yes	Overall College Admit Rate: 59% Undergrad Enrollment: 4,892 Total Enrollment: 6,920	BS, MS, Ph.D. Aerospace Eng, BME, Mechanical & Materials Eng, Robotics Engineering MS, Ph.D. Fire Protection Eng, Manufacturing Eng
Princeton University Princeton University, Princeton, NJ 08544	GPA: 3.93 SAT (ERW): 710-770 SAT (M): 740-800 ACT (C): 32-35 ED: No, but Restrictive Early Action (REA) available	Overall College Admit Rate: 6% Undergrad Enrollment: 4,774 Total Enrollment: 7,853	AB, Ph.D. Aerospace Eng, Astrophysical Science, Chemical & Bio Eng, Enviro Eng, Mechanical Engineering, Robotics Eng; MS, Ph.D. Manufacturing Eng, Materials Science Eng

NORTHEAST

MECHANICAL ENGINEERING PROGRAMS

School	Avg. GPA, SAT Evidence-Based Reading Writing (ERW), SAT Math (M), and ACT Composite (C) Early Decision (ED): Yes/No	Admission Statistics	Selected Program(s)
Stevens Institute of Technology 1 Castle Point Terrace, Hoboken, NJ 07030	GPA: N/A SAT (ERW): 640-710 SAT (M): 680-770 ACT (C): 31-34 ED: Yes	Overall College Admit Rate: 53% Undergrad Enrollment: 3,791 Total Enrollment: 7,257	BS, MS, MEng, Ph.D. Mechanical Engineering, Naval Engineering MS/MEng Artificial Intelligence, Robotics, Sustainability Management, Space Systems Engineering
Columbia University 1130 Amsterdam Avenue, New York, NY 10027	GPA: N/A SAT (ERW): 720-770 SAT (M): 740-800 ACT (C): 33-35 ED: Yes	Overall College Admit Rate: 4% Undergrad Enrollment: 8,448 Total Enrollment: 31,455	BS, MS, Ph.D. Civil & Mechanical Engineering, Applied Physics & Eng Mgmt Systems, Engineering Mechanics MA Climate & Society
Cooper Union 30 Cooper Sq, New York, NY 10003	GPA: 3.75 SAT (ERW): 650-740 SAT (M): 655-790 ACT (C): 30-35 ED: Yes	Overall College Admit Rate: 18% Undergrad Enrollment: 806 Total Enrollment: 887	BEng, MEng Mechanical Engineering BS General Engineering
Cornell University 430 College Ave., Ithaca, NY 14850	GPA: N/A SAT (ERW): 680-750 SAT (M): 720-790 ACT (C): 32-35 ED: No	Admit Rate: 11% Undergrad Enrollment: 14,743 Total Enrollment: 23,620	BS, MEng, Ph.D. Aerospace Eng, Biological Eng, BME, Chemical Engineering, Materials Science, Mechanical Engineering
Rensselaer Polytechnic Institute (RPI) 110 8th Street, Greene Bldg., Troy, NY 12180	GPA: 3.91 SAT (ERW): 620-720 SAT (M): 680-780 ACT (C): 29-34 ED: Yes	Overall College Admit Rate: 57% Undergrad Enrollment: 6,283 Total Enrollment: 7,501	BS, MS, MEng, DEng, Ph.D. Aeronautical Eng, Industrial & Mgmt Eng; Mechanical Engineering, MS, MEng, DEng, Ph.D. Transportation Eng

MECHANICAL ENGINEERING PROGRAMS

School	Avg. GPA, SAT Evidence-Based Reading Writing (ERW), SAT Math (M), and ACT Composite (C) Early Decision (ED): Yes/No	Admission Statistics	Selected Program(s)
Syracuse University 401 University Place, Syracuse, NY 13244-2130	GPA: 3.67 SAT (ERW): N/A SAT (M): N/A ACT (C): N/A ED: Yes	Overall College Admit Rate: 69% Undergrad Enrollment: 14,479 Total Enrollment: 21,322	BS, BS/MS, MS, Ph.D. Aerospace Eng, BME, Chemical Eng, Comp Eng, Computer Science, Electrical Eng, Mechanical Engineering
University of Rochester 300 Wilson Boulevard, Rochester, NY 14627	GPA: N/A SAT (ERW): 650-720 SAT (M): 680-790 ACT (C): 30-34 *Test-optional ED: Yes	Overall College Admit Rate: 35% Undergrad Enrollment: 6,521 Total Enrollment: 11,741	BS, MS, Ph.D. Biomedical Engineering, Chemical Engineering, Biology, Chemistry, Computer Science, Mechanical Engineering
Bucknell University One Dent Dr, Lewisburg, PA 17837	GPA: 3.61 SAT (ERW): 610-690 SAT (M): 610-710 ACT (C): N/A *Test-optional ED: Yes	Overall College Admit Rate: 38% Undergrad Enrollment: 3,695 Total Enrollment: 3,726	BS Biomedical Eng, Computer Engineering, Comp Sci; BS, BS/MS, MS Chemical Eng, Civil Eng, Electrical Eng, Environmental Eng, Mechanical Engineering
Carnegie Mellon University 5000 Forbes Avenue, Pittsburgh, PA 15213	GPA: 3.85 SAT (ERW): 700-760 SAT (M): 760-800 ACT (C): 33-35 ED: Yes	Overall College Admit Rate: 17% Undergrad Enrollment: 7,073 Total Enrollment: 14,189	BS, MS, Ph.D. BME, Chemical Eng, Civil Engineering, EE, Mechanical Eng; BS/MS and MS/MBA Integrated Degrees

NORTHEAST

MECHANICAL ENGINEERING PROGRAMS

School	Avg. GPA, SAT Evidence-Based Reading Writing (ERW), SAT Math (M), and ACT Composite (C) Early Decision (ED): Yes/No	Admission Statistics	Selected Program(s)
Drexel University 3250 Chestnut Street, MacAlister Hall, Suite 4020, Philadelphia, PA 19104	GPA: N/A SAT (ERW): 590-680 SAT (M): 590-700 ACT (C): 25-31 ED: No	Admit Rate: 77% Undergrad Enrollment: 14,616 Total Enrollment: 23,589	BS, MS, Ph.D. Mechanical Engineering & Mechanics MS Robotics & Autonomy
Lafayette College 730 High St., Easton, PA 18042	GPA: 3.53 SAT (ERW): 640-720 SAT (M): 660-740 ACT (C): 30-33 ED: Yes	Overall College Admit Rate: 41% Undergrad Enrollment: 2,725 Total Enrollment: 2,725	BS BME, Chemical Eng, Civil Eng, Comp Eng, Electrical Engineering, Environmental & Energy Engineering, Mechanical Engineering, Robotics Engineering
Lehigh University 27 Memorial Drive West, Bethlehem, PA 18015	GPA: N/A SAT (ERW): 645-730 SAT (M): 680-760 ACT (C): 30-34 ED: Yes	Overall College Admit Rate: 46% Undergrad Enrollment: 5,451 Total Enrollment: 7,263	BS, BS/MS, MS, MEng, Ph.D. Mechanical Eng, Chemical Eng, Comp Sci, Computer Eng, Electrical Engineering, Materials Science & Engineering
Pennsylvania State University (Penn State) 124 Borland Building, University Park, PA 16802	GPA: N/A SAT (ERW): 580-670 SAT (M): 580-700 ACT (C): 25-30 ED: No	Overall College Admit Rate: 49% Undergrad Enrollment: 40,639 Total Enrollment: 47,223	BS, MS, Ph.D. Aerosp, Eng, Chem Eng, Mechanical Eng, Nuclear Engineering; MS, Ph.D. Eng Science & Mechanics, MEng Eng Mechanics, MS Additive Manuf. & Design Engineering

MECHANICAL ENGINEERING PROGRAMS

School	Avg. GPA, SAT Evidence-Based Reading Writing (ERW), SAT Math (M), and ACT Composite (C) Early Decision (ED): Yes/No	Admission Statistics	Selected Program(s)
University of Pennsylvania (UPenn) 3535 Market Street, Philadelphia, PA 19104	GPA: 3.9 SAT (ERW): 710-770 SAT (M): 750-800 ACT (C): 33-35 ED: Yes	Overall College Admit Rate: 9% Undergrad Enrollment: 11,155 Total Enrollment: 26,552	BS, AM/MSE, Ph.D. Bioeng, Chemical Eng, Molecular Eng, Mechanical Eng, EE, Materials Science & Eng MSE Data Sci, Comp Graphics & Game Tech, Nanotech, Robotics, Product Design
Villanova University 800 E. Lancaster Avenue, Villanova, PA 19085	GPA: 4.23 SAT (ERW): 650-710 SAT (M): 670-750 ACT (C): 30-33 ED: Yes	Overall College Admit Rate: 31% Undergrad Enrollment: 7,037 Total Enrollment: 11,032	BS, MS, Ph.D.. Chem Eng, Civil Eng, Comp Eng, Electrical Eng, Mechanical Engineering; MS, Ph.D. Biochemical Eng, Sustainable Eng
Brown University 198 Dyer Street, Providence, RI 02903	GPA: N/A SAT (ERW): 710-770 SAT (M): 730-790 ACT (C): 33-35 ED: Yes	Admit Rate: 8% Undergrad Enrollment: 6,792 Total Enrollment: 9,948	AB, Sc.B., Sc.B./Sc.M., MS, Ph.D. BME, Chemical Eng, Computer Eng, EE, Environmental Eng, Materials Science & Eng, Mechanical Eng

NORTHEAST

BOSTON UNIVERSITY

Address: Boston University College of Engineering, 44 Cummington Mall, Room 601, Boston, MA 02215
Website: *https://www.bu.edu/eng/*
Contact: *https://www.bu.edu/eng/about/contact/*
Phone: (617) 353-8068
Email: engineering@bu.edu

COST OF ATTENDANCE:

Tuition & Fees: $61,050 | **Addl Exp:** $21,710 | **Total:** $82,760
Financial Aid: https://www.bu.edu/finaid/

ADDITIONAL INFORMATION:

Available Degree(s)
- BS, MS, Ph.D. Mechanical Engineering, Concentrations in Aerospace Engineering, Energy Technologies
- MS Artificial Intelligence, Computer Science, Materials Science & Engineering, Robotics & Autonomous Systems, Product Design & Manufacture
- MS, Ph.D. Computer Engineering, Electrical Engineering, Materials Science & Engineering, Systems Engineering

Related Research Centers
Advanced Materials Process Control Lab, AI Res Init, BU Robotics Lab, Ctr for Space Physics, Ctr for Sys Nanoscience, Data Science & Machine Learning Lab, Inst of Sustainable Energy, Multimedia Comm Lab, Optimization & Machine Learning Lab, Performance & Energy Aware Computing Lab, Reliable Computing Lab, Security Lab, Signal Transformation & Information Representation Group, Smart Lighting Engineering Research, Visual Information Processing Lab

Scholarships Offered
BU meets 100% of a student's financial need. BU awards merit-based scholarships to recognize academic, athletic, or artistic achievement regardless of need. The Trustee's Scholarship provides a full-tuition grant. Apply by Dec. 1st – no FAFSA or CSS Profile req. BU's Presidential Scholarship is $25,000. The College of Engineering offers $25,000 FIRST Robotics scholarships to applicants who have participated in at least 1 season w/a FIRST Robotics team (Apply by Dec. 1). Merit scholarships are also offered for international students.

Special Opportunities
Co-ops, internships, research projects, Innovate@BU, BostonHacks, Make_BU, Build Lab Student Innovation Center, 24-hour (spring) and 36-hour (fall) Hackathons. Become a Dean's Host, Engineering Ambassador, EK 100 Student Advisor, Sophomore Mentor, TRAC Mentor, Engineers' Week host, or member of the Engineering Student Government.

Sophomore year (2nd semester) abroad in Spain or Australia. Junior year study abroad: National University of Singapore, Dublin City University, or Sydney University

Orgs: American Institute of Aeronautics & Astronautics, American Society of Mechanical Eng, Cleantech Club, Dean's Imagineering Comp, Engineers w/o Borders, Global Engineering Brigade, National Soc of Black Eng, Soc of Asian Sci & Eng, Soc of Automotive Eng, Soc of Hispanic Prof Eng, Soc of Manufacturing Eng, Soc of Women Eng

Teams: BU Racing Formula SAE Team, BU Rocket Propulsion Team, Catapult Challenge, Chess Club, Cubing Club, COVID Solution Design Comp, Lutron Lighting Comp, New Venture Comp, Satellite Team, Task Machine Competition, Unmanned Aerial Vehicles Team

Notable Alumni
Doris Blake, David Ciardi, James Cockee, John Couris, Ruth Daly, Bogdan Dobrescu, Harold Dorschug, Michael Katze, Michael Leitman

HARVARD UNIVERSITY

Address: Harvard University, School of Engineering & Applied Sciences, 29 Oxford Street, Cambridge, MA 02138
Website: *https://www.seas.harvard.edu/*
Contact: *https://college.harvard.edu/contact-us*
Phone: (617) 496-9567
Email: dean@seas.harvard.edu

COST OF ATTENDANCE:

Tuition & Fees: $57,261 | **Addl Exp:** $24,739 | **Total:** $82,000

Financial Aid: https://college.harvard.edu/financial-aid

ADDITIONAL INFORMATION:

Available Degree(s)
- AB Mechanical Engineering
- MS, MS/MBA, Ph.D. Engineering Sci, Appl Mathematics, Appl Physics, Computational Science & Eng, Comp Sci, Data Sci

Related Research Areas
Applied Computational Science, Biofilm, Biomimetic Materials, Brain Science, Computational Science, Data Privacy, Data Science, Energy, Disease Reprogramming, Entrepreneurship, Environment, Ethics, Human Performance, Internet & Society, Microbial Science, Microdevices, Microrobots, Nanoscale Systems, Quantum Biology, Quantum Materials, Quantum Optics, Risk Analysis, Robotics, Science & Cooking, Solar Geoengineering

Scholarships Offered
Harvard does not award merit-based financial aid. However, Harvard does meet 100% of need-based aid. Harvard's average need-based scholarship is over $50,000. Students with family incomes less than $75,000 are not expected to pay. Most students with family incomes less than $150,000 pay less than $10,000.

Special Opportunities
State-of-the-art Allston facilities (Bioengineering, Computer Science, Data Science, Computational Science & Engineering programs) include a maker space, teaching labs, labs for experimentalists, and an Engineering Yard. Harvard has an Innovation Lab, Life Lab, & ArtLab.

Learning Incubator, Program for Researcha in Science & Engineering (PRISE), Research Experience for Undergrads (REU), Undergraduate Research & Fellowships, The Harvard Undergraduate Research Journal (THURJ), David Rockefeller International Experience Grants

Orgs: Aeronautics Club, Appl Math Society, Biomedical Engineering Society, Engineering Society, Engineers w/o Borders, Global Alliance for Medical Innovation, MakeHarvard, Society for Black Scientists & Engineers, Society of Hispanic Professional Engineers, Quantum Computing Association, Society of Women Engineers, Students for the Exploration & Development of Space, Video Game Development Club, Wireless Club, Women in Computer Science

Teams: Chem-E Car, Chess, College Bowl, Cyber Defense, Club, Hackathon, Hyperloop, Human-Powered Vehicle Team, iGEM Team, Mock Trial Team, Model Congress, Model United Nations, Robotics Club, Satellite Team, Science Olympiad, Solar Decathlon Team

Notable Alumni
Darius Adamczyk, Daniel Burke, Hardy Cross, Rollin King, James McNerney, Charles Moorman, Don Ross, Frank Shrontz, Neil deGrasse Tyson, Rick Wagoner, Arne Wilhelmsen, and Mark Zuckerberg (8 presidents, over 150 Nobel Prize winners)

CONNECTICUT
MAINE
MASSACHUSETTS
NEW HAMPSHIRE
NEW JERSEY
NEW YORK
PENNSYLVANIA
RHODE ISLAND
VERMONT

NORTHEAST

MASSACHUSETTS INSTITUTE OF TECHNOLOGY (MIT)

Address: MIT School of Engineering, Building 1-206, 77 Massachusetts Avenue, Cambridge, MA 02139-4307
Website: *https://engineering.mit.edu/*
Contact: *https://engineering.mit.edu/contact-us/*
Phone: (617) 253-3291
Email: engineering@mit.edu

COST OF ATTENDANCE:

Tuition & Fees: $58,416 | **Addl Exp:** $22,669 | **Total:** $81,085

Financial Aid: https://sfs.mit.edu/

ADDITIONAL INFORMATION:

Available Degree(s)
- SB, SM, ScD, and Ph.D. Mechanical Engineering
- ScD, Ph.D. Transportation Engineering

Related Research Centers
Artificial Intelligence Laboratory, Center for Global Change Science, Entrepreneurship, Internet Policy Research Initiative, Kavli Institute for Astrophysics & Space Research, Kuwait-MIT Center for Natural Resources & the Environment, Materials Research Laboratory, Microsystems Technology Labs, MIT Energy Initiative, MIT.nano, MIT Portugal Program, Technological Innovation, Transportation & Logistics, and World Wide Web Consortium

Scholarships Offered
MIT is need-blind and awards families with full-need. Approximately 60% of MIT students receive aid. "And for most students with family incomes under $140,000 a year (and typical assets), we ensure that scholarship funding will allow them to attend MIT tuition-free." The average MIT scholarship was $45,146.

Special Opportunities
Passionate students, rigorous education, remarkable professors, cutting-edge research, top reputation, successful graduates, and amazing facilities underscore the reasons to attend MIT. You will study, get stuck, create, collaborate, laugh, and make close bonds with a tight-knit friend group. Though nerdy, quirky, unconventional, and intense MIT offers limitless potential for success.

Teams: Arcturus - Autonomous Surface Vehicle (ASV) and Drone Group, Collegiate Inventors Competition, Collegiate Programming Contests, Combat Robotics, Concrete Canoe, Design-Build-Fly (AIAA Competition team), Design for America, Driverless/Autonomous Vehicle Building, Electric Vehicle, Engineers w/o Borders, Hyperloop III Team, MADMEC Team, Marine Robotics team, Motorsports Team, MIT Lincoln Lab Cubesat Team, NASA Competition Team, Robotics Team, Rocket Team, Satellite Team, Solar Electric Vehicle Team, Space Development, Spokes Cycling, QL+, Tech Model Railroad Club, Rubik's Cube Club, Science Bowl, Steel Bridge Team

Notable Alumni
Buzz Aldrin, Colin Angle, Kofi Annan, Satya N. Atluri, Shiva Ayyadurai, Ben Bernanke, Karel Bossart, Amar Bose, Vanu Bose, Jimmy Doolittle, Mario Draghi, Charles Stark Draper, Esther Duflo, Richard Feynman, Jose Figueres Ferre, Carly Fiorina, Jon Kabat-Zinn, Sal Khan, Bill Koch, Charles Koch, Francis Lynch, Thomas Massie, Ronald McNair, Benjamin Netanyahu, Ngozi Okonjo-Iweala, Neri Oxman, Henry Paynter, I.M. Pei, Nicholas A. Peppas, Jonah Peretti, Raghuram Rajan, Claude Shannon, William Shockley, George Shultz, Joseph Stiglitz, Lisa Su, Lawrence Summers, Tom Wolf, and James Woods

NORTHEASTERN UNIVERSITY

Address: College of Engineering, Northeastern University, 360 Huntington Ave., Snell Engineering Center, Boston, Massachusetts 02115
Website: https://coe.northeastern.edu/
Contact: https://coe.northeastern.edu/request-information/
Phone: (617) 373-6300
Email: dean@coe.northeastern.edu

COST OF ATTENDANCE:
Tuition & Fees: $59,572 | **Addl Exp:** $23,445 | **Total:** $83,017
Financial Aid: https://studentfinance.northeastern.edu/

ADDITIONAL INFORMATION:

Available Degree(s)
- BS, BS/MS, MS, Ph.D.: Mechanical Engineering, Industrial Eng, Computer Engineering, Comp Sci, Electrical Engineering
- Master's Programs: Applied Physics & Engineering, Operations Research, Advanced & Intelligent Manufacturing
- Ph.D. Programs: Cybersecurity, Network Science

Related Research Areas
Center for Microwave Magnetic Materials and Integrated Circuits, Center for Nano and Microcontamination Control, Center for Research Innovation, Contamination Threats, Electronic Materials Research, Experiential Robotics, High-rate Nanomanufacturing, NULab for Texts, Maps, and Networks, Renewable Energy Technology, Soft Target Engineering to Neutralize the Threat Reality, Versatile Onboard Traffic Embedded Roaming Sensors

Scholarships Offered
Northeastern meets 100% of need-based aid with 78% of first-year students receiving financial aid. More than $300,000,000 in aid is provided each year. NU awards merit scholarships, including the prestigious Dean's first-year scholarship of $10,000 to $28,000.

Special Opportunities
Undergraduate/graduate experiential co-ops, student research, service learning, and global learning

The Egan Engineering/Science Research Center is a state-of-the-art research facility housing more than a dozen engineering labs and the Interdisciplinary Science and Engineering Complex (ISEC).

Orgs: American Inst of Aeronautics & Astronautics, AerospaceNU, Alliance for Diversity in Science & Eng, Amer Institute of Chemical Engineers, Amer Society of Civil Eng, Amer Soc for Eng Mgmt, Amer Society of Mechanical Eng, Black Eng Student Society, Bioengineers GSC, Biomedical Eng Society, CEE GSC, ChemE GSC, Data Analytics, Engineering Student Organization, Enabling Engineering, Engineers w/o Borders, ESS, Generate, IEEE, Innovators for Global Health, IISE, INFORMS, IoT Connect, ISPE, Material Advantage, NEPSA, NEWEA, NGSEA, SHPE, SASE, NUAGE, NUITE, NUMC, NUMCAA, NUSBO, NUSound, NUToys, oSTEM, SAC, SEEDS, SEWERS, SFB, STEMout, Society of Women Engineers, ViTAL, Wireless Club

Teams: Baja SAE Team, Chem-E Car, Concrete Canoe, Geothermal Collegiate Competition, Hackathons, iGEM Team (Intl Genetically Eng Machine), International Robotics Competition - XPrize Avatar Challenge, Mars Society's University Rover Challenge, NU Electric Racing, NU Hacks, NU's Hyperloop Team in the SpaceX Hyperloop Pod Competition, Roxbury Robotics, Solar Decathlon, Steel Bridge

Notable Alumni
Hans Baumann, George Behrakis, Jeff Bornstein, Robert Brooks, Han Camenzind, Jeff Clark, Jeff Cooper, Bob Davis, Richard Egan, Shawn Fanning, Jerald Fishman, Richard Gabriel, Gregory Jarvis, Amin Khoury, Eugene Lally, Roger Marina, Alan McKim, Yale Patt, Jeffrey Rosen, Albert Sacco, and Biz Stone

CONNECTICUT
MAINE
MASSACHUSETTS
NEW HAMPSHIRE
NEW JERSEY
NEW YORK
PENNSYLVANIA
RHODE ISLAND
VERMONT

NORTHEAST

OLIN COLLEGE OF ENGINEERING

Address: Olin College of Engineering, 1000 Olin Way, Needham, MA 02492
Website: *https://www.olin.edu/*
Contact: *https://www.olin.edu/contact-us*
Phone: (781) 292-2300
Email: adva.waranyuwat@olin.edu

COST OF ATTENDANCE:

Tuition & Fees: $68,250 | **Addl Exp:** $14,235 | **Total:** $82,485

Financial Aid: https://www.olin.edu/admission

ADDITIONAL INFORMATION:

Available Degree(s)
- BS Bioengineering, Engineering Computing, Engineering Design, Engineering Robotics, Engineering Sustainability, Electrical Engineering, Mechanical Engineering

Related Research Areas
Aircraft & Spacecraft Mechanisms, Amazon Remote Manipulation Systems, Amazon Robotics, Apps to Help Blind Students, Asteroid Hunting, Blockchain, Brain-Machine Interfaces, Catalyzing the Transition to Electrical Vehicles, Climate Science, Energy-Efficient Desalination, Energy Harvesting, Environmental Epidemiology, Future of Water Infrastructure, Human Factors, Materials Informatics, Manufacturing, Medical Equipment Packaging, Microbial Community Dynamics, Miniature Marine Robots, Modeling & Simulation, National Transportation Center, Olin Robot Lab, Risk Control, Robotic Assisted Surgery, Robotics & Automation, Textiles, Scenario-Based Self-Defense Training, Self-Defense Armor for Full-Force Impact, Software and Data Analysis, Technology & the Return to Manufacturing in the U.S., Thermal Conductivity of Quilts, User Experience, Waste Water Reuse, Water Technologies

Scholarships Offered
Every accepted student as of 2023 receives $110,000+ (over 8 FT semesters) in merit-based aid covering half the annual tuition charges. This scholarship recognizes achievement in/out of the classroom. Grants + Scholarships in 2022 ranged from $27,806 yearly to $82,485. Need-based aid covers up to all expenses paid; 48% qualified for need-based aid.

Special Opportunities
Olin looks for bold, entrepreneurial risk-takers! The college's close-knit community works together in research, laboratory, and social spaces using seven buildings around "the oval". Dorms have living rooms, semi-private bathrooms, cable, Ethernet and fiber-optic capability. The student body buzzes with energy and activity. The Babson College campus is steps away where students can take classes in entrepreneurship. Approximately third of Olin's student create startup companies.

Job/internship fairs, employer/graduate school info sessions, campus interviews, career exploration workshops, SCOPE, a unique industry-university collaboration (Senior Capstone project).

Teams: Olin Aquatic Robotic Systems, Olin Baja Formula SAE, Olin Design-Build-Fly, Olin Electric Motor Sports, Olin PowerChords (Acappella Group), Olin Running Club, Olin Rocketry, Society of Women Engineers, The MIX (Multicultural Innovators eXperience)

Notable Alumni
Andy Barry, Etosha Cave, Kate Garrett, Ollie Haas, Frances Haugen, Brendan Quinlivan, and Kevin Tostado

---

CONNECTICUT

MAINE

MASSACHUSETTS

NEW HAMPSHIRE

NEW JERSEY

NEW YORK

PENNSYLVANIA

RHODE ISLAND

VERMONT

TUFTS UNIVERSITY

Address: Tufts University, Science and Engineering Complex, Anderson Hall, Room 105, 200 College Avenue, Medford, MA 02155
Website: *https://engineering.tufts.edu/*
Contact: *https://admissions.tufts.edu/connect-with-us/contact/*
Phone: (617) 627-3237
Email: engineering.inquiry@tufts.edu

COST OF ATTENDANCE:

Tuition & Fees: $65,222 | **Addl Exp:** $19,378 | **Total:** 84,600

Financial Aid: https://students.tufts.edu/financial-services/financial-aid

ADDITIONAL INFORMATION:

Available Degree(s)
- BS, MS, Ph.D. Mechanical Engineering
- BS, MS Human-Factors Engineering
- MS Human-Robot Interaction
- Joint Ph.D. Mechanical Engineering with Materials Science & Engineering, Mechanical Engineering with Human-Robot Interaction
- Certificates: Assistive Design, Human-Robot Interaction, Human Factors in Data Science, Human Factors in Medical Devices & Systems, Manufacturing Engineering

Related Research Areas
Advanced Materials Center, Applied Brain & Cognitive Sciences, Energy Water, & the Environment, Human Health & Bioengineering, Human-Technology Interface, Intelligent Systems, Neural Science, Disease, & Engineering, STEM Diversity

Scholarships Offered
Tufts meets 100% of demonstrated need regardless of citizenship status. Students with family incomes less than $60,000 typically receive a student aid package with no student loans. Tufts does not award merit-based financial aid.

Special Opportunities
Tufts University's Science & Engineering houses state-of-the-art Advanced Microscopic Imaging Center, Epitaxial Facility and Materials Characterization Lab, Micro Characterization Facility, and the Micro- and Nano-Fabrication Facility.

Orgs: American Society of Chemical Engineers, American Society of Civil Engineers, American Society for Engineering Education, American Society of Mechanical Engineers, BioMed Engineering Society, Biomedical Engineering and Chemical Engineering Society, Civil & Environmental Engineering Graduate Student Organization, Engineering Student Council, Engineers w/o Borders, Human Factors & Ergonomics Society, Institute for Electrical & Electronic Engineers, National Society of Black Engineers, Society of LatinX Engineers & Scientists, Society of Women Engineers, Computer Science Exchange, National Society of Black Engineers, oSTEM, Society of LatinX Engineers & Scientists, Society of Women Engineers, Student Teacher Outreach Mentorship Program, Women in Computer Science

Teams: Chem-E Car Team, Chess, Concrete Canoe Team, Debate Team, Electric Racing, Jumbo Code, Mock Trial, MUN, MAKE, Robotics. Solar Racing Team, Rubik's Cube, Steel Bridge Team

Notable Alumni
Saleem Ali, Anthony Cortese, Macy DuBois, Margaret Floyd, Rick Hauck, Robert Kayen, Frederick Nelson, and C. David Welch

CONNECTICUT
MAINE
MASSACHUSETTS
NEW HAMPSHIRE
NEW JERSEY
NEW YORK
PENNSYLVANIA
RHODE ISLAND
VERMONT

NORTHEAST

WORCESTER POLYTECHNICAL UNIVERSITY

Address: Worcester Polytechnic Institute, School of Engineering, 100 Institute Road, Worcester, MA 01609-2280
Website: https://www.wpi.edu/academics/engineering
Contact: https://www.wpi.edu/contact?url=https%3A//www.wpi.edu/academics/engineering
Phone: (508) 831-5000
Email: admissions@wpi.edu

COST OF ATTENDANCE:

Tuition & Fees: $57,096 | **Addl Exp:** $19,994 | **Total:** $77,040

Financial Aid: https://www.wpi.edu/admissions/tuition-aid

ADDITIONAL INFORMATION:

Available Degree(s)
- BS, MS, Ph.D. Aerospace Engineering, Architectural Eng, Biomedical Eng, Chemical Engineering, Civil Engineering, Computer Eng, Electrical Engineering, Environmental Eng, Industrial Eng, Mechanical Engineering, Robotics Engineering
- MS, Ph.D. Fire Protection Engineering, Manufacturing Engineering, Materials Process Engineering, Materials Science & Engineering, Systems Engineering

Related Research Areas
Center for Advanced Research in Drying, Center for Heat Treating Excellence, Center for Resources Recovery & Recycling, Center for Wireless Information Network Studies, Energy Research Group, Integrative Materials Design Center, Metal Processing Institute, Water Resource Center

Labs: Automation & Interventional Medicine Robotics Lab, Combustion Lab, Embedded Computing Lab, Holographic Studies & Laser Micro-MechaTronics Lab, Optomechanics Lab, NanoEnergy Lab, Navigation, Environment, Signal Processing & Information Networking Lab, Soft Robotics Lab, Surveillance, & Transportation Lab, Wireless Information Network Studies Lab

Scholarships Offered
All incoming first-year students receive a Global Scholarship for up to $5,000, to complete a project at one of WPI's 50+ project centers domestically and abroad. WPI offers FIRST & VEX robotics scholarships; graduate fellowships & assistantships. Engineering scholarships for top students typically range bet $10,000-$25,000 and are renewable for four years.

Special Opportunities
Internships & Co-ops; Career Development Center help you land an internship; Grand Challenges Scholars Program, Interdisciplinary Groups, Student Teams

Orgs: American Institute of Aeronautics & Astronautics, American Society for Biochem & Molecular Bio, Association for Computing Machinery, Biomedical Eng Society, Bionics Club, Biotech Club, ChemE Grad Org, CollabLab, Computer & Tech Club, Cyber Security Club, Data Sci Club, Galactic Senate: A Star Wars Club, Greenhouse & Horticulture Club, Inst of Elect & Electronic Eng, International Game Develpmt. Assoc, Intl Society of Pharmaceutical Eng, SciFi Society, Society of Automotive Engineers, Video Game Club, WPI Lego Club

Teams: Autonomous Underwater Vehicle, Concrete Canoe, Esports Club, Model Railroading Club, Motorsports Club, Robokids, Robotics Club, Rubik's Cube Club, Steel Bridge, Surveillance UAV/Drones

Notable Alumni
Harold Black, Karen Casella, Robert Goddard, Dan Itse, Yiqi Mei, Nancy Pimental, Kotaro Shimomura, James Smith, Robert Stempel, Gilbert Vernam, and Richard Whitcomb

---

CONNECTICUT

MAINE

MASSACHUSETTS

NEW HAMPSHIRE

NEW JERSEY

NEW YORK

PENNSYLVANIA

RHODE ISLAND

VERMONT

PRINCETON UNIVERSITY

Address: Princeton School of Engineering and Applied Science, Engineering Quadrangle, C207, Princeton, New Jersey 08544
Website: *https://engineering.princeton.edu/*
Contact: *https://engineering.princeton.edu/about*
Phone: (609) 258-4554
Email: bogucki@princeton.edu

COST OF ATTENDANCE:

Tuition & Fees: $57,410 | **Addl Exp:** $24,835 | **Total:** $82,245

Financial Aid: https://finaid.princeton.edu/

ADDITIONAL INFORMATION:

Available Degree(s)
- AB, Ph.D. Astrophysical Sciences, Chemical & Biological Engineering, Mechanical & Aerospace Engineering, Engineering & Applied Science
- Certificate: Robotics & Intelligent Systems

Related Research Areas
Applied Physics, Biomechanics & Biomaterials, Control, Robotics, and Dynamical Systems, Fluid Mechanics, Materials Science, Propulsion & Energy Sciences

Scholarships Offered
Princeton University admissions is need-blind with a no-loan policy that replaces student loans with grant aid that students do not pay back. Approximately 62% of undergraduates receive aid with an average grant of $62,200. Families whose income is less than $65,000 do not pay for tuition, room, or board.

Special Opportunities
Internships, Summer Programs, Co-ops, Study Abroad, Seminar Programs, Corporate Research Partnerships; Summer Undergraduate Research Fellows; NSF-Funded Summer REU Program in Biophysics; Machine Learning Theory Summer Program

Orgs: American Institute of Aeronautics & Astronautics, American Institute of Chemical Engineers, American Society of Civil Engineers, American Society of Mechanical Engineers, Association for Computing Machinery, Aviation Club Drone Project, Engineering Council, Engineers w/o Borders, Institute of Electrical and Electronics Engineers, Material Research Society, National Society of Black Engineers, Operations Research Society, Princeton Engineering Education for Kids, Society of Hispanic Professional Engineers, Women in Computer Science, Society of Women Engineers

Teams: Alexa Competition (selected for $100,000 stipend), Amazon Robotics Challenge, Autonomous Underwater Vehicle, Chem-E Car, Chess Team, Concrete Canoe, Cubesat, Electric Car Competition, HackPrinceton, iGEM Team (Intl Genetically Engineered Machines), International Math Modeling Competition, IRoM-Lab Robots, Micro-g Neutral Buoyancy Experimental Design Team, Mock Trial, Model Congress, Model United Nations, Princeton Electric Racing, Quiz Bowl, Robotics Competitions, Rocketry Team, Science Olympiad, TigerSats - Satellite Systems, Unmanned Aerial Vehicle Team

Notable Alumni
James Adamson, Norman Augustine, Ben Baldanza, Daniel Barry, Brian Binnie, Gerald Carr, Charles Coker, Richard Felder, William Ford, Jr., Brian Kernighan, Gregory Linteris, James McDonnell, Red Whittaker, and Ben Zinn

CONNECTICUT
MAINE
MASSACHUSETTS
NEW HAMPSHIRE
NEW JERSEY
NEW YORK
PENNSYLVANIA
RHODE ISLAND
VERMONT

NORTHEAST

CONNECTICUT

MAINE

MASSACHUSETTS

NEW HAMPSHIRE

NEW JERSEY

NEW YORK

PENNSYLVANIA

RHODE ISLAND

VERMONT

STEVENS INSTITUTE OF TECHNOLOGY

Address: Charles V. Schaefer, Jr. School of Engineering and Science, Edwin A. Stevens Hall (EAS), 24 5th Street, Hoboken, NJ 07030
Website: https://www.stevens.edu/schaefer-school-engineering-science
Contact: https://www.stevens.edu/schaefer-school-engineering-science/about/office-dean
Phone: (201) 216-8233
Email: kishore.pochiraju@stevens.edu

COST OF ATTENDANCE:

Tuition & Fees: $58,624 | **Addl Exp:** $20,330 | **Total:** $78,954

Financial Aid: https://www.stevens.edu/admissions/tuition-financial-aid

ADDITIONAL INFORMATION:

Available Degree(s)
- BS, MS, MEng, Ph.D. Biomedical Engineering, Chemical Engineering, Civil Engineering, Computer Engineering, Computer Science, Electrical Engineering, Environmental Engineering, Mechanical Engineering, Naval/Optical Eng
- MS/MEng Artificial Intelligence, Construction Engineering, Cybersecurity, Information Systems, Machine Learning, Quantum Engineering, Pharmaceutical Manufacturing/Eng, Robotics, Sustainability Management, Software Engineering, Space Systems Engineering, Technology Management
- MS, Ph.D. Data Science, Engineering Management, Materials Science & Engineering, Ocean Engineering, Systems Engg

Related Research Areas
Center for Complex Systems & Enterprises, Center for the Advancement of Secure Systems & Information Assurance, Center for Quantum Science & Engineering, Center for Environmental Systems, MicroDevice Lab, Center for Healthcare Innovation, Center for Innovation in Engineering & Science Education, Center for Neuromechanics, Highly Filled Materials Institute, Maritime Security Center, Center for Microchemical Systems, Institute for Artificial Intelligence, Systems Engineering Research Center

Scholarships Offered
Stevens Institute offers merit-based scholarships for academically talented freshmen who are NJ and non–NJ residents; NJ Dreamers can apply for need-based government aid; Tuition Aid Grant (TAG) offers additional need-based grants; veterans scholarships are also available. NJ Residents may also qualify for the Governor's Urban Scholarship, NJ World Trade Center Scholarship, Law Enforcement Officer Memorial Scholarship

Special Opportunities
Internships, Externships, Co-ops, Study abroad program, Pre-College Program, STEP Program. Facilities include the Mass Spectrometry Laboratory and the High-Performance Computing Cluster.

Orgs: Engineers w/o Borders, Stevens Environmental Engineering Professional Society, Safe Autonomous Systems Lab hack protection, emergency landing equipment, AI camera systems, prevention of malicious cyberattacks, and situational intelligence.

Teams: 1st Place winners in ASCE Ultra-High Performance Concrete Team (2019), Formula SAE Racing Team, Underwater Robot Submarine mapping in dangerous marine environments

Notable Alumni
Igor Bensen, David Farber, Gerard Joseph Foschini, Greg Gianforte, Gerald Goertzel, Peter Cooper Hewitt, Beatrice Hicks, Sandeep Mathrani, Chadwell O'Connor, Richard H. Rice, and Zehev Tadmor

COLUMBIA UNIVERSITY

Address: Columbia, Fu Foundation School of Engineering & Applied Science, 500 W 120th St., Mudd 510, New York, NY 10027
Website: *https://www.engineering.columbia.edu/*
Contact: *https://www.engineering.columbia.edu/contact*
Phone: (212) 854-2993
Email: sfchang@ee.columbia.edu

COST OF ATTENDANCE:

Tuition & Fees: $66,139 | **Addl Exp:** $19,928 | **Total:** $85,967

Financial Aid: https://www.sfs.columbia.edu/fin-aid

ADDITIONAL INFORMATION:

Available Degree(s)
- Fu Foundation SEAS: BS, MS, Ph.D. Civil & Mechanical Engineering, Applied Physics & Applied Mathematics, Electrical Engineering, Engineering Management Systems, Engineering Mechanics, Material Science & Engineering
- BA Applied Physics, Chemical Physics, Sustainable Development
- MA Climate & Society, 3-2 BA/MS Engineering, MA Biotechnology, MS Sustainability Management

Related Research Areas
Artificial Intelligence, Cybersecurity, Data, Media, & Society, Data Science, Optimization Res, Sense, Collect, & Move Data, Smart Cities

Scholarships Offered
Most students from families whose annual income is less than $150,000 attend Columbia tuition-free. Columbia awards more than $177 million annually in scholarships and grants from all sources; 50% of Columbia students receive grants; the average amount awarded is $62,850; Incoming first-year students from low-income families receive a start-up grant of $2,000 to ease their transition to college. Students are expected to borrow $0 to attend Columbia.

Special Opportunities
Internships, Summer Programs, Co-ops, Study Abroad, Seminar Programs, State-of-the-Art Facilities, Corporate Partnerships

The cornerstone of Columbia's Fu Foundation is a strong engineering background with a liberal arts core. Columbia's intellectual mission is to provide wide-ranging knowledge in ideas & achievements in music, art, literature, philosophy, history, & science. Students choose from 17 areas enriched by 20 liberal arts minors and 15+ engineering minors.

Orgs: American Chemical Society, American Institute of Aeronautics & Astronautics, American Institute of Chemical Engineers, American Medical Students Assoc, American Physician Scientists Association, American Society of Civil Engineers, American Society of Mechanical Engineers, Biomedical Engineering Soc, Bioethics Society, Columbia Space Initiative, National Society of Black Engineers, Neuroscience Society, Pre-Medical Society, Society of Hispanic Professional Engineers, Society of Women Engineers, Women in Computer Science

Teams: Chess, Columbia Space Initiative, CubeSat, Debate Team, Formula SAE Team, Hackathon for Humanity, MAP Project48 – Data Science Competition, Mock Trial, Model Congress, Model United Nations, Quiz Bowl, Robotics Club, Space Team, Steel Bridge Team

Notable Alumni
Kenneth Bowersox, Shu Chien, Kevin Chilton, Amelia Earhart, Joseph Engelberger, James Fletcher, Ferdinand Freudenstein, William Gregory, Herman Hollerith, Gregory Johnson, Rudolf Kálmán, Kai-Fu Lee, John Marchetti, Michael Massimino, Story Musgrave, Rebecca Oppenheimer, Stephen Schneider, Eugene Trinh, John Trump, Neil DeGrasse Tyson, and Victor Wouk

CONNECTICUT
MAINE
MASSACHUSETTS
NEW HAMPSHIRE
NEW JERSEY
NEW YORK
PENNSYLVANIA
RHODE ISLAND
VERMONT

NORTHEAST

COOPER UNION

Address: Cooper Union School of Engineering, 41 Copper Sq., New York, NY 10003
Website: https://cooper.edu/engineering
Contact: https://cooper.edu/about/contact
Phone: (212) 353-4285
Email: engineering@cooper.edu

COST OF ATTENDANCE

Tuition & Fees: $48,007 | **Addl Exp:** $15,500 | **Total:** $63,507

Financial Aid: https://cooper.edu/students/financial-aid

ADDITIONAL INFORMATION:

Available Degree(s)
- Bachelor of Engineering in Mechanical Engineering
- Master of Engineering in Mechanical Engineering
- BS General Engineering

Related Research Areas
Materials & Fluids Research, Autonomy, Control, Cyber-Physical Systems Research, Machine Learning, Data Science & Artificial Intelligence, Sustainability, Theoretical & Computational Sciences, Signal Processing & Communications

Scholarships Offered
Benjamin Menschel Fellowship Program to Support Creative Inquiry, The Cooper Union Internal Grant Program, The IDC Foundation Innovation Fellowship (engineering – full scholarship plus $1,000 stipend), Travel Fellowships, AACE Lab Grant

Cooper Union offers generous financial aid/scholarship support to all admitted undergraduate, full-time students—awarding students a half-tuition scholarship valued at $22,275. Students may also receive additional merit awards & financial aid based on eligibility.

Special Opportunities
Summer Writing Program, Summer STEM Program, STEM Outreach, Summer Art Intensive, STEM Saturdays, Introduction to Architecture Intensive

The AACE Lab Grant Program allows students to apply for funding to further explore digital fabrication, and increase engagement with the AACE Lab, including free materials to experiment. If accepted, Cooper Union will purchase material for you.

The Vertically Integrated Projects (VIP) Program provides interdisciplinary research opportunities.

Orgs: Association for Computing Machinery, American Institute of Chemical Engineers, American Society of Civil Engineers, American Society of Mechanical Engineers, AEEE, Biomedical Engineering Soc, Engineers w/o Borders, Inst of Electrical & Electronic Engineers, Nat Soc of Black Eng, Soc of Hispanic Prof Eng, Soc of Women Engineers

Teams: Chem-E Car, Create@Cooper, Cooperloop (Compete in the SpaceX Hyperloop Competition), Cooper Motorsports (Compete at the Michigan International Speedway), Cooper Cube Team, Formula SAE, iGEM (Genetically Engineered Machines) Steel Bridge Team

Notable Alumni
Stan Allen, Shigeru Ban, Karen Bausman, John Walters Christie, Joshua Lionel Cowen, Freda Diamond, Thomas Edison, Joel H. Ferziger, Chuck Hoberman, Bruce Pasternack, William Gardner Pfann, Charles Rosen, Richard Schwartz, Sy Schulman, Samuel R. Scottron, Edwin King Stodola, Eric E. Sumner, Nina Tandon, Louis Waldman, Edward J. Wasp, and Jackie Yi-Ru Ying

---

CONNECTICUT

MAINE

MASSACHUSETTS

NEW HAMPSHIRE

NEW JERSEY

NEW YORK

PENNSYLVANIA

RHODE ISLAND

VERMONT

CORNELL UNIVERSITY

Address: Cornell Engineering, Carpenter Hall, 313 Campus Rd., Ithaca, New York 14853
Website: *https://www.engineering.cornell.edu/*
Contact: *https://www.engineering.cornell.edu/contact-us*
Phone: (607) 255-4326
Email: engr_generalinfo@cornell.edu

COST OF ATTENDANCE:

Tuition & Fees: $63,200 | **Addl Exp:** $20,096 | **Total:** $85,967
Financial Aid: https://finaid.cornell.edu/

ADDITIONAL INFORMATION:

Available Degree(s)
- BS, MEng, Ph.D. Mechanical Engineering, Aerospace Engineering, Chemical Engineering, Materials Science
- Minors: Aerospace Engineering, Business for Engineering Students, Computer Science, Earth & Atmospheric Science, Entrepreneurship & Innovation, Eng Comm, Game Design

Related Research Areas
Aerodynamics & Aeroacoustics, Bioenergy, Biomaterials, Biomass Combustion, Combustion Dynamics of Biofuels, Computational Fluid Mech, Geotextiles, Immunotherapy & Cell Eng, Microfluidic Device Design, Mechanics of Biological Materials, Nano- & Micro-Scale Engineering, Robotics & Computer Controlled Machinery, Satellite Systems, Self-Assembling Chemical Reactors, Solar & Renewable Energy, Thermofluids, Turbulence, Turbine Management, Environmental Eng, Game Design, Industrial Sys & Information Technology, Information Science, Materials Science & Engineering, Mechanical Eng, Operations Research & Management Science, Robotics, Smart Cities, Sustainable Energy Systems

Scholarships Offered
Most students with family annual incomes less than $150,000 attend Cornell tuition-free. Cornell awards more than $177 million scholarships/grants; 50% of Cornell students receive grants; average amount awarded is $62,850; Incoming 1st-year students from low-income families receive a start-up grant of $2,000 to ease transition. Students expected to borrow $0.

Special Opportunities
Internships, Summer Programs, Co-ops, Study Abroad, Seminar Programs, State-of-the-Art Facilities, Corporate Partnerships

Orgs: Eng for a Sustainable World, Eng in Action, Eng w/o Borders

Teams: AutoBoat Team, Autonomous Underwater Vehicle Team, Baja SAE Racing Team, ChemE Car, Chess Team, Combat Robotics @Cornell, Competitive Programming Team, Concrete Canoe Team, Cornell AppDev, Cornell Autonomous Bicycle, Cornell Cup Robotics, Cornell FSAE Racing, Cornell Mars Rover, Custom Silicon Systems (C2S2) team, Data Science Team, Design Build Fly, Design & Tech Initiative Team, Electric Vehicle Team, iGEM Genetically Engineered Machine Research Team, GeoData Team, Hack4Impact, Hyperloop Team, Rocketry Team, SailBot International Robotic Sailboat Regatta, Unmanned Air Systems Team, World Health (EWH) Project Team, Seismic Design Team, Steel Bridge Team, Solar Boat Team

Notable Alumni
Eric Betzig, Joseph Boardman, Samuel Bodman, Heather Cho, Joseph Coors, Kenneth Derr, Tom Dinwoodie, Pawan Goenka, Leroy Grumman, Jeff Hawkins, F. Kenneth Iverson, Irwin Jacobs, Robert Kennedy, Robert Langer, Douglas Leone, Kenneth Nichols, Spencer Olin, Thomas Reed, Clarence Spicer, John Swanson, Tien Tzuo, Jay Walker, and David Welch

CONNECTICUT
MAINE
MASSACHUSETTS
NEW HAMPSHIRE
NEW JERSEY
NEW YORK
PENNSYLVANIA
RHODE ISLAND
VERMONT

NORTHEAST

RENSSELAER POLYTECHNIC INSTITUTE

Address: School of Engineering, Rensselaer Polytechnic Institute, 110 8th Street Troy, NY 12180 USA
Website: https://eng.rpi.edu/
Contact: https://eng.rpi.edu/contact
Phone: (518) 279-6298
Email: gardes@rpi.edu

COST OF ATTENDANCE:

Tuition & Fees: $60,074 | **Addl Exp:** $20,360 | **Total:** $80,434

Financial Aid: https://admissions.rpi.edu/aid

ADDITIONAL INFORMATION:

Available Degree(s)
- BS, MS, MEng, DEng, Ph.D. Aeronautical Eng, Biomedical Eng, Chemical Eng, Civil Eng, Computer & Systems Eng, Comp Sci, EE, Environmental Eng, Industrial and Management Eng, Materials Engineering, Mechanical Engineering, Nuclear Eng
- MS, MEng, DEng, Ph.D. Transportation Engineering
- ME Systems Engineering & Technology Management
- Ph.D. Decision Sciences & Engineering Systems, Nuclear Engineering & Science

Related Research Areas
More than 30 research centers, including The Design Lab, Center for Earthquake Engineering Simulation, the Network Science & Technology Center (NeST), & Gaerttner Linear Accelerator Center

Focus Areas: Climate Change, Disease Mitigation, Energy, Water, & Food, Infrastructure, National/Global Security, Resilience, Sustainability

Scholarships Offered
Multiple scholarships available (amounts vary): Rensselaer Grant, Rensselaer Leadership Award (outstanding academic/personal achievements), Rensselaer Medal Scholarship; $7,500 nuclear engineering awards

Special Opportunities
Grand Challenges Program, K-12 Outreach, Engineering Ambassadors, Study Abroad, Co-ops, Internships available. Summer and school year internships available

Orgs: American Helicopter Society, American Institute of Aeronautics & Astronautics, American Institute of Chemical Engineers, American Nuclear Society, American Society of Civil Engineers, American Society of Heating, Refrigeration, & Air Conditioning Engineers, American Society of Mechanical Engineers, Biomedical Engineering Society, Institute of Electrical & Electronics Engineers, Rensselaer Aeronautical Federation, Society of Automotive Engineers

Teams: ChemE Car Team, Chess Club, Design-Build-Fly Team, RPI Formula Hybrid Team, Rensselaer Electric Vehicle Team, Formula SAE Team, iGEM (Intl Genetically Engineered Machines), Model Railroad Society, OSCaR ("Obsolete Spacecraft Capture and Removal"), the semi-autonomous craft, Quiz Bowl, RPI Rock Raiders, RPISEC "Capture the Flag" Competition Team, Solar Car Racing Team (entered in the North American Solar Challenge and Cross-Australia World Solar Challenge)

Notable Alumni
Marshall Brain, Leffert Buck, Nicholas Donofrio, Allen DuMont, George Ferris Jr., Joseph Gerber, Lois Graham, William Gurley, Ted Hoff, J. Erik Jonsson, Theodore Judah, Keith Millis, David Noble, Sheldon Roberts, Washington Roebling, Steven Sasson, Robert Scaringe, John Schenck, Bert Sutherland, Massood Tabib-Azar, Raymond Tomlinson, John Waddell, and Robert Widmer

---

CONNECTICUT

MAINE

MASSACHUSETTS

NEW HAMPSHIRE

NEW JERSEY

NEW YORK

PENNSYLVANIA

RHODE ISLAND

VERMONT

SYRACUSE UNIVERSITY

Address: Syracuse University, College of Engineering & Computer Science, 223 Link Hall, Syracuse, NY 13244
Website: *https://www.syracuse.edu/academics/career-pathways/engineering/*
Contact: *https://www.syracuse.edu/admissions/request-information/*
Phone: (315) 443-2545
Email: orange@syr.edu

COST OF ATTENDANCE:
Tuition & Fees: $58,440 | **Addl Exp:** $22,574 | **Total:** $81,014
Financial Aid: https://www.syracuse.edu/admissions/cost-and-aid/

ADDITIONAL INFORMATION:

Available Degree(s)
- BS, BS/MS, MS, Ph.D. Aerospace Engineering, Biomedical Engineering, Chemical Engineering, Computer Engineering, Computer Science, Electrical Eng, Mechanical Engineering
- MS Cybersecurity
- Minors: Computer Engineering, Computer Science, Computer Science Management, Electrical Engineering, Energy Systems, Civil Engineering, Infrastructure, Cities, & the Future

Related Research Areas
BioInspired Institute, Building Energy & Environmental Systems Lab, Cognitive Wireless Systems & Networks, Center for Advanced Systems & Engineering, Center for Environmental Systems Eng, Center for Info & Systems Assurance & Trust, Center for Sustainable Eng, Composite Materials Lab, Cyber Engineering & Security, Energy Sources, Conversion, Conservation, Envir. Finance Center, Geofoam Research Ctr, Green Data Ctr, Industrial Assessment Center, Institute for Manufacturing Enterprises, Rehabilitative & Regenerative Eng, Smart Materials in Healthcare, SU Center of Excellence in Environmental Energy Systems, SU Infrastructure Institute

Scholarships Offered
SU offers 83% of the students financial support; numerous scholarships

Special Opportunities
SU has 13 schools/coll; 200 customizable majors; 100 minors; online degrees; 300 student orgs; comm engagement. Partnerships; law school on campus; SUNY Upstate med school next to campus; SUNY Forestry within steps of SU; domed stadium on the quad

SU has educational centers in Florence, London, Madrid, Santiago, and Strasbourg; Summer Research Program in Strasbourg

Orgs: American Institute of Aeronautics & Astronautics, American Institute of Chemical Engineers, American Society of Civil Engineers, Biomedical Engineering Society, Ambassadors, Engineering World Health, Institute of Electrical & Electronic Engineers, National Society of Black Engineers, oSTEM, Society of Asian Scientists & Engineers, Society of Hispanic Professional Engineers, Society of Women Eng

Teams: Citrus Racing, CuseHacks, Formula SAE, Hackathons, Orange Robotics Team, Unmanned Aerial Systems Club

Notable Alumni
Joseph Ahearn, Ishfaq Ahmad, John Archbold, Albert Baez, Ben Baldanza, Andrew Carnegie, Eileen Collins, Dennis Crowley, Tesfaye Dinka, Nick Donofrio, Nina Fedoroff, Joan Feynman, Edith Flanigen, George Fox, Robert Jarvik, Sean O'Keefe, Giles Martin, Lowell Paxson, Pierre Ramond, Kirthiga Reddy, MarkReed, Else Reichmanis, Charles Rosen, Rainer Sachs, Sultan bin Salman, James Tour, Vishal Sikka, Lyman Smith, and Thomas Watson

CONNECTICUT
MAINE
MASSACHUSETTS
NEW HAMPSHIRE
NEW JERSEY
NEW YORK
PENNSYLVANIA
RHODE ISLAND
VERMONT

NORTHEAST

UNIVERSITY OF ROCHESTER

Address: University of Rochester, Office of Admissions, P.O. Box 270251, Rochester, NY 14627-0251
Website: https://www.hajim.rochester.edu/
Contact: https://www.hajim.rochester.edu/contact.html
Phone: (585) 275-3221
Email: wendi.heinzelman@rochester.edu

COST OF ATTENDANCE:

Tuition & Fees: $61,678 | **Addl Exp:** $20,790 | **Total:** $82,468

Financial Aid: https://www.rochester.edu/financial-aid/

ADDITIONAL INFORMATION:

Available Degree(s)
- BS, MS, Ph.D. Biomedical Engineering, Chemical Engineering, Biology, Chemistry, Computer Science, Mechanical Engineering, Optical Engineering, Audio & Music Engineering
- BA Computer Science, BS Electrical & Computer Engineering,

Related Research Areas
Center for Matter at Atomic Pressures, Institute for Matter at Extreme Energy Density, Institute of Optics, Integrated Nanosystems Center, Laboratory for Laser Energetics

Scholarships Offered
Arts, Sciences, & Engineering offers merit-based scholarships ($2,000 – full tuition), including First Robotics Scholarship, Prince Street Scholarship, Simon Scholars Case Award, Steve Harrison Scholarship, and Whipple Sciences & Research Scholarship. International students may receive scholarships from $2,000 to full tuition per year regardless of nationality. Study abroad scholarships include project-based, business-focused, and major-specific scholarships. UR undergraduates can earn the $5,000 Drucker Scholarship to study in Japan, Gilman International Scholarship, and Boren critical language acquisition scholarship.

Special Opportunities
Internships, Fellowships, Research, Study Abroad, The Grand Challenges, Senior Scholars Program, Photon Camp for prospective HS students, Engineers for a Sustainable World

Orgs: American Institute of Chemical Engineers, American Society of Mechanical Engineers, Astronomy Club, Audio Engineering Society, Aviation in Rochester, Biomedical Engineering Society, Girls Who Code, Google Development Club, Institute of Electrical & Electronics Engineers, Makers, National Society of Black Engineers, Neuroscience Undergrad Council, Optical Society of America, Red Cross, Society of Earth & Environmental Science Students, Society of Hispanic Professional Engineering, Society of Physics Students, Society of Women Engineering, Society of Women in Astronomy & Physics, STEM Initiative, Undergraduate Chemistry Society, Undergrad Data Science Council, Women & Minorities in Computing

Teams: Baja SAE Team, Esports, Mock Trial, Model United Nations, Navigation Challenge, Quiz Bowl, Robotics Team, UR Lunabotics (automated mining robot for lunar landscapes) at NASA's Kennedy Space Center, Solar Drone Project, UAV Autonomous Team, UR Biomedical Data Science Hackathon, Up-Stat Data Competition, UR Next Gen Challenge

Notable Alumni
Stephen Burns, Josh Cassada, Esther Conwell, Julian Earls, Edward Gibson, Amit Goyal, William Harkness, William May, Paul Murdin, James Pawelczyk, Stephen Roessner, and Avie Tevanian

---

CONNECTICUT

MAINE

MASSACHUSETTS

NEW HAMPSHIRE

NEW JERSEY

NEW YORK

PENNSYLVANIA

RHODE ISLAND

VERMONT

BUCKNELL UNIVERSITY

Address: Bucknell University, College of Engineering, One Dent Drive, 235 Dana Engineering Building, Lewisburg, PA 17837
Website: https://www.bucknell.edu/academics/college-engineering
Contact: https://www.bucknell.edu/azdirectory?t=faculty_staff&s=All
Phone: (570) 577-2000
Email: engineering@bucknell.edu

COST OF ATTENDANCE:

Tuition & Fees: $61,408 | **Addl Expenses:** $18,822 | **Total:** $80,230
Financial Aid: https://www.bucknell.edu/admissions-aid/tuition-fees-financial-aid

ADDITIONAL INFORMATION:

Available Degree(s)
- BS Biomedical Engineering, Computer Engineering, Computer Science
- BS, BS/MS, MS Chemical Engineering, Civil Engineering, Electrical Engineering, Environmental Engineering, Mechanical Engineering

Related Research Areas
Atm Chemistry, Biological Engineering, Biomaterials, Biotechnology, Chemical Process Eng, Chemical Transport, Computer & Data Science, Environ Eng, Hazardous Waste Management, Intelligent Systems, Machine Learning, Materials Engineering, Pharmaceutical Process Engineering, Polymer Science, Predictive Analytics, Product & Process Chemistry, Center for Sustainability & the Environment

Scholarships Offered
Merit scholarships require the submission of Bucknell's scholarship application; the deadline is the same as the application deadline. Merit scholarships, renewable for eight fall/spring semesters, are awarded at the time of admission and are only available for incoming first-year students. Most funding is awarded to students who demonstrate institutional need, but a few are awarded to those without financial need or do not complete the FAFSA. Scholarships include: Arts Merit Scholarship, Bucknell Women in Science & Engineering, Charles T. Bauer Scholarship, Community Engagement Scholarship, Mathematics Scholarship, Presidential Fellows Scholarship, PricewaterhouseCoopers Scholarship

Special Opportunities
Corporate Relations & Industry Collaborations, Study Abroad, Davis United World Coll Scholars Prog, Grand Challenges Scholars Prog; 7th Street Studio & MakerSpace & tech-equipped playgrounds for investigative/innovative minds, outfitted with vinyl/laser cutters, design software, 3D printers, computer-controlled mills; welding, soldering, woodworking tools, and printed circuit board equipment.

Bucknell's Small Business Devt Center hires eng majors as product development consultants to work on engineering design, analysis, & prototype development w/startups & companies seeking to expand.

The 5-week, on-campus summer Engineering EXCELerator program allows students to attend an Engineering Camp, develop skills in prototyping/fabrication, and get ahead in calculus & physics.

Bucknell's facilities, include a research green roof, structural testing lab, and sustainability monitoring center. Bucknell Engineering is teaming with Amazon Robotics on projects and internships.

Notable Alumni
Steven DeKosky, Dennis Dougherty, Marc Hauser, Marc Lore, Marty Makary, Takeo Shiina, Greg Skibiski, Amos Smith, Trisha Torrey, Bill Westenhofer, and David Wood

CONNECTICUT

MAINE

MASSACHUSETTS

NEW HAMPSHIRE

NEW JERSEY

NEW YORK

PENNSYLVANIA

RHODE ISLAND

VERMONT

NORTHEAST

CARNEGIE MELLON UNIVERSITY

Address: 5000 Forbes Avenue, Pittsburgh, PA 15213
Website: https://engineering.cmu.edu/
Contact: https://admission.enrollment.cmu.edu/pages/contact-us
Phone: (412) 268-2354
Email: admission@andrew.cmu.edu

COST OF ATTENDANCE:

Tuition & Fees: $60,634 | **Addl Exp:** $19,906 | **Total:** $80,540

Financial Aid: https://www.cmu.edu/admission/aid-affordability

ADDITIONAL INFORMATION:

Available Degree(s)
- BS, MS, and Ph.D. Mechanical Engineering
- BS, MS, and Ph.D. Civil Engineering
- BS/MS and MS/MBA Integrated Degrees

Related Research Centers
Electricity Industry, Air, Climate, and Energy Solutions, Climate and Energy Decision Making, Complex Fluids Engineering, Engineering and Resilience for Climate Adaptation, Iron and Steelmaking Research, Mechanics and Engineering of Cellular Systems, Computing On Network Infrastructure for Pervasive Perception, CyLab Security and Privacy, Data Storage Systems Center, Green Design, Manufacturing Futures, Mobility21, National USDOT University Transportation Center for Mobility of People and Goods, NextManufacturing, Smart Infrastructure, and Energy Innovation

Scholarships Offered
CMU offers need-based grant and endowed scholarships. Undergrad, graduate, and alumni awards are available as well. Current students can win design, sustainability, research, and engagement scholarships ($75,000 additional awarded each year).

Special Opportunities
The College of Engineering offers research projects, 1st-class facilities.

Orgs: Amer Society of Civil Engineers, American Society of Mechanical Engineers, American Institute of Chemical Engineers, Biomedical Engineering Society, Engineers w/o Borders, Engineering Student Council, Green Design Inst, Inst of Electrical & Electronics Eng, Materials Advantage, National Society of Black Eng, oSTEM, National Robotics Engineering Ctr, Society of Automotive Engineers, Soc of Asian Sci & Eng, Society of Hisp Prof Eng, Society of Women Engineers, WinECE

Teams: Abu Dhabi Robotics Challenge, Autonomous Aerial Vehicle Team, Autonomous Underwater Vehicle Team, Build 18, Chem-E Car Team, Chess, College Bowl, Cubesat Team, Debate Team, Formula SAE Electric Car Team, Mock Trial, Model United Nations, Quiz Bowl, Rocket Command (NASA Student Launch Competition, Solar Racing Team, CMU Hacking Team Wins DEF CON "Superbowl of Hacking" for 6th Time in 2022; $2 million Defense Adv Research Projects Agency (DARPA) Subterranean Challenge (multi-year robotics competition)

Notable Alumni
Alex Acero, Raymond Betler, Gloria Chen, Giorgio Coraluppi, Anirudh Devgan, Anthony DiGioia III, Scott Griffith, Anand Iyer, Raj Kapoor, David Kelley, Vinod Khosla, William Lee, William Leone, Candace Matthews, George Mueller, Gerald Meyers, Drew Perkins, Ana Pinczuk, James Rogers, Matt Rogers, Jonathan Rothberg, Jane Rudolph, Mark Russinovich, Barb Samardzich, Ivan Sutherland, Daniel Swanson, Carol Williams, Charles Wilson, and Amit Zavery

---

CONNECTICUT

MAINE

MASSACHUSETTS

NEW HAMPSHIRE

NEW JERSEY

NEW YORK

PENNSYLVANIA

RHODE ISLAND

VERMONT

DREXEL UNIVERSITY

Address: Drexel University, 3141 Chestnut Street, Philadelphia, PA 19104
Website: https://drexel.edu/engineering/
Contact: https://drexel.edu/engineering/contact-directories
Phone: (215) 895-2210
Email: engineering@drexel.edu

COST OF ATTENDANCE

Tuition & Fees: $38,390 | **Addl Exp:** $16,186 | **Total:** $51,151

Financial Aid: https://drexel.edu/drexelcentral/finaid/overview/

ADDITIONAL INFORMATION:

Available Degree(s)
- BS, MS, Ph.D. Mechanical Engineering & Mechanics
- MS Robotics & Autonomy
- Minors in Engineering Leadership, Engineering Policy Analysis, Global Engineering, Green Energy & Sustainability, Robotics & Automation
- Certificate NAE Grand Challenge Scholars Program, Peace Engineering, Reliability Engineering, Systems Engineering, Sustainability & Green Construction

Related Research Areas
A.J. Drexel Nanotechnology Institute, C & J Nyheim Plasma Institute, Center for Electric Power Engineering, Expressive and Creative Interaction Technologies, Materials Center of Excellence, CAD Lab, Design & Manufacturing Lab, Machine Shop, Mesoscale Materials Lab, Multiscale Computational Mechanics and Biomechanics LAB, Theoretical and Applied Mechanics Group

Scholarships Offered
100% of new students were given scholarships at Drexel University, averaging $28,332 per person

Special Opportunities
Students alternate classes with full-time employment through University-approved employers. Eight different tools are available for internship jobs. Fellowships and volunteer opportunities are also available.

Orgs: American Institute of Aeronautics & Astronautics, American Institute of Chemical Engineers, American Society for Engineering Education, American Society of Civil Engineers, American Society of Mechanical Engineers, American Society of Heating, Refrigeration, and Air-Conditioning Engineers, Biomedical Engineering Society, Construction Management Association, Engineers w/o Borders, Icarus Insterstellar, Institute of Electrical & Electronics Engineers, Material Advantage, National Society of Black Engineers, Smart House, Society of Asian Scientists & Engineers, Society of Hispanic Professional Engineers, Society of Manufacturing Engineers, Society of Women Engineers, TechServ

Teams: Aero SAE, Chess, Concrete Canoe Team, CyberDragons, Debate Union, Esports, Formula SAE Electric Race Car Team, Hackathons, Mock Trial, Model United Nations, Philly Codefest, Robotics Team, Solar Car Team, Steel Bridge Team

Notable Alumni
Sirous Asgari, Paul Baran, Michael Baum, Michael Behe, Lin Bin, Douglas Briggs, Kenneth Dahlberg, Ranjan Dash, Bruce Eisenstein, Lex Fridman, Eli Fromm, David Geiger, Lex Fridman, Walter Golaski, John Gruber, Jon Hall, Vasant Honavar, Moshe Kam, Cynthia Maryanoff, Jiang Mianheng, James Nell, Paul Richards, Alia Sabur, Bernard Silver, and Norman Woodland.

CONNECTICUT

MAINE

MASSACHUSETTS

NEW HAMPSHIRE

NEW JERSEY

NEW YORK

PENNSYLVANIA

RHODE ISLAND

VERMONT

NORTHEAST

LAFAYETTE COLLEGE

Address: 730 High St, 308 Acopian Engineering Center, Easton, PA 18042
Website: *https://engineering.lafayette.edu/*
Contact: *https://www.lafayette.edu/contact-lafayette/*
Phone: (610) 330-5403
Email: engineering@lafayette.edu

COST OF ATTENDANCE:

Tuition & Fees: $59,368 | **Addl Exp:** $20,236 | **Total:** $79,604

Financial Aid: https://admissions.lafayette.edu/financial-aid/

ADDITIONAL INFORMATION:

Available Degree(s)
- BS Bioengineering, Chemical Engineering, Civil Engineering, Computer Engineering, Electrical Engineering, Engineering International Studies Dual Degree, Engineering Studies, Environmental and Energy Engineering, Mechanical Engineering, Robotics Engineering

Related Research Areas
Atmospheric Aerosols, Biofuels, Biosynthesis, Cold-Flow Properties of Biofuels, Extraction/Conversion of Materials, Minimization of Waste Products, Molecular Engineering, Offshore petroleum extraction, Sustainable Biodiesel Production

Scholarships Offered
Scholarships support tuition, travel, & special projects. NSF Grad Research Fellowship Program. Merit Scholarships (need/non-need awards) - Full tuition Marquis Fellowship, Half-Tuition Marquis Scholarship & Lafayette Scholarship ($5,000 - $30,000) are available. Candidates seeking financial aid whose demonstrated need exceeds the amount of a Marquis or Lafayette Award will receive additional need-based aid up to their level of demonstrated need.

Special Opportunities
Internships & Co-ops, Study Abroad, Scholars Programs, Grand Challenges, Summer programs & funding. Juniors in Engineering Studies are encouraged to undertake internships with local businesses or public sector agencies. Students spend one day a week throughout the semester at the internships, for which they receive academic credit. The internships are arranged and supervised by faculty in the Engineering Studies program.

Orgs: American Society of Civil Engineers, American Society of Mechanical Engineers, American Institute of Chemical Engineers, Association for Computing Machinery Dyer Center for Innovation & Entrepreneurship, Engineering Student Council, Engineers w/o Borders, Institute of Electrical & Electronics Engineers, National Society of Black Engineers, Neuroscience Club, Society of Environmental Engineers & Scientists, Society of Hispanic Professional Engineers, Society of Women Engineers

Teams: Chess, Concrete Canoe Team, Design Build Fly Team, Esports Team, Formula SAE Vehicle Team, Lafayette Hacks, Mock Trial, Model United Nations, Motorsports Team, National Collegiate Cyber Defense Competition Team, Rocketry Team, Speech and Debate Team, Steel Bridge Team

Notable Alumni
William Cattell, William Durand, Edgar Jadwin, Don Lancaster, and James Porter III

LEHIGH UNIVERSITY

Address: P.C. Rossin College of Engineering & Applied Science, 19 Memorial Drive W., Lehigh University, Bethlehem, PA 18015
Website: https://engineering.lehigh.edu/
Contact: https://engineering.lehigh.edu/contact
Phone: (610) 758-4025
Email: engineering@lehigh.edu

COST OF ATTENDANCE:

Tuition & Fees: $60,690 | **Addl Exp:** $17,955 | **Total:** $78,645

Financial Aid: https://www2.lehigh.edu/financial-aid

ADDITIONAL INFORMATION:

Available Degree(s)
- BS, BS/MS, MS, MEng, Ph.D. Mechanical Engineering, Chemical Engineering, Computer Science, Computer Engineering, Electrical Engineering, Materials Science & Engineering
- Minors: Aerospace Engineering, Biotech, Business, Chemical & Biomolecular Eng, Comp Sci, Data Sci, Electrical Eng, Energy Eng, Eng Leadership, Entrepreneurship, Environmental Eng, Manufacturing Sys Eng, Materials Science & Eng, Mechanics of Materials, Music, Nanotechnology, Polymer Science & Eng

Related Research Areas
Institute for Cyber Physical Infrastructure & Energy, Institute for Data, Intelligent Systems, & Computation, Institute for Functional Materials & Devices

Scholarships Offered
Lehigh offers renewable merit scholarships (automatic) considered and others require a separate application

Alice P. Gast STEM Scholarship ($12,500 for selected women in STEM careers), Dean's Scholars ($15,000/yr based on academics & leadership), Founder's & Trustees' Scholarships (full or half tuition for top students); engineering scholarships are available. ROTC scholarships include full tuition, book allowance of $1,200, & monthly stipend (room & board free for students who commit to becoming an Army officer); Greer Scholars Program provides funding & support network for African American & Hispanic students pursuing engineering

Special Opportunities
Experiential learning/internships, high-tech res ctrs & labs, Lehigh CHOICES Program, and Lehigh Univ Summer Engineering Institute for K-12 students. Study abroad options in Belgium, England, France, the Czech Republic, Italy, & China. Winter-term programs have been offered in England, Italy, Costa Rica, Spain, & Ghana.

Teams: F1TENTH Virtual Global Autonomous Racing Competition Head-to-Head Race (1st place in 2022) Precast/Prestressed Concrete Institute's Engineering Student Design Competition (3rd overall in 2020), Modeling & Optimization Theory & Applications Competition, National ChemE Competition Team

Notable Alumni
Ali Al-Naimi, William Amelio, Walter Bachman, John-David Bartoe, Stephen Benkovic, William Bowie, Morris Cooke, Stacey Cunningham, Harry Diamond, William Elmore, Martin Faga, Terry Hart, Marc Holtzman, Lee Iacocca, Kevin Kennedy, Andrew Knoll, Reginald Lenna, Judy Marks, Fred Mackenzie, Daniel Moore, John Patrick, Roger Penske, Jordan Ritter, Robert Serber, John Texter, Fred Trump, Jr.

CONNECTICUT
MAINE
MASSACHUSETTS
NEW HAMPSHIRE
NEW JERSEY
NEW YORK
PENNSYLVANIA
RHODE ISLAND
VERMONT

NORTHEAST

PENNSYLVANIA STATE UNIVERSITY

Address: College of Engineering, Office of the Dean, 101 Hammond Building, University Park, PA 16802
Website: *https://www.engr.psu.edu/*
Contact: *https://www.engr.psu.edu/directory/index.aspx*
Phone: (814) 865-7537
Email: dean@engr.psu.edu

COST OF ATTENDANCE:

Tuition & Fees: $18,898 (in-state), $36,476 (out-of-state)
Addl Exp: $17,580 | **Total:** $36,278 (in-state), $53,856 (out-of-state)

Financial Aid: https://www.psu.edu/tuition-and-financial-aid/

ADDITIONAL INFORMATION:

Available Degree(s)
- BS, MS, Ph.D. Aerospace Engineering, Mechanical Engineering, Nuclear Engineering
- MS, Ph.D. Engineering Science & Mechanics, MEng Engineering Mechanics
- MEng, MS Additive Manufacturing & Design, Engineering Design,
- D.Eng. Doctor of Engineering
- Minors: Biol Eng, Biomed Eng, Eng Leadership Development, Engineering Mechanics, Entrepreneurship & Innovation, Environmental Eng, International Eng, Nanotechnology

Related Research Areas
Autonomous Vehicles, Optimized, & Adaptive Infra Systems, Energy Sourcing & Production, Ethical Water-Energy-Food Policies & Social Resp, Food Production Optimization, Infrastructure Sys Integration, Resilient Infrastructure Sys, Tri-System Modeling, Optimization, & Mgmt, Water-Energy-Food Nexus, Water Resource Sustainability

Scholarships Offered
To be eligible for any Penn State scholarship, students must submit a FAFSA form. The Provost's Award grants $5,000 for 1st & 2nd years and $7,000 for years 3 and 4 (PA and non-PA residents are considered). The Discover Penn State Award grants $6,000 for 1st & 2nd years and $7,000 for years 3 and 4. Students must be residents of Del., MD, OH, NJ, NY, VA, WV, & DC.

Special Opportunities
Engineering House (E-House), Engineering Student Council, Engineering Leadership Society, Engineering Peer Advising Leaders

Orgs: American Inst of Aeronautics & Astronautics, American Society of Civil Engineers, American Society of Mechanical Engineers, Concrete Institute, Engineering Ambassadors, Eng Consulting Collaborative, Engineers for a Sustainable World, Engineers w/o Borders, Global Engineering Fellows, Helicopter Society, Institute of Transportation Eng, Korean-Amer Scientists & Eng Association, Lunar Lion, Materials Research Society, National Society of Black Engineers, oSTEM, Society for Automotive Engineers, Society of Eng Science, Society of Hispanic Prof Eng, Society of Women Engineers, Solar Energy Society, Theme Park Eng Group, Wind Energy Club

Teams: Advanced Vehicles (Autonomous Vehicles, AutoDrive Challenge), Aero Design-Build-Fly Team, Chess Squad, College Bowl, Concrete Canoe, Cubesat, Formula SAE, HackPSU, Hybrid Electric Vehicle, LionTech Rocket Team, Lunar Lion Google Lunar X Prize Team, Mock Trial, Robotics Club, Robo X, Rubik's Cube Club, Soaring Club, Steel Bridge Team, Unmanned Aerial Systems

Notable Alumni
Elliott Abrams, Guion Bluford, David Bohm, Robert Cenker, Jane Charlton, Shawn Domagal-Goldman, Robert Eberly, Gregory Forbes, Paul Julian, Jim Keller, Joel Myers, James Pawelczyk, Jef Raskin, Harry Shoemaker, John Surma, Ben Wang, Paul Weitz, and Patricia Woertz

UNIVERSITY OF PENNSYLVANIA

Address: School of Engineering & Applied Science, 220 South 33rd Street, 107 Towne Building, Philadelphia, PA 19104-6391
Website: https://www.seas.upenn.edu/
Contact: https://www.seas.upenn.edu/about/school-leadership/
Phone: (215) 898-7246
Email: ras@seas.upenn.edu

COST OF ATTENDANCE:

Tuition & Fees: $63,452 | **Addl Exp:** $22,286 | **Total:** $85,738

Financial Aid: https://srfs.upenn.edu/financial-aid

ADDITIONAL INFORMATION:

Available Degree(s)
- BSE, MEng, Ph.D. Mechanical Engineering, Electrical Engineering, Materials Science & Engineering
- MSE Data Science, Computer Graphics & Game Technology, Nanotechnology, Robotics, Product Design
- Minors: Computer & Information Science, Data Science, Electrical & Systems Engineering, Energy & Sustainability, Engineering Entrepreneurship, Materials Science & Eng

Related Research Areas
Center for Engineering MechanoBiology, General Robotics, Automation, Sensing, and Perception, Visual Analysis & Re-Synthesis

Scholarships Offered
Approximately 57% of freshmen received financial aid with an average amount of $44,232 in 2022. UPenn's undergraduate aid is entirely need-based. No scholarships are awarded based on academic or athletic merit.

Special Opportunities
Rachleff Scholars Program, Clark Scholars Program, CG@Penn Summer Research, CIS Undergraduate Summer Research Program, NSF Research Experience for Undergrads, Minority Participation Undergraduate Research Program, Summer Undergraduate Fellowship in Sensor Technologies, Penn Engineering Scholars Program Center for Undergraduate Research & Fellowships, Senior Design Project Competition (Technology & Innovation Prize, Social Impact Prize, Leadership Prize, Judge's Choice Award)

Nanoscale Characterization Facility, Nanofabrication Facility, Scanning & Local Probe Facility, Center for Computer Graphics, Soft Lithography Lab, Student-Run Technical Innovation Hub

Study abroad program, engagement opportunities. Penn's cutting-edge research spans from biotechnology & robotics, to computer animation & nanotechnology

Orgs: ACM SIGGRAPH, ASCE, ASME, Nat Soc of Black Eng, oSTEM, Engineers w/o Borders, Soc of Hispanic Prof Eng, Soc of Systems Eng, Society of Women Eng, Technology Entrepreneurship Club, Underrep Stud Advisory Board in Eng, Women in Computer Science

Teams: Chess, Debate Society, Formula SAE - Penn Electric Racing, iGEM, Mock Trial, MUN, Quiz Bowl, Robotics, Science Olympiad

Notable Alumni
Alfred Boller, Warren Buffett, Noam Chomsky, Jeffrey Chu, John Durham, J. Presper Eckert, George Heilmeier, J. Clarence Karcher, David Kuhl, Christian Lambertsen, Robert Lanza, John Legend, Yueh-Lin Loo, Ollie Luba, Elon Musk, Mehmet Oz, I.M. Pei, Mary Pennington, Sundar Pichai, Frank Piasecki, Fairman Rogers, Gregg Semenza, George Smith, Benjamin Tilghman, Bert Vogelstein, Jack Wolf, Horatio Wood, Nathaniel Wyeth, and Ahmed Zewail

CONNECTICUT
MAINE
MASSACHUSETTS
NEW HAMPSHIRE
NEW JERSEY
NEW YORK
PENNSYLVANIA
RHODE ISLAND
VERMONT

NORTHEAST

VILLANOVA UNIVERSITY

Address: Villanova University, 800 E. Lancaster Ave., Villanova, PA 19085
Website: *https://www1.villanova.edu/university/engineering.html*
Contact: *https://www1.villanova.edu/villanova/contact.html*
Phone: (610) 519-4500
Email: gotovu@villanova.edu

COST OF ATTENDANCE:

Tuition & Fees: $61,618 | **Addl Exp:** $16,087 | **Total:** $77,705

Financial Aid: https://www1.villanova.edu/villanova/enroll/finaid/process.html

ADDITIONAL INFORMATION:

Available Degree(s)
- BS, MS, Ph.D.. Chemical Engineering, Civil Eng, Computer Engineering, Electrical Engineering, Mechanical Engineering
- MS, Ph.D. Cybersecurity, Biochemical Engineering, Sustainable Engineering, and Water Resources & Environmental Engineering
- Minors: Aerospace Eng, Biochemical Eng, Biomedical Eng, Comp Architecture, Computer Engineering, Cybersecurity, Cybersecurity w/a Concentration In Cyber-Physical & Control Systems Security, Electrical Engineering, Engineering Entrepreneurship, Humanitarian Engineering, Mechatronics, Real Estate Development, Sustainability, Sustainable Eng

Related Research Areas
Center for Advanced Communications, Center for Cellular Engineering (NovaCell), Center for Energy-Smart Electronic Systems, Center for Humanitarian Engineering and International Development, Center for Nonlinear Dynamics and Control, Villanova Center for Analytics of Dynamic Systems, Villanova Center for Resilient Water Systems

Scholarships Offered
The Presidential Scholarship (transformational leadership): merit-based award covering full tuition, room, board, general fee, and the cost of textbooks for eight consecutive semesters. Students must be nominated by a HS official or home school entity or non-profit CBO leader by Dec. 1, complete an application by Dec 5, and complete the scholarship app by Jan 2.

St. Martin de Porres Scholarships is a full scholarship to attract a diverse & talented student population. The Anthony Randazzo Endowed Presidential Scholarship (African American candidate) covers the full cost of tuition & general fees. More scholarships and appl at https://www1.villanova.edu/university/undergraduate-admission/Financial-Assistance-and-scholarship.html

Special Opportunities
Orgs: American Institute of Chemical Engineers, American Society of Civil Engineers, American Society of Mechanical Engineers, Institute of Electrical and Electronic Engineers, Institute of Transportation Engineers, National Society of Black Engineers, National Society of Professional Engineers, Society of Asian Scientists & Engineers, Society of Hispanic Professional Eng, Society of Women Engineers

Teams: Amateur Radio, Chem E Car Team, CubeSat Club (Nanosatellites), Debate Union, Formula SAE Team, Maritime RobotX Challenge, Mock Trial, NovaCANE

Notable Alumni
Andrew Allen, Ayman Asfari, Sean Carroll, Dominic Caruso, Steve Chen, Nance Dicciani, John Drosdick, Edward Guinan, Jamie Hyneman, Deirdre Imus, John Jones, James Kim, Christopher Lee, James Mullen, and Emanuel Rubin

---

CONNECTICUT

MAINE

MASSACHUSETTS

NEW HAMPSHIRE

NEW JERSEY

NEW YORK

PENNSYLVANIA

RHODE ISLAND

VERMONT

BROWN UNIVERSITY

Address: Department of Engineering, Brown University, 69 Brown St Box 1822, Providence, RI 02912
Website: https://engineering.brown.edu/
Contact: https://engineering.brown.edu/get-involved/contact-us
Phone: (401) 863-1000
Email: Carolyn_Harris@brown.edu

COST OF ATTENDANCE:
Tuition & Fees: $65,146 | Addl Exp: $20,837 | Total: $85,983

Financial Aid: https://finaid.brown.edu/

ADDITIONAL INFORMATION:

Available Degree(s)
- AB, Sc.B., Sc.B./Sc.M., MS, Ph.D. Biomedical Engineering, Chemical Engineering, Computer Engineering, Electrical Engineering, Environmental Engineering, Materials Science & Engineering, Mechanical Engineering
- MA Data Enabled Computational Engineering & Science, Design Eng, Entrepreneurship, Fluids & Thermal Sciences, Mechanics of Solids & Structures, Technology Leadership

Related Research Areas
Biomaterials, Biomechanics, & Biophysics, Computational Mechanics, Computer Vision, Image, & Medical Image Processing, Digital Fabrication, Energy Science, Mechanics of Materials for Energy Storage, Mechanics of Soft Materials, Mechanics of Thin Films & Surface Engineering, Nano & Micro-Mechanics, Robotics & Industrial Automation, Sensor Networks, Smart Cameras, Networked Systems, & Signal Processing, Structural Materials, Wireless Communications & Power Transmission

Scholarships Offered
Approximately 44% of incoming students receive financial aid, mostly in scholarships/grants amounting to $55,862/year. Brown fully covers tuition for families earning $125,000 or less with typical assets. For families earning less than $60,000 with typical assets, Brown covers tuition, room, board, books, and an additional scholarship.

Special Opportunities
Design@Brown, Handshake at Brown, BrownConnect, Royce Fellowship, RI Space Consortium Grant, DiMase Fellowship, NSF Research Experience for Undergraduates, Brown Design Workshop, Joint Engineering Physics Instrument Shop, MRI Research Facility, Nanoelectronics Central Facility

Orgs: American Academy of Environmental Engineers & Scientists, American Institute of Chemical Engineers, American Society of Mechanical Engineers, Biomedical Eng Society, EngnDug, National Society of Black Engineers, oSTEM, Scientists for a Sustainable World, Society of Asian Scientists & Engineers, Society of Hispanic Professional Engineers, Society of Women Engineers, STEAM

Teams: Brown Space Engineering Team, Chess, Brown Debate Union, Formula Racing Team, iGEM (Intl Genetically Eng Machines), Mock Trial, Model United Nations, Robotics Team, Quiz Bowl, Rubik's Cube Competitions, Science Olympiad, Space Eng Team

Notable Alumni
Willis Adcock, Zachariah Allen, Brian Binnie, Bernard Budiansky, Walter Cady, Michael Dickinson, James Garvin, Lillian Gilbreth, David Grinspoon, Morton Gurtin, Andy Hertzfeld, Alexander Holley, Wesley Huntress, Adam Leventhal, Victor Li, Byron Lichtenberg, Sarah Milkovich, Jessica Meir, Ken Silverman, Ellen Stofan, Suzanne Smrekar, Paul Spudis, Winslow Upton, and Maria Zuber

CONNECTICUT

MAINE

MASSACHUSETTS

NEW HAMPSHIRE

NEW JERSEY

NEW YORK

PENNSYLVANIA

RHODE ISLAND

VERMONT

NORTHEAST

CHAPTER 12

REGION TWO
MIDWEST

ILLINOIS
INDIANA
IOWA
KANSAS
MICHIGAN
MINNESOTA
MISSOURI
NEBRASKA
NORTH DAKOTA
OHIO
SOUTH DAKOTA
WISCONSIN

14 Programs | 9 States

1. IL – Northwestern University
2. IL - University of Illinois, Urbana-Champaign
3. IN - Purdue University
4. IN - Rose-Hulman Institute of Technology
5. IN - University of Notre Dame
6. MI - Kettering University
7. MI - Michigan State University
8. MI - Michigan Technological University
9. MI - University of Michigan
10. MN - University of Minnesota, Twin Cities
11. MO - Washington University in St. Louis
12. OH - Case Western Reserve University
13. OH - The Ohio State University
14. WI - University of Wisconsin, Madison

MECHANICAL ENGINEERING PROGRAMS

School	Avg. GPA, SAT Evidence-Based Reading Writing (ERW), SAT Math (M), and ACT Composite (C) Early Decision (ED): Yes/No	Admission Statistics	Selected Program(s)
Northwestern University 633 Clark St, Evanston, IL 60208	GPA: N/A SAT (ERW): 700-760 SAT (M): 730-790 ACT (C): 33-35 ED: No	Overall College Admit Rate: 9% Undergrad Enrollment: 8,194 Total Enrollment: 22,072	BS, MS, Ph.D. BME, Chem Eng, Mechanical Engineering, Materials Science & Engineering MS Manufacturing & Design Engineering, Robotics
University of Illinois Urbana-Champaign (UIUC) 901 West Illinois Street, Urbana, IL 61801	GPA: N/A SAT (ERW): 590-700 SAT (M): 620-770 ACT (C): 27-33 ED: Yes	Overall College Admit Rate: 50% Undergrad Enrollment: 34,559 Total Enrollment: 56,257	BS, MS, Ph.D. Aerosp. Eng, ChemE, Mech Eng BA/BS Aviation (8 core aviation courses, flight training, transp analysis, airport mgmt + capstone)
Purdue University Purdue University, West Lafayette, IN 47907	GPA: 3.67 SAT (ERW): 590-690 SAT (M): 600-740 ACT (C): 25-33 ED: No	Overall College Admit Rate: 67% Undergrad Enrollment: 34,920 Total Enrollment: 45,869	BS, MS, Ph.D. Aero & Astro Engineering; Mechanical Eng BS Airport Mgmt & Ops, Prof Flight, UAV; BS, MS, Ph.D. Aviation & Aerospace Mgmt
Rose-Hulman Institute of Technology 5500 Wabash Avenue, Terre Haute, IN 47803	GPA: 4.03 SAT (ERW): 620-710 SAT (M): 650-770 ACT (C): 28-33 ED: No	Overall College Admit Rate: 77% Undergrad Enrollment: 2,081 Total Enrollment: 2,101	BS, MS/MEng BME, Chemical Eng, Civil Eng, Comp Eng, Comp Sci, Data Science, EE, Eng Design, Enviro Eng, Mechanical Eng, Software Engineering
University of Notre Dame University of Notre Dame, Notre Dame, IN 46556	GPA: N/A SAT (ERW): 690-760 SAT (M): 710-790 ACT (C): 32-35 ED: Yes	Overall College Admit Rate: 19% Undergrad Enrollment: 8,874 Total Enrollment: 12,809	BS, BS/MS, MS, Ph.D. Aerospace Eng, Chemical Eng, Civil Eng, Comp Eng, Comp Science, Electrical Eng, Environmental Eng, Mechanical Eng

MECHANICAL ENGINEERING PROGRAMS

School	Avg. GPA, SAT Evidence-Based Reading Writing (ERW), SAT Math (M), and ACT Composite (C) Early Decision (ED): Yes/No	Admission Statistics	Selected Program(s)
Kettering University 1700 University Avenue, Flint, MI 48504	GPA: N/A SAT (ERW): 580-660 SAT (M): 600-700 ACT (C): 25-30 ED: No	Admit Rate: 74% Undergrad Enrollment: 1,659 Total Enrollment: 2,030	BS, BS/MS, MS ChemE, Computer Eng, EE, Mechanical Engineering MS AI, Industrial Eng, Mobility Systems, Robotic Systems
Michigan State University Michigan State University, East Lansing, MI 48824	GPA: 3.74 SAT (ERW): 550-640 SAT (M): 550-660 ACT (C): 23-29 ED: No	Admit Rate: 76% Undergrad Enrollment: 38,491 Total Enrollment: 49,695	BS, BS/MS, MS, Ph.D. Biosystems Eng, ChemE, Civil Eng, Comp Eng Comp Sci, EE, Environmental Eng, Materials Sci & Eng, Mechanical Eng
Michigan Technical University 1400 Townsend Dr, Houghton, MI 49931	GPA: 3.78 SAT (ERW): 560-660 SAT (M): 570-670 ACT (C): 25-31 ED: No	Admit Rate: 86% Undergrad Enrollment: 5,778 Total Enrollment: 7,009	BS, MS/MEng, MEng, DEng, Ph.D. BME, ChemE, CivilE, Comp Eng, Comp Sci, EE, Mat Sci, Mechanical Eng, Mining Engineering, BS Robotics Engineering
University of Michigan 500 S. State St., Ann Arbor, MI 48109	GPA: 3.87 SAT (ERW): 660-740 SAT (M): 680-780 ACT (C): 31-34 ED: No	Overall College Admit Rate: 26% Undergrad Enrollment: 31,329 Total Enrollment: 47,907	BS, BS/MS, MS, Ph.D. Aerospace Eng, BME, ChemE, Civil Eng, EE, Mechanical Eng, Naval Architecture & Marine Eng, Robotics, Space Science & Engineering
University of Minnesota, Twin Cities 330 21st Ave S., Minneapolis, MN 55455	GPA: N/A SAT (ERW): 600-700 SAT (M): 640-760 ACT (C): 25-31 ED: No	Overall College Admit Rate: 70% Undergrad Enrollment: 36,061 Total Enrollment: 52,017	BS, MS, Ph.D. Aerosp. Eng & Mechanics, Chemical Eng, Food Science, Materials Sci & Eng, Mechanical Engineering MS, Ph.D. Nuclear Eng

MIDWEST

MECHANICAL ENGINEERING PROGRAMS

School	Avg. GPA, SAT Evidence-Based Reading Writing (ERW), SAT Math (M), and ACT Composite (C) Early Decision (ED): Yes/No	Admission Statistics	Selected Program(s)
Washington University in St. Louis 1 Brookings Dr, St. Louis, MO 63130	GPA: 4.21 SAT (ERW): 720-760 SAT (M): 760-800 ACT (C): 33-35 ED: Yes	Overall College Admit Rate: 16% Undergrad Enrollment: 7,653 Total Enrollment: 15,449	BS, MS, Ph.D. Mechanical Eng Minors: Human-Computer Interaction, Mechatronics, Quantum Engineering, Robotics
Case Western Reserve University 10900 Euclid Ave., Cleveland, Ohio 44106	GPA: 3.75 SAT (ERW): 640-730 SAT (M): 700-790 ACT (C): 31-34 ED: Yes	Overall College Admit Rate: 30% Undergrad Enrollment: 5,430 Total Enrollment: 11,465	BS, BS/MS, MS, Ph.D. Aerospace Eng, BME, ChemE, Civil Eng, EE, Materials Science & Engineering, Mechanical Eng, Systems & Control Eng
The Ohio State University 1849 Cannon Drive, Columbus, OH 43210	GPA: N/A SAT (ERW): 590-690 SAT (M): 620-740 ACT (C): 26-32 ED: No	Overall College Admit Rate: 87% Undergrad Enrollment: 19,284 Total Enrollment: 25,714	BS, MS, Ph.D. Aerosp. Eng, BME, Chem Eng, Mat Sci & Engineering Mechanical Eng, BA/BS Aviation (8 aviation courses, flight training, transp analysis, airport mgmt + capstone)
University of Wisconsin 702 West Johnson Street, Madison, WI 53715	GPA: 3.87 SAT (ERW): 610-690 SAT (M): 650-770 ACT (C): 27-32 ED: No	Overall College Admit Rate: 57% Undergrad Enrollment: 32,688 Total Enrollment: 44,640	BS Eng Mechanics, Engineering Physics, Naval Science BS, MS, Ph.D. BME, Civil Eng, Chem Eng, EE, Enviro Eng, Industrial Engineering, Materials Science & Eng, Mechanical Eng

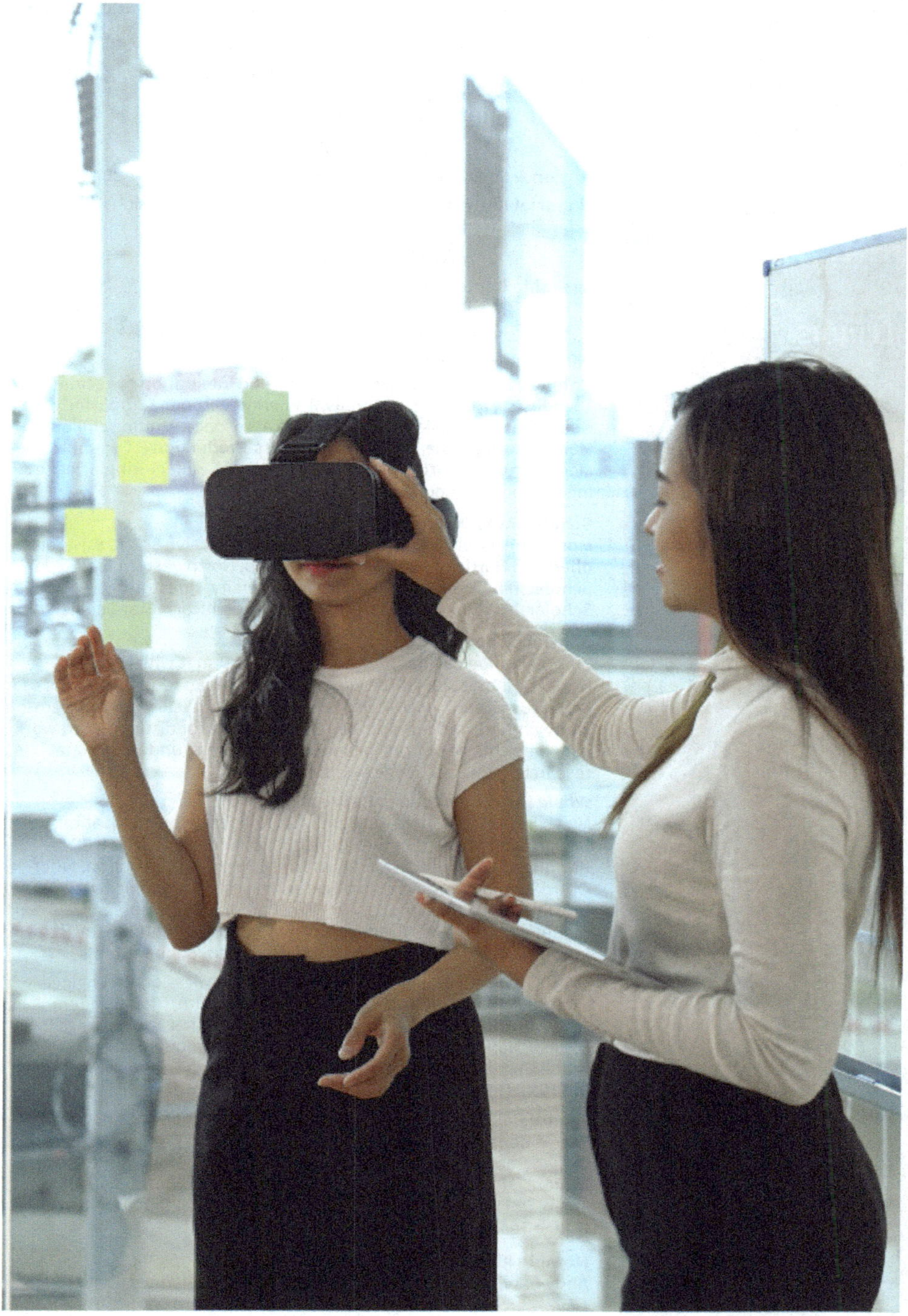

NORTHWESTERN UNIVERSITY

Address: Northwestern University, Robert R. McCormick School of Engineering and Applied Science Technological Institute, 2145 Sheridan Road, Evanston, IL 60208
Website: https://www.mccormick.northwestern.edu/
Contact: https://www.mccormick.northwestern.edu/contact/index.html
Phone: (847) 491-5220
Email: jm-ottino@northwestern.edu

COST OF ATTENDANCE:
Tuition & Fees: $63,468 | **Addl Exp:** $24,336 | **Total:** $87,804

Financial Aid: https://www.northwestern.edu/admissions/financial-aid-offices.html

ADDITIONAL INFORMATION:

Available Degree(s)
- BS, MS, Ph.D. Mechanical Engineering
- MS Manufacturing & Design Engineering, Robotics

Related Research Areas
Materials Design Approach for Accelerated Integration of Technology To Industry, Medicine, Materials, & Energy, Methods & Tools for Heavy Machinery, Metal Processing, & Aerospace, Multidisciplinary Manufacturing Research To Impact Mass-Production & Customized Manufacturing, Northwestern Initiative For Manufacturing Science & Innovation, Transportation Center

Scholarships Offered
Most families with incomes under $150,000 receive $48,328. NU also offers the Northwestern Univ Scholarship, Northwestern Endowed Scholarship, Good Neighbor, Great University, Questbridge, Founder's Scholarship, Karr Achievement Award, and Chicago Star Scholarship

Special Opportunities
The Technological Institute features 850,000 sq ft with research facilities, labs, state-of-the-art equipment, clean rooms, robotics lab, & computer labs. NU also offers internships, summer programs, study abroad, and research seminars. Awards for distinguished work including college honors, major-specific honors, undergraduate research grants, & college awards.

Whole Brain Engineering Approach
Northwestern Initiative for Manufacturing Science & Innovation, Design & Manufacturing Group. Acoustic Microscopes, CLIP 3D Printing, Cyberphysical Manufacturing, Design Optimization, Fiber-Optic Sys, Functional Surface Texturing, Laser Ultrasonic Systems, mHUB (Innovation center for physical product development & manufacturing) Mass Production Manufacturing, Material Design, Rapid Flexible Manufacturing, Ultrasonic Inspection Systems

Orgs: Council of Supply Chain Management Professionals, Engineers for a Sustainable World, Engineering World Health, Global Water Brigades, Institute of Industrial Engineers, National Engineering Honor Society, National Society of Black Engineers, National Society of Professional Engineers, Society of Manufacturing Engineering, Society of Hispanic Professional Engineers, Society of Women Engineers

Teams: Baja Racing Team, Chess, Computer Science Team, Concrete Canoe Consulting Competitions, Cubesat Team, Design for America, Design Competitions, eSports, Mock Trial Team, Model United Nations, NU Formula Racing, NUSolar Car Team, Quiz Bowl, Robotics Team, Rocket Team, Science Olympiad, Speech & Debate Team, Steel Bridge Team, Wildhacks Hackathon

Notable Alumni
Andy Carvin, K. T. Chau, Sugun Dawodu, Larry Gladney, Amy Gooch, Gary Kremen, Kermit Krantz, Vid Latham, Richard Lerner, Irene Kong, Joseph Staten, Jacques Vallee, Edward Weiler, and John Wharton

UNIVERSITY OF ILLINOIS URBANA-CHAMPAIGN (UIUC)

Address: The Grainger College of Engineering, University of Illinois, 306 Engineering Hall MC 266, 1308 West Green Street, Urbana, IL 61801
Website: https://grainger.illinois.edu/
Contact: https://www.admissions.illinois.edu/request-more
Phone: (217) 333-2280
Email: engineering@illinois.edu

COST OF ATTENDANCE:
Tuition & Fees: $17,660 (in-state), $38,132 (out-of-state)
Addl Exp.: $16,500 | **Total:** $34,160 (in-state), $54,632 (out-of-state)

Financial Aid: https://admissions.illinois.edu/Invest/financial-aid

ADDITIONAL INFORMATION:

Available Degree(s)
- BS, MS, Ph.D. Aerospace Engineering, Mechanical Engineering,
- BA/BS Aviation (8 core aviation courses, flight training, transportation analysis, airport management + capstone)
- Online Master of Engineering Mgmt, MS Global Engineering Leadership, MS Welding Engineering
- Minor in Humanitarian Engineering

Related Research Centers
Advanced Materials & Evaluation Lab, Aeroacoustics, Aeroelasticity, Aerodynamics, AI for Future Resil., Management, & Sustainability Inst, Center for Autonomy, Ctr for Hypersonics & Entry Systems Students, Combustion & Prop, Computational Fluid Dynamics, Exp Robotics Lab, Gas Dynamics Lab, Human-Centered Design, Hypersonics, IBM-IL Disc Accelerator Inst, IL Center for Transportation, Info Trust Inst, Inst for Carbon-Neutral Energy Res, Inst for Sustainability, Energy, & Envir, Intelligent Robotics Lab, Laser & Optical Diagnostics, Power Optimization of Electro-Thermal Systems, Quantum Info Sci & Tech, Satellite Design & Manufacturing, Space Sys, Tech Entrepreneur Ctr

Scholarships Offered
UIUC applicants are automatically considered for merit-based scholarships. The supplemental form for need-based scholarships may be found at https://secure.osfa.illinois.edu/scholarshipsupp/ Note: 70% of UIUC undergraduates receive aid.

For graduate students, there are scholarships, assistantships, hourly positions, engineering school opportunities, and student loans.

Special Opportunities
K-12 programs incl WYSE, I-STEM, & Engineering Ambassadors, as well internships/co-ops starting in the summer of your freshman year. The College partners w/Zhejiang Univ (ZJU) Intl Campus.

UIUC offers students cutting-edge resources, facilities, such as the Engineering Library & Idea Lab, Innovation Studio, & MakerLab, & specialization courses, research projects, and a joint minor with the Gies College of Business. Additionally, UIUC offers the City Scholars program, study abroad in 50+ countries.

Orgs: Engineers w/o Borders, ARISE, AWARE, Eng Ambassadors, Eng Council, MEP, NSBE, NSPE, Society of Women Eng, Women in Eng

Teams: Robobrawl (iRobotics) Team, Midwest Robotics Design Comp, Illini Formula Electric, Illini Motorsports, Offroad Illini, Eco Illini Supermileage, Shell EcoMarathon Americas, Illini EV Concept, Solar Car Competition, Math contests open to all UIUC students

Notable Alumni
Marc Andreessen, Bruce Artwick, Arnold Beckman, Eric Bina, Steve Chen, James DeLaurier, Fazlur Khan, Chris Lattner, Ray Ozzie, H. Gene Slottow, Bill Stumpf, and Kevin Warwick

ILLINOIS
INDIANA
IOWA
KANSAS
MICHIGAN
MINNESOTA
MISSOURI
NEBRASKA
NORTH DAKOTA
OHIO
SOUTH DAKOTA
WISCONSIN

MIDWEST

PURDUE UNIVERSITY

Address: Purdue University Office of Future Engineers Welcome Center, Neil Armstrong Hall of Engineering, Room 1085, 701 W. Stadium Ave., West Lafayette, IN 47907-2045
Website: https://engineering.purdue.edu/Engr
Contact: https://engineering.purdue.edu/Engr/AboutUs/contact_us
Phone: (765) 494-3975
Email: future-engineers@purdue.edu

COST OF ATTENDANCE:

Tuition & Fees: $9,992 (in-state), $28,794 (out-of-state)
Addl Exp: $12,930 | **Total:** $22,922 (in-state), $41,724 (out-of-state)
Financial Aid: https://www.purdue.edu/dfa/

ADDITIONAL INFORMATION:

Available Degree(s)
- BS, MS, Ph.D. Aeronautical/Astronomical Eng, Mechanical Eng
- BS Aeronautical Engineering Technology, Aerospace Financial Analysis, Airline Management & Operations, Airport Mgmt & Operations, Aviation Mgmt, Prof Flight, Unmanned Aerial Sys
- MS, Ph.D. Aviation & Aerospace Management
- Ph.D. in Tech; Humanitarian Engineering Concentration
- Minor in Sustainable Engineering

Related Research Centers
Focus Areas: Acoustics & Noise Control, Advanced Materials, Combustion, Dynamics & Vibration, Fluid Mechanics, Heat & Mass Transfer, Human-Machine Interaction, Measurements & Controls, Micro & Nanotechnology, Propulsion, Robotics, Sustainable Energy, Thermodynamics, Transportation

Scholarships Offered
College of Engineering awards $3.8 million in undergraduate scholarships yearly in addition to institutional and private options.

Special Opportunities
First-Year Engineering Program; Grand Challenges in Aviation & Transportation Technology; internships with airline industry partners, Project Bloom, Study Abroad, Global Programs. Facilities include the Birck Nanotechnology Center (BNC), Bowen Laboratory, and FlexLab

Summer Undergraduate Research Fellowship (SURF) Program, INSPIRE Research Institute for Pre-College Engineering, and co-op programs like EPICS, a service-learning design program where teams of students partner with community organizations; internships available in each degree program.

Orgs: ABE Ambassadors, ASABE, AAPS, AIChE, ASM, Engineers w/o Borders, IEEE, IFT, iGEM, NSBE, NSHE, Nanotechnology Student Advisory Council, PSEF, SAE, Society of Women Engineers

Teams: Aerial Robotics Team, Algorithmic Prog Team, Autonomous Motorsports, Business Case Competitions, Chem-E Car Team, Chess, Concrete Canoe Team, Cubesat, Cyber Security Events and Comp, Data Analytics Competition, Formula SAE & Baja SAE Competition Teams, iGEM Team, Lunabotics, Mock Trial, Model United Nations, NASA Student Launch Team, National Marine Energy Collegiate Competition, Purdue Hackers - Hack Nights, Purdue Electric Racing, Purdue Solar Racing Team, Quiz Bowl, Remotely Operated Underwater Vehicle Team, Rube Goldberg Machine Contest, Rubik's Cube, Science Olympiad, TechCrunch Disrupt's Startup Battlefield, Steel Bridge Team

Notable Alumni
Sue Abreu, Neil Armstrong, Gregory Ayers, Stephen Bechtel Jr., Eugene Cernan, Paul Cloyd, Clarence Cory, Richard Dauch, Kevin Granata, "Gus" Grissom, Larry Howell, Marshall Larsen, Arthur Lefebvre, John Martin, Herman Pevler, Orville Redenbacher, David R. Schwind, Thomas Sheridan, "Sully" Sullenberger, III, John Wooden

ROSE HULMAN INSTITUTE OF TECHNOLOGY

Address: Office of Admissions, Rose-Hulman Institute of Technology, 5500 Wabash Avenue, Terre Haute, Indiana 47803
Website: *https://www.rose-hulman.edu/*
Contact: *https://www.rose-hulman.edu/about-us/get-to-know-rose-hulman/contact-RHIT.html*
Phone: (800) 248-7448
Email: admissions@rose-hulman.edu

COST OF ATTENDANCE:

Tuition & Fees: $52,119 | **Addl Exp:** $22,107 | **Total:** $74,226

Financial Aid: https://www.rose-hulman.edu/admissions-and-aid/index.html

ADDITIONAL INFORMATION:

Available Degree(s)
- BS, MS/MEng Biomedical Engineering, Chemical Eng, Civil Eng, Computational Science, Computer Eng, Comp Sci, Data Science, EE, Engineering Design, Environmental Engineering, Mechanical Engineering, Software Engineering
- MS Engineering Management, Optical Engineering

Related Research Areas
Artificial Intelligence, Aerodynamics, Aerospace Design, Automotive Electronics, Dynamic Systems, Electromagnetics, Embedded Systems, Energy Production, Information Security, Kinematics, Power Systems, Propulsion Systems, Renewable Energy, Robot Dynamics, Thermal Fluid Systems, Turbomachinery, Vibration Analysis

Scholarships Offered
Rose-Hulman Merit Scholarship (automatic consideration), Named Scholarships (automatic consideration, specific restrictions) Rose-Hulman Need-Based Grant, Noblitt Scholars Program (4-year, invitation-only), Bakota Family Scholarship (1-year scholarship for students in electrical, mechanical, or chemical engineering – additional steps), FIRST Robotics Scholarship (3 merit-based scholarships $10,000/year for 4 years –apply by February 1st), Trueb Scholarship for freshmen who were in Boy Scouts (apply by Feb 1st), Rose-BUD Scholarship (diversity program, $10,000/year for EE & computer engineering), Conru Scholarship for freshmen entrepreneurial types ($10,000/year for 4 years – apply by Feb 1st)

Facilities: Branam & Kremer Innovation Centers, MiNDs Lab, Oakley Observatory, and Rose-Hulman Ventures

Special Opportunities
K-12 programs, like Operation Catapult camps and FIRST Robotics; Study Abroad & International Exchange/Global E3, study in Germany; Industry-Sponsored Projects, Internships & Co-ops locally and internationally through Handshake and Career Services.

Orgs: Aeronautics & Astronautics Club, AIChE, American Society of Civil Engineers, American Society of Mechanical Engineers, Assoc of Black Engineers, Engineers for a Sustainable World, Engineers w/o Borders, Rose Innovative Student Entrepreneurs, Society of Asian Scientists and Engineers, Society of Women Engineers

Teams: Chem-E Car, Concrete Canoe Team, Cyber Defense Team, Design-Build-Fly, Efficient Vehicle, FIRST Robotics, Formula SAE, Human-Powered Vehicle, Make It Happen, Maker Lab, Robotics, Rocketry, Rose Grand Prix Engineering, Rose-Hulman Efficient Vehicle Team, Rose Grand Prix Engineering, Team Rose Motorsports

Notable Alumni
Tim Cindric, Andrew Conru, Benjamin Cook, Robert Marks, Abe Silverstein, Mat Thompson, and Bernard Vonderschmitt

ILLINOIS
INDIANA
IOWA
KANSAS
MICHIGAN
MINNESOTA
MISSOURI
NEBRASKA
NORTH DAKOTA
OHIO
SOUTH DAKOTA
WISCONSIN

MIDWEST

UNIVERSITY OF NOTRE DAME

Address: University of Notre Dame, College of Engineering, 257 Fitzpatrick Hall of Engineering, Notre Dame, IN 46556
Website: *https://engineering.nd.edu*
Contact: *https://admissions.nd.edu/visit-engage/request-information/*
Phone: (574) 631-5530
Email: engineer@nd.edu

COST OF ATTENDANCE:

Tuition & Fees: $60,301 | **Addl Exp:** $19,910 | **Total:** $80,211

Financial Aid: https://financialaid.nd.edu/how-aid-works/cost-of-attendance/

ADDITIONAL INFORMATION:

Available Degree(s)
- BS, BS/MS, MS, Ph.D. Aerospace Engineering, Chemical Eng, Civil Engineering, Computer Engineering, Computer Science, Electrical Eng, Environmental Eng, Mechanical Engineering
- Ph.D. Bioengineering, Materials Science & Engineering
- Minors: Bioengineering, Computational Eng, Energy Eng, Energy Studies, Eng Corporate Practice, Environmental Earth Sciences, Resiliency & Sustainability of Engineering Systems

Related Research Areas
Aero-Optics Core Facility, Aerospace Research Lab, Analytical Science, Biophysics Instrumentation Core, Center for Environmental Science & Tech, Chemical Synthesis & Drug Discovery, Chemistry Nitrogen Core, Computer-Aided Molecular Design, Machine Shops, Environmental Research Center, Flow Cytometry, Fluorescence Asst Cell Sorting Core, Genomics & Bioinformatics Core, Helium Recovery & Liquefaction, Integrated Imaging, Exp Ecosystem, Mag Resonance Res Center, Mass Spec & Proteomics, Materials Char, Nanofabrication, Nitrogen Core, MicroCT Facility, Molecular Science & Engineering, Multidisciplinary Eng Research, Radiation Lab/Glassblowing, Turbomachinery Lab

Scholarships Offered
Notre Dame Scholars Program ($25,000/year merit$ for 20 students), Hesburgh-Yusko Scholars Program (350 student scholarships), Notre Dame Stamps Scholarship (full tuition + $12,000 additional money)

Special Opportunities
Engineering Innovation Hub, Grand Challenges Scholars Program, Edison Lecture Series; Integrated Engineering & Business Practices Program, Study Abroad

Orgs: Association for Computing Machinery, American Institute of Aeronautics & Astronautics, American Society of Civil Engineers, American Institute of Chemical Engineers, American Society of Mechanical Engineers, EES, HES, Institute of Electrical & Electronics Engineers, E-NABLE ND, CS for Good, NDSeed, Engineers w/o Borders, National Society of Black Engineers, Society of Hispanic Professional Engineers, Society of Women Engineers, Women in Engineering

Teams: Baja SAE Racing Team, ChemE Car, Chess Club, Concrete Canoe Team, Cyber Threat Competition Team, Debate Team, Design/Build/Fly Team, FIRST Robotics, Notre Dame Hackathons, Hybrid Electric Car, Hydroplane Team, Innovative Robotics & Interactive Systems, Irish Cubesat, I-Robotics, Lego Robotics, Mock Trial, Model United Nations, NASA Student Research Challenge (Dronehook - won 2021), Quiz Bowl, Robotic Football Club, Rocketry Team (NASA Student Launch Competition), Science Olympiad, Solar Car Team, Steel Bridge Team, Unmanned Aerial Vehicle Team (AUVSI SUAS Mission Team)

Notable Alumni
John Burgee, Frank Ching, Marianne Cusato, Anthony Earley, Jr., John Goodwine, Holly Michael, Edward Noonan, and Charles Pell

KETTERING UNIVERSITY

Address: Kettering University, University Communications, 1700 University Avenue, Flint, MI 48504
Website: https://www.kettering.edu/academics/college-engineering
Contact: https://www.kettering.edu/contact-us
Phone: (810) 762-9856
Email: choff@kettering.edu

COST OF ATTENDANCE:
Tuition & Fees: $44,380 | **Addl Expenses:** $14,221 | **Total:** $58,601
Financial Aid: https://www.kettering.edu/admissions-aid/financial-aid

ADDITIONAL INFORMATION:

Available Degree(s)
- BS, BS/MS, MS Chemical Engineering, Computer Engineering, Electrical Engineering, Mechanical Engineering
- MS AI, Industrial Eng, Mobility Systems, Robotic Systems
- Concentrations: Alternative Energy, Automotive Engineering Design, Bioengineering Applications, Machine Design & Advanced Materials, Manufacturing Systems, Mechatronic Systems

Related Research Areas
Advanced Energy Storage & Applications, Advanced Microscopy, Advanced Machines & Power Electronics Design, AI of Things, Autonomous Driving & Artificial Intelligence, Crash Safety, High-Performance Computing Center, High Voltage, Human Interfaces & Ergonomics, Mobility Research, Mobile Systems, Noise, Vibration, and Harshness, Experimental Mechanics, Haptics, Vehicle Controls

Scholarships Offered
Kettering U Merit Scholarship ($8,500 - $17,500) – transcripts/test scores submitted by February 1st; Affinity Scholarship ($3,000); Ford STEM Scholarship; Account Spark STEM Scholarship ($2,500-$10,000 - 2nd generation Arab American students); Oumedian Engineering Scholarship, Ebeid Scholarships, Society of Women Eng Scholarship; American Axle & Manufacturers Scholars Prog, GM STEM Incl Scholarship, BorgWarner Scholars Prog, Lear Scholars Program, Navistar Scholars Program, Endowed Scholarships, Esports Scholarship, KU Coding & Prog Scholarship, KU DECA/BPA/FBLA Scholarship, KU Recognizes Excellence Scholarship, KU Mobility/Vehicle Competition Scholarship, KU Robotics Scholarship

Special Opportunities
Formerly GM Inst of Tech requires students to complete 5+ Co-Ops. Impressive list of internships/co-ops available: 60% of students go from Co-Op to employment upon grad - https://drive.google.com/file/d/1e2vSr1VZceaHOd-blD9o8nuxgXv_V2ac/view. Kettering Univ concentrates on applied learning, insisting on paid internships while attending the University (starting your freshman year).

Kettering Univ is committed to robotics with 20+ years in FIRST and VEX Robotics, a FIRST Comm Center, hosts robotics comp, awards robotics scholarships, & offers robotics programs. Students at Kettering pursue robotic interests in academic programs, compete in collegiate robotics and serve as mentors for K-12 robotic teams.

Teams: Combat Robotics, Esports, and SAE competitions including Formula, Autodrive, Baja and Clean Snowmobiling

Notable Alumni
Mary Barra, Larry Burns, Don Chaffin, Edward Cole, Pete Estes, Jason Forcier, David Hermance, Major Horton, Chet Huber, Tim Lee, Rex Luzader, James McCaslin, F. James McDonald, John Middlebrook, Raj Nair, Marissa Peterson, Robert Reiss, Derica Rice, Dennis Schraeder, Diana Tremblay, and Greg Tyus

ILLINOIS
INDIANA
IOWA
KANSAS
MICHIGAN
MINNESOTA
MISSOURI
NEBRASKA
NORTH DAKOTA
OHIO
SOUTH DAKOTA
WISCONSIN

MIDWEST

MICHIGAN STATE UNIVERSITY

Address: Engineering Building, 428 S. Shaw Lane, East Lansing, MI 48824-1226
Website: *https://www.egr.msu.edu/*
Contact: *https://www.egr.msu.edu/contact-engineering*
Phone: (517) 355-5113
Email: https://www.egr.msu.edu/contact-engineering

COST OF ATTENDANCE:
Tuition & Fees: $16,844 (in-state), $43,674 (out-of-state)
Additional Expenses: $14,984 (in-state), $15,794 (out-of-state)
Total: $31,828 (in-state), $59,468 (out-of-state)

Financial Aid: https://finaid.msu.edu/

ADDITIONAL INFORMATION:
Available Degree(s)
- BS Applied Engineering Science
- BS, BS/MS, MS, Ph.D. Biosystems Engineering, Chemical Engineering, Civil Engineering, Computational Data Science, Computer Engineering, Computer Science, Electrical Eng, Environmental Eng, Materials Sci & Eng, Mechanical Eng
- MS, Ph.D. Biomedical Engineering
- Concentrations: Global Engineering

Related Research Areas
Automotive Research Experiment Station, BEACON Center for the Study of Evolution in Action, Center for Anti-Counterfeiting & Product Protection, Composite Materials & Structures Center, Composite Vehicle Research Center, Fraunhofer Center for Coatings & Diamond Technologies, Great Lakes Bioenergy Research Center

Scholarships Offered
MSU Spartan Advantage Program, MSU Student Aid Grant; Engineering Scholarships are offered with no additional application required. Students receive notice during the first two weeks of April.

The MSU College of Engineering offers more than 300 scholarships to undergrad students each year, and numerous graduate scholarships.

Special Opportunities
CoRe Experience – Integrated first-year living-learning engineering academic program (tutoring, peer mentors, professional & recreational field trips, evening presentations, projects, and service opportunities; Engineering Abroad and Future Engineers programs

Global Core - Information & Communication Technology for Development (applying ICT in developing countries with a field exp

Orgs: Amateur Radio Club, American Ceramic Society, American Chemical Society, American Inst of Chemical Engineers, American Society of Agricultural & Biological Engineers, American Society of Civil Engineers, American Society of Mechanical Engineers, American Institute of Aeronautics & Astronautics, Association for Computing Machinery, Audio Enthusiasts & Eng, Biosystems Engineering Club, Biomedical Society, CSEGA, Environmental Engineering Society, Institute of Electrical & Electronics Engineers, Institute of Food Technologists, Institute of Transportation Engineers, Minerals, Metals, and Materials Society, National Society of Black Engineers, NOBCChE, Spartasoft, Society of Hispanic Professional Eng, Soc of Automotive Engineers, Society of Women Eng, Women in Computing

Teams: Baja Team, Steel Bridge Team, MSU Formula SAE Racing Team, MSU Rocketry, Solar Car Racing, SparaHack, MSU Hackathon

Notable Alumni
Montie Brewer, Louis Carpenter, Rolla Carpenter, Don Jones, Charles Fems, T.A. Heppenheimer, Michael Lamach, and Robert Stempel

---

ILLINOIS

INDIANA

IOWA

KANSAS

MICHIGAN

MINNESOTA

MISSOURI

NEBRASKA

NORTH DAKOTA

OHIO

SOUTH DAKOTA

WISCONSIN

MICHIGAN TECHNOLOGICAL UNIVERSITY

Address: College of Engineering, 712 Minerals and Materials Building, 1400 Townsend Drive, Houghton, Michigan 49931
Website: *https://www.mtu.edu/engineering/*
Contact: *https://www.mtu.edu/engineering/about/contact/*
Phone: (906) 487-2005
Email: engineering@mtu.edu

COST OF ATTENDANCE:

Tuition & Fees: $17,995 (in-state), $40,240 (out-of-state)
Addl Exp: $15,316 | **Total:** $33,311 (in-state), $55,556 (out-of-state)

Financial Aid: https://www.mtu.edu/finaid/

ADDITIONAL INFORMATION:

Available Degree(s)
- BS, MS/MEng, MEng, DEng, Ph.D. Biomedical Engineering, Chem Eng, Civil Eng, Computer Eng, Comp Sci, Electrical Eng, Geological Eng, Materials Science, Mech Eng, Mining Eng
- BS Geospatial Engineering, Robotics Eng, Software Eng
- BS, MS Cybersecurity, Environmental Engineering
- Certificate: Electric Power Engineering
- Minor: Aerospace Eng, Bioprocess Eng, Humanitarian Eng, MechE Tech, Polymer Sci & Eng, Nanoscale Sci & Eng, Naval Systems Engineering, Systems Eng, Tissue & Stem Cell Eng

Related Research Areas
Advanced Power Systems Research Center, Center for Agile & Interconnected Microgrids, Center for Quantum Phenomena, Health Research Institute, Institute of Computing & Cybersystems, Institute of Materials Processing, MTU Aerospace Engineering Research Center, MTU Transportation Inst, Multi-Scale Technologies Institute

Scholarships Offered
Alumni Legacy Award, Eng Technology Scholars, FIRST/VEX Robotics, Intl Ambassador, Leading Scholar Award, National Scholars Program, Presidential Scholars Program, Sponsored Schol., Summer Youth Scholars Award, Transfer Scholarships, Working Families Scholarship

Special Opportunities
Co-Ops, Internship Opportunities; STEM Opportunities in Michigan; Global campus/study abroad. Enterprise Program; K-Day, Winter Carnival, Spring Fling, Parade of Nations

Orgs: American Chemical Society, American Institute of Chemical Engineers, American Institute of Professional Geologists, American Institute of Steel Construction, American Society for Engineering Management, American Society of Civil Engineers, American Society of Mechanical Engineers, Audio Engineering Society, Biomedical Engineering Society, Chemical Engineering Student Advisory Board, Engineers w/o Borders, Institute of Electrical & Electronic Engineers, Materials United, Mind Trekkers, National Society of Black Engineers, Optics & Photonics Society, Society for Environmental Engineers, Society for Mining, Metallurgy & Exploration, Society of Asian Scientists & Engineers, Society of Automotive Engineers, Society of Hispanic Professional Engineers, Society of Women Engineers, Systems Engineering Association, Theme Park Engineering Group

Teams: AutoDrive Challenge (autonomous vehicle design competition), Chem-E Car Team, Concrete Canoe Team, Copper Country Coders, Copper Country Robotics, Cybersecurity Competitions, Formula SAE Team, Hackathons, Keweenaw Rocket Range, Quiz Bowl, Railroad Engineering, SAE Aero Design Team, Satellite Team, Steel Bridge Team

Notable Alumni
Iver Anderson, William Bernard, Jr., Markus Buehler, Melvin Calvin, Paul Fernstrum, Julie Fream, Susan Kiehl, Bhakta Rath, Melvin Visser

ILLINOIS
INDIANA
IOWA
KANSAS
MICHIGAN
MINNESOTA
MISSOURI
NEBRASKA
NORTH DAKOTA
OHIO
SOUTH DAKOTA
WISCONSIN

MIDWEST

UNIVERSITY OF MICHIGAN

Address: Michigan Engineering, 1221 Beal Ave. Ann Arbor, MI 48109-2102
Website: *https://www.engin.umich.edu/*
Contact: *https://www.engin.umich.edu/about/contact-us/*
Phone: (734) 647-7000
Email: engin-info@umich.edu

COST OF ATTENDANCE:

Tuition & Fees: $17,560 (in-state), $55,336 (out-of-state)
Addl Exp: $16,819 | **Total:** $34,379 (in-state), $72,155 (out-of-state)
Financial Aid: https://finaid.umich.edu/

ADDITIONAL INFORMATION:

Available Degree(s)
- BS, BS/MS, MS, Ph.D. Aerospace Engineering, Biomedical Eng, Chemical Eng, Civil Eng, Climate and Meteorology, Computer Eng, Comp Science, Data Science, Electrical Eng, Eng Physics, Environmental Eng, Industrial & Ops Eng, Materials Science & Eng, Mechanical Eng, Naval Architecture & Marine Eng, Nuclear Eng & Radiological Sciences, Robotics, Space Sciences & Eng

Related Research Areas
3D Culture, Automotive Research Center, Center for Entrepreneurship, Center for Ergonomics, Ctr for Solar & Thermal Energy Conversion, Center for Wireless Integrated Microsensing & Systems, Electron Microscope Analysis Lab, Energy Institute, Engineering Education, Immuno-Therapeutics, Ion Beam Lab, Laser Aided Intelligent Manufacturing, Manufacturing Research Center, Michigan Materials Research Institute, Micro-Nanotechnology & Molecular Engineering, Nanofabrication Facility, Naval Engineering, Predictive Integrated Structural Materials Science Center, Transportation Research Institute

Scholarships Offered
International Student Scholarships, Merit Scholarships, Need-Based Scholarships, Study Abroad Scholarship; Approximately 70% of UMich students receive some aid

Ph.D. students receive full funding, which includes a tuition waiver, monthly living stipend, and health insurance.

Special Opportunities
ATLAS Digital, Automotive Future, Alternate Reality Initiative, Alternative Spring Break - Chicago

Orgs: American Soc of Mechanical Eng, Bio-Tech, Entrepreneurship, and Coding Organization, Audio Engineering Society, Blockchain at Michigan, Climate Blue, Eng Elementary Partnerships, Engaging Scientists in Policy & Advocacy, eTrek, FAMNM, Girls Teaching Girls to Code. Genes in Diseases & Systems, INvent, MECC Consulting, MedLaunch, M-Fab, Michigan Transportation Student Org, National Organization for Business & Engineering, Pre-Med Hub, Sling Health

Teams: Aerospace Vehicle Engineering, American Solar Challenge, Autonomous Robotic Vehicle, Autonomous Aerial Vehicles, Baja SAE Racing Team, Concrete Canoe Team, Debate Team, Drone Racing, Electric Boat, Electric Jetski, Formula SAE Electric Car Racing Team, Green Team, HackBlue, Human-Powered Submarine Team, Intl Aerial Robotics, iGEM (Intl Genetically Engineered Mach), Michigan Hackers, NASA Rocket Launching, MESI Environmental Project Team, M-Fly, M-HEAL, Mars Rover Team, MHacks, Mock Trial, Model United Nations, Personal Vertical Flight Competition, Quiz Bowl, Rainworks Challenge, RoboSub Team, Rubik's Cube, Science Olympiad, Steel Bridge Team

Notable Alumni
Frances Allen, Benjamin Bailey, Aisha Bowe, Robert Cailliau, Willian Crossley, Paul Debevec, Tess Hatch, Barbara Johnston, Thomas Knoll, Anne Marinan, Eugene McAllaster, Matthew McKeown, Larry Page, Dan Patt, Steve Sandoval, Claude Shannon, Tia Sutton, and Niklas Zennström

UNIVERSITY OF MINNESOTA, TWIN CITIES

Address: The University of Minnesota, College of Science and Engineering, 117 Pleasant St, Minneapolis MN 55455
Website: *https://cse.umn.edu/*
Contact: *https://cse.umn.edu/college/cse-directories*
Phone: (612) 624-2006
Email: cseinfo@umn.edu

COST OF ATTENDANCE:
Tuition & Fees: $16,108 (in-state), $35,348 (out-of-state)
Addl Exp: $18.500 | **Total:** $34,608 (in-state), $53,848 (out-of-state)
Financial Aid: https://admissions.tc.umn.edu/cost-aid/financial-aid

ADDITIONAL INFORMATION:
Available Degree(s)
- BS, MS, Ph.D. Aerospace Engineering, Mechanical Engineering

Related Research Centers
Center for Compact & Efficient Fluid Power, Drones & Driverless Cars, Earthquake Engineering Simulation, Energy Science Catalytic Materials, Fluid Mechanics Lab, Microelectromechanical Systems, Minnesota Robotics Institute, Multi-Axial Subassemblage Testing Lab, Nanotechnology, Spintronic Materials, Interfaces & Novel Architectures, Plastic Electronics, Renewable Energy

Scholarships Offered
$50 million is awarded in university-wide and major-specific scholarships to freshman applicants each year; no additional form is required for academic scholarships; scholarship opportunities exist for undocumented and international students; 77% of UM students receive some aid.

Special Opportunities
Study Abroad, Volunteer Opportunities; Earthquake Simulation Center, Nanotechnology Lab, First-in-the-World Ultrafast Electron Microscope, Medical Device Center, Fluid Mechanics Lab

Machine shop with fabrication, machining, stainless steel welding, silver soldering, on-site inspection, SolidWorks for Computer Aided Design (CAD), Helium leak detector, & prototype repair equipment. CAD design equipment create machine code for accurate and reproducible results. Available materials include aluminum, brass, copper, stainless steel, and miscellaneous engineering plastics.

Internships, Co-ops, Career Services, Summer Camps, Outreach, and K-12 Enrichment Programs; Engineers w/o Borders

Orgs: American Chemical Society, American Indian Science & Eng Society, American Inst of Aeronautics & Astronautics, Amer Inst of Chemical Eng, APWA, ASABE, American Soc of Civil Eng, American Society of Mechanical Engineers, ASHRAE, ACM, Assoc for Women in Math, Biomedical Engineering Society, Institute of Electrical & Electronics Eng, IISE, Material Advantage, National Society of Black Engineers, oSTEM, Society for Mining, Metallurgy & Exploration, Society of Asian Scientists & Engineers, Society of Hispanic Professional Engineers, SIAM, Society of Women Engineers

Teams: Baja SAE Team, Chem-E Car Team, Chess, Collegiate Drone Sports, Concrete Canoe, Design/Build/Fly Team, Esports, Forensics Team, Gopher Motorsports, iGEM (Intl Genetically Engineered Machines) MinneHack, Minn Electric Racing, Mock Trial, Model United Nations, Quiz Bowl, Robotics Team, Rocket Team, Sales Team Championship, Steel Bridge Team, UMinn Solar Vehicle Proj

Notable Alumni
J Edward Anderson, John Barry, Lloyd Berkner, Arthur Bulbulian, Satish Dhawan, John Eastwood, Robert Gore, Mark Gorenberg, Robert Henle, John Hilliard, Sanjay Mittal, George Prudden, Avtar Saini, Bill Smith, William Stout, and Clarence Syvertson

ILLINOIS
INDIANA
IOWA
KANSAS
MICHIGAN
MINNESOTA
MISSOURI
NEBRASKA
NORTH DAKOTA
OHIO
SOUTH DAKOTA
WISCONSIN

MIDWEST

WASHINGTON UNIVERSITY IN ST. LOUIS

Address: Washington University in St. Louis, McKelvey School of Engineering, MSC: 1100-122-303, 1 Brookings Drive, St. Louis, MO 63130-4899
Website: https://engineering.wustl.edu/
Contact: https://engineering.wustl.edu/about/contact-us.html
Phone: (314) 935-6100
Email: admissions@wustl.edu

COST OF ATTENDANCE:

Tuition & Fees: $60,590 | **Addl Exp:** $22,886 | **Total:** $83,476
Financial Aid: https://financialaid.wustl.edu/

ADDITIONAL INFORMATION:

Available Degree(s)
- BS, MS, Ph.D. Bioinformatics, Chemical Engineering, Electrical Engineering, Energy Engineering, Geochemistry, Mechanical Engineering, Systems Engineering
- Minors: Human-Computer Interaction, Mechatronics, Quantum Engineering, Robotics

Related Research Areas
Boeing Center for Technology & Information Management, Ctr for Air Pollution Impact & Trend Analysis, Center for Collaborative Human-AI Learning and Operation, Ctr for Optimization & Semantic Control, Intl Ctr for Adv Renewable Energy & Sustainability, Ctr for the Space Sciences, NSF Science & Tech Center for Engineering MechanoBiology

Scholarships Offered
Alexander S. Langsdorf Fellowships, Ampersand Scholarships, Annika Rodriguez Scholars Program, Danforth Scholars Program, Enterprise Holdings Scholars Program, James M. McKelvey Undergraduate Research Award, John B. Ervin Scholars Program

WUSTL is Need Blind; WUSTL meets 100% of demonstrated need

Special Opportunities
Study Abroad, Seminars & Events, Cybersecurity Boot Camp, BioEntrepreneurship Core

Orgs: American Institute of Aeronautics and Astronautics, American Institute of Chemical Engineers, American Society of Civil Engineers, American Society of Mechanical Engineers, Association for Computing Machinery, Assoc for Women in Science, Biomedical Engineering Society, Diversity in Clean Energy, Engineering Societies Council, Engineering Test Kitchen, Engineers w/o Borders, Engineering World Health, Girls Who Code, National Society for Black Engineers, oSTEM, Sling Health, Society for Hispanic Professional Engineers, Society for Industrial & Applied Mathematics, Society for Women Engineers, Water Environment Federation, Women in Materials Science & Engineering, Women in Science & Engineering, Women in Computer Science, Young Scientist Program

Teams: CM International Collegiate Programming Contest, AI Genomics Hackathon, ArchHacks, Autonomous Vehicles, Big Ideas Competition, Chess, Collegiate Bridge Bowl Team, Cubesat, Debate Team, Design-Build-Fly, Team, Formula SAE Race Car, GlobalHack, HackWashU, IEEE Drone Competition, iGEM Team (Genetically Engineered Machine), Mock Trial, Model United Nations, NASA CubeSat Team, Quiz Bowl, Rubik's Cube Championship, Solar Decathlon, Vertical Flight Society, Robotics Club, WU Rocketry Team

Notable Alumni
Geoffrey Ballard, Col. Robert Behnken, Lee Harrison III, Marc Kamionkowski, Edwin Krebs, Ben Moreell, Fred Olsen, Michael Phelps, Rob Phillips, Larry Robinson, Michael J. Wendl, Ernst Zinner

---

ILLINOIS

INDIANA

IOWA

KANSAS

MICHIGAN

MINNESOTA

MISSOURI

NEBRASKA

NORTH DAKOTA

OHIO

SOUTH DAKOTA

WISCONSIN

CASE WESTERN RESERVE UNIVERSITY

Address: Case School of Engineering, Nord Hall, Suite 500, 10900 Euclid Avenue, Cleveland, OH 44106
Website: *https://www.engineering.case.edu/*
Contact: *https://engineering.case.edu/about/contact-visit*
Phone: (216) 368-4436
Email: lms159@case.edu

COST OF ATTENDANCE:

Tuition & Fees: $62,234 | **Addl Exp:** $20,784 | **Total:** $81,824
Financial Aid: https://case.edu/financialaid/

ADDITIONAL INFORMATION:

Available Degree(s)
- BS, BS/MS, MS, Ph.D. Aerospace Engineering, Biomedical Engineering, Chemical Engineering, Civil Engineering, Computer Engineering, Computer Science, Data Science & Analytics, Electrical Engineering, Materials Science & Engineering, Mechanical Engineering, Systems & Control Engineering
- Minor Applied Data Science, Artificial Intelligence, Computer Gaming, Electronics, Entrepreneurship, Mechanical Design & Manufacturing

Related Research Areas
Biomechanics & Biomaterials, Energy Storage & Renewable Energy, Energy-Efficient Buildings & Systems, Engineering Mechanics & High-Rate Testing, Fluids & Thermal Sciences, Machine Learning & Data Science, Robotics & Mechatronics, Smart & Sustainable Manufacturing

Scholarships Offered
All first-year applicants are considered for scholarships. Some are based on academic achievement, test scores, leadership, and talent. Scholarships include the University Scholarship, Michelson-Morley STEM Scholarship, Phi Theta Kappa ($20,000 transfer scholarship), Austin E. Knowlton Endowed Memorial Scholarship Fund (Ohio residents)

CWRU meets 100 percent of demonstrated need.

Special Opportunities
Study Abroad, Exchange Programs, Industrial and Governmental Partners; Labs include the Advanced Manufacturing and Mechanical Reliability Center (AMMRC), the Case Metal Processing Laboratory (CMPL), Center for Advanced Polymer Processing (CAPP).

Orgs: American Institute of Chemical Engineers, American Society of Civil Eng, American Society of Mechanical Engineers, Association of Computing Machinery, Amateur Radio Club, Biomedical Engineering Society, Case Engineers Council, CWRU Hacker Society, CWRU MedWish, Humanitarian Design Corps, Institute of Electrical & Electronics Engineers, Macromolecular Student Organization, National Society of Black Engineers, Society of Hispanic Professional Engineers, Society of Professional Engineers, Undergraduate Materials Society, Women in Science & Engineering Roundtable

Teams: Avatar Team (xPrize Foundation), Baja SAE, Battle of the Rockets, Case Rocket Team, Chess, Design for America, CWRU Motorsports, Formula SAE Electric Car Team, Hack CWRU, iGEM (Intl Genetically Engineered Machine) Team, NASA Robotics Mining Competition, National Robotics Challenge, RC Aircraft Team

Notable Alumni
Hans Baumann, Elizabeth Cosgriff-Hernandez, Xyla Foxlin, Donald Glaser, Siegfried Hecker, Bambang Hidayat, Robert Kearns, Lawrence Krauss, Sidney McCuskey, Salvatore Pais, Frederick Reines, John Ruhl

ILLINOIS
INDIANA
IOWA
KANSAS
MICHIGAN
MINNESOTA
MISSOURI
NEBRASKA
NORTH DAKOTA
OHIO
SOUTH DAKOTA
WISCONSIN

MIDWEST

THE OHIO STATE UNIVERSITY

Address: The Ohio State College of Engineering, 122 Hitchcock Hall, 2070 Neil Ave., Columbus, OH 43210
Website: https://engineering.osu.edu/
Contact: https://engineering.osu.edu/about-college/contacts
Phone: (614) 292-2836
Email: howard.1727@osu.edu

COST OF ATTENDANCE:

Tuition & Fees: $12,462 (in-state), $36,698 (out-of-state)
Addl Exp: $18,000 | **Total:** $30,162 (in-state), $55,216 (out-of-state)

Financial Aid: http://undergrad.osu.edu/cost-and-aid/financial-aid

ADDITIONAL INFORMATION:

Available Degree(s)
- BS, MS, Ph.D. Aerospace Engineering, Mechanical Engineering
- BA/BS Aviation (8 core aviation courses, flight training, transportation analysis, airport management + capstone)
- Online Master of Engineering Management, MS Global Engineering Leadership, MS Welding Engineering
- Minor in Humanitarian Engineering

Related Research Centers
Accelerated Maturation of Materials, Advanced Materials & Manuf, Automotive Components, Aviation Research, Carbon Management & Sequestration, Climate, Energy, & the Environment, Computational Mechanics, Corrosion Ctr, Ergonomics, Gas Dynamics & Turbulence, Gas Turbine Lab, Gear & Power Transmission Lab, Industrial Sensors & Measurements, Integrative Materials, Mapping & GIS, Mechatronic/Electromechanical Sys, Occupational Health in Auto Manufacturing, Polar & Climate Research, Propulsion & Power Center, Satellite Positioning & Inertial Navigation, Simulation Innovation & Modeling, Smart Vehicle Concepts Center, Space Geodesy & Remote Sensing, Spatial & Environmental Statistics, Sustainability, Transportation for Tomorrow's Economy, Turbulence & Combustion Research

Scholarships Offered
Approximately 30 scholarships for STEM students with specialized scholarships for minorities and women in engineering. Scholarships to study abroad; Summer Research Fellowships.

Special Opportunities
Co-op and internship opportunities through Buckeye Engineering Career Services (ECS). About 75% of engineering students participate in a co-op or internship before they graduate. Approximately 45% of OSU students receive aid.

Students have access to state-of-the-art facilities: the Scott Lab 080, Honda Interdisciplinary Lab - a 24-hour lab; Engineers w/o Borders; corporate partnerships, & capstone projects; students may participate in student-driven Humanitarian Engineering Innovation Lab to research, design, & solve community problems. Specialized initiatives to collaborate on projects in Japan & Tanzania.

Teams: BajaSAE, Buckeye Solar Racing, Buckeye Space Launch Init, Buckeye Vertical, Chem-E Car, Code 4, Competitive Programming Team, Concrete Canoe, Cyber Security, Design/Build/Fly, EcoCAR Challenge Team, FIRST Robotics, Formula SAE, Maker Club, Science Olympics, Steel Bridge, Tractor Design, Underwater Robotics Team

Notable Alumni
Homer Adkins, James Bobbitt, Jacqueline Chen, Anjan Contactor, Kristen Hammer, Lara Harrington, Charles Kettering, Benjamin Lamme, Maria Martinez, Ralph Mershon, Margaret Mkhosi, Curtis Moody, Jeff Morosky, Jackie O'Brien, Bob Patel, Frederick Patterson, Karl Probst, R. Tom Sawyer, Michael Snyder, and William White

UNIVERSITY OF WISCONSIN, MADISON

Address: University of Wisconsin-Madison, Department of Engineering, 1415 Engineering Drive, Madison, WI 53706
Website: https://engineering.wisc.edu/
Contact: https://directory.engr.wisc.edu/services/staff/
Phone: (608) 262-3471
Email: contact-us@engr.wisc.edu

COST OF ATTENDANCE:

Tuition & Fees: $12,440.92 (in-state), $40,328.92 (out-of-state)
Additional Expenses: $16,764 (in-state), $17,234 (out-of-state)
Total: $29,204.92 (in-state), $57,562.92 (out-of-state)
Financial Aid: https://financialaid.wisc.edu/

ADDITIONAL INFORMATION:

Available Degree(s)
- BS Engineering Mechanics, Engineering Physics, Naval Sci
- BS, MS, Ph.D. Biomedical Eng, Civil Eng, Environmental Engineering, Geological Engineering, Industrial Engineering, Materials Science & Engineering, Mechanical Engineering
- Certificates: Eng for Energy Sustainability, Eng Thermal Energy Systems, Intl Eng, Manufacturing Engineering, Nuclear Engineering Materials, Technical Communication

Related Research Areas
Additive Manufacturing & Design, Advanced Manufacturing, Manufacturing & Production Systems, Mechanics of Materials, Electronic & Quantum Materials, Fusion Science, Materials for Constructed Facilities, Materials for Extreme Environments, Materials Transport, Plasma Science & Fusion Energy, Soft & Hybrid Materials, Structural Engineering

Scholarships Offered
Engineering Freshman Award, Departmental Scholarship Award, LEED Scholars Program, Scholarships for Continuing Students, STAR Scholarship Program. More scholarships are found in the Wisconsin Scholarship Hub (WiSH) which requires a login to access. Approximately half of the freshman class receives aid with an average aid package of approximately $16,000.

Special Opportunities
Grainger Institute for Engineering (Incubator for transdisciplinary research), Engineering Student Council

Facilities: Microelectronics, Nano-Fabrication, Electron Microscopy, Micro-Analysis, Soft Materials Characterization

Orgs: Amateur Radio Society, American Society of Civil Engineers, American Society of Mechanical Engineers, American Society of Heating, Refrigerating and Air-Conditioning Engineers, Construction Club, Business & Entrepreneurship, Engineers for a Sustainable World, Environmental Engineering Club, Insight Washington, Material Ethics Club, Railroad Society, Transcend Engineering, Wisconsin Engineer Magazine

Teams: Autonomous Self-Driving Vehicles, BadgerLoop (pseudo-startup setting), BAJA SAE Team, Clean Snowmobile IC & ZE – SAE, Concrete Canoe Team, Electric Vehicle, Formula SAE, Human-Powered Vehicle, Steel Bridge Team, Robotics Team, Space Race, WiscWind (wind-driven power systems for off-grid applications)

Notable Alumni
Chris Bangle, Robert Bird, Clarence Chamberlin, Chow Chung-Kong, John Clark, Laurel Clark, William Davidson, Michael Dhuey, Louis Friedman, David Geiger, William Harley, Charles Hart, Charles Lindbergh, Parry Moon, Keith Nosbusch, Richard Rhode, Digvijai Singh, Reuben Trane, Patrick Widdick, and Samuel Wonders

ILLINOIS
INDIANA
IOWA
KANSAS
MICHIGAN
MINNESOTA
MISSOURI
NEBRASKA
NORTH DAKOTA
OHIO
SOUTH DAKOTA
WISCONSIN

MIDWEST

CHAPTER 13
REGION THREE
SOUTH

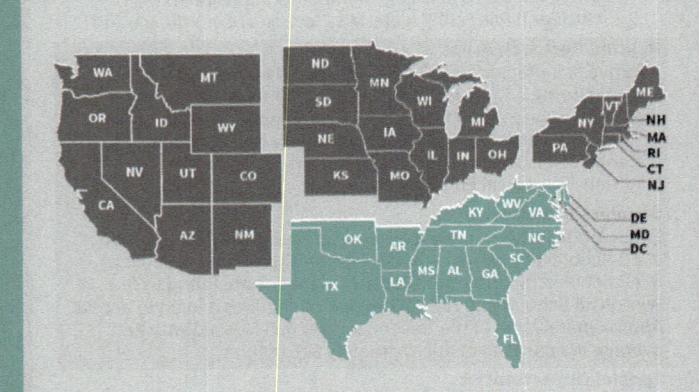

ALABAMA

ARKANSAS

DELAWARE

DISTRICT OF COLUMBIA

FLORIDA

GEORGIA

KENTUCKY

LOUISIANA

MARYLAND

MISSISSIPPI

NORTH CAROLINA

OKLAHOMA

SOUTH CAROLINA

TENNESSEE

TEXAS

VIRGINIA

WEST VIRGINIA

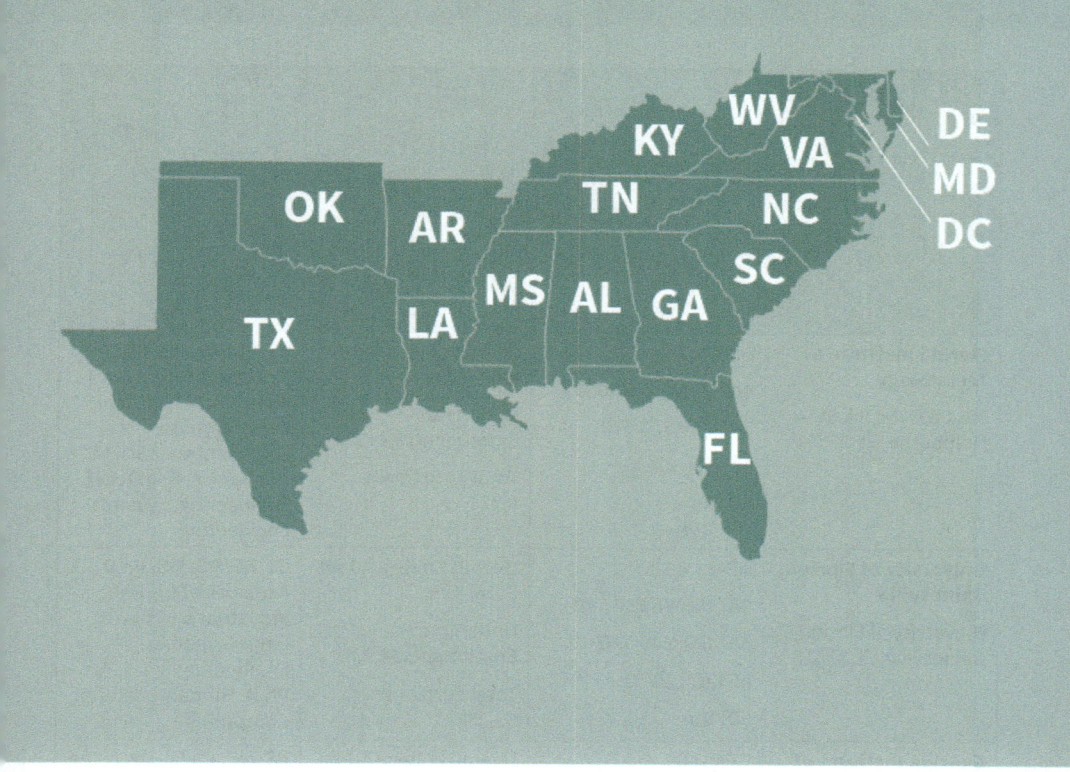

14 Programs | 16 States

1. FL - Florida Institute of Technology
2. FL - University of Florida, Gainesville
3. GA - Georgia Institute of Technology (Georgia Tech)
4. MD - Johns Hopkins University
5. MD - University of Maryland, College Park
6. NC - Duke University
7. NC - North Carolina State University
8. TN - Vanderbilt University
9. TX - Rice University
10. TX - Southern Methodist University
11. TX - Texas A&M University
12. TX - The University of Texas at Austin (UT Austin)
13. VA - University of Virginia, Charlottesville
14. VA - Virginia Tech

MECHANICAL ENGINEERING PROGRAMS

School	Avg. GPA, SAT Evidence-Based Reading Writing (ERW), SAT Math (M), and ACT Composite (C) Early Decision (ED): Yes/No	Admission Statistics	Selected Program(s)
Florida Institute of Technology 3011 S Babcock St, Melbourne, FL 32901	GPA: N/A SAT (ERW): 550-660 SAT (M): 570-670 ACT (C): 23-30 ED: No	Overall College Admit Rate: 69% Undergrad Enrollment: 3,475 Total Enrollment: 6,775	BS, BS/MS, MS, Ph.D. Aerospace Eng, Biomedical Eng, Civil Eng, Computer Eng, Computer Sci, EE, Mechanical Eng Ocean Engineering, Systems Engineering
University of Florida, Gainesville University of Florida, Gainesville, FL 32611	GPA: 3.88 SAT (ERW): 650-720 SAT (M): 640-740 ACT (C): 29-33 ED: No	Overall College Admit Rate: 31% Undergrad Enrollment: 34,931 Total Enrollment: 53,372	BS, BS/MS, MS, Ph.D. Aerospace Eng, BME, Industrial & Systems Eng, Mechanical Engineering Ph.D. Human-Centered Computing
Georgia Institute of Technology (Georgia Tech) Georgia Institute of Technology, North Ave NW, Atlanta, GA 30332	GPA: 4.09 SAT (ERW): 670-740 SAT (M): 700-790 ACT (C): 31-35 ED: No	Overall College Admit Rate: 21% Undergrad Enrollment: 16,561 Total Enrollment: 39,771	BS, MS, Ph.D. Mech Eng & Mechanics BS Nuclear & Radiologic Engineering MS, Ph.D. Nuclear Eng Minors in Aerospace Engineering
Johns Hopkins University 3400 N. Charles St., Mason Hall, Baltimore, MD 21218-2683	GPA: N/A SAT (ERW): 720-760 SAT (M): 750-800 ACT (C): 34-36 ED: Yes	Admit Rate: 11% Undergrad Enrollment: 6,331 Total Enrollment: 28,890	BS, BS/MS, MS, Ph.D. Mechanical Eng MS Bioengineering Innovation & Design, Robotics, Space Sys Eng Systems Eng, Technical Mgmt
University of Maryland, College Park 7999 Regents Dr., College Park, MD 20742	GPA: 4.34 SAT (ERW): 650-730 SAT (M): 680-780 ACT (C): 30-34 ED: No	Admit Rate: 52% Undergrad Enrollment: 30,922 Total Enrollment: 41,272	BS, BS/MS, MS, Ph.D. Aerospace Engineering, Chemical Engineering, Materials Science & Engineering, Mechanical Eng; BS Embedded Systems & Internet of Things

MECHANICAL ENGINEERING PROGRAMS

School	Avg. GPA, SAT Evidence-Based Reading Writing (ERW), SAT Math (M), and ACT Composite (C) Early Decision (ED): Yes/No	Admission Statistics	Selected Program(s)
Duke University Duke University, Durham, NC 27708	GPA: N/A SAT (ERW): 720-770 SAT (M): 750-800 ACT (C): 34-35 ED: Yes	Overall College Admit Rate: 8% Undergrad Enrollment: 6,717 Total Enrollment: 16,172	BS, BS/MS, MS, Ph.D. Mechanical Engineering Minors: Machine Learning, Artificial Intelligence, Energy Engineering
North Carolina State University (NC State) 50 Pullen Road, Raleigh, NC 27695	GPA: 3.8 SAT (ERW): 620-690 SAT (M): 630-730 ACT (C): 27-32 ED: No	Overall College Admit Rate: 46% Undergrad Enrollment: 26,150 Total Enrollment: 36,042	BS Mechanical Eng, Mechanical Engineering Systems, Mechatronics Eng, Aerospace Eng MS, Ph.D. Mechanical Eng, Aerospace Engineering
Vanderbilt University 2305 West End Avenue, Nashville, TN 37203	GPA: 3.86 SAT (ERW): 720-770 SAT (M): 750-800 ACT (C): 33-35 ED: Yes	Admit Rate: 12% Undergrad Enrollment: 7,057 Total Enrollment: 13,537	BS, BS/MS, MS, Ph.D. Mechanical Engineering, Biomedical Eng MS Eng Mgmt, Risk, Reliability, & Resilience Engineering
Rice University 6100 Main Street, Houston, TX 77005	GPA: N/A SAT (ERW): 710-770 SAT (M): 750-800 ACT (C): 34-36 ED: Yes	Overall College Admit Rate: 11% Undergrad Enrollment: 4,076 Total Enrollment: 7,643	BS, BS/MS, MS, Ph.D. Biomedical Engineering, Chemical Engineering, Civil Engineering, Computer Eng, Electrical Eng, Environmental Eng, Materials Science & Nano Engineering, Mechanical Engineering

SOUTH

MECHANICAL ENGINEERING PROGRAMS

School	Avg. GPA, SAT Evidence-Based Reading Writing (ERW), SAT Math (M), and ACT Composite (C) Early Decision (ED): Yes/No	Admission Statistics	Selected Program(s)
Southern Methodist University (SMU) 6425 Boaz Lane, Dallas, TX 75205	GPA: 3.64 SAT (ERW): 640-720 SAT (M): 660-760 ACT (C): 29-33 ED: Yes	Admit Rate: 53% Undergrad Enrollment: 6,827 Total Enrollment: 12,373	BS, BS/MS, MS, Ph.D. Civil Eng, Computer Eng, Comp Sci, Data Science, Electrical Eng, Environmental Eng, Mechanical Eng, Ops Res/Mgmt Science
Texas A&M University 400 Bizzell St, College Station, TX 77843	GPA: N/A SAT (ERW): 580-680 SAT (M): 580-800 ACT (C): 26-32 ED: No	Overall College Admit Rate: 63% Undergrad Enrollment: 55,568 Total Enrollment: 70,418	BS, MS, Ph.D. Civil Eng Environmental Eng Interdisciplinary Eng, Materials Science & Eng, Mechanical Eng, Nuclear Eng, Ocean Eng, Petroleum Eng
The University of Texas at Austin (UT Austin) 310 Inner Campus Drive, Austin, TX 78712	GPA: N/A SAT (ERW): 610-720 SAT (M): 600-750 ACT (C): 26-33 ED: No	Overall College Admit Rate: 32% Undergrad Enrollment: 40,048 Total Enrollment: 50,476	BS, MS, Ph.D. Aerosp. Eng, Architectural Eng, Civil Eng, EE, Enviro Eng, GeoSystems Eng & Hydrogeology, Mechanical Engineering & Petroleum Eng
University of Virginia University of Virginia, Charlottesville, VA 22904	GPA: 4.31 SAT (ERW): 660-740 SAT (M): 660-770 ACT (C): 30-34 ED: Yes	Overall College Admit Rate: 23% Undergrad Enrollment: 17,310 Total Enrollment: 25,628	BS, MS, Ph.D. Aerospace Eng, Civil Engineering, Systems Engineering MS Materials Science & Engineering, Mechanical Engineering
Virginia Tech 1325 Perry Street, Blacksburg, VA 24061	GPA: 3.96 SAT (ERW): 590-680 SAT (M): 580-690 ACT (C): 25-31 ED: Yes	Overall College Admit Rate: 66% Undergrad Enrollment: 30,020 Total Enrollment: 37,024	BS, MS, MEng, Ph.D. Aerospace Engineering, Civil Engineering, EE, Engineering Mechanics, Mechanical Engineering, Meteorology, Ocean Engineering

189

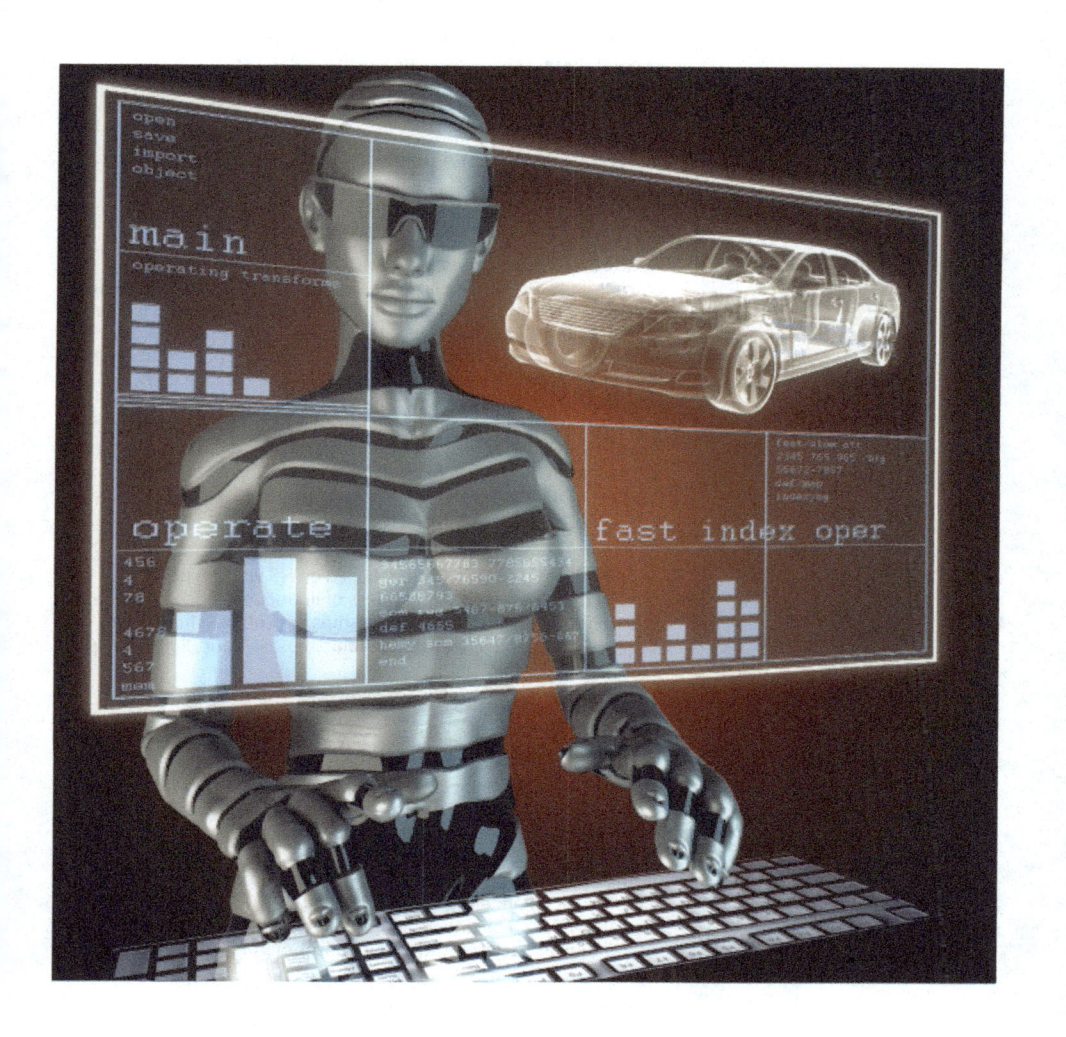

FLORIDA INSTITUTE OF TECHNOLOGY

Address: FIT College of Engineering & Science, 150 W. University Blvd., Melbourne, FL 32901
Website: https://www.fit.edu/engineering-and-science/
Contact: https://www.fit.edu/engineering-and-science/connect-with-us/contact-us/
Phone: (321) 674-8020
Email: https://www.fit.edu/contact/

COST OF ATTENDANCE:

Tuition & Fees: $14,400 | **Addl Exp:** $17,978 | **Total:** $32,378

Financial Aid: https://www.fit.edu/financialaid/

ADDITIONAL INFORMATION:

Available Degree(s)
- BS, BS/MS, MS, Ph.D. Aerospace Engineering, Biomedical Engineering, Civil Engineering, Computer Engineering, Computer Science, Electrical Engineering, Mechanical Engineering, Ocean Engineering, Systems Engineering

Related Research Areas
Astrobiology, Bio-Mechanics Lab, Center for Corrosion & Biofouling Control, Computational Modeling Lab, Computer-Aided Engineering Lab, Center for Advanced Manufacturing & Innovative Design, Dynamic Systems & Controls Lab, Energy Research, Fire Lab, Flight Test Engineering, Fluids & Aerodynamics Lab, Geospace Physics Lab, Human Space Flight Lab, Human-Centered Design Institute, Intelligent Design & Engineering, Internet of Things Security & Privacy Lab, Laser, Optics, & Instrumentation Lab, Massive Binary Stars, Thermal Sciences & Clean Energy Lab, Transportation Systems Engineering, Wind & Hurricane Impact Lab

Scholarships Offered
All domestic applicants a considered for a Panther Fund Merit Scholarship (up to 50% tuition) based on HS wt. GPA plus standardized test scores regardless of financial need, Also offered are Florida Resident Merit Scholarships, Incentive Scholarships, Legacy Scholarships, Transfer Scholarships, Athletic, Scholarships, Florida Tech Grants

Special Opportunities
Hands-On Research, Ortega Telescope, Machine & Welding Shop, Olin Engineering Complex, nearby the Kennedy Space Center

Orgs: American Chemical Society, American Institute of Aeronautics & Astronautics, American Institute of Chemical Engineers, American Society of Civil Engineers, American Society of Mechanical Engineers, Associated Builders & Contractors, Association for Computing Machinery, Astrobiological Research & Education, Biomedical Engineering Society, Society of Automotive Engineers, Society of Ocean Engineers, Marine Biology Society, Student Astronomical Society, Student Organization for Sustainability Action

Teams: Airport Design Competition Team, Baja SAE Team, Concrete Canoe Team, Cubesat, Cybersecurity Club, eSports Teams, FITSEC Cybersecurity Championship Team, Formula Drag Racing Team, Formula SAE Combustion Team, Formula Electric Car Team, Hybrid Rocket Competition Team, Society of Automotive Engineers, Steel Bridge Team, U.S. Cyber Team Member, WxChallenge

Notable Alumni
Albert Crossfield, Wassim Haddad, Joan Higginbotham, Kathryn Hire, David King, Christopher Loria, Julius Montgomery, Mike Moses, Jim Quinn, Frederick Sturckow, Felix Toro, Sunita Williams, George Zamka

UNIVERSITY OF FLORIDA GAINESVILLE

Address: University of Florida, Herbert Wertheim College of Engineering, 300 Weil Hall, 1949 Stadium Road, P.O. Box 116550, Gainesville, FLA 32611-6550
Website: *https://www.eng.ufl.edu/*
Contact: *https://www.eng.ufl.edu/about/contact/*
Phone: (352) 392-0944
Email: info@eng.ufl.edu

COST OF ATTENDANCE:
Tuition & Fees: $6,380 (in-state), $28,658 (out-of-state)
Addl Exp: $15,050 | **Total:** $21,430 (in-state), $43,708 (out-of-state)
Financial Aid: https://www.sfa.ufl.edu/?p=home

ADDITIONAL INFORMATION:
Available Degree(s)
- BS, MS, Ph.D. Aerospace Eng, Mechanical Eng & Mechanics
- BS, BS/MS, MS, Ph.D. Aerospace Engineering, Biomedical Engineering, Industrial & Systems Engineering, Materials Science & Engineering, Mechanical Engineering
- Ph.D. Human-Centered Computing

Related Research Areas
Areas: Dynamics, Systems, & Control, Solid Mechanics, Design, & Manufacturing, Thermal Science & Fluid Dynamics

Scholarships Offered
Bright Futures Scholarship, Florida Assistance Grant, UF Grant, First-Gen Matching Grant

Approximately 90% of incoming freshmen receive aid; grants are awarded for those in need; merit scholarships available; academic scholarships are awarded by academic achievement

Special Opportunities
Study abroad. State-of-the-art facilities include a Biotech lab, prototyping labs, and a global teleconferencing lab.

Orgs: American Institute of Chemical Engineers, American Society of Civil Engineers, American Society of Mechanical Engineers, Biomedical Engineering Society, Engineers w/o Borders, Game Developers' Association, Theme Park Engineering & Design Org, Institute of Electrical and Electronics Engineers, Packaging Club, Power & Energy Club, Society of Automotive Engineers, Society for Environmental Engineers, Society of Women Engineers

Teams: Aggregator Team, Autonomous Maritime System (RobotX Challenge), Battlebots Team, Ceramic Mug Drop Design Team, Chess Club, Concrete Canoe, Concrete Design Team, Cyber Defense Team, Design-Build-Fly Team, Electric Racing/Motorsports Team, Formula SAE Race Car Team, Human-Powered Vehicle Design Team (recumbent bike competition), iGEM Team (International Genetically Engineered Machine), Information Security Team, Liquid Propulsion Development Team, Mock Trial, Model United Nations, Quiz Bowl, Roaring Riptide Robotics, Robotics Teams, Rubik's Cube, Science Olympiad, Solar Gator Formula Sun Grand Prix Team, Space Systems Design Team, Speech & Debate Team, Steel Bridge Team, Swamp Launch Rocket Team, VexU Robotics Team

Notable Alumni
Andrew Allen, John Anderson, Brian Caffo, Amitava Chattopadhyay, Jack Clemons, Jonathan Earle, William Fisher, Kevin Ford, Fitzhugh Fulton, Ronald Garan, Jesse Garrett, Herbert Gursky, Pramod Khargonekar, Donald Mallick, Bill Nelson, Ronald Parise, Anil Rajvanshi, Michael Reynolds, Lesa Roe, Michael Ryschkewitsch, Norman Thagard, James Thompson, Maryly Van Leer Peck, Eva Vertes

ALABAMA
ARKANSAS
DELAWARE
DISTRICT OF COLUMBIA
FLORIDA
GEORGIA
KENTUCKY
LOUISIANA
MARYLAND
MISSISSIPPI
NORTH CAROLINA
OKLAHOMA
SOUTH CAROLINA
TENNESSEE
TEXAS
VIRGINIA
WEST VIRGINIA

SOUTH

GEORGIA TECH

Address: College of Engineering Dean's Office, 225 North Avenue, 3rd Floor Tech Tower, Atlanta, GA 30332-0360
Website: *https://coe.gatech.edu/*
Contact: *https://coe.gatech.edu/about/find-college-engineering*
Phone: (404) 894-3350
Email: rbeyah@coe.gatech.edu

COST OF ATTENDANCE

Tuition & Fees: $10,258 (GA) $31,370 (Non-GA) | **Additional Expenses:** $17,908 | **Total:** $28,166/$49,278

Financial Aid: http://finaid.gatech.edu/

ADDITIONAL INFORMATION:

Available Degree(s)
- BS, MS, Ph.D. Aerospace Eng, Mechanical Eng & Mechanics
- BS Nuclear & Radiological Eng & MS, Ph.D. Nuclear Eng
- MS Medical Physics, Paper Science & Engineering
- Minors in Aerospace Eng, Biomedical Engineering, Global Engineering Leadership, Engineering & Business, Materials Science Engineering, and Nuclear & Radiological Engineering

Related Research Areas
Acoustics/Dynamics, Automation, Robotics & Control, CAE & Design, Center for Nonlinear Sci, Relativistic Astrophysics, Sustainable Sys, Manufacturing Institute, Elect & Nanotech Fluid Mechanics, Health & Humanitarian Sys, Mechanics of Materials, Medical Physics, Micro & Nano Eng, Nuclear & Radiological Eng, People & Tech, Robotics & Intelligent Machines, Renewable Bioproducts Institute, Strategic Energy Institute, Space Technology & Res, Graphics, Visualization, & Usability Center, Research on Active Surfaces & Interfaces, & Tribology

Scholarships Offered
Georgia Tech awards $105+ million in need/merit-based aid to undergrads; 66% rec aid w/an average financial aid pkg of $20,131. The Provost Scholarship awards 40 1st-year, non-resident students an out-of-state tuition waiver for 8 sem. Georgia Tech's 4-year, full-ride Stamps President's Scholarship - top 1% of 1st-year stud. The Gold Scholarship - top 2% of 1st-year students. Also, many in-state students are eligible for the Hope & Zell Miller merit scholarships.

Special Opportunities
Georgia Tech's Co-op Program is a five-year, academic program with paid practical work experience. The Internship Program complements a student's formal education with "real world" applications. Georgia Tech also has a campus in France.

Orgs: Assoc of Enviro Eng & Sci, Amer Soc of Civil Eng, Amer Society of Mechanical Eng, American Soc for Health Care Eng, Construction Engineering Association, Earthquake Engineering Research Institute, Engineers for a Sustainable World, Engineers w/o Borders, Geotechnical Society, Institute of Transportation Engineers, Water Environment Federation, Women's Transportation Seminar

Teams: ASME-CIE Hackathon, Chem-E Car Team, Cubesat, Debate Team, GT Motorsports, HyTech Racing (Formula SAE), GT Off-Road (Baja SAE), GT Solar Racing, EcoCAR (EcoCAR Mobility Challenge), iGEM (International Genetically Engineered Machines), Mock Trial, Model United Nations, Robotics (7 world competitions), Wreck Racing (Grassroots Motorsports Challenge), a top team in the National Security Innovation Network's Visualization Cyber Ops Hackathon

Notable Alumni
Eric Boe, Joe Brooks, Michael Clifford, Wallace Coulter, Jan Davis, James Deese, Ben Epps, Gabriel Georgiades, Don Giddens, Samuel Graham, John Jureit, Dean Kamen, Susan Kilrain, Timothy Kopra, Sandra Magnus, Michel Malti, William McArthur, Gary May, Lane Mitchell, Bryan Nesbitt, Richard Truly, B.N. Wilson, and John Young.

ALABAMA
ARKANSAS
DELAWARE
DISTRICT OF COLUMBIA
FLORIDA
GEORGIA
KENTUCKY
LOUISIANA
MARYLAND
MISSISSIPPI
NORTH CAROLINA
OKLAHOMA
SOUTH CAROLINA
TENNESSEE
TEXAS
VIRGINIA
WEST VIRGINIA

JOHNS HOPKINS UNIVERSITY

Address: Johns Hopkins University, Whiting School of Engineering, 3400 North Charles Street Baltimore, MD 21218
Website: *https://engineering.jhu.edu/*
Contact: *https://engineering.jhu.edu/contact/*
Phone: (410) 516-4050
Email: wsecommunications@jhu.edu

COST OF ATTENDANCE:
Tuition & Fees: $60480 | **Addl Exp:** $21,005 | **Total:** $81,485
Financial Aid: https://www.jhu.edu/admissions/financial-aid/

ADDITIONAL INFORMATION:

Available Degree(s)
- BS, BS/MS, MS, Ph.D. Mechanical Engineering
- MS/MSE Bioengineering Innovation & Design, Cybersecurity, Data Science, Engineering Management, Robotics, Security Informatics, Space Systems Engineering, Systems Engineering, Technical Management

Related Research Areas
Additive Manufacturing & Architected Materials, Cold-Formed Steel, Computational Sensing & Robotics., Environmental & Applied Fluid Mechanics, Hopkins Extreme Materials Institute, Integrated Structure-Materials Modeling & Simulation, Materials in Extreme Dynamic Environments, Sustainable Energy Institute

Scholarships Offered
JHU meets 100% need; most of the grants are need-based including the Clark Scholarship & Hodson Gilliam Success Scholarship; merit-based awards include The Hodson Trust Scholarship, Charles R. Westgate Scholarship in Engineering, National Fellowships Program, ROTC

Special Opportunities
Design Studios for prototyping, building, testing products (aesthetic, financial, material, theoretical, environmental, and practical); JHU Engineering Design Day

Orgs: American Institute of Chemical Engineers, American Society of Civil Engineers, American Society of Mechanical Engineers, Association for Computing Machinery, Civil & Systems Engineers Graduate Association, Earthquake Engineering Research Center, Engineers' Council, Engineers w/o Borders, Habitat for Humanity, National Society of Black Engineers, oSTEM, Students for the Exploration & Development of Space, Society for Biological Engineering, Society of Hispanic Professional Engineers, Society of Women Engineers, Women in Computer Science, WoMEn

Teams: AstroJays, Blue Jay Racing Team, BME Healthcare Design Team, Chem-E Car Competition, Collegiate Inventors Competition, Concrete Canoe Team, Cubsat Team, Design-Build-Fly, Freshman Mechanical Engineering Design Competition, HopHacks, Hopkins Baja, HopStart Competition, Humanitarian Design Hackathon, IDIES Hackathon, IEEEXtreme Programming Competition, Information Security Institute Competition, JHU Business Plan Competition, JHU Robo Challenge, Leading Innovation Design Team, MedHacks, Mock Trial, Model United Nations, Quiz Bowl, Robotics Team, Rocketry Competition, Rubik's Cube, Science Olympiad, Steel Bridge Team, Sustainable Solutions Competition, Tower of Power Competition, Unmanned Aerial Vehicle Team

Notable Alumni
Frederick Billig, Jared Cohon, William George, Ellis Johnson, Joeng Kim, George Nemhauser, Nina Patel, Richard Potember, Erika Taylor, Michael Thomas, Reid Wiseman, Bang Wong

ALABAMA
ARKANSAS
DELAWARE
DISTRICT OF COLUMBIA
FLORIDA
GEORGIA
KENTUCKY
LOUISIANA
MARYLAND
MISSISSIPPI
NORTH CAROLINA
OKLAHOMA
SOUTH CAROLINA
TENNESSEE
TEXAS
VIRGINIA
WEST VIRGINIA

SOUTH

UNIVERSITY OF MARYLAND, COLLEGE PARK

Address: University of Maryland, 3110 Jeong H. Kim Engineering Building, 8228 Paint Branch Dr., College Park, MD 20742
Website: https://eng.umd.edu/
Contact: https://eng.umd.edu/contact
Phone: (301) 405-8335
Email: futureengineer@umd.edu

COST OF ATTENDANCE:

Tuition & Fees: $11,232 (in-state), $39,468 (out-of-state)
Addl Exp: $18,404 | **Total:** $29,636 (in-state), $57,872 (out-of-state)

Financial Aid: https://financialaid.umd.edu/

ADDITIONAL INFORMATION:

Available Degree(s)
- BS, BS/MS, MS, Ph.D. Aerospace Engineering, Chemical Eng, Materials Science & Engineering, Mechanical Engineering
- BS Embedded Systems & Internet of Things
- MS Fire Protection Engineering, Systems Engineering
- MS, Ph.D. Reliability Engineering
- MS, MEng, Ph.D. Project Management

Related Research Areas
Bridge Engineering Software & Tech Center, Ctr for Adv Life Cycle Eng, Ctr for Adv Transportation Tech, Ctr for Disaster Resilience, Center for Engineering Concepts Development, Center for Minorities in Sci & Eng, Ctr for Risk & Reliability, Center for Tech & Systems Mgmt, Rotorcraft Ctr Inst for Systems Research, MD NanoCenter, MD Robotics Center, MD Transportation Institute, Center for Harmonic Analysis & Appl

Scholarships Offered
Ave need-based scholarship - $11,838. Merit Scholarships -apply by Nov 1; Banneker/Key Scholarship – Full tuition, room/board, fees, book allowance, & admit to Honors College; President's Scholarship – 4-yr awards ($2,000 - $12,500) for in-state & out-of-state students; Dean's Scholarship ($1,500 - $4,500) only for in-state students.

Special Opportunities
Alternative Spring Break, Workshops; Keystone Program. Pre-college and K-12 programs; State-of-the-art labs & centers.

Orgs: American Inst of Aeronautics & Astronautics, American Inst of Chemical Engineers, American Helicopter Society, American Society of Civil Engineers, American Society of Engineers of Indian Origin, American Society of Mechanical Eng, ASHRAE, Asian Engineering Students Association, Black Engineers Society, Biomedical Engineering Society, Electrochemical Society, Eng Student Council, Engineers w/o Borders, Engineering World Health, Inst of Electrical & Electronics Eng, Net Impact STEM, oSTEM, Society of Asian Scientists & Eng, Society of Automotive Eng, Society of Fire Protection Eng, Society of Hispanic Professional Eng, MatES, Society of Women Engineers, Undergrad Quantum Association, Women in Aeronautics & Astronautics, Women in Electrical and Computer Engineering

Teams: Autonomous Micro Air Vehicle, Chem-E Car, Concrete Canoe Team, Cybersecurity Team, FIRST Robotics, Formula SAE Teams, Helicopter Design Comp Team, Hovercraft Competition, Hyperloop Team, iGEM Team (International Genetically Engineered Machines), Info Challenge Competition, Info Challenge Summer Camp for HS Students, Robotics@Maryland, Robotic Exploration of Solar System (RASC-AL), Solar Decathlon, Steel Bridge Team, Terps Racing, Terps Hackers, Rocket Team

Notable Alumni
Richard Arnold, Frederick Billig, Sergey Brin, James Clark, Jeanette Epps, Michael Griffin, Chris Kubasik, Tobin Marks, William McCool, Judith Resnik, Paul Richards, Alex Severinsky, and Barbara Williams

---

ALABAMA
ARKANSAS
DELAWARE
DISTRICT OF COLUMBIA
FLORIDA
GEORGIA
KENTUCKY
LOUISIANA
MARYLAND
MISSISSIPPI
NORTH CAROLINA
OKLAHOMA
SOUTH CAROLINA
TENNESSEE
TEXAS
VIRGINIA
WEST VIRGINIA

DUKE UNIVERSITY

Address: Pratt School of Engineering, Duke University, 305 Nello L. Teer Engineering Building, Box 90271, Durham, NC 27708-0271
Website: https://pratt.duke.edu/
Contact: https://pratt.duke.edu/directory
Phone: (919) 660-5386
Email: prattdeansoffice@duke.edu

COST OF ATTENDANCE:

Tuition & Fees: $62,973 | **Addl Exp:** $18,364 | **Total:** $81,337

Financial Aid: https://financialaid.duke.edu/

ADDITIONAL INFORMATION:

Available Degree(s)
- BS, BS/MS, MS, Ph.D. Mechanical Engineering
- Minors: Machine Learning, Artificial Intelligence, Energy Engineering

Related Research Areas
Aerospace/Transp. Vehicle Industries, Mechanics & Biomechanics, Nonlinear Dynamics & Control, Thermal & Fluids Systems

Scholarships Offered
At Duke, 21% of the first-year class attends tuition-free and meets 100% of their demonstrated need. Other expenses include study away, summer study, and equipment. Merit scholarships are awarded by the Office of Undergraduate Financial Aid, with input from the Pratt School of Engineering.

A.James Clark Scholars (10 4-year scholarships), Baquerizo Innovation Grant ($20,000 grants)

Special Opportunities
Duke-In Global Education – 6 continents, Intl Internships & Research

Student Founders - Innovation Venture Program, Duke Innovation & Entrepreneurship Institute, Duke Engineering Entrepreneurship (Signature Undergraduate Experience) – develop an entrepreneurial mindset with advice, education, resources, & connections

Orgs: American Institute of Aeronautics & Astronautics, American Institute of Chemical Engineers, American Society of Civil Engineers, American Society of Mechanical Engineers, Assoc for Computing Machinery, Biomedical Engineering Society, Duke Aviators, Duke Conservation Tech, Duke Undergrad Machine Learning, Engineering Student Government, Engineering World Health, Engineering & Science, Engineers w/o Borders, Females Excelling More in Math, Girls Engineering Change, Institute of Electrical & Electronics Engineers, National Society of Black Engineers, Pratt Peer Advisors, Quantum Information Society, Society of Hispanic Professional Engineers, Society of Women Engineers, Tech for Equity

Teams: Academy for Model Aeronautics, Chess, Combat Robotics, Design for America, Duke Electric Vehicles, DukEngineer Magazine, Duke Engineers for International Development, Duke Hyperloop, Duke Motorsports Team, eNable, HackDuke, Innoworks, MEDesign, Project Tadpole, Mock Trial, Model United Nations, Quiz Bowl, Robotics Team, Runway of Dreams, Science Olympiad, Smart Home

Notable Alumni
Luis von Ahn, Adrian Bejan, Jack Bovender, Jr., John Browne, Lewis Campbell, George Church, Daniel Clancy, Tim Cook, Eddy Cue, William DeVries, Fred Ehrsam, William Hawkins, Mark Humayun, Robert Malkin, Aubrey McClendon, Terry Myerson, Peter Nicholas, Victoria Nneji, Edmund Pratt, Jr., Bert O'Malley, Olaf von Ramm, Rick Wagoner, Jeff Williams, R. Sanders Williams, and Blake Wilson

ALABAMA
ARKANSAS
DELAWARE
DISTRICT OF COLUMBIA
FLORIDA
GEORGIA
KENTUCKY
LOUISIANA
MARYLAND
MISSISSIPPI
NORTH CAROLINA
OKLAHOMA
SOUTH CAROLINA
TENNESSEE
TEXAS
VIRGINIA
WEST VIRGINIA

SOUTH

NORTH CAROLINA STATE UNIVERSITY

Address: North Carolina State College of Engineering, Fitts-Woolard Hall, 915 Partners Way, Raleigh, NC 27695-7901
Website: *https://www.engr.ncsu.edu/*
Contact: *https://www.engr.ncsu.edu/about/contact/*
Phone: (919) 515-3263
Email: engineering@ncsu.edu

COST OF ATTENDANCE:

Tuition & Fees: $9,128 (in-state), $30,869 (out-of-state)
Addl Exp: $16,700 | **Total:** $25,752 (in-state), $47,757 (out-of-state)

Financial Aid: https://studentservices.ncsu.edu/your-money/financial-aid/

ADDITIONAL INFORMATION:

Available Degree(s)
- BS Aerospace Engineering, Mechanical Engineering, Mechatronics Engineering
- MS, Ph.D. Aerospace Engineering, Mechanical Engineering

Related Research Centers
Accelerated Real-Time Analytics, Additive Manufacturing & Logistics, Advanced Analytics, Broadband Wireless Access & Applications, Clean Energy Tech, Dielectrics & Piezoelectrics, Environmental & Human Health Effects, Environmental Policy, Ergonomics, Geospatial Analytics, Highway Safety, Next Gen Power Electronics, Power Engineering, Renewable Electric Energy Delivery & Management, Self-Powered Systems of Sensors & Technologies, Smart Manufacturers Innovation Institute, Textile Protection & Comfort, Transportation Research & Education

Scholarships Offered
Scholarships available through PackAssist. Freshman engineering scholarships: Park Scholarship, General Hugh Shelton Leadership Initiative Scholarship, Chancellor's Leadership Scholarship, Goodnight Scholars Prog; Caldwell Fellows Prog for cont students.

Special Opportunities
The Engineering Place & summer camp for K-12 students are held on campus. Academic enrichment includes the Living/Learning Villages and the Grand Challenges-Focused Research Experiences for Teachers (RET) with Stratified Teaming Program; Design Day

NCSU's Clean Energy Center offers students opportunities to incorporate renewable energy, clean power, industrial efficiencies, clean transp, policy options, & sustainability into their projects.

Orgs: Air/Waste Management Association, American Concrete Inst, American Indian Science & Engineering Society, American Railway Engineers, American Society of Civil Engineers, American Society of Mechanical Engineers, ASHRAE, Amer Water Research Assoc, Assoc Gen Contractors, CEGSA, Coasts, Oceans, Ports & Rivers Institute, Earthquake Eng Research Inst, Eng Ambassadors, Eng Entrepreneurs Program, Engineers w/o Borders, Engineers' Council, Institute Transportation Engineers, American Society of Highway Engineers, National Association of Home Builders, National Society of Black Engineers, Society of Asian Scientists & Eng, Society of Hispanic Professional Eng, Society of Women Engineers, Student Energy Club

Teams: Aerial Robotics, AquaPack Robotics (Underwater Vehicle) Biome Robotics, Concrete Canoe Team, Esports Team, HackPack, High-Powered Rocketry, Pack Motorsports Team, Rubik's Cube, SolarPack (Sun Grand Prix), Steel Bridge Team, VEXU Robotics Team

Notable Alumni
Mechanical - Anthony Barr, James Goodnight, Terry Hershner, Dean Kamen, Christina Koch, Hal Lawton, Jackie Moreland, James Owens, Rajendra Pachauri, Katharine Stinson, and Gregory Washington

---

ALABAMA
ARKANSAS
DELAWARE
DISTRICT OF COLUMBIA
FLORIDA
GEORGIA
KENTUCKY
LOUISIANA
MARYLAND
MISSISSIPPI
NORTH CAROLINA
OKLAHOMA
SOUTH CAROLINA
TENNESSEE
TEXAS
VIRGINIA
WEST VIRGINIA

VANDERBILT UNIVERSITY

Address: Vanderbilt University, School of Engineering, 2301 Vanderbilt Place, PMB 351826, Nashville, TN 37235-1826
Website: *https://engineering.vanderbilt.edu/*
Contact: *https://engineering.vanderbilt.edu/contact/*
Phone: (615) 343-3773
Email: Michele.bender@vanderbilt.edu

COST OF ATTENDANCE:
Tuition & Fees: $63,991 | **Addl Exp:** $25,064 | **Total:** $89,005
Financial Aid: https://www.vanderbilt.edu/financialaid/

ADDITIONAL INFORMATION:
Available Degree(s)
- BS, BS/MS, MS, Ph.D. BME, ChemE, Mechanical Engineering
- MS Engineering Mgmt, Risk, Reliability, & Resilience Engineering, Surgery & Intervention
- Minors: Comp Sci, Data Sci, Digital Fabr, Electrical & Comp Eng Energy & Enviro Sys, Eng Mgmt, EnviroEng, Materials Sci & Eng, Nanoscience & Nanotech, Scientific Computing

Related Research Areas
Adv Robotics & Mechanism Appl, Assistive Tech, Electro-Mechanical Devices, Robot Architectures, Micro/Macro Telemanipulators, Modeling Cardiovascular System, Multiscale Modeling & Simulation Center, Nanotech, Piezoelectrically-Actuated Small-Scale Mobile Robots, Rehabilitation, Risk, Reliability, & Resilience, Space & Defense Systems, Transportation & Operational Resiliency

Scholarships Offered
250 Merit-Based Scholarship Winners/year - Apply after submitting application: Ingram Scholars (Due Dec 1 – Full Tuition) civic-minded service, innovation, entrepreneurial spirit, & leadership; Cornelius Vanderbilt Scholarship (Dec 1 – Full Tuition) - outstanding academic achievement with strong leadership and contributions outside the classroom; Chancellor's Scholarship (Dec 1 – Full Tuition) - bridging gaps among economically, socially, & racially diverse groups & demonstrated significant interest in issues of diversity education, tolerance, & social justice; Carell Family Scholarship for students who worked PT in HS and demonstrate need (Full Tuition); Clark Scholars Program - $15,000/year + summer aid for engineering students; Curb Leadership Scholarship - $8,000/year – creative students transforming communities; John Seigenthaler Scholarship

Special Opportunities
Freshman Mentor Program, Internships, Robotics, Study Abroad

Orgs: American Society of Civil Engineers, American Society of Mechanical Engineers, American Institute of Chemical Eng, Assoc Society of Metals, Association of Computing Machinery, Biomedical Engineering Society, Engineering Council, Engineers w/o Borders, Engineering World Health, Institute of Electrical & Electronics Eng, International Society of Optics & Photonics, National Society of Black Eng, Society of Automotive Eng, Society of Hispanic Professional Eng, Society of Engineering Science, Society of Women Engineers

Teams: Aerospace Design Team, Concrete Canoe, Cubesat, Data Science, Debate Team, Formula SAE Electric Vehicle, iGEM (Intl Genetically Engineered Machine), Mock Trial, Model United Nations, Motorsports, Quiz Bowl, Robotics Team, Rubik's Cube, Steel Bridge Team, Vanderbilt Rocketry (NASA Student Launch Competition)

Notable Alumni
James L Barnard, Bob Boniface, Yvonne Clark, Baratunde Cola, William Davis Jr., Eric Eidsness, Jordan French, Kenneth Galloway, Michael Gernhardt, G. Scott Hubbard, Param Jaggi, William Lucas, Thiago Olson, Philip Porter, J. Robert Sims, and Li Yang

ALABAMA
ARKANSAS
DELAWARE
DISTRICT OF COLUMBIA
FLORIDA
GEORGIA
KENTUCKY
LOUISIANA
MARYLAND
MISSISSIPPI
NORTH CAROLINA
OKLAHOMA
SOUTH CAROLINA
TENNESSEE
TEXAS
VIRGINIA
WEST VIRGINIA

SOUTH

RICE UNIVERSITY

Address: George R. Brown School of Engineering, MS-364, P.O. Box 1892, Houston, Texas 77251-1892
Website: https://engineering.rice.edu/
Contact: https://engineering.rice.edu/about/contact-rice-engineering
Phone: (713) 348-4955
Email: engrnews@rice.edu

COST OF ATTENDANCE:
Tuition & Fees: $54,960 | **Addl Exp:** $19,150 | **Total:** $74,110

Financial Aid: https://financialaid.rice.edu/

ADDITIONAL INFORMATION:

Available Degree(s)
- BS, BS/MS, MS, Ph.D. Biomedical Engineering, Chemical Engineering, Civil Engineering, Computer Engineering, Electrical Engineering, Environmental Engineering, Material Science & Nano Engineering, Mechanical Engineering

Related Research Areas
Alliance for Innovation & Entrepreneurship, Atomic & Molecular Collisions Group, Climate Water & Energy Lab, Computational Science, Computer-Aided Programing@Rice, Computer Security, Digital Signal Processing, Electron Microscopy Center, Environmental & Applied Geophysics, Experimental Petrology, Hazardous Substances Research, Integrated Systems & Circuits Lab, Laser Cooling & Trapping of Atoms, Mechatronics & Haptic Interfaces Lab, Nanophotonics Lab, Robots for Hazardous Environments Group, Seismic Data Processing, Severe Storm Prediction, Space Institute, Transformation of Data to Knowledge

Scholarships Offered
Eligible students with family incomes below $75,000 receive grant aid covering at least their full tuition, mandatory fees, room and board; students with family incomes between $75,000 and $140,000 receive grants covering at least full tuition; and students with family incomes between $140,000 and $200,000 receive grants covering at least half of their tuition.

Special Opportunities
Rice has 11 self-governing residential colleges w/living, dining, and activities. A faculty member & spouse serve as liaisons w/the univ, cultivating student interests in activities, & eating w/the students.

Traditions: Beer Bike (bike race), Hello Hamlet, Sallyport, Baker 13, research, service, Rice 'Jacks' (pranks), Valhalla - 'hobbit hole', "Gratuitous Friday Cheer", Honor Code

Orgs: American Chemical Society, American Institute of Chemical Eng, American Society of Civil Engineers, Amer Society of Mech Eng, Biomedical Engineering Society, CSters: Women in Computing, Design for America, DREAM, Engineers w/o Borders, GoBabyGo (Power Wheels), Institute of Electrical & Electronics Eng, Materials Science & Nanoengineering Undergrad Society, National Society of Black Engineers, oSTEM, Computer Science Club, Robotics Club, ShELECs, Society of Asian Scientists & Engineers, Society of Hispanic Professional Eng, Society of Petroleum Engineers, Society of Women Engineers, Students for the Exploration & Development of Space

Teams: Concrete Canoe Team, Electric Vehicle Team, Esports OwlNest, FIRST Robotics, HackRice, Hyperloop Team, SpaceX Hyperloop Pod Competition, Owl Cubesat, Rocketry Team

Notable Alumni
Kwatsi Alibaruho, Brian Armstrong, Jay Bailey, John Bull, Takao Doi, Mark Durcan, Wanda Gass, Wayne Hale, Howard Hughes, Tamara Jernigan, Howard Johnson, Larry Lake, James Newman, John Olivas, Fred Stalkup, Janice Voss, Shannon Walker, Peggy Whitson

SOUTHERN METHODIST UNIVERSITY

Address: Southern Methodist University, Lyle School of Engineering, PO Box 750339, Dallas, TX 75205
Website: https://www.smu.edu/lyle
Contact: https://www.smu.edu/Lyle/About-Lyle/Get-in-Touch
Phone: (214) 768-3050
Email: dean@lyle.smu.edu

COST OF ATTENDANCE:

Tuition & Fees: $61,980 | **Addl Exp:** $21,226 | **Total:** $83,206

Financial Aid: https://www.smu.edu/EnrollmentServices/FinancialAid

ADDITIONAL INFORMATION:

Available Degree(s)
- BS, BS/MS, MS, Ph.D. Civil Engineering, Computer Engineering, Computer Science, Data Science, Electrical Engineering, Environmental Engineering, Mechanical Engineering, Operations Research/Management Science
- MS Cybersecurity, Data Engineering, Datacenter Systems Engineering, Information Engineering & Management, Network Engineering, Software Engineering, Systems Eng

Related Research Areas
AT&T Center for Virtualization, Center for Engineering Leadership, Institute for Cyber Security, Institute for Engineering & Humanity, Research Center for Advanced Manufacturing

Additive Manufacturing, Automation, Bio-Micro-Nano-Fluidics, Dynamic Behavior of Materials & Structures, Fluid Dynamics, Materials Testing, Mechanics of Materials, Nanotechnology, Robotics, Solid & Structural Mechanics

Scholarships Offered
77% of undergraduates receive financial aid

Merit scholarships include the President's Scholars Program which provides full tuition and fees as well as study abroad; Hunt Leadership Scholars Program $46,000/year plus airfare & tuition for international leadership-based experience (additional essay required); Founders', Second Century Scholarship, SMU Distinguished Scholarship, and Provost Scholarships are awarded students who demonstrated outstanding academic success.

Special Opportunities
SMU-in-Taos, with skiing, hiking, and a stunning New Mexico forest backdrop, engages the body, mind, and spirit. Small class sizes and a "classroom without walls" philosophy encourages deep dives into subjects w/tight bonds with faculty and classmates.

JanTerm (France, Morocco, Spain), MayTerm, Summer Term

Laser Micromachining, Laser Materials Processing Lab, Micro Sensing Devices, Porous Media Systems Lab

Orgs: American Society of Civil Engineers, Artificial Intelligence Club, Biomedical Engineering Society, Business in Healthcare Club, Computer Science Club, Cyber Security, Debate, Engineers w/o Borders, Entrepreneurship Club, Global Medical Brigades, National Society of Black Engineers, SciFi Buddies, Society of Hispanic Professional Eng, Society of Women Eng, Women in Science & Eng

Teams: Debate and Speech, Drone Competition Team, eSports, Formula SAE, Mock Trial, Robotics Team, Mustang Rocketry

Notable Alumni
John Christmann, Michael Bunnell, Alex Cruz, C. David Cush, Donald Holmquest, Thomas Horton, Jack James, Jerry Junkins, and Paul Loyd, Jr.

ALABAMA
ARKANSAS
DELAWARE
DISTRICT OF COLUMBIA
FLORIDA
GEORGIA
KENTUCKY
LOUISIANA
MARYLAND
MISSISSIPPI
NORTH CAROLINA
OKLAHOMA
SOUTH CAROLINA
TENNESSEE
TEXAS
VIRGINIA
WEST VIRGINIA

SOUTH

ALABAMA
ARKANSAS
DELAWARE
DISTRICT OF COLUMBIA
FLORIDA
GEORGIA
KENTUCKY
LOUISIANA
MARYLAND
MISSISSIPPI
NORTH CAROLINA
OKLAHOMA
SOUTH CAROLINA
TENNESSEE
TEXAS
VIRGINIA
WEST VIRGINIA

TEXAS A&M UNIVERSITY

Address: Zachry Engineering Education Complex, 125 Spence St., Suite 481, 3127 TAMU, College Station, TX 77843-3127
Website: *https://engineering.tamu.edu/*
Contact: *https://engineering.tamu.edu/contact/index.html*
Phone: (979) 845-7200
Email: easa@tamu.edu

COST OF ATTENDANCE:

Tuition & Fees: $13,406.30 (in-state), $41,291.60 (out-of-state)
Additional Expenses: $18,950 (in-state) $20,350 (out-of-state)
Total: $32,356.30 (in-state), $61,641.60 (out-of-state)

Financial Aid: https://financialaid.tamu.edu/

ADDITIONAL INFORMATION:

Available Degree(s)
- BS, MS, Ph.D. Aerospace Eng, Biological & Agricultural Eng, BME, Chemical Eng, Civil Eng, Comp Eng, Computer Science, Electrical Eng, Environmental Eng, Industrial Engineering, Interdisciplinary Engineering, Materials Science & Eng, Mechanical Eng, Nuclear Eng, Ocean Eng, Petroleum Eng
- Minor: Cybersecurity, Game Design & Development

Related Research Centers
Algorithms, Artificial Intelligence, Computational Fabrication, Computer Architecture, Computer Vision, Cyber-Physical Systems, Cybersecurity, Electronic Design Automation & VSLI, Embedded Systems, Gaming, Graphics & Visualization, Health, Human-Ctrd Sys, Human-Computer Interactions, Human-Robot Connections, Intelligent Sys, Machine Learning, Robotics, Technical Reporting

Scholarships Offered
20+ Endowed Engineering/Comp Sci/Data Sci Scholarships, Travel Grants, Continuing Student Scholarships, Corporate-Sponsored Scholarships; 81% receive aid; 64% receive grants or scholarships

Special Opportunities
Orgs: 12th Astronaut Lab, Aggie Aerospace Women in Engineering, AggieSat Lab, Aggies Communicate through Engineering, Aggie Club of Eng, American Institute of Aeronautics & Astronautics, American Concrete Institute, American Society of Civil Engineering, American Society of Mechanical Engineers, American Water Resources Assoc, Association of Environmental Engineering Students, Civil Materials Student Org, Council for Undergraduate Research in Eng, Eng Honor Society, Eng Serving the Community, Eng w/o Borders, Freshmen Reaching Excellence in Engineering, Geo-Inst of ASCE, Institute of Transportation Eng, Marine Technology Society, National Society of Black Eng, oSTEM, Soc of Civil Eng, Soc of Flight Test Eng, Society of Naval Architects & Marine Eng, Soc of Women in Space Exploration, Soc of Mexican Amer in Eng & Scientists, Student Engineers' Council, Society of Asian Scientists & Eng, Society of Hispanic Professional Eng, Society of Women Eng, Students for the Exploration & Development of Space, Structural Engineering Association of Texas, T-Minus

Teams: AERO Design Team, Aggie Robotics, AggieSat, Baja SAE Team, Concrete Canoe Team, Cybersecurity Competition Team, DOE CyberForce, Embedded Security Systems Team, Esports Team, Formula Electric Car, G-I GeoWall Competition, High-Altitude Balloon, Human-Powered Submarine Team, Robotics Team, Rocket Engine Design, Robomaster Robotics, Speech & Debate Team, Solar Motorsports Team, Sounding Rocketry Team, Vertical Flight Society

Notable Alumni
Khalid Al-Falih, Richard Battin, Michael Bonsignore, Michael Fossum, Joe Foster, John Junkins, Mavis Kelsey, Jack Kilby, John Kinealy, Edward Knipling, Maurice Lukefahr, Byran Lunney, Frank Malina, William Pailes, Steven Swanson, and Henry "Pat" Zachry

UNIVERSITY OF TEXAS AT AUSTIN

Address: The University of Texas at Austin, 301 E. Dean Keeton St. C2100, Austin, Texas 78712-2100
Website: *https://cockrell.utexas.edu/*
Contact: *https://cockrell.utexas.edu/contact*
Phone: (512) 471-1166
Email: mbcates@mail.utexas.edu

COST OF ATTENDANCE:

Tuition & Fees: $13,576 (in-state), $46,498 (out-of-state)
Additional Expenses: $19,770 (in-state) $20,970 (out-of-state)
Total: $33,346 (in-state), $ 67,468 (out-of-state)
Financial Aid: https://finaid.utexas.edu/

ADDITIONAL INFORMATION:

Available Degree(s)
- BS, MS, Ph.D. Aerospace Eng, GeoSystems Engineering & Hydrogeology, Mechanical Engineering, Petroleum Eng
- Minors: Materials Science & Eng, Sustainable Energy
- MS, Ph.D. Materials Science & Engineering, Operations Research & Industrial Engineering

Related Research Centers
Ctr for Additive Manuf & Design Innov, Ctr for Electromechanics, Ctr for Energy & Environmental Res, Center for Engineering Education, Structures, & Materials, Ctr for Nanomanufacturing Sys for Mobile Computing & Mobile Energy Tech, Ctr for Subsurface Energy & the Environment, Center for Water & the Environment, Construction Industry Inst, Energy Inst, Structural Eng Lab, Texas Materials Inst

Scholarships Offered
UT offers over 3,000 scholarships to incoming & current students. To be considered for merit-based scholarships, complete the Engineering Honors Program Application by December 1.

Special Opportunities
Texas Innovation Center: This STEM-focused entrepreneurial area works synergistically between the Cockrell School of Engineering and the College of Natural Sciences to get products launched, manufactured, and to the marketplace. The Center provides commercialization support through networking, industry connections, specialized events, lectures, dedicated coworking space, a wet lab incubator, and Longhorn community resources. Study abroad opportunities with faculty allow Texas Engineers to innovate technology, cross cultural borders, and implement

Orgs: American Institute of Aeronautics & Astronautics, American Institute of Chemical Engineers, American Association of Drilling Engineering, American Society of Civil Engineering, American Society of Mechanical Engineering, Biomedical Engineering Society, Biomedical Outreach & Leadership Team, Institute of Electrical & Electronics Engineers, Society of Petroleum Engineers, Society of Petrophysicists & Well Log Analysts, Women in BME, Women in Mechanical Eng, Women in Petroleum & Geosystems Engineering

Teams: Computer Programming Team, Concrete Canoe Team, Cyber Policy Team, Design/Build/Fly (AIAA RC Aircraft), Hack Texas Hackathon, Longhorn Electric Vehicle Racing Team, Makeathon, Longhorn Rocketry Association, UAV (Autonomous Flight), Texas Aerial Robotics, Texas Rocket Engineering Lab, Solar Racing Team, Steel Bridge Team, Texas Spacecraft Lab, UT Programming Team

Notable Alumni
Michael Baker, Alan Bean, Robert Crippen, Gary Kelly, Phil Ligrani, Paul Lockhart, Carl Meade, Frederick Leslie, Austin Ligon, Andreas Mogensen, "Poppy" Northcutt, Karen Nyberg, H. Grady Rylander, James Truchard, Neil deGrasse Tyson, and Michael Webber

ALABAMA
ARKANSAS
DELAWARE
DISTRICT OF COLUMBIA
FLORIDA
GEORGIA
KENTUCKY
LOUISIANA
MARYLAND
MISSISSIPPI
NORTH CAROLINA
OKLAHOMA
SOUTH CAROLINA
TENNESSEE
TEXAS
VIRGINIA
WEST VIRGINIA

SOUTH

UNIVERSITY OF VIRGINIA

Address: Thornton Hall, Room A124, 351 McCormick Rd., P.O. Box 400246, Charlottesville, VA 22904-4246
Website: https://engineering.virginia.edu/
Contact: https://engineering.virginia.edu/about/visit-us
Phone: (434) 924-3593
Email: engrdean@virginia.edu

COST OF ATTENDANCE:

Tuition & Fees: $28,020 (in-state), $64,504 (out-of-state)
Additional Expenses: $17,862 (in-state) $19,352 (out-of-state)
Total: $45,882 (in-state), $83,856 (out-of-state)

Financial Aid: https://sfs.virginia.edu/

ADDITIONAL INFORMATION:

Available Degree(s)
- BS, MS, Ph.D. Aerospace Engineering, BME, Chemical Eng, Civil Eng, Computer Eng, Computer Science, Electrical Engineering, Mechanical Engineering, Systems Engineering
- MS Materials Science & Engineering

Related Research Centers
Center for Advanced Biomanufacturing, Center for Advanced Logistic Systems, Center for Advanced Manufacturing, Center for Applied Biomechanics, Center for Transportation Studies, Center for Visual & Decision Informatics, Multi-Functional Integrated Systems Tech, nanoSTAR Inst, Nanosystems Engineering Research Ctr for Adv Self-Powered Sys of Integrated Sensors & Tech, Rolls-Royce Tech Center

Scholarships Offered
UVA Student Financial Services (SFS) offers privately endowed (individual & foundations) need-based scholarships; several awards include merit aid. In most cases, students are automatically considered. Scholarships for current engineering students as well as hardship scholarships are available.

Special Opportunities
UVA Engineering provides free, scheduled on-demand tutoring with student tutors. 3-D Bioprinting, Industry-Quality Distillation Column, Machine Shops, Microfab Laboratories, Nanoscale Materials Characterization Facility, flight simulator, and rapid prototyping

Study Abroad: Eng/commerce design in Argentina; eng in Spain; "Exploring German Engineering" at Mercedes-Benz, Bosch, the Max Planck Institutes, & research labs; real-world sustainability in Sweden.

Orgs: 3D Printing Club, American Inst of Aeronautics & Astronautics, American Inst of Chemical Eng, Amer Soc Civil Eng, Assoc for Comp Mach, Biomedical Eng Soc, Comp Network Security Club, Engineers Going Global, Eng Student Council, Genomics Society, Gizmologists, Mechatronics & Robotics Society, Nat Soc of Black Eng, oSTEM, Soc of Asian Sci & Eng, Society of Hispanic Prof Eng, Society of Women Eng, Spectra, SURE, Student Game Developers, Women in Computing Sci

Teams: Academic Comp Club, Aero Design "Hoos Flying", Chem-E Car Team, Chess, Collaborative Robotics Lab, Coop of autTOnomous Robots; CubeSat, High-Powered Rocketry Team, HooHacks, Human-Powered Vehicle Team, GEM (Intl Genetically Engineered Machines); Mock Trial, MUN, National Cybersecurity Comp; NSF I-Corps; Pike Eng Entrepreneurship Challenge, Programming Comp, Smart-City Innovation, Solar Car Team, Virginia Motorsports (Formula SAE)

Notable Alumni
Eric Anderson, Daniel Barringer, Algernon Buford, Richard Byrd, W. Graham Claytor, Jr., Norman Crabill, Heber Curtis, Elmer Gaden, Robert Hagood, Karl Henize, Thomas Marshburn, Leland Melvin, Edward Ney, Bill Nelson, Gregory Olsen, William Page, Samuel Spencer, Kathryn Thornton, and Robert Young

VIRGINIA TECH

Address: Virginia Tech College of Engineering, 212 Hancock Hall, Blacksburg, VA 24061
Website: https://eng.vt.edu/
Contact: https://vt.edu/academics/contacts/major-contact-general-engineering-1.html
Phone: (540) 231-3244
Email: engris@vt.edu

COST OF ATTENDANCE:

Tuition & Fees: $12,102 (in-state), $31,754 (out-of-state)
Addl Exp: $20,172/21,004 | **Total:** $32,274/$52,758

Financial Aid: https://finaid.vt.edu/

ADDITIONAL INFORMATION:

Available Degree(s)
- BS, MS, MEng, Ph.D. Aerospace Engineering, EE, Engineering Mechanics, Mechanical Engineering, Meteorology, Ocean Eng

Related Research Centers
Computational Mechanics, Construction Engineering Management, Cyber-Physical Security, Dynamics, Control, & Estimation, Environmentally Responsible Systems, Environmental & Water Resources Engineering, Fabrication, Geotechnical Engineering, Prototyping, & Additive Manufacturing, National Security, Renewable Energy, Small Satellites & Space-Based Sensing, Structural Engineering & Materials, Sustainable Land Development, Transportation & Systems Manufacturing

Scholarships Offered
Davenport Leadership Scholarships ($7,000/year – separate appl), Merit & Need-Based Scholarships (complete the General University Scholarship Application), A. James Clark Scholars Program for engineering students; SEC-Global Engineering Access Scholarship,. More than 70% receive aid with a typical package of $17,634.

Special Opportunities
The Frith Lab: first-year students learn by dissecting, designing, making, & analyzing engineering products. Other facilities include the InVents Studio, Ware Lab, & Advanced Engineering Design Lab.

International Research Experiences include Global Engineering Ambassador, International Internships, Rolls-Royce International Internship Program, Engineering Research Experience in China, Global Design & Construction in Rwanda, Coastal Engineering in Australia, Semester Abroad in Switzerland

Partnership with Hamburg University for junior spring semester abroad to gain knowledge of German engineering.

Engineering Class: Bridges, Builders & Society class, taught by ASU professors in Spring 2023, includes travel from May 14-26, 2023 to Italy, Austria, & Switzerland. Students travel to Europe with profs.

Orgs: Amer Indian Scientists & Eng Soc, Amer Inst of Aeronautics & Astronautics, Amer Inst of Chemical Eng, Amer Soc of Ag & Bio Eng, Amer Soc of Civil Eng, Amer Soc of Mechanical Eng, Amer Society of Naval Eng, Assoc for UAV Systems Intl, Assoc for Women in Comp, Engineers w/o Borders, Nat Society of Black Eng, Society of Hispanic Prof Eng, Soc of Asian Sci & Eng, Society of Flight Test Eng, Society of Naval Architects & Marine Eng, Society of Women in Aviation & Space Exploration, Society of Women Eng, Theme Park Eng & Design Group

Teams: Baja SAE, e-NABLE, Hybrid Electric Vehicle Team, iGEM, Mock Trial, Model United Nations, Rocketry Team, TEK Robotics

Notable Alumni
Regina Dugan, Deborah Hersman, Paige Kassalen, Michelson, Enid Montague, George Nolen, and Joseph Ware, Jr.

ALABAMA
ARKANSAS
DELAWARE
DISTRICT OF COLUMBIA
FLORIDA
GEORGIA
KENTUCKY
LOUISIANA
MARYLAND
MISSISSIPPI
NORTH CAROLINA
OKLAHOMA
SOUTH CAROLINA
TENNESSEE
TEXAS
VIRGINIA
WEST VIRGINIA

SOUTH

CHAPTER 14
REGION FOUR
WEST

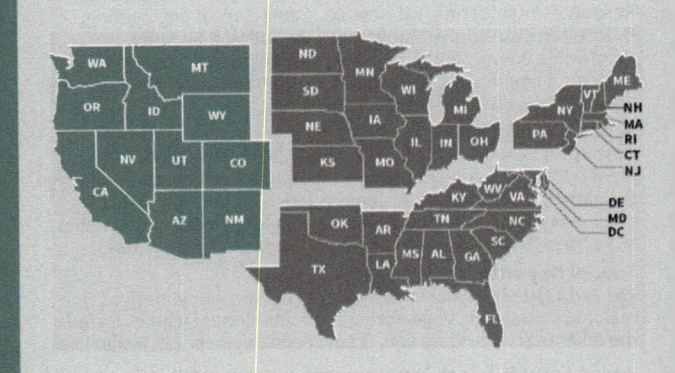

ALASKA
ARIZONA
CALIFORNIA
COLORADO
HAWAII
IDAHO
MONTANA
NEVADA
NEW MEXICO
OREGON
UTAH
WASHINGTON
WYOMING

13 Programs | 13 States

1. AZ – Arizona State University
2. CA - California Institute of Technology (CalTech)
3. CA - California Polytechnic State University, San Luis Obispo (Cal Poly, SLO)
4. CA - Harvey Mudd College
5. CA - Loyola Marymount Univ (LMU)
6. CA - Santa Clara University
7. CA - Stanford University
8. CA - University of California, Berkeley
9. CA - University of California, Los Angeles
10. CA - University of Southern California
11. CO - Colorado School of Mines
12. CO - University of Colorado, Boulder
13. WA - University of Washington

MECHANICAL ENGINEERING PROGRAMS

School	Avg. GPA, SAT Evidence-Based Reading Writing (ERW), SAT Math (M), and ACT Composite (C) Early Decision (ED): Yes/No	Admission Statistics	Selected Program(s)
Arizona State University 1151 S. Forest Ave. Tempe, AZ 85281	GPA: N/A SAT (ERW): 550-650 SAT (M): 550-670 ACT (C): 21-28 *Test-optional ED: No	Admit Rate: 88% Undergrad Enrollment: 63,124 Total Enrollment: 74,795	BSE, MS, Ph.D. Civil Eng, Enviro Eng, Mechanical Eng; MS, Ph.D. Constr Mgmt, Sustainable Eng; Accel 5-year, 4+1 BSE/MS Enviro Eng, Robotics & Autonomous Systems
California Institute of Technology (CalTech) 383 S. Hill Avenue, Pasadena, CA 91125	GPA: N/A SAT (ERW): 740-780 SAT (M): 790-800 ACT (C): 35-36 ED: No	Overall College Admit Rate: 7% Undergrad Enrollment: 901 Total Enrollment: 2,240	BS, MS, Ph.D. Chem Eng, Environmental Science & Eng, Materials Science & Eng; MS, Ph.D. Aerospace Engineering, Civil Eng, Mechanical Eng Medical Eng, Space Engineering
California Polytechnic State University, San Luis Obispo (Cal Poly SLO) 1 Grand Avenue, San Luis Obispo, CA 93407	GPA: 3.99 SAT (ERW): 610-690 SAT (M): 610-720 ACT (C): 26-32 ED: No	Overall College Admit Rate: 38% Undergrad Enrollment: 21,456 Total Enrollment: 22,440	BS, MS Aerospace Eng, Biomedical Eng, Civil Eng, Computer Eng, Comp Sci, Electrical Eng, Industrial Eng, Materials Science & Eng, Mechanical Eng
Harvey Mudd College 301 Platt Blvd., Claremont, CA 91711	GPA: N/A SAT (ERW): 710-760 SAT (M): 770-800 ACT (C): 34-36 ED: Yes	Admit Rate: 10% Undergrad Enrollment: 905 Total Enrollment: 905	BS Biology, Chemistry, Computer Science, Engineering, Mathematics, Physics, and Joint Majors
Loyola Marymount University (LMU) 1 LMU Dr., Los Angeles, CA 90045	GPA: 3.92 SAT (ERW): 620-700 SAT (M): 630-720 ACT (C): 28-32 ED: Yes	Overall College Admit Rate: 46% Undergrad Enrollment: 7,127 Total Enrollment: 10,184	BS, MSE, 4+1 BS/MSE: Civil Engineering, Computer Eng, Computer Science Data Science, Electrical Engineering, Mechanical Eng, Systems Engineering

MECHANICAL ENGINEERING PROGRAMS

School	Avg. GPA, SAT Evidence-Based Reading Writing (ERW), SAT Math (M), and ACT Composite (C) Early Decision (ED): Yes/No	Admission Statistics	Selected Program(s)
Santa Clara University 407 Palm Dr, Santa Clara, CA 95053	GPA: 3.68 SAT (ERW): 630-700 SAT (M): 640-750 ACT (C): 28-32 ED: Yes	Admit Rate: 51% Undergrad Enrollment: 5,608 Total Enrollment: 8,616	BS, BS/MS, MS BME, Civil Eng, Computer Science & Eng, Mechanical Eng; MS Aerospace Eng, Power Systems & Sustainable Energy, Robotics & Automation
Stanford University 355 Galvez Street, Stanford, CA 94305	GPA: 3.96 SAT (ERW): 720-770 SAT (M): 750-800 ACT (C): 34-35 ED: No	Admit Rate: 4% Undergrad Enrollment: 7,645 Total Enrollment: 17,680	BS Aeronautics & Astronautics, Enviro Systems Eng, Civil Eng, Mechanical Eng; MS, Ph.D. Environmental Eng, Structural Eng & Geomechanics
University of California, Berkeley University of California, Berkeley, Berkeley, CA 94720	GPA: 3.87 SAT (ERW): 650-740 SAT (M): 660-790 ACT (C): 30-35 ED: No	Overall College Admit Rate: 17% Undergrad Enrollment: 30,799 Total Enrollment: 42,327	BS, MS, Ph.D. Aerospace Engineering, Civil Eng, Energy Eng, Engineering Physics, Environmental Eng, Materials Science, Mechanical Eng
University of California, Los Angeles (UCLA) 405 Hilgard Avenue, Los Angeles, CA 90095	GPA: 3.9 SAT (ERW): 650-740 SAT (M): 640-780 ACT (C): 29-34 ED: No	Overall College Admit Rate: 14% Undergrad Enrollment: 31,636 Total Enrollment: 44,589	BS, MS, Ph.D. Aerospace Eng, Bioengineering, Chemical Eng, Civil Engineering, Comp Eng, Comp Sci, Electrical Eng, Materials Science & Eng, Mechanical Engineering

WEST

MECHANICAL ENGINEERING PROGRAMS

School	Avg. GPA, SAT Evidence-Based Reading Writing (ERW), SAT Math (M), and ACT Composite (C) Early Decision (ED): Yes/No	Admission Statistics	Selected Program(s)
University of Southern California (USC) Watt Hall, Suite 204, Los Angeles, CA 90089	GPA: 3.83 SAT (ERW): 660-740 SAT (M): 680-790 ACT (C): 30-34 ED: No	Overall College Admit Rate: 16% Undergrad Enrollment: 19,786 Total Enrollment: 46,287	BS, MS, Ph.D. Aerospace Eng, Astronautical Eng, Civil Eng, Computer Eng, Computer Science, Construction Eng, Data Science, EE, Environmental Eng, Mechanical Engineering
Colorado School of Mines 1812 Illinois Street, Golden, CO 80401	GPA: 3.8 SAT (ERW): 620-700 SAT (M): 650-740 ACT (C): 28-33 *Test-optional ED: No	Admit Rate: 55% Undergrad Enrollment: 5,216 Total Enrollment: 6,754	BS, MS, Ph.D. Civil Engineering, Geological Eng, Geophysics, Materials Science & Engineering, Mechanical Engineering, Mining Engineering, Petroleum Engineering
University of Colorado, Boulder Regent Administrative Center, Boulder, CO 80305	GPA: 3.67 SAT (ERW): 570-670 SAT (M): 560-680 ACT (C): 24-31 *Test-optional ED: No	Admit Rate: 84% Undergrad Enrollment: 30,300 Total Enrollment: 36,956	BS, MS, Ph.D. Aerospace Eng Science, Architectural Eng, Civil Eng, Computer Science, Electrical & Comp Eng, Environmental Eng, Integrated Eng Design, Mechanical Engineering
University of Washington 1400 NE Campus Parkway, Seattle, WA, 98195	GPA: 3.82 SAT (ERW): 590-700 SAT (M): 610-753 ACT (C): 27-33 ED: No	Overall College Admit Rate: 56% Undergrad Enrollment: 32,244 Total Enrollment: 48,149	BS, MS, Ph.D. Civil Engineering, Environmental Engineering, Mechanical Engineering

209

ARIZONA STATE UNIVERSITY

Address: Ira A. Fulton Schools of Engineering, P.O. Box 879309, Tempe, AZ 85287-9309
Website: *https://engineering.asu.edu https://engineering.asu.edu/contact/*
Contact: *https://engineering.asu.edu/contact/*
Phone: (480) 965-2272
Email: FultonSchools@asu.edu

COST OF ATTENDANCE:
Tuition & Fees: $11,600 (in-state), $28,800 (out-of-state)
Addl Exp: $21,489 | **Total:** $32,200 (in-state) $50,300 (out-of-state)

Financial Aid: https://students.asu.edu/financialaid

ADDITIONAL INFORMATION:

Available Degree(s)
- BS, MS, and Ph.D. Mechanical Engineering
- MS Robotics and Autonomous Systems
- Accelerated 5-year, 4+1 BSE and MS Mechanical Engineering

Related Research Centers
Adaptive Intelligent Materials and Systems, Accelerating Operational Efficiency, Complex System Safety, Efficient Vehicles & Sustainable Transportation Systems, Embedded Systems, Human, Artificial Intelligence, Robot Teaming, Negative Carbon Emissions, Integrated Circuits, Systems, and Sensors, Flexible Electronics and Display, Information Assurance, Infrastructure and Sustainable Engineering, Excellence on SMART INNOVATIONS, Power Systems Engineering, Quantum Energy, and Sustainable Solar Technologies, Secure, Trusted, and Assured Microelectronics

Scholarships Offered
ASU Engineering Tutoring Center offers free tutoring in engineering, math, physics, & chemistry.

Engineering Projects in Community Service (EPICS): Design, build, & deploy systems to solve engineering-based probs for nonprofit orgs.

Fulton Grand Challenge Scholars Program: Combine classes with cutting-edge, problem-solving research.

Fulton Undergraduate Research Initiative provides hands-on lab exp, independent & thesis-based research, & conference travel.

Tooker House: ASU's "dorm built for engineers" has on-site digital classrooms & state-of-the-art maker spaces with 3D printers, laser cutters, and cutting edge tools.

Orgs: Ambassadors, Amer Concrete Inst, Amer Indian Sci & Eng Soc, Amer Inst of Aeronautics & Astronautics, Amer Inst of Chemical Eng, American Society of Civil Engineers, American Society of Mechanical Eng, Associated General Contractors of America, Assoc for Computer Systems Security, Biomedical Eng Soc, Bridges to Prosperity, Constr Students Abroad, Engineering World Health, Engineers w/o Borders, INFORMS, Inst of Electrical & Electronics Eng, IIE, Nat Soc of Black Eng, SAE Soc of Hispanic Prof Eng, MAES, Soc of Women Eng, SoDA, WCS

Teams: Air Devils, Alka Rocketeers, ChemE Car, Combat Robotics, Daedalus Astronautics, DIYBio, Electric Car, Formula SAE, Game Dev Studio, Helios Rocketry, iGEM, Mock Trial, MUN, Motorsports, Next Level Devils, Rossum Rumblers Robotics Team, Satellite Team, Solar Devils, Speech & Debate Team, SunHacks, Underwater Robotics Team

Notable Alumni
David Allais, Stephen Basila, Craig Berge, Stephen DeTommaso, Kent Dibble, Michael Fann, Kim Fox, George Geiser, Richard Guthrie, Thomas Hardwicke, LeRoy Hanneman Jr., Ron Harper, Paul Henry, Enamul Hoque, Geza Kmetty, Debra Larson, Hisha Mahmoud, Harriet Nembhard, Douglas Nicholls, John Nicklow, Ravi Prasher, Valerie Roberts, Michael Roy, Janaka Ruwanpura, and Margaret Woodward

CALIFORNIA INST OF TECHNOLOGY (CALTECH)

Address: California Institute of Technology, Division of Engineering and Applied Science, 1200 E. California Blvd., MC 155-44, Pasadena, California 91125-2100
Website: https://eas.caltech.edu/
Contact: https://eas.caltech.edu/contact
Phone: (626) 395-4101
Email: maria.cervantes@caltech.edu

COST OF ATTENDANCE:

Tuition & Fees: $58,479 | **Addl Exp:** $25,119 | **Total:** $83,598

Financial Aid: https://www.finaid.caltech.edu/

ADDITIONAL INFORMATION:

Available Degree(s)
- BS, MS, Ph.D. Bioengineering, Chemical Eng, Computational & Neural Science, Comp Sci, EE, Environmental Science & Eng, Info/Data Science, Materials Science & Eng, Mechanical Eng
- MS, Ph.D. Aerospace Engineering, Civil Engineering, Medical Engineering, Space Engineering
- Minors: Aerospace, Control/Dynamical Systems, Neurobiology, Structural Mechanics, Visual Culture

Related Research Areas
Autonomous Systems and Technologies, Environmental Microbial Interactions, Artificial Photosynthesis, Quantum Entanglement

Caltech Microanalysis Center, Infrared Processing & Analysis Center, Keck Institute for Space Studies, Laser Interferometer Gravitational-wave Observatory, Owens Valley Radio Observatory, Palomar Observatory, Space Radiation Laboratory, W. M. Keck Observatory

Scholarships Offered
Summer Research & Internships; Summer Programs. Caltech has 1,000 undergrads; you will not be anonymous; everyone works hard, takes breaks, and finds outlets – theatre, sports, 16 NCAA DIII teams, 100 clubs, art, music, competition teams, and 5 NASA facilities

Orgs: A Capella, Amateur Radio Club, American Institute of Aeronautics & Astronautics, Anime, American Institute of Chemical Engineers, American Society of Civil Engineers, American Society of Mechanical Engineers, Black Scientists & Engineers at CalTech, BlockTech, Computing Club, Engineers w/o Borders, Institute of Electrical & Electronics Engineers, MedLife, Origami Club, Sci-Fi, Scuba, Society of Women Engineers

Teams: Amateur Radio, Ballroom Dance, Blocktech, Board Game Competitions, Bridge Club, Caltech Racing, Chess, Cubesat, Cybersecurity Bootcamp, Engineering Design Team, Formula SAE Team, Gaming, Hacktech, iGEM Team (Intl Genetically Engineered Machines), Poker, Quiz Bowl, RC Aircraft, Robotics Team, Rocketry Team, Science Olympiad, Solar Decathlon, Speed Cubing, Triathlon

Annual Sumobot Competition - Student teams are challenged to design, build, and field robots for each of the three Sumobot categories: (1) Autonomous wheeled, (2) Radio-controlled (R/C) wheeled, and (3) (R/C) Strandbot, i.e., a linkage, mechanism-based walking robot.

Notable Alumni
Mark Adler, Mihran Agbabian, Irving Ashkenas, David Bohm, Frank Borman, David Brin, James Broadwell, James Daily, Sidney Gottlieb, David Ho, Howard Hughes, Donald Knuth, Fei-Fei Li, Fred Lindvall, Amy Mainzer, Benoit Mandelbrot, John McCarthy, Charlie Munger, Frank Oppenheimer, Linus Pauling, Charles Richter, William Shockley, Peter Shor, Pol Spanos, Kip Thorne, Vito Vanoni, Stephen Wolfram

ALASKA
ARIZONA
CALIFORNIA
COLORADO
HAWAII
IDAHO
MONTANA
NEVADA
NEW MEXICO
OREGON
UTAH
WASHINGTON
WYOMING

WEST

CAL POLY SAN LUIS OBISPO

Address: Cal Poly San Luis Obispo, College of Engineering, 1 Grand Avenue, Building 192, Room 301, San Luis Obispo, CA 93407
Website: https://ceng.calpoly.edu/
Contact: https://ceng.calpoly.edu/contact/#contact-our-office
Phone: (805) 756-2131
Email: engineeringdean@calpoly.edu

COST OF ATTENDANCE:
Tuition & Fees: $11,022 (in-state), $30,942 (out-of-state)
Addl Exp: $20,599 **Total:** $31,621 (in-state), $51,541 (out-of-state)
Financial Aid: https://www.calpoly.edu/financial-aid

ADDITIONAL INFORMATION:

Available Degree(s)
- BS, MS Aerospace Engineering, Biomedical Engineering, Civil Engineering, Computer Engineering, Computer Science, Electrical Engineering, Industrial Engineering, Materials Science & Engineering, Mechanical Engineering
- MS Fire Protection Engineering

Related Research Centers
California Cybersecurity Inst, Center for Applications in Biotechnology, Center for Coastal Marine Sciences, Center for Construction Engineering, Center for Expressive Technologies, Center for Health Research, Center for Innovation & Entrepreneurship, Center for Sustainability, Electric Power Institute, Global Waste Research Inst, Inst for Adv Technology & Public Policy, Lab for Global Automatic Identification Technologies, Western Coatings Technology Center

Scholarships Offered
Students are automatically considered for most scholarships; additional scholarships available once enrolled; continuing students complete a scholarship application in My Cal Poly Portal for major-based scholarships; internal department scholarships also available.

Special Opportunities
Free Peer-to-Peer Tutoring (Course Assts, Prob Sets, Exam Prep, Gen Study Skills), Group Study Sessions, Supplemental Workshops, Study Skills Library, Research 101, Career Services, Internships, Summer Undergrad Research Program, Facilities, 80 Labs, Tools/Technology, Plastics, AI, Engineering Student Services, Multicultural Eng Prog, Intl Exchange Program, Women in Engineering Program, 397 Clubs

Orgs: Amateur Radio, Ambassadors, American Chemical Society, American Foundry Society, American Indian Science & Engineering Society, American Institute of Aeronautics & Astronautics, American Society of Civil Eng, Amer Soc of Mechanical Engineers, Biomedical Engineering Society, Biotech Club, CalGeo Club, Computer Eng Society, Computer Science & AI, Data Science Club, Engineering Student Council, Environmental Science Club, Game Development Club, Institute of Transport Eng, Materials Engineering Student Society, National Society of Black Engineers, oSTEM, PolyHacks, Power & Engineering Society, Quantum Comp Club, Society of Hispanic Professional Engineers, Society of Civil Engineers, Society of Environmental Engineering, Society of Manufacturing Engineering

Teams: Supermileage Team won 2022 Shell Eco-Marathon, Cal Poly Steel Bridge Team won 2nd at ASCE, SLO Concrete Canoe Team wins 6th national title in 2022, Sustainable Packaging Design Team won 1st Place in 2022 national competition, Animal Science Team won 1st Place in ASAS Competition for 3rd consecutive time, Formula SAE, Cal Poly Hackathon, Baja Racing Team, CSU Student Research Competition; also Hack4Impact competitions

Notable Alumni
Michael Alsbury, Tory Bruno, Victor Glover, Noel Lee, Mark Lucovsky, Alison Murray, Farid Nazem, Peter Oppenheimer, Aaron Peckham, Burt Rutan, Peter Siebold, Frederick Sturckow, William Swanson

---

ALASKA
ARIZONA
CALIFORNIA
COLORADO
HAWAII
IDAHO
MONTANA
NEVADA
NEW MEXICO
OREGON
UTAH
WASHINGTON
WYOMING

HARVEY MUDD

Address: Department of Engineering, Harvey Mudd College, 301 Platt Blvd., Claremont, CA 91711
Website: https://www.hmc.edu/engineering/
Contact: https://www.hmc.edu/engineering/faculty-staff/
Phone: (909) 621-8019
Email: engineering@hmc.edu

COST OF ATTENDANCE:

Tuition & Fees: $62,817 | **Addl Exp:** $21,408 | **Total:** $84,225

Financial Aid: https://www.finaid.caltech.edu/

ADDITIONAL INFORMATION:

Available Degree(s)
- BS Biology, Chemistry, Computer Science, Engineering, Mathematics, Physics, and Joint Majors

Related Research Areas
Center for Climate and the Environment, Center for Design Education, Program for Responsive Science and Engineering

Scholarships Offered
Seven Engineering Fellowship Programs are available at Harvey Mudd. The Department of Engineering hosts several research programs, each focuses on a different aspect of engineering. Many faculty send an email to the engineering majors in the middle of the fall semester. Eleven scholarships & awards for engineering students, such as the Johnson Excellence in Engineering Award.

Special Opportunities
Office of Career Services internships, career fairs, HMC Alumni Association Group, numerous job opportunities, study abroad.

Muddraker Student Newspaper

HMC Machine Shop offers opportunities to turn ideas into reality with additive manufacturing machines, conventional and CNC lathes and mills, furnaces for heat-treating, a full wood shop and advanced fabrication machines. Flexible curriculum allowing students to spend a semester/year studying away.

The Engineering Clinic unites teams working w/faculty advisors and external liaison engineers to solve real problems for clients in the public/private sector. Programs and facilities are funded by private foundations and government agencies including NSF, the Hearst Foundation, and NIH.

Harvey Mudd frequently ranks in PayScale.com's top highest paid graduates of the colleges and universities in the United States.

Orgs: 5C LatinX in Technology, 5C Pre-Vet Club, American Chemical Society, Amer Inst of Chem Eng, American Soc of Civil Eng, American Society of Mechanical Eng, Assoc for Computing Machinery, Black Lives at Mudd, Claremont Astronomical Society, Claremont Journal of Medicine & Social Justice, Claremont Journal of STEM & Social Science, Doctors w/o Borders, Exploring Pan-Asian Identity & Culture, IEEE, Innovation Lab, Pre-Health Club, Pre-PA Club, Society of Professional Latinos in STEM, Society of Hispanic Prof Engineers, Society of Women Engineers, Women & Minority Voices in STEM, Women in Computer Science, Women of Color in Pre-Health Society

Teams: 5C Hack, Artificial Intelligence Group, Chess Club, Claremont EMT, Intl Programming Contest, Model United Nations, MuddSub, Organic Farm, Quiz Bowl, Robotics Team, TERMINAL Global Championship, Urbanscape Club, Wind Turbine Competition Team

Notable Alumni
Donald D. Chamberlin, Joseph Costello, Ned Freed, Robert Freitas, Nabeel Gareeb, Jonathan Gay, Dominic Mazzoni, Bruce Nelson, Sage Weil

ALASKA
ARIZONA
CALIFORNIA
COLORADO
HAWAII
IDAHO
MONTANA
NEVADA
NEW MEXICO
OREGON
UTAH
WASHINGTON
WYOMING

WEST

LOYOLA MARYMOUNT UNIVERSITY

Address: Loyola Marymount University College of Science & Engineering 1 LMU Drive, Los Angeles, CA 90045
Website: https://admission.lmu.edu/
Contact: https://www.lmu.edu/about/contact/
Phone: (310) 338-2750
Email: admission@lmu.edu

COST OF ATTENDANCE:

Tuition & Fees: $55,441 | **Add Expenses:** $21,525 | **Total:** $76,966

Financial Aid: https://financialaid.lmu.edu/

ADDITIONAL INFORMATION:

Available Degree(s)
- BS, MSE, 4+1 BS/MSE: Civil Engineering, Computer, Computer Science, Data Science Electrical Engineering, Mechanical Engineering, Systems Engineering
- Certificates: Additive Manufacturing, Aeronautics & Space Systems, Climate Change Solutions, Cybersecurity, Engineering Project Management, Groundwater Management, Software Architecture, Sustainability, Water & Wastewater Treatment, Water Quality Management

Related Research Centers
Aerospace Propulsion Lab, Bioethics Institute, Coastal Research Institute, Fred Kiesner Center for Entrepreneurship, Howard Hughes Medical Institute, Institute for Business, Ethics, and Sustainability

Scholarships Offered
LMU Endowed Scholarships, LMU Athletic Grant-in-Aid, Gates Millennium; 86.9% of students receive financial aid; continuing scholarships are also available to currently enrolled students

Special Opportunities
Alternative Breaks, Co-ops, Internships, Research, Scholar Programs (Noyce 8-week Summer STEM internship; McNair Scholars Program), Study Abroad. Trimble Technology Lab

Orgs: American Institute of Aeronautics & Astronautics (AIAA), American Society of Civil Engineers (ASCE), American Society of Mechanical Engineers (ASME), Association for Computing Machinery (ACM), Associated General Contractors, Biomedical Engineering Society (BMES), Energy Club, Engineering for Humanity, Engineers w/o Borders (EWB), Institute of Electrical & Electronic Engineers (IEEE), Lions Mechanical & Aerospace Research Society, LMU Aerospace Research Society (LoyolaMARS), National Society of Black Engineers (NBSE), Quality of Life Plus (QL+),Society Society of Hispanic Professional Engineers (SHPE), Society of Industrial & Applied Mathematics (SIAM), Society of Women Engineers (SWE)

Teams: ASME Student Design Competition, Baja SAE Competition Team, Chess, Computer Science Competition, Cubesat, Debate Team (Parliamentary & Lincoln-Douglas Debate), Design/Tech Comp, Human-Powered Vehicle Challenge, Esports, LMU Pitch Competition, Meta Hackathon, Mock Trial, Model United Nations, Moot Court, OC "World's Fair of Sustainability", NASA Student Launch Competition, NSF Convergence Accelerator Competition, Robotics Team, Society of Automotive Engineers AeroDesign Competition

Notable Alumni
Corey Epstein and Tom Mueller

SANTA CLARA UNIVERSITY

Address: Santa Clara University, School of Engineering, 500 El Camino Real, Santa Clara, CA 95053
Website: *https://www.scu.edu/engineering/*
Contact: *https://phonebook.scu.edu/*
Phone: (408) 554-4000
Email: rdavis@scu.edu

COST OF ATTENDANCE:

Tuition & Fees: $57,534 | **Addl Exp:** $21,315 | **Total:** $78,849
Financial Aid: https://www.scu.edu/financialaid/

ADDITIONAL INFORMATION:

Available Degree(s)
- BS, BS/MS, MS Biomedical Engineering, Civil Engineering, Computer Science & Engineering, Electrical & Computer Engineering, Mechanical Engineering
- BS Web Design & Engineering
- MS Aerospace Engineering, Power Systems & Sustainable Energy, Robotics & Automation
- Ph.D. Computer Science, Electrical & Computer Engineering, Mechanical Engineering

Related Research Areas
Multimedia Compression (Image & Video Coding), Cluster Space Control of Multiple Mobile Robots & Model-Based Anomaly Management, Dynamics & Control Systems, Ctr for Nanostructures

Scholarships Offered
First-year applicants can receive merit-based awards with no additional application (international students eligible), including Johnson Scholars Award (up to full tuition, room & board, books & supplies, summer stipend, renewable for 12 quarters); SCU Presidential at Entry Scholarship (full-tuition for 12 quarters); SCU Provost Scholarship (half-tuition for 12 quarters); SCU Dean's Scholarship (award amounts vary – 12 quarters)

Special Opportunities
Commitment to climate neutrality: compost pails, terracycle, reusable goods, tree trackers, sustainable energy/building materials, share shelf, environmental protection badges, gardens, thrift shop, lectures.

Labs: BioInnovation & Design Lab, 3D Bioprinting, Center for Nanostructures, Engineering Computing Center, Frugal Innovation Hub, Latimer Energy Lab, Maker Lab, Nanoscale Technologies for testing drinking water, Robotic Systems Lab, TENT Lab

Orgs: American Institute of Aeronautics & Astronautics, American Society of Civil Engineers, American Society of Mechanical Engineers, Amer Soc of Heating, Refrig, & AC Engineers, Assoc for Computing Machinery, Associated General Contractors, Biomedical Engineering Society, Energy Club, Engineers w/o Borders, Engineering World Health, Institute of Electrical & Electronic Engineers, Maker Club, National Society of Black Engineers, SCU Innovation & Design Club, Society of Hispanic Professional Engineers, Society of Women Engineers, Women in STEM, Grand Challenges Scholars Program

Teams: Aerial Robotics, Business Pitch Comp, Chess, Esports Team, Formula SAE Electric Vehicle Team, Hack for Humanity, iGEM Team (International Genetically Engineered Machine), Maker Group, Mock Trial, Philalethic Debating Society, Robotics Competitions, Satellite Team, Venture Capital Investment Competition, Vex Robotics Team

Notable Alumni
Frank Cepollina, David Drummond, Brendan Eich, Fred Franzia, Robert Freitas, Pat Gelsinger, Richard Justice, Jack Kuehler, David Merritt, Boris Murmann, John Mullin, Peter Oppenheimer, and George Reyes

ALASKA
ARIZONA
CALIFORNIA
COLORADO
HAWAII
IDAHO
MONTANA
NEVADA
NEW MEXICO
OREGON
UTAH
WASHINGTON
WYOMING

WEST

STANFORD UNIVERSITY

Address: Stanford Engineering, 475 Via Ortega, Suite 227, Stanford, CA 94305
Website: https://engineering.stanford.edu/
Contact: https://engineering.stanford.edu/contact-us
Phone: (650) 723-2091
Email: tkenny@stanford.edu

COST OF ATTENDANCE:
Tuition & Fees: $56,169 | **Addl Exp:** $22,110 | **Total:** $77,279
Financial Aid: https://financialaid.stanford.edu/

ADDITIONAL INFORMATION:
Available Degree(s)
- BS, MS, Ph.D. Aeronautics & Astronautics, Bio Eng, Chemical Eng, Materials Science & Engineering, Mechanical Engineering

Related Research Areas
Aerospace Robotics, AI Lab, Aircraft Aerodynamics, Air Traffic Control, Autonomous Systems, Extreme Environment Microsystems Lab, Flow Physics & Aeroacoustics Lab, GPS Laboratory, Haptics & Robotics, Institute for Energy, Intelligent & Composites Lab, Mapping & Navigation in Extreme Environments, Morphing Space Structures Lab, Navigation & Autonomous Systems Lab, Planning & Control for Agile Robotic Systems, Plasma Dynamics Modeling, Reconfigurable Structures, Robotic Transportation Networks, Space Environment & Satellite Systems, Space Rendezvous, Space Robotics, Structures & Composites Lab, Sustainable Energy, Technology Ventures

Scholarships Offered
Families with incomes of $150,000 or less attend college tuition free. Stanford does not offer merit scholarships. Graduate students study for free and receive an additional stipend through a special program. Students are encouraged to apply for the Rhodes, Marshall, and Mitchell Scholarships, Fulbright Grants, Churchill Scholarships, Gates Cambridge Scholarships, German Academic Exchange (DAAD) Awards, and Think Swiss Research Scholarship.

Special Opportunities
Over 50 institutes, labs, and centers with the College of Engineering; state-of-the-art engineering equipment.

Global internships, Cardinal Quarter, Study Tours, Faculty-Initiated Travel Programs, Bing Overseas Study Program (Australia, Berlin, Cape Town, Florence, Madrid, Kyoto, NYC, Oxford, Paris, Santiago), and Chinese Undergraduate Visiting Research Program

The France-Stanford Center for Interdisciplinary Studies partners with the French Ministry of Foreign Affairs to bridge the Humanities, STEM, Business, and Law.

Teams: Concrete Canoe Team, Chess, CubeSat, Debate Society, Esports, Formula SAE, iGEM (Intl Genetically Engineered Machine) Team, Mock Trial, Model United Nations, NASA Student Launch Competition Team, National Collegiate Cyber Defense Competition, Rubik's Cube, Solar Car, Stanford Racing Team, Stanford Student Robotics, Student Space Initiative, Unmanned Aerial Vehicle Team

Notable Alumni
Norman Abramson, Scott Anderson, Mary Barra, Ronald N. Bracewell, Robert Cannon, Jr., Eileen Collins, Ray Dolby, Roland Dore, Charles Stark Draper, Charbel Farhat, Mike Fincke, William Fisher, Bill Franke, Owen Garriott, Susan Helms, Michael Hopkins, G. Scott Hubbard, Mae Jemison, Elizabeth Jens, Tamara Jernigan, Stanley Kennedy Sr., Gregory Linteris, A. Louis London, Edward Lu, John Macready, Bruce McCandless II, Stephen McLin, Barbara Morgan, Rodney O'Neal, Raj Reddy, Kathleen Rubins, Ellen Ochoa, Scott Parazynski, Sally Ride, Stephen Robinson, Debbie Senesky, Steve Smith, Stephen Timoshenko, and Jeff Wisoff

UNIVERSITY OF CALIFORNIA, BERKELEY

Address: UC Berkeley College of Engineering, Dean's Office, 320 McLaughlin Hall, Berkeley, CA 94720-1700
Website: *https://engineering.berkeley.edu/*
Contact: *https://engineering.berkeley.edu/contact/*
Phone: (510) 642-5771
Email: engineeringdean@berkeley.edu

COST OF ATTENDANCE:

Tuition & Fees: $15,352 (in-state), $47,926 (out-of-state)
Addl Exp: $25,700 | **Total:** $41,052 (in-state), $73,626 (out-of-state)
Financial Aid: https://financialaid.berkeley.edu/

ADDITIONAL INFORMATION:

Available Degree(s)
- BS Aerospace Engineering (new in 2022)
- BS, MS, Ph.D. Bioeng, Chemical Eng, Civil Eng, Computer Sci, Electrical Eng, Energy Eng, Eng Math/Statistics, Eng Physics, Environmental Engineering, Industrial Eng, Materials Science, Mechanical Eng, Nuclear Eng, Operations Research

Related Research Centers
BRAVO Autonomous Vehicle Research, Institute of Transportation Studies, Jacobs Institute for Design Innovation, Pacific Earthquake Engineering Research Center, Partners for Adv Transportation Tech, SWARM Lab, Team for Research in Ubiquitous Secure Technology

Scholarships Offered
Berkeley, Fiat Lux, & Middle-Class Scholarships - no addl app required Complete the FAFSA or CA Dream Act Application. Regents and Chancellor's Scholarships - $2,500 for scholars w/o financial need.

Special Opportunities
Berkeley Engineering holds classes/research/activities in dozen buildings using 1,000,000 sq w/large-scale facilities, include one of the world's largest earthquake simulators. Berkeley Innovators, Engineering Research Support Organization, The Foundry@ CITRIS, Intellectual Property & Industry Research Alliances, SkyDeck

Labs: Berkeley Research IT, Biomolecular Nanotech Center, Invention Lab, Marvell Nanofabrication Lab, Lawrence Berkeley National Lab, Lawrence Livermore National Lab

Orgs: American Nuclear Society, American Society of Civil Engineers, American Society of Mechanical Engineers, Biomedical Engineering Society, Engineers for a Sustainable World, Engineers w/o Borders, Environmental Team, Institute of Electrical & Electronics Engineers, Institute of Transportation Engineers, Materials Science & Eng Assoc, NAE Grand Challenges Scholars Program, Society of Eng Scientists

Teams: Bike Builders, Biofuels Tech, Bioprinting@Berkeley, Cal Construction, Cal Seismic Design Team, CalSol, Cal Super Mileage Vehicle Team, Chem-E Car Team, Concrete Canoe, Cyber Security Competition Team, Debate Society (British Parliamentary & American Parliamentry), Enable Tech, Environmental Team, Extended Reality, Formula SAE Electric Vehicle, Human-Powered Vehicle, iGEM (Intl Genetically Engineered Machines), Mock Trial, MUN, Seismic Design Team, Space Enterprise, Space Tech & Rocketry, Steel Bridge Team Competition Team, Sustainable Housing at Cal, Transportation Team, Unmanned Aerial Vehicle Team, Underwater Robotics Team

Notable Alumni
Frances Arnold, Thomas Cech, Robert Curl, Andrew Fire, Jim Gray, Carol Greider, Alan Heeger, David Julius, Butler Lampson, Yuan Lee, Silvio Micali, Mario Molina, Kary Mullis, Gordon Moore, Loren Ryder, Margret Schmidt, Glenn Seaborg, Hamilton Smith, Henry Taube, Charles Thacker, & Steve Wozniak

ALASKA
ARIZONA
CALIFORNIA
COLORADO
HAWAII
IDAHO
MONTANA
NEVADA
NEW MEXICO
OREGON
UTAH
WASHINGTON
WYOMING

WEST

UNIVERSITY OF CALIFORNIA, LOS ANGELES

Address: UCLA Samueli School of Engineering, 7400 Boelter Hall, Los Angeles, CA 90095
Website: https://samueli.ucla.edu/
Contact: https://samueli.ucla.edu/contact-us
Phone: (310) 825-9580
Email: engrdean@seas.ucla.edu

COST OF ATTENDANCE:

Tuition & Fees: $15,352 (in-state), $47,926 (out-of-state) | **Addl Expenses:** $25,700 | **Total:** $41,052 (in-state), $73,626 (out-of-state)

Financial Aid: https://financialaid.ucla.edu/

ADDITIONAL INFORMATION:

Available Degree(s)
- BS, MS, Ph.D. Aerospace Engineering, Bioeng, Chemical Eng, Civil Eng, Computer Eng, Comp Sci, Electrical Engineering, Materials Science & Engineering, Mechanical Engineering
- MS Computer Networking, Manufacturing & Design, Quantum Science & Technology, Signal Processing, Structural Materials

Related Research Centers
Breakthrough Tech Artificial Intelligence, Center for Domain-Specific Computing, Ctrfor Encrypted Functionalities, Center of Excellences for Green Nanotechnologies, Center for Function Accelerated nanoMaterial Engineering, Center for Information & Computation Sec, Center for Translational Apps of Nanoscale Multiferroic Systems, Inst for Carbon Management, Inst for Technology Law & Policy, Inst for Technology & Advancement, Scalable Analytics Inst, Sci Hub for Humanity & Artificial Intelligence, UCLA Center for Heterogeneous Integration & Performance Scaling, Western Inst of Nanoelectronics

Scholarships Offered
Regents/Chancellor's Scholarships offer $2,500 for scholars w/o financial need. For need-based scholarships, complete online "UCLA Scholarship Application" through MyUCLA & submit a FAFSA or Dream Act application by the March 2 priority deadline each year.

Special Opportunities
UCLA Samueli expanded facilities include Boelter Hall, Engineering-IV, V & VI, exploretech.la, Student Creativity Ctr, & Innovation Lab

Orgs: Amer Indian Sci & Eng Soc, Amer Inst of Aero & Astronautics, Amer Inst of Chemical Eng, Amer Soc of Mechanical Eng, Arab Amer Assoc of Eng & Architects, Blockchain @ UCLA, Bruin Consulting, Bruin Entrepreneurs, Bruin Home Solutions, Bruin Space Group, Building Eng & Mentors, Design Create Solar, Eng Ambassador Prog, Eng & Entrepreneurial Group & UCLA, Eng Society UC, Eng w/o Borders, Inst of Transportation Eng, Korean-Amer Sci & Eng Assoc, LA Blueprint, Materials Res Soc, MentorSEAS, National Soc of Black Eng, NoCode, Nova, Pilipinos in Eng & Science (PIES), QSTEM, Renewable Energy Assoc, Soc of Asian Sci & Eng, Soc of Automotive Eng, Soc of Latino Eng & Sci, Society of Women Eng, Supermileage Vehicle SA

Teams: AIAA Design/Build/Fly, Baja SAE, BattleBots, Chess, College Bowl, Concrete Canoe Team, CubeSat, Cubing Club (Rubik's Cube), DARPA Challenge, DevX, Hack/Build/Innovate, Department Of Energy Solar Decathlon, Formula SAE Bruin Racing, iGEM Team (International Genetically Engineered Machines), National Collegiate Cyber Defense Comp Team, FIRST Robotics Team, Quiz Bowl, RoboCup (Robotic Soccer), Rocket Project Team, Science Olympiad, Steel Bridge Team

Notable Alumni
Allen Adham, Barry Boehm, Vince Brand, Vinton Cerf, Steve Crocker, Walter Cunningham, Charles Elachi, Anna Fisher, Ed Krupp, Nita Ing, K. Megan McArthur, Michael Morhaime, Story Musgrave, Frank Pearce, Henry Samueli, Elliot See, Steven Soter, Ronald Sugar, Taylor Wang, Jessica Watkins, and James Yenbamroong

UNIVERSITY OF SOUTHERN CALIFORNIA

Address: University of Southern California, Viterbi School of Engineering, Olin Hall of Engineering, Room 106, 3650 McClintock Ave, Los Angeles, CA 90089
Website: *https://viterbischool.usc.edu/*
Contact: *https://viterbischool.usc.edu/contact-us/*
Phone: (213) 740-4488
Email: sath@usc.edu

COST OF ATTENDANCE:
Tuition & Fees: $64,726 | **Addl Exp:** $20,922 | **Total:** $85,648
Financial Aid: https://financialaid.usc.edu/

ADDITIONAL INFORMATION:

Available Degree(s)
- BS, MS, Ph.D. Aerospace Engineering, Astronautical Engineering, Biomedical Engineering, Chemical Engineering, Civil Engineering, Computer Engineering, Computer Science, Construction Engineering, Data Science, Electrical Engineering, Environmental Engineering, Industrial & Systems Engineering, Intelligence & Cyber Operations, Materials Science, Mechanical Engineering, Petroleum Engineering

Related Research Centers
Airbus Inst for Eng Res, Center for Adv Manuf, Ctr for Computational Modeling of Cancer, Ctr for Dark Energy Biosphere Investigations, Ctr for Intelligent Environments, Ctr for Interactive Smart Oilfield Tech, Ctr for Risk & Economic Analysis of Threats & Emergencies, Ctr for Sustainability Solutions, Ctr for Systems & Control, Energy Inst, Foundation for Cross-Connection Control & Hydraulic Res, M.C. Gill Composites Ctr, Inst for Collaborative Eng, Robotics & Autonomous Sys Ctr, Space Eng Res Ctr, Visualizing Narrative Forms - Quantum Physics, AI, & Sustainability, Wrigley Inst for Environmental Studies

Scholarships Offered
For a full list of USC merit scholarships for w/special qualifications - academic, athletic or artistic talent see: https://issuu.com/esdwebm/docs/scholarship_grid_issuu_?fr=sMzE0NDM2NzY5Njk

Trojan Transfer Program - Some students are chosen to be provisionally accepted for a subsequent term based upon successful completion of the university's requirements.

Special Opportunities
Internships, fellowships, summer research; Global Summit, Eng + Program, Grand Challenges; labs, institutes, centers, competition, & entrepreneurship; Viterbi Entrepreneurship Ed (freshman core)

Orgs: 3D4E, ASPEN, ADT, AAEES, AIAA, AIChE, AISC, ASCE, AIMC, CAISS++, CybOrg, CTC, CMAA, EERI, EWB, GIT, IEEE, IISE, KIUEL, KSEA, NSBE, QuEST, RPL, SIGC, SASE, SHPE, SWE, WIC, WCHE

Teams: Athena Hacks, ChemE Car, Chess, Concrete Canoe, CubeSat, Cyber Defense Team, Esports, Formula SAE Car, Hack-IoT Team, iGEM, Mock Trial, MUN, MEDesign Team, Quiz Bowl, Recumbent Veh, Rubik's Cube Team, SC Racing, Science Olympiad, Solar Car Team, Steel Bridge, Underwater Vehicles, USC Makers, VEX Robotics Team

2022 USC AeroDesign Team came in 4th out of 97 teams in AIAA Comp; Maseeh Entrepreneurship Prize Competition (startups), Min Family Challenge; ABC Innovation Prize Competition (solutions in atoms, bits, & cells); Global Engineering Design Studio (8-week international collaboration); Viterbi Startup Garage Incubator

Notable Alumni
Neil Armstrong, Douglas Bergeron, George Chilingar, Fred Cohen, Chris DeWolfe, Andrew Frank, Robert Gray, Ayanna Howard, Jeff Kaplan, Barry Kerzin, Satinder Kessar, Mike Markkula, Thom Mayne, Edward Raymund, Andrew Viterbi, Bernard Zimmerman

ALASKA
ARIZONA
CALIFORNIA
COLORADO
HAWAII
IDAHO
MONTANA
NEVADA
NEW MEXICO
OREGON
UTAH
WASHINGTON
WYOMING

WEST

COLORADO SCHOOL OF MINES

Address: The Ohio State College of Engineering, 122 Hitchcock Hall, 2070 Neil Ave., Columbus, OH 43210
Website: *https://engineering.osu.edu/*
Contact: *https://engineering.osu.edu/about-college/contacts*
Phone: (614) 292-2826
Email: howard.1727@osu.edu

COST OF ATTENDANCE:
Tuition & Fees: $19,986 (in-state), $41,903 (out-of-state)
Addl Exp: $17,750 | **Total:** $37,736 (in-state), $59,653 (out-of-state)
Financial Aid: https://finaid.mines.edu/

ADDITIONAL INFORMATION:

Available Degree(s)
- BS, MS, Ph.D. Chemical Engineering, Civil Engineering, Computer Science, Electrical Engineering, Geological Engineering, Geophysics, Materials Science & Engineering, Mechanical Engineering, Mining Engineering, Petroleum Eng

Related Research Centers
Bioethics & Medical Humanities, Carbon Mgmt & Sequestration, Chemical Instrumentation, Climate, Energy, & the Environment, Diabetes & Metabolism Research, Electron Microscope & Analysis, Electronic & Magnetic Nanoscale Composite Multifunctional Materials, Emergent Materials, Global Water Institute, Manufacturing & Materials Innovation, Nanoengineering, Nuclear Reactor Lab, Polymer & Composite Engineering, Physics, Innovation, & Entrepreneurship, Plant Sciences, Polar & Climate Research, Polymer NanoMaterials & Devices, Propulsion & Power Center, Radiosurgery for Brain & Spine, Regenerative Medicine, Spectroscopy

Scholarships Offered
All first-year students are considered for merit scholarships. ROTC scholarships available. Visit https://finaid.mines.edu/scholarships/ for more information on finding & applying for additional scholarships.

Special Opportunities
Jobs, co-ops, & internships available through the Career Center https://www.mines.edu/careers/jobs-and-internships/

Design@Mines - This program is a coordinated sequence of courses that are incrementally sophisticated in developing creativity and a problem-solving mentality in the design of useful/beneficial products and processes and organized into introductory cornerstone and upper level capstone project experiences. Study abroad programs available https://www.mines.edu/global/study-abroad-student-exchange/

Orgs: American Institute of Aeronautics & Astronautics, American Association of Drilling Engineers, American Association of Petroleum Geologists, American Chemical Society, American Institute of Chemical Engineers, ASHRAE, American Society of Mechanical Engineers, Mines Maker Society, Society of Automotive Engineers, Society of Women Eng

Teams: Angry Vehicle Competition, Baja Racing Team - Society for Automotive Engineering (SAE), Beetleweight Robotics Challenge, Board Games, Capture-the-Flag Security Games, Chem-E Car Team, Chess, Concrete Canoe Team, DOE Solar Decathlon Team, Equestrian, Formula SAE Racing, iGEM (Intl Genetically Engineered Machines) Intercollegiate Mining Games (Mucking, Trackstand, Jackleg, Handsteel, Survey, Gold Pan, & Swede Saw), Mines Robotics, Mines Rover Autonomous Vehicle, National Cyber Defense Competition, Racing Club, Society for Mechanical Engineering (SME) Student Design Competition, Steel Bridge Team

Notable Alumni
John Allen, William Arbegast, Fred Bond, Shane Carwin, Derrick Jensen, Jan Miller, and Robert Waterman Jr.

ALASKA
ARIZONA
CALIFORNIA
COLORADO
HAWAII
IDAHO
MONTANA
NEVADA
NEW MEXICO
OREGON
UTAH
WASHINGTON
WYOMING

UNIVERSITY OF COLORADO, BOULDER

Address: University of CO, Boulder, College of Engineering & Applied Sciences, 1111 Engineering Dr., 422 UCB, Boulder, CO 80309-0422
Website: *https://www.colorado.edu/engineering/*
Contact: *https://www.colorado.edu/engineering/contact-us*
Phone: (303) 492-5071
Email: cueng@colorado.edu

COST OF ATTENDANCE:

Tuition & Fees: $16,658 (in-state), $43,636 (out-of-state)
Addl Exp: $17,346 | **Total:** $34,004 (in-state), $60,982 (out-of-state)
Financial Aid: https://www.colorado.edu/financialaid/

ADDITIONAL INFORMATION:

Available Degree(s)
- BS, MS, Ph.D. Aerospace Eng Sci, Architectural Engineering, Biomedical Eng, Chem & Biological Eng, Chem Eng, Civil Eng, Computer Science, Electrical & Computer Eng, Electrical Eng, Environmental Eng, Integrated Eng Design, Mechanical Eng
- Minors: Biomedical Eng, Comp Sci, Computer Eng, Creative Technology & Design, Electrical Eng, Eng Management, Energy Eng, Global Eng, Quantum Engineering, Signals & Systems
- Certificates: Digital Media, Energy, Eng for Developing Comm, Eng Leadership, Eng Mgmt & Entrepreneurship, Eng, Science & Society, Global Eng, International Eng, Telecommunication

Related Research Centers
Aerospace Mech Res Ctr, AeroSpace Ventures, ATLAS Inst, Ctr for Res & Educ in Wind, Center for Software & Soc, Ctr for Unmanned Aircraft Systems, CO Ctr for Astrodynamics Res, Coop Institute for Research in Environmental Science, Design Center, Joint Inst for Lab Astrophysics, Lab for Atmosphere & Space Physics, Membrane Applied Science & Technology Center, Optical Lab, Power Electronics Ctr, Renewable & Sustainable Energy Institute, Research & Eng Center for Unmanned Vehicles, Soft Materials Research Center, Space Grant Consort

Scholarships Offered
CU Boulder's scholarship application (opens Nov 1; some close Feb 1; others close March 1): https://www.colorado.edu/scholarships/cuboulder-scholarship-app.

Special Opportunities
Co-Ops, Internships, Earth Lab, Env Std Prog, Entrepreneurship & Eng, Global Exp, Leadership, National Center for Women & Info Tech, Our Future, Space Mobility; Space Weather Technology, Telecom Program, Undergraduate Research, Senior Design Projects, Service Learning

Orgs: American Institute of Aeronautics & Astronautics, American Indian Science & Engineering Society, American Institute of Chemical Engineers, American Society of Civil Engineers, American Society of Mechanical Engineers, Architectural Engineering Institute, Associated General Contractors, Assoc for Computing Machinery, Biomedical Eng Society, CO Engineering Magazine, Eng Council, CU Energy Club, Eng w/o Borders, Illuminating Eng Society, Intl Society for Pharmaceutical Eng, National Society of Black Eng, Society of Asian Scientists and Eng, Society of Hispanic Eng, Society of Mexican Amer Eng & Scientists, Society of Environmental Engineering, Society of Women Engineers

Teams: Coding Buffs, Cyber Team, Design-Build-Fly, Formula SAE Baja Racing, Grand Challenge – Our Space, iGEM (Intl Genetically Engineered Machines), HackCU, Hyperloop, Mock Trial, Model United Nations, Physics Olympiad, Racing Team, Robotics Team, RoboSub Team, Rover Team, Solar Decathlon, Sounding Rocketry, SpaceForce, T9hacks

Notable Alumni
Sidney Altman, Steve Chappell, W. Edwards Deming, Moriba Jah, Alan Kay, Tom Maniatis, Craig Mello, Norman Ramsey, Ellen Sileaf, Leon Silver, Gary Stormo, Steve Swanson, Joe Tanner

ALASKA
ARIZONA
CALIFORNIA
COLORADO
HAWAII
IDAHO
MONTANA
NEVADA
NEW MEXICO
OREGON
UTAH
WASHINGTON
WYOMING

WEST

UNIVERSITY OF WASHINGTON

Address: University of Washington, Seattle, WA 98195
Website: https://www.engr.washington.edu/
Contact: https://admit.washington.edu/contact/
Phone: (206) 543-9686
Email: Contact via contact link.

COST OF ATTENDANCE:

Tuition & Fees: $12,076 (in-state) $39,906 (out-of-state)
Addl Exp: $18,564 | **Total:** $30,640(in-state), $58,470 (out-of-state)
Financial Aid: https://www.washington.edu/financialaid/

ADDITIONAL INFORMATION:

Available Degree(s)
- BS, MS, Ph.D. Aeronautics & Astronautics, Bioengineering, Chemical Engineering, Civil Engineering, Electrical & Comp Eng, Environmental Engineering, Mechanical Engineering
- Online Master's in Construction Engineering, Supply Chain, Sustainable Transportation, and Energy Infrastructure

Research Centers & Institutes
Adv Composites Ctr, AI Inst, Biofab Center, Bloedel Hearing Research Center, Boeing Adv Res Ctr, Ctr for Collab. Sys for Security, Safety, & Regional Resilience, Center for Medical & Industrial Ultrasound, Ctr for Neurotech, Center for Translational Muscle Res, Clean Energy Inst, Center on Satellite Multimedia & Connected Vehicles, Center for Digital Fabrication, Inst for Foundations of Data Sci, Inst of Stem Cell & Regenerative Medicine, JT Ctr for Aerospace Tech Innov, Molecular Eng Materials Center, Nanofab Facility, Pacific Marine Energy Center, Pacific NW Transportation Consortium, Plasma Sci & Innovation Ctr, QuantumX, Supply Chain Transp & Logistics Ctr for Accessible Tech

Scholarships Offered
Presidential Scholarship valued at $10,000 available for high achieving Washington students; Purple & Gold Scholarship. UW Diversity Scholarship - $10,000 per year for four years.

Special Opportunities
Internships, externships, career services, summer programs for K-12 students. Study abroad programs: Grand Challenges Impact Lab – India; Valle Scholarship & Scandinavian civil & environmental engineering; Engineering Jordan – water engineering.

Orgs: American Institute of Chemical Engineering, American Public Works Assn, American Society of Civil Engineers, American Society of Mechanical Engineers, Association for Computing Machinery for Women, ACES, Bioengineers w/o Borders, Bioexplore, Biomedical Engineering Society, Engineers w/o Borders, GRID, HuskyADAPT, Institute of Industrial & Systems Engineering, National Society of Black Engineers, NEXUS Builders, Project Indoor Farm, Science & Eng Business Association, Society for the Advancement of Material Process Engineering, Society for Advanced Rocket Propulsion, Society of Asian Scientists & Engineers, Students for the Exploration & Development of Space, Society of Hispanic Professional Engineers, Synaptech, Society of Women Engineers, WA Wave

Teams: Capture-the-Flag Team (Batman's Kitchen), Chem-E Car, ChemE Brew, Chess, Concrete Canoe, Cubesat Team, Cyber Defense Competition Team, Design-Build-Fly, DubHacks, DubsTech, Formula Motorsports Electric Car Racing Team, Human-Powered Submarine Team, iGEM, Mock Trial, Model United Nations, Satellite Team, Hyperloop, Quiz Bowl, Robotics Team, Science Olympiad, Solar Car Team, Sounding Rocket Team, Steel Bridge Team, WOOF3D

Notable Alumni
Basel Alomair, Jeff Dean, Earl Eisenhower, Muhammad Iqbal, Irving Kanarek, George Martin, Lina Nilsson, Harley Nygren, Stefan Savage, Phil Spencer, Rao Varanasi, Usha Varanasi, and Victor Wong

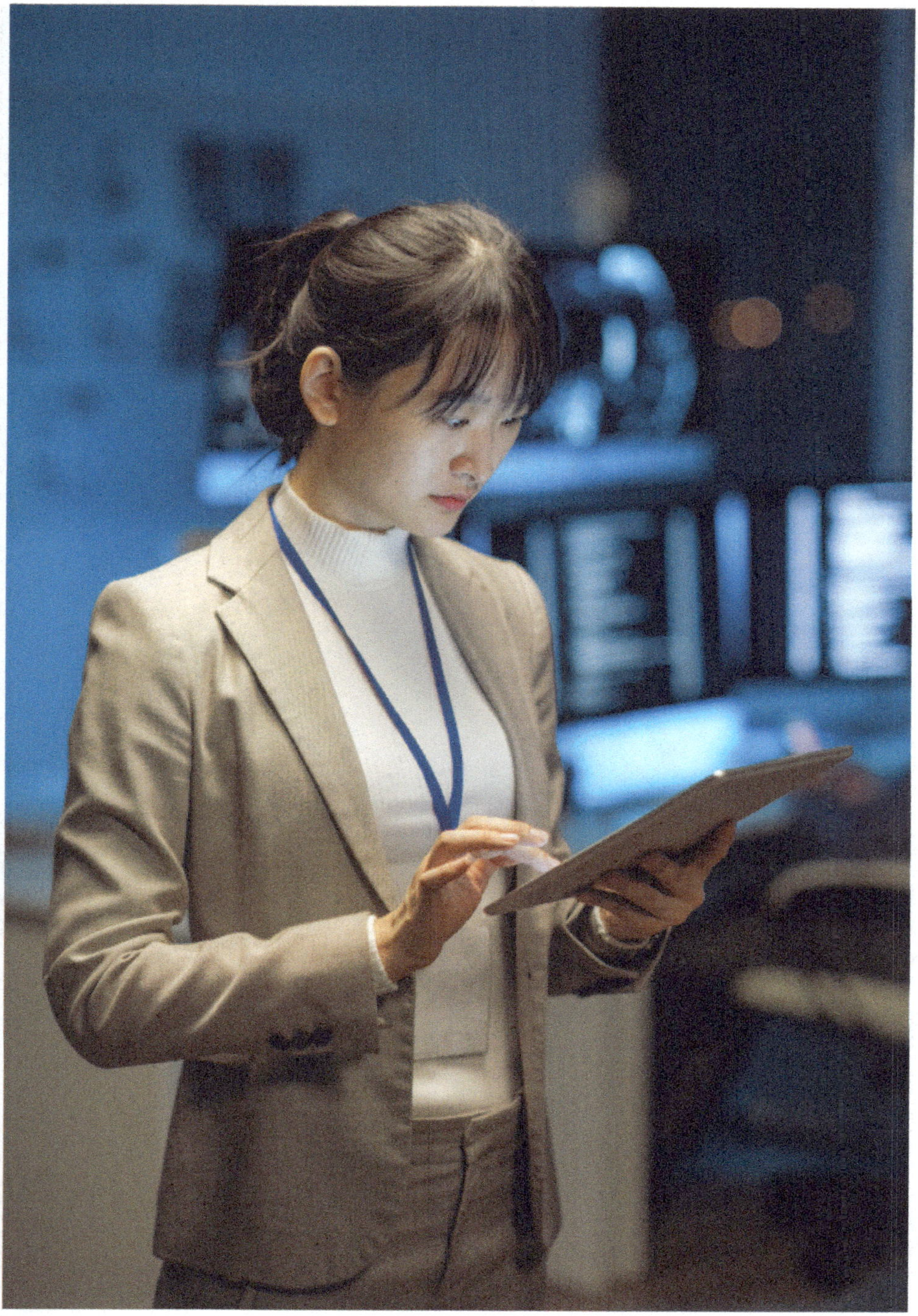

CHAPTER 15

TOP 12 MECHANICAL ENGINEERING PROGRAMS

S/N	School
1.	Massachusetts Institute of Technology (MIT)
2.	Georgia Institute of Technology (Georgia Tech)
3.	Stanford University
4.	University of California, Berkeley
5.	California Institute of Technology (CalTech)
6.	University of Michigan, Ann Arbor
7.	University of Illinois, Urbana-Champaign (UIUC)
8.	Purdue University, West Lafayette
9.	Carnegie Mellon University
10.	Cornell University
11.	The University of Texas, Austin
12.	Texas A&M University, College Station

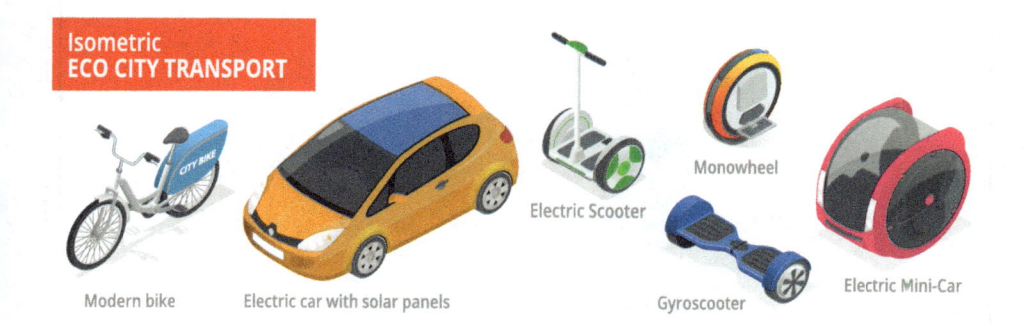

Isometric
ECO CITY TRANSPORT

Modern bike Electric car with solar panels Electric Scooter Monowheel Gyroscooter Electric Mini-Car

CHAPTER 16

TOP MECHANICAL ENGINEERING SCHOOLS – ALPHABETICAL BY STATE

School	State
Arizona State University	Arizona
California Institute of Technology (CalTech)	California
California Polytechnic State University, San Luis Obispo (Cal Poly, SLO)	California
Harvey Mudd College	California
Loyola Marymount University (LMU)	California
Santa Clara University	California
Stanford University	California
University of California, Berkeley	California
University of California, Los Angeles	California
University of Southern California	California
Colorado School of Mines	Colorado
University of Colorado, Boulder	Colorado
Florida Institute of Technology	Florida
University of Florida, Gainesville	Florida
Georgia Institute of Technology	Georgia
Northwestern University	Illinois
University of Illinois, Urbana-Champaign	Illinois
Purdue University	Indiana
Rose-Hulman Institute of Technology	Indiana
University of Notre Dame	Indiana
Johns Hopkins University	Maryland
University of Maryland, College Park	Maryland
Boston University	Massachusetts
Harvard University	Massachusetts
Massachusetts Institute of Technology (MIT)	Massachusetts
Northeastern University	Massachusetts
Olin College of Engineering	Massachusetts
Tufts University	Massachusetts
Worcester Polytechnic Institute (WPI)	Massachusetts
Kettering University	Michigan
Michigan State University	Michigan
Michigan Technological University	Michigan
University of Michigan	Michigan
University of Minnesota, Twin Cities	Minnesota
Washington University in St. Louis	Missouri
Princeton University	New Jersey
Stevens Institute of Technology	New Jersey

School	State
Columbia University	New York
Cooper Union for the Advancement of Science and Arts	New York
Cornell University	New York
Rensselaer Polytechnic Institute (RPI)	New York
Syracuse University	New York
University of Rochester	New York
Duke University	North Carolina
North Carolina State University	North Carolina
Case Western Reserve University	Ohio
The Ohio State University	Ohio
Bucknell University	Pennsylvania
Carnegie Mellon University	Pennsylvania
Drexel University	Pennsylvania
Lafayette College	Pennsylvania
Lehigh University	Pennsylvania
Pennsylvania State University	Pennsylvania
University of Pennsylvania (UPenn)	Pennsylvania
Villanova University	Pennsylvania
Brown University	Rhode Island
Vanderbilt University	Tennessee
Rice University	Texas
Southern Methodist University	Texas
Texas A&M University	Texas
The University of Texas at Austin (UT Austin)	Texas
University of Virginia, Charlottesville	Virginia
Virginia Tech	Virginia
University of Washington, Seattle	Washington
University of Wisconsin, Madison	Wisconsin

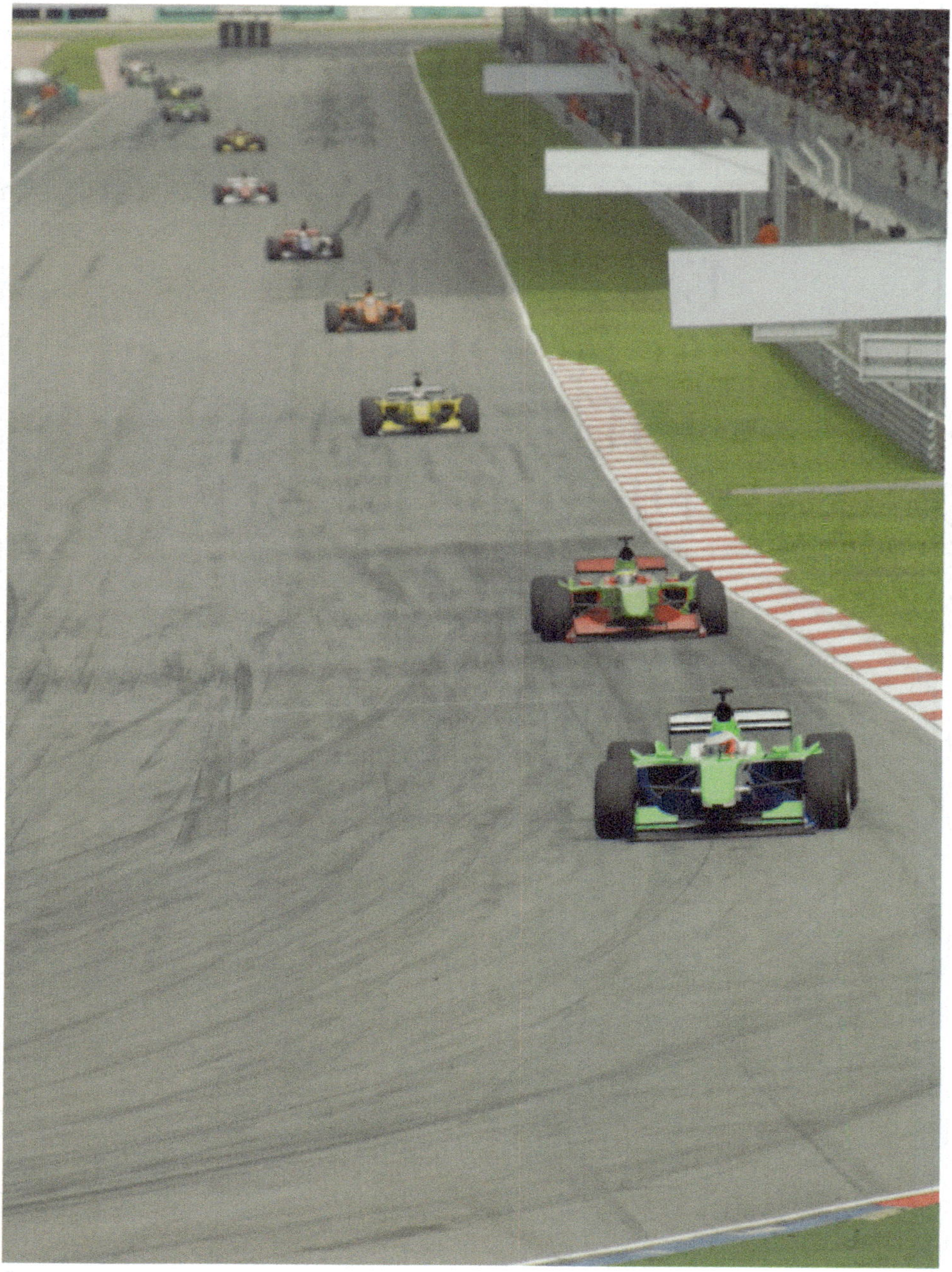

CHAPTER 17

TOP MECHANICAL ENGINEERING SCHOOLS BY ADMIT RATE AND UNDERGRADUATE ENROLLMENT

School	Admit Rate
Columbia University	4%
Stanford University	4%
Harvard University	5%
Princeton University	6%
Massachusetts Institute of Technology (MIT)	7%
California Institute of Technology (CalTech)	7%
Brown University	8%
Duke University	8%
University of Pennsylvania	9%
Northwestern University	9%
Harvey Mudd College	10%
Cornell University	11%
Johns Hopkins University	11%
Rice University	11%
Tufts University	11%
Vanderbilt University	12%
University of California, Los Angeles	14%
University of Southern California	16%
Washington University in St. Louis	16%
Carnegie Mellon University	17%
University of California, Berkeley	17%
Cooper Union	18%
Olin College of Engineering	18%
University of Notre Dame	19%
Boston University	20%
Northeastern University	20%
Georgia Institute of Technology	21%
University of Virginia, Charlottesville	23%
University of Michigan	26%
Case Western Reserve University	30%
Villanova University	31%
University of Florida, Gainesville	31%
The University of Texas at Austin (UT Austin)	32%
University of Rochester	35%
Bucknell University	38%
California Polytechic State University, San Luis Obispo (Cal Poly SLO)	38%
Lafayette College	41%

School	Admit Rate
Lehigh University	46%
Loyola Marymount University (LMU)	46%
North Carolina State University	46%
Pennsylvania State University	49%
University of Illinois, Urbana-Champaign	50%
Santa Clara University	51%
University of Maryland, College Park	52%
Southern Methodist University	53%
Stevens Institute of Technology	53%
Colorado School of Mines	55%
University of Washington, Seattle	56%
Rensselaer Polytechnic Institute (RPI)	57%
University of Wisconsin, Madison	57%
Worcester Polytechnic Institute	59%
Texas A&M University	63%
Virginia Tech	66%
Purdue University	67%
Florida Institute of Technology	69%
Syracuse University	69%
University of Minnesota, Twin Cities	**70%**
Kettering University	**74%**
Michigan State University	**76%**
Drexel University	**77%**
Rose-Hulman Institute of Technology	**77%**
University of Colorado, Boulder	**84%**
Michigan Technical University	**86%**
The Ohio State University	**87%**
Arizona State University	**88%**

TOP MECHANICAL ENGINEERING SCHOOLS BY UNDERGRADUATE ENROLLMENT

School	Enrollment
Olin College of Engineering	382
Cooper Union	806
California Institute of Technology (CalTech)	901
Harvey Mudd College	905
Kettering University	1,659

School	Enrollment
Rose-Hulman Institute of Technology	2,081
Lafayette College	2,725
Florida Institute of Technology	3,475
Bucknell University	3,695
Stevens Institute of Technology	3,791
Rice University	4,076
Massachusetts Institute of Technology (MIT)	4,361
Princeton University	4,774
Worcester Polytechnic Institute	4,892
Colorado School of Mines	5,216
Case Western Reserve University	5,430
Lehigh University	5,451
Santa Clara University	5,608
Michigan Technical University	5,778
Rensselaer Polytechnic Institute (RPI)	6,283
Johns Hopkins University	6,331
University of Rochester	6,521
Tufts University	6,676
Duke University	6,717
Brown Univrersity	6,792
Southern Methodist University	6,827
Villanova University	7,037
Vanderbilt University	7,057
Carnegie Mellon University	7,073
Loyola Marymount University (LMU)	7,127
Stanford University	7,645
Washington University in St. Louis	7,653
Northwestern University	8,194
Columbia University-	8,448
Harvard University	8,527
University of Notre Dame	8,874
University of Pennsylvania	11,155
Cornell University	14,743
Syracuse University	14,479
Drexel University	14,616
Northeastern University	15,156
Georgia Institute of Technology	16,561

School	Enrollment
Boston University	16,872
University of Virginia, Charlottesville	17,310
The Ohio State University	19,284
University of Southern California	19,786
California Polytechnic State University, San Luis Obispo (Cal Poly SLO)	21,456
North Carolina State University	26,150
Virginia Tech	30,020
University of Colorado, Boulder	30,300
University of California, Berkeley	30,799
University of Maryland, College Park	30,922
University of Michigan	31,329
University of California, Los Angeles	31,636
University of Washington, Seattle	32,244
University of Wisconsin, Madison -	32,688
University of Illinois, Urbana-Champaign	34,559
Purdue University	34,920
University of Florida, Gainesville	34,931
University of Minnesota, Twin Cities	36,061
Michigan State University	3,491
The University of Texas at Austin (UT Austin)	40,048
Pennsylvania State University	40,639
Texas A&M University	55,568
Arizona State University	63,124

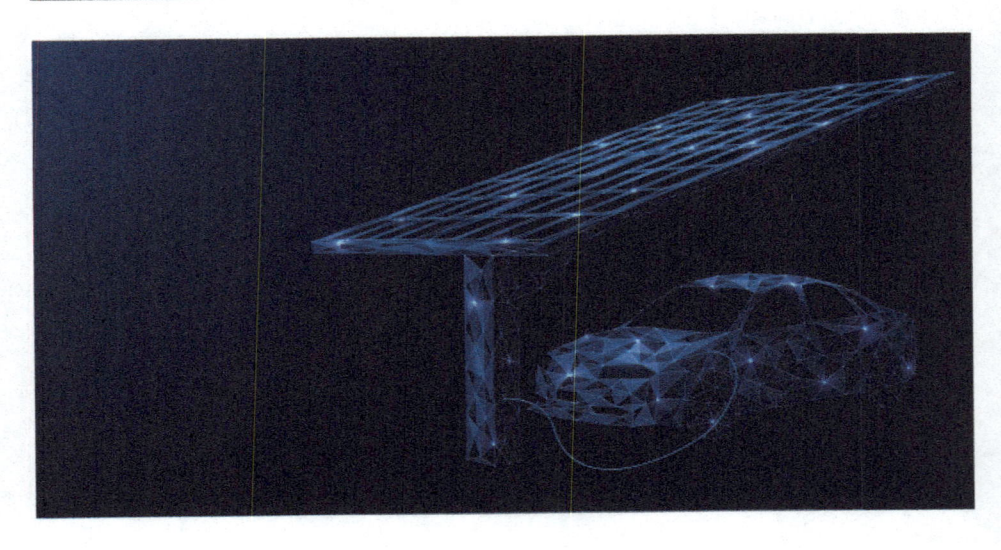

235

CHAPTER 18

ABET ACCREDITED MECHANICAL ENGINEERING PROGRAMS

School	Degree	Year Accredited
Alabama A&M University - Huntsville, AL	BSME	Oct 1, 1998 – Present
Alfred University - Alfred, NY	BS	Oct 1, 1988 – Present
Anderson University - Anderson, IN	BS	Oct 1, 2016 – Present
Angelo State University - San Angelo, TX	BSME	Oct 1, 2020 – Present
Arizona State University - Tempe, AZ	BSE	Oct 1, 1961 – Present
Arkansas State University - Jonesboro, AR	BSME	Oct 1, 2010 – Present
Arkansas Tech University - Russellville, AR	BSME	Oct 1, 1999 – Present
Auburn University - Auburn, AL	BME	Oct 1, 1939 – Present
Baylor University - Waco, Texas, United States	BSME	Oct 1, 1999 – Present
Benedictine College - Atchison, KS	BS	Oct 1, 2014 – Present
Boise State University - Boise, ID	BS	Oct 1, 1997 – Present
Boston University - Boston, MA	BS	Oct 1, 1983 – Present
Bradley University - Peoria, IL	MSBE	Oct 1, 1951 – Present
Brigham Young University - Provo, UT	BS	Oct 1, 1960 – Present
Brigham Young University - Rexburg, ID	BS	Oct 1, 2004 – Present
Brown University - Providence, RI	BS	Oct 1, 1936 – Present
Bucknell University - Lewisburg, PA	BSME	Oct 1, 1939 – Present
California Baptist University - Riverside, CA	BSME	Oct 1, 2010 – Present
California Institute of Technology - Pasadena, CA	BS	Oct 1, 2002 – Present
California State University Maritime Academy - Vallejo, CA	BS	Oct 1, 2001 – Present
California Polytechnic State University, San Luis Obispo, CA	BS	Oct 1, 1959 – Present
California State Polytechnic University, Pomona, CA	BS	Oct 1, 1970 – Present
California State University, Chico, CA	BS	Oct 1, 1971 – Present
California State University, Fresno, CA	BS	Oct 1, 1955 – Present
California State University, Fullerton, CA	BS	Oct 1, 1985 – Present
California State University, Long Beach, CA	BS	Oct 1, 1963 – Present
California State University, Los Angeles, CA	BS	Oct 1, 1965 – Present
California State University, Northridge, CA	BS	Oct 1, 1994 – Present
California State University, Sacramento, CA	BSME	Oct 1, 1965 – Present
Carnegie Mellon University - Pittsburgh, PA	BSME	Oct 1, 1936 – Present
Case Western Reserve University - Cleveland, OH	BSE	Oct 1, 1936 – Present
Catholic University - Washington, DC	BSME	Oct 1, 1938 – Present
Cedarville University - Cedarville, OH	BSME	Oct 1, 1993 – Present
Central Connecticut State University - New Britain, CT	BS	Oct 1, 2008 – Present
Central Michigan University - Mount Pleasant, MI	BSME	Oct 1, 2007 – Present
Christian Brothers University - Memphis, TN	BS	Oct 1, 1970 – Present
Citadel - Charleston, SC	BSME	Oct 1, 2015 – Present

School	Degree	Year Accredited
City University of New York, City College - New York, NY	BE	Oct 1, 1936 – Present
Clarkson University - Potsdam, NY	BS	Oct 1, 1936 – Present
Clemson University - Clemson, SC	BS	Oct 1, 1936 – Present
Cleveland State University - Cleveland, OH	BSME	Oct 1, 1948 – Present
College of New Jersey - Ewing, NJ	BSME	Oct 1, 2001 – Present
Colorado School of Mines - Golden, CO	BS	Oct 1, 2012 – Present
Colorado State University - Fort Collins, CO	BS	Oct 1, 1938 – Present
Columbia University - New York, NY	BS	Oct 1, 1936 – Present
Cooper Union - New York, NY	BSME	Oct 1, 1936 – Present
Cornell University - Ithaca, NY	BS	Oct 1, 1936 – Present
Drexel University - Philadelphia, PA	BSME	Oct 1, 1936 – Present
Duke University - Durham, NC	BSE	Oct 1, 1936 – Present
Dunwoody College of Technology - Minneapolis, MN	BSME	Oct 1, 2019 – Present
Eastern Michigan University - Ypsilanti, MI	BS	Oct 1, 2018 – Present
Eastern Washington University - Cheney, WA	BS	Oct 1, 2011 – Present
Embry-Riddle Aeronautical University - Daytona Beach, FL	BS	Oct 1, 2005 – Present
Embry-Riddle Aeronautical University - Prescott, AZ	BSME	Oct 1, 2009 – Present
Fairfield University - Fairfield, CT	BS	Oct 1, 1992 – Present
Florida A&M University - Florida State - Tallahassee, FL	BS	Oct 1, 1986 – Present
Florida Atlantic University - Boca Raton, FL	BSME	Oct 1, 1977 – Present
Florida Institute of Technology - Melbourne, FL	BS	Oct 1, 1974 – Present
Florida International University - Miami, FL	BS	Oct 1, 1988 – Present
Florida Polytechnic University - Lakeland, FL	BS	Oct 1, 2017 – Present
Franklin W. Olin College of Engineering - Needham, MA	BS	Oct 1, 2005 – Present
Gannon University - Erie, PA	BSME	Oct 1, 1965 – Present
George Mason University - Fairfax, VA	BSME	Oct 1, 2015 – Present
The George Washington University - Washington, DC	BS	Oct 1, 1940 – Present
Georgia Institute of Technology - Atlanta, GA	BSME	Oct 1, 1936 – Present
Georgia Southern University - Statesboro, GA	BSME	Oct 1, 2012 – Present
Kettering University - Flint, MI	BS	Oct 1, 1977 – Present
Gonzaga University - Spokane, WA	BSME	Oct 1, 1985 – Present
Grace College and Seminary - Winona Lake, IN	BS	Oct 1, 2020 – Present
Grand Canyon University - Phoenix, AZ	BSME	Oct 1, 2018 – Present
Grand Valley State University - Allendale, MI	BSE	Oct 1, 1997 – Present
Grove City College - Grove City, PA	BSME	Oct 1, 1989 – Present
Harding University - Searcy, AR	BS	Oct 1, 2007 – Present
Harvard University - Cambridge, MA	BS	Oct 1, 2013 – Present

School	Degree	Year Accredited
Hofstra University - Hempstead, NY	BS	Oct 1, 1988 – Present
Howard University - Washington, DC	BS	Oct 1, 1936 – Present
Idaho State University - Pocatello, ID	BS	Oct 1, 1993 – Present
Illinois Institute of Technology - Chicago, IL	BS	Oct 1, 1935 – Present
Indiana Institute of Technology - Fort Wayne, IN	BS	Oct 1, 1995 – Present
Indiana University - Indianapolis, IN	BSME	Oct 1, 1973 – Present
Inter American University - Bayamon, Puerto Rico	BS	Oct 1, 2009 – Present
Iowa State University of S&T - Ames, IA	BS	Oct 1, 1936 – Present
John Brown University - Siloam Springs, AR	BSME	Oct 1, 2019 – Present
Johns Hopkins University - Baltimore, MD	BSME	Oct 1, 1989 – Present
Kansas State University - Manhattan, KS	BS	Oct 1, 1936 – Present
Kennesaw State University - Kennesaw, GA	BS	Oct 1, 2012 – Present
King's College - Wilkes Barre, PA	BS	Oct 1, 2018 – Present
Lafayette College - Easton, PA	BS	Oct 1, 1936 – Present
Lake Superior State University - Sault Ste. Marie, MI	BS	Oct 1, 1999 – Present
Lamar University - Beaumont, TX	BSME	Oct 1, 1961 – Present
Lawrence Technological University - Southfield, MI	BS	Oct 1, 1975 – Present
Lehigh University - Bethlehem, PA	BSME	Oct 1, 1936 – Present
LeTourneau University - Longview, TX	BS	Oct 1, 2014 – Present
Liberty University - Lynchburg, VA	BS	Oct 1, 2017 – Present
Lipscomb University - Nashville, TN	BS	Oct 1, 2008 – Present
Louisiana State U. and A&M College - Baton Rouge, LA	BSME	Oct 1, 1936 – Present
Louisiana Tech University - Ruston, LA	BSME	Oct 1, 1948 – Present
Loyola Marymount University - Los Angeles, CA	BSE	Oct 1, 1967 – Present
Manhattan College - Riverdale, NY	BS	Oct 1, 1967 – Present
Minnesota State University - Mankato, MN	BS	Oct 1, 1992 – Present
Marquette University - Milwaukee, WI	BSME	Oct 1, 1936 – Present
Marshall University - Huntington, WV	BSME	Oct 1, 2016 – Present
Merrimack College - North Andover, MA	BS	Oct 1, 2015 – Present
Miami University - Oxford, OH	BSE	Oct 1, 2003 – Present
Michigan State University - East Lansing, MI	BS	Oct 1, 1936 – Present
Michigan Technological U. - Houghton, MI	BS	Oct 1, 1936 – Present
Midwestern State University - Wichita Falls, TX	BSME	Oct 1, 2007 – Present
Milligan University - Milligan, TN	BS	Oct 1, 2019 – Present
Milwaukee School of Engineering - Milwaukee, WI	BS	Oct 1, 1980 – Present
Mississippi State University - Mississippi State, MS	BS	Oct 1, 1941 – Present
Missouri University of Science and Technology - Rolla, MO	BS	Oct 1, 1950 – Present

School	Degree	Year Accredited
Montana Technological University - Butte, MT	BS	Oct 1, 2017 – Present
Montana State University - Bozeman, MT	BS	Oct 1, 1936 – Present
Naval Postgraduate School - Monterey, CA	MS	Oct 1, 1973 – Present
New Jersey Institute of Technology - Newark, NJ	BS	Oct 1, 1936 – Present
New Mexico Institute of Mining and Technology - Socorro, NM	BS	Oct 1, 2003 – Present
New Mexico State University - Las Cruces, NM	BSME	Oct 1, 1938 – Present
New York Institute of Technology - Old Westbury, NY	BS	Oct 1, 1986 – Present
New York University - Brooklyn, NY	BS	Oct 1, 1936 – Present
North Carolina A&T State University - Greensboro, NC	BS	Oct 1, 1969 – Present
North Carolina State University - Raleigh, NC	BS	Oct 1, 1936 – Present
North Dakota State University - Fargo, ND	BS	Oct 1, 1940 – Present
Northeastern University - Boston, MA	BSME	Oct 1, 1939 – Present
Northern Arizona University - Flagstaff, AZ	BSE	Oct 1, 1974 – Present
Northern Illinois University - Dekalb, IL	BS	Oct 1, 1988 – Present
Northwestern University - Evanston, IL	BS	Oct 1, 1938 – Present
Norwich University - Northfield, VT	BS	Oct 1, 1949 – Present
Oakland University - Rochester Hills, MI	BSE	Oct 1, 1979 – Present
Ohio Northern University - Ada, OH	BSME	Oct 1, 1954 – Present
The Ohio State University - Columbus, OH	BSME	Oct 1, 1936 – Present
Ohio University - Athens, OH	BSME	Oct 1, 1951 – Present
Oklahoma Christian University - Edmond, OK	BSME	Oct 1, 1989 – Present
Oklahoma State University - Stillwater, OK	BSME	Oct 1, 1936 – Present
Old Dominion University - Norfolk, VA	BS	Oct 1, 1967 – Present
Oregon Institute of Technology - Klamath Falls, OR	BS	Oct 1, 2007 – Present
Oregon State University - Corvallis, OR	BS & HBS	Oct 1, 1936 – Present
Pennsylvania State University - University Park, PA	BS	Oct 1, 1936 – Present
Pennsylvania State University, Behrend College - Erie, PA	BS	Oct 1, 1995 – Present
Pennsylvania State University, Berks Campus - Reading, PA	BSME	Oct 1, 2014 – Present
Pennsylvania State University, Harrisburg - Middletown, PA	BS	Oct 1, 2010 – Present
Point Park University - Pittsburgh, PA	BS	Oct 1, 2018 – Present
Polytechnic University - San Juan, Puerto Rico	BS	Oct 1, 1994 – Present
Portland State University - Portland, OR	BS	Oct 1, 1982 – Present
Prairie View A&M University - Prairie View, TX	BSME	Oct 1, 1972 – Present
Princeton University - Princeton, NJ	BSE	Oct 1, 1936 – Present
Purdue University - West Lafayette, IN	BSME	Oct 1, 1936 – Present
Purdue University - Fort Wayne, IN	BSME	Oct 1, 1989 – Present
Purdue University Northwest - Hammond, IN	BS	Oct 1, 1980 – Present

School	Degree	Year Accredited
Quinnipiac University - Hamden, CT	BS	Oct 1, 2015 – Present
Rensselaer Polytechnic Institute - Troy, NY	BS	Oct 1, 1936 – Present
Rice University - Houston, TX	BSME	Oct 1, 1936 – Present
Rochester Institute of Technology - Rochester, NY	BS	Oct 1, 1969 – Present
Rockhurst University - Kansas City, MO	BS	Oct 1, 2019 – Present
Rose-Hulman Institute of Technology - Terre Haute, IN	BS	Oct 1, 1936 – Present
Rowan University - Glassboro, NJ	BS	Oct 1, 1999 – Present
Rutgers University - New Brunswick, NJ	BS	Oct 1, 1936 – Present
Saginaw Valley State University - University Center, MI	BSME	Oct 1, 1989 – Present
Saint Martin's University - Lacey, WA	BSME	Oct 1, 1992 – Present
San Diego State University - San Diego, CA	BS	Oct 1, 1964 – Present
San Francisco State University - San Francisco, CA	BS	Oct 1, 1986 – Present
San Jose State University - San Jose, CA	BS	Oct 1, 1963 – Present
Santa Clara University - Santa Clara, CA	BS	Oct 1, 1936 – Present
Seattle Pacific University - Seattle, WA	BSME	Oct 1, 2017 – Present
Seattle University - Seattle, WA	BSME	Oct 1, 1962 – Present
South Dakota School of Mines and Technology - Rapid City, SD	BS	Oct 1, 1950 – Present
South Dakota State University - Brookings, SD	BS	Oct 1, 1936 – Present
Southern Illinois University - Carbondale, IL	BS	Oct 1, 1988 – Present
Southern Illinois University - Edwardsville, IL	BS	Oct 1, 1992 – Present
Southern Methodist University - Dallas, TX	BSME	Oct 1, 1939 – Present
Southern New Hampshire University - Manchester, NH	BSE ME	Oct 1, 2016 – Present
Southern University and A&M College - Baton Rouge, LA	BSME	Oct 1, 1970 – Present
Southern Utah University - Cedar City, UT	BS	Oct 1, 2018 – Present
St. Ambrose University - Davenport, IA	BSME	Oct 1, 2014 – Present
St. Cloud State University - St. Cloud, MN	BS	Oct 1, 2002 – Present
St. Mary's University - San Antonio, TX	BS	Oct 1, 2016 – Present
Saint Louis University - Saint Louis, MO	BS	Oct 1, 1996 – Present
Stanford University - Stanford, CA	BS	Oct 1, 1936 – Present
Stony Brook University - New York, NY	BS	Oct 1, 1979 – Present
Stevens Institute of Technology - Hoboken, NJ	BS	Oct 1, 1984 – Present
SUNY Binghamton - Vestal, NY	BS	Oct 1, 1988 – Present
SUNY Maritime College - Bronx, NY	BS	Oct 1, 2009 – Present
SUNY - New Paltz, NY	BS	Oct 1, 2016 – Present
SUNY, Polytechnic Institute - Utica, NY	BS	Oct 1, 2016 – Present
Syracuse University - Syracuse, NY	BS	Oct 1, 1936 – Present
Tarleton State University - Stephenville, TX	BS	Oct 1, 2017 – Present

School	Degree	Year Accredited
Temple University - Philadelphia, PA	BS	Oct 1, 1988 – Present
Tennessee State University - Nashville, TN	BS	Oct 1, 1977 – Present
Tennessee Technological University - Cookeville, TN	BSME	Oct 1, 1966 – Present
Texas A&M University – Kingsville - Kingsville, TX	BSME	Oct 1, 1978 – Present
Texas A&M University - College Station, TX	BS	Oct 1, 1936 – Present
Texas A&M University - Corpus Christi, TX	BS	Oct 1, 2011 – Present
Texas Tech University - Lubbock, TX	BS	Oct 1, 1937 – Present
Thomas Jefferson University - Philadelphia, PA	BSE	Oct 1, 2009 – Present
Trine University - Angola, IN	BSME	Oct 1, 1971 – Present
Tufts University - Medford, MA	BS	Oct 1, 1936 – Present
Tuskegee University - Tuskegee, AL	BS	Oct 1, 1965 – Present
Union College - Schenectady, NY	BS	Oct 1, 1957 – Present
US Air Force Academy - USAFA, CO	BS	Oct 1, 1989 – Present
US Coast Guard Academy - New London, CT	BS	Oct 1, 1994 – Present
US Military Academy - West Point, NY	BS	Oct 1, 1985 – Present
US Naval Academy - Annapolis, MD	BS	Oct 1, 1970 – Present
Universidad Ana. G. Mendez - Gurabo, Puerto Rico	BS	Oct 1, 2003 – Present
University of Akron - Akron, OH	BS in ME	Oct 1, 1941 – Present
University of Alabama - Birmingham, AL	BSME	Oct 1, 1983 – Present
University of Alabama - Huntsville, AL	BSME	Oct 1, 1976 – Present
University of Alabama - Tuscaloosa, AL	BSME	Oct 1, 1936 – Present
University of Alaska Anchorage, AK	BS	Oct 1, 2007 – Present
University of Alaska Fairbanks, AK	BS	Oct 1, 1980 – Present
University of Arkansas - Fayetteville, AR	BSME	Oct 1, 1936 – Present
University of Arkansas at Little Rock, AR	BS	Oct 1, 2016 – Present
University of Arizona - Tucson, AZ	BSME	Oct 1, 1936 – Present
University of Bridgeport - Bridgeport, CT	BS MEEG	Oct 1, 2020 – Present
University at Buffalo, SUNY - Buffalo, NY	BS	Oct 1, 1964 – Present
University of California, Berkeley, CA	BS	Oct 1, 1936 – Present
University of California, Davis, CA	BS	Oct 1, 1965 – Present
University of California, Irvine, CA	BS	Oct 1, 1978 – Present
University of California, Los Angeles, CA	BS	Oct 1, 1985 – Present
University of California, Merced, CA	BS	Oct 1, 2012 – Present
University of California, Riverside, CA	BS	Oct 1, 1997 – Present
University of California, San Diego, CA	BS	Oct 1, 1987 – Present
University of California, Santa Barbara, CA	BS	Oct 1, 1967 – Present
University of Central Florida - Orlando, FL	BSME	Oct 1, 1972 – Present

School	Degree	Year Accredited
University of Central Oklahoma - Edmond, OK	BS	Oct 1, 2012 – Present
University of Cincinnati - Cincinnati, OH	BS	Oct 1, 1936 – Present
University of Colorado Boulder, CO	BS	Oct 1, 1936 – Present
University of Colorado at Colorado Springs, CO	BS	Oct 1, 2002 – Present
University of Colorado Denver, CO	BSME	Oct 1, 1982 – Present
University of Connecticut - Storrs, CT	BSE	Oct 1, 1941 – Present
University of Dayton - Dayton, OH	BSE	Oct 1, 1951 – Present
University of Delaware - Newark, DE	BSE	Oct 1, 1936 – Present
University of Denver - Denver, CO	BSME	Oct 1, 1988 – Present
University of Detroit Mercy - Detroit, MI	BSE	Oct 1, 1936 – Present
University of the District of Columbia - Washington, DC	BS	Oct 1, 1988 – Present
University of Evansville - Evansville, IN	BSME	Oct 1, 1970 – Present
University of Florida - Gainesville, FL	BS	Oct 1, 1936 – Present
University of Georgia - Athens, GA	BSME	Oct 1, 2016 – Present
University of Hartford - West Hartford, CT	BSME	Oct 1, 1967 – Present
University of Hawaii at Manoa - Honolulu, HI	BS	Oct 1, 1967 – Present
University of Houston - Houston, TX	BSME	Oct 1, 1957 – Present
University of Houston - Clear Lake - Houston, TX	BS	Oct 1, 2019 – Present
University of Idaho - Moscow, ID	BSME	Oct 1, 1936 – Present
University of Illinois - Champaign, IL	BS	Oct 1, 1936 – Present
University of Illinois - Chicago, IL	BS	Oct 1, 1985 – Present
University of Indianapolis - Indianapolis, IN	BSME	Oct 1, 2019 – Present
University of Iowa - Iowa City, IA	BSE	Oct 1, 1937 – Present
University of Jamestown - Jamestown, ND	BS	Oct 1, 2019 – Present
University of Kansas - Lawrence, KS	BS	Oct 1, 1936 – Present
University of Kentucky - Lexington, KY	BSME	Oct 1, 1940 – Present
University of Kentucky - Lexington, KY	BSME	May 1, 2001 – Present
University of Louisiana - Lafayette, LA	BSME	Oct 1, 1956 – Present
University of Louisville - Louisville, KY	BSME	Oct 1, 2008 – Present
University of Louisville - Louisville, KY	Meng in ME	Oct 1, 1936 – Present
University of Massachusetts - Lowell, MA	BSE	Oct 1, 1952 – Present
University of Maine - Orono, ME	BS	Oct 1, 1936 – Present
University of Maryland - Baltimore, MD	BS	Oct 1, 1936 – Present
University of Maryland - College Park, MD	BS	Oct 1, 1936 – Present
University of Massachusetts - Amherst, MA	BS	Oct 1, 1950 – Present
University of Massachusetts - Dartmouth, MA	BS	Oct 1, 1970 – Present
University of Memphis - Memphis, TN	BSME	Oct 1, 1973 – Present

School	Degree	Year Accredited
University of Miami - Coral Gables, FL	BSME	Oct 1, 1962 – Present
University of Michigan - Ann Arbor, MI	BSE	Oct 1, 1936 – Present
University of Michigan - Dearborn, MI	BSE	Oct 1, 1975 – Present
University of Michigan - Flint, MI	BSE	Oct 1, 2011 – Present
University of Minnesota - Duluth, MI	BSME	Oct 1, 2003 – Present
University of Minnesota - Minneapolis, MI	BME	Oct 1, 1936 – Present
University of Mississippi - University, MS	BSME	Oct 1, 1959 – Present
University of Missouri - Columbia, MO	BSME	Oct 1, 1936 – Present
University of Missouri - Kansas City, MO	BSME	Oct 1, 1978 – Present
University of Missouri - St. Louis, MO	BSME	Oct 1, 1999 – Present
University of Mount Union - Alliance, OH	BS	Oct 1, 2013 – Present
University of Nebraska - Lincoln, NE	BS	Oct 1, 1936 – Present
University of Nevada - Las Vegas, NV	BSE	Oct 1, 1987 – Present
University of Nevada - Reno, NV	BSME	Oct 1, 1938 – Present
University of New Hampshire - Durham, NH	BSME	Oct 1, 1936 – Present
University of New Haven - West Haven, CT	BS	Oct 1, 1970 – Present
University of New Mexico - Albuquerque, NM	BS	Oct 1, 1936 – Present
University of New Orleans - New Orleans, LA	BSME	Oct 1, 1977 – Present
University of North Carolina - Charlotte, NC	BS	Oct 1, 1984 – Present
University of North Dakota - Grand Forks, ND	BSME	Oct 1, 1936 – Present
University of North Florida - Jacksonville, FL	BS	Oct 1, 2002 – Present
University of Notre Dame - Notre Dame, IN	BS	Oct 1, 1942 – Present
University of Oklahoma - Norman, OK	BS	Oct 1, 1936 – Present
University of the Pacific - Stockton, CA	BS	Oct 1, 1986 – Present
University of Pittsburgh - Pittsburgh, PA	BSE	Oct 1, 1936 – Present
University of Pittsburgh - Johnstown, PA	BSE	Oct 1, 2018 – Present
University of Portland - Portland, OR	BSME	Oct 1, 1974 – Present
University of Puerto Rico - Mayaguez, Puerto Rico	BSME	Oct 1, 1960 – Present
University of Rhode Island - Kingston, RI	BSME	Oct 1, 1936 – Present
University of Rochester - Rochester, NY	BS	Oct 1, 1936 – Present
University of San Diego - San Diego, CA	BS/BA ME	Oct 1, 2006 – Present
University of South Alabama - Mobile, AL	BS	Oct 1, 1983 – Present
University of South Carolina - Columbia, SC	BSE	Oct 1, 1948 – Present
University of South Florida - Tampa, FL	BSME	Oct 1, 1972 – Present
University of Southern California - Los Angeles, CA	BS	Oct 1, 1942 – Present
University of Southern Indiana - Evansville, IN	BSME	Oct 1, 2016 – Present
University of Southern Maine - Portland, ME	BS	Oct 1, 2013 – Present

School	Degree	Year Accredited
University of St. Thomas - Saint Paul, MN	BSME	Oct 1, 1999 – Present
University of Tennessee - Chattanooga, TN	BSME	Oct 1, 2002 – Present
University of Tennessee - Knoxville, TN	BS	Oct 1, 1936 – Present
University of Texas - Arlington, TX	BSME	Oct 1, 1967 – Present
University of Texas - Austin, TX	BS	Oct 1, 1936 – Present
University of Texas - El Paso, TX	BSME	Oct 1, 1966 – Present
University of Texas, Permian Basin - Odessa, TX	BS	Oct 1, 2010 – Present
University of Texas - Richardson, TX	BSME	Oct 1, 2011 – Present
University of Texas Rio Grande Valley - Edinburg, TX	BSME	Oct 1, 1995 – Present
University of Texas - San Antonio, TX	BS	Oct 1, 1986 – Present
University of Texas - Tyler, TX	BSME	Oct 1, 2001 – Present
University of Toledo - Toledo, OH	BS	Oct 1, 1950 – Present
University of Tulsa - Tulsa, OK	BS	Oct 1, 1965 – Present
University of Utah - Salt Lake City, UT	BSME	Oct 1, 1936 – Present
University of Vermont - Burlington, VT	BSME	Oct 1, 1936 – Present
University of Virginia - Charlottesville, VA	BS	Oct 1, 1936 – Present
University of Washington - Seattle, WA	BSME	Oct 1, 1936 – Present
University of Washington - Bothell, WA	BS	Oct 1, 2015 – Present
University of West Florida - Pensacola, FL	BSME	Oct 1, 2017 – Present
University of Wisconsin - Madison, WI	BS	Oct 1, 1936 – Present
University of Wisconsin - Milwaukee, WI	BSE	Oct 1, 1969 – Present
University of Wisconsin - Platteville, WI	BS	Oct 1, 1986 – Present
University of Wisconsin - Menomonie, WI	BS	Oct 1, 2017 – Present
University of Wyoming - Laramie, WY	BSME	Oct 1, 1941 – Present
Utah State University - Logan, UT	BS	Oct 1, 1961 – Present
Utah Valley University - Orem, UT	BSME	Oct 1, 2019 – Present
Valparaiso University - Valparaiso, IN	BSME	Oct 1, 1958 – Present
Vanderbilt University - Nashville, TN	BE	Oct 1, 1939 – Present
Vaughn College of Aeronautics and Technology - Flushing, NY	BS	Oct 1, 2018 – Present
Villanova University - Villanova, PA	BSME	Oct 1, 1941 – Present
Virginia Commonwealth University - Richmond, VA	BS	Oct 1, 1999 – Present
Virginia Military Institute - Lexington, VA	BSME	Oct 1, 1987 – Present
Virginia Tech - Blacksburg, VA	BSME	Oct 1, 1936 – Present
Washington State University - Pullman, WA	BSME	Oct 1, 1936 – Present
Washington State University - Richland, WA	BS	Oct 1, 2013 – Present
Washington State University - Vancouver, WA	BS	Oct 1, 2006 – Present
Washington University - Saint Louis, MO	BS	Oct 1, 1936 – Present

School	Degree	Year Accredited
Wayne State University - Detroit, MI	BSME	Oct 1, 1944 – Present
Weber State University - Ogden, UT	BS	Oct 1, 2019 – Present
Wentworth Institute of Technology - Boston, MA	BS	Oct 1, 2013 – Present
West Texas A&M University - Canyon, TX	BS	May 1, 2006 – Present
West Virginia University Institute of Technology - Beckley, WV	BS	Oct 1, 1968 – Present
West Virginia University - Morgantown, WV	BSME	Oct 1, 1936 – Present
Western Illinois University - Macomb, IL	BS	Oct 1, 2016 – Present
Western Kentucky University - Bowling Green, KY	BS	Oct 1, 2003 – Present
Western Michigan University - Kalamazoo, MI	BSE	Oct 1, 1985 – Present
Western New England University - Springfield, MA	BS	Oct 1, 1971 – Present
Wichita State University - Wichita, KS	BSME	Oct 1, 1961 – Present
Widener University - Chester, PA	BS	Oct 1, 1985 – Present
Wilkes University - Wilkes-Barre, PA	BS	Oct 1, 1995 – Present
Worcester Polytechnic Institute - Worcester, MA	BS	Oct 1, 1936 – Present
Wright State University - Dayton, OH	BS	Oct 1, 1988 – Present
Yale University - New Haven, CT	BS	Oct 1, 1936 – Sep 30, 1965, Oct 1, 1985 – Present
York College of Pennsylvania - York, PA	BS	Oct 1, 1998 – Present
Youngstown State University - Youngstown, OH	BSME	Oct 1, 1954 – Present

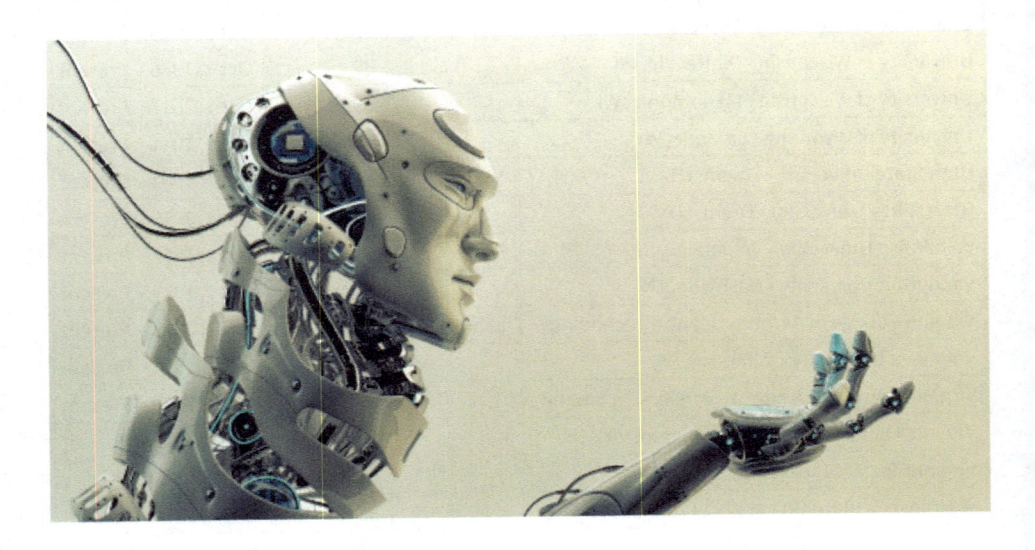

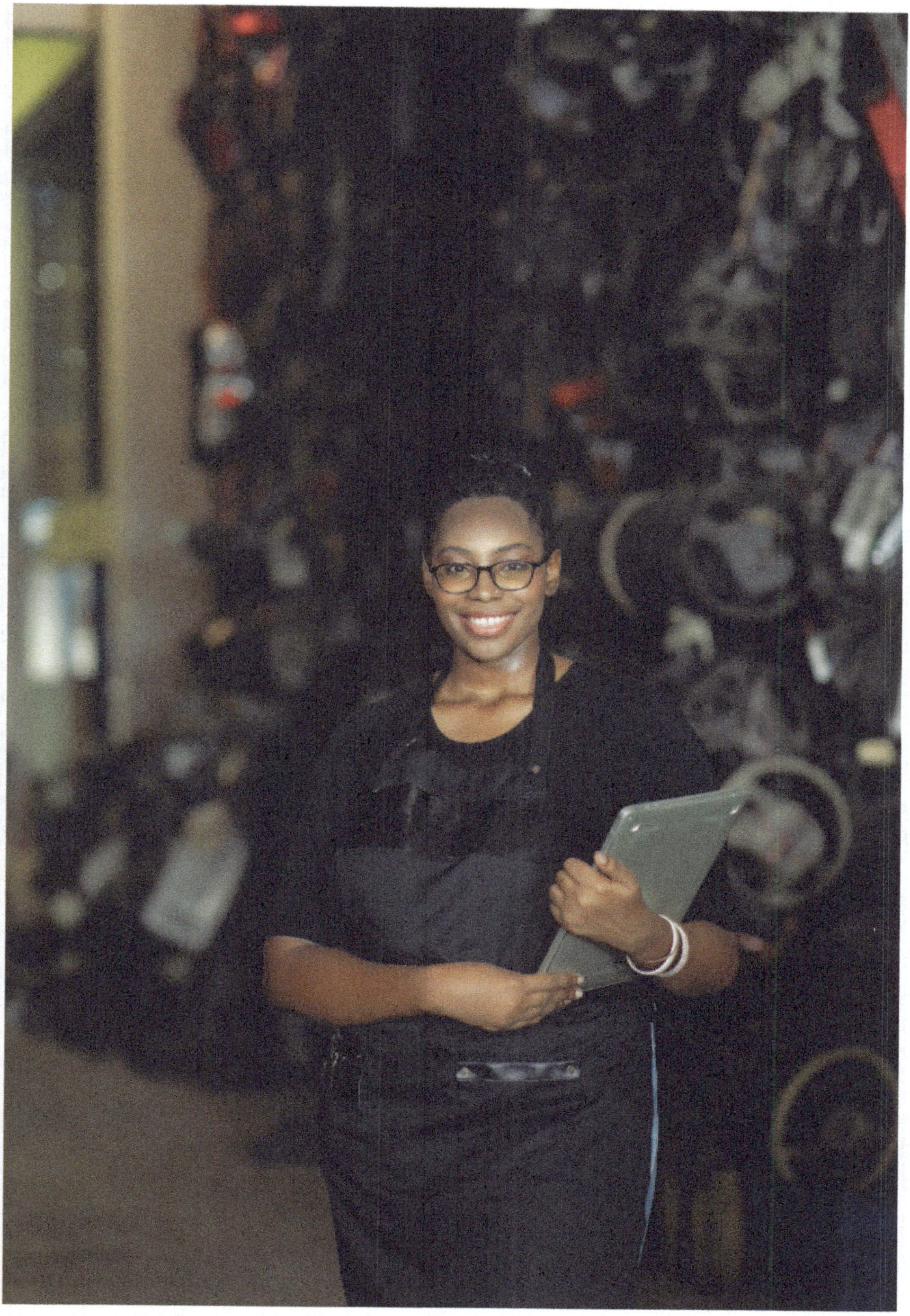

CHAPTER 19

TOP PROGRAMS FOR AEROSPACE ENGINEERING

Arizona State University	Notes
Auburn University	
Boston University	
California Institute of Technology (CalTech)	
California Polytechnic State University, San Luis Obispo	
California State Polytechnic University, Pomona	
California State University, Long Beach (CSULB)	
Case Western Reserve University	
Cornell University	
Embry-Riddle Aeronautical University	
Florida Institute of Technology	
Georgia Institute of Technology	
Iowa State University	
Massachusetts Institute of Technology	
Oklahoma State University	
Pennsylvania State University, University Park	
Princeton University	
Purdue University	
Rensselaer Polytechnic Institute (RPI)	
Rice University	
Rutgers University, New Brunswick	
San Diego State University	
San José State University (SJSU)	
Stanford University	
Syracuse University	
Texas A&M University	
The Ohio State University, Columbus	
The University of Oklahoma, Norman	
The University of Texas at Austin (UT Austin)	
The University of Texas, Arlington	
United States Air Force Academy	
United States Naval Academy	
University of California, Berkeley	
University of California, Davis	
University of California, Irvine	
University of California, Los Angeles	
University of California, San Diego	
University of Colorado, Boulder	

250

Arizona State University	Notes
University of Florida, Gainesville	
University of Illinois, Urbana-Champaign	
University of Kansas	
University of Maryland, College Park	
University of Miami	
University of Michigan	
University of Notre Dame	
University of Southern California	
University of Virginia, Charlottesville	
University of Washington	
Virginia Polytechnic Institute and State University (Virginia Tech)	
Washington University in St. Louis	
Worcester Polytechnic Institute	

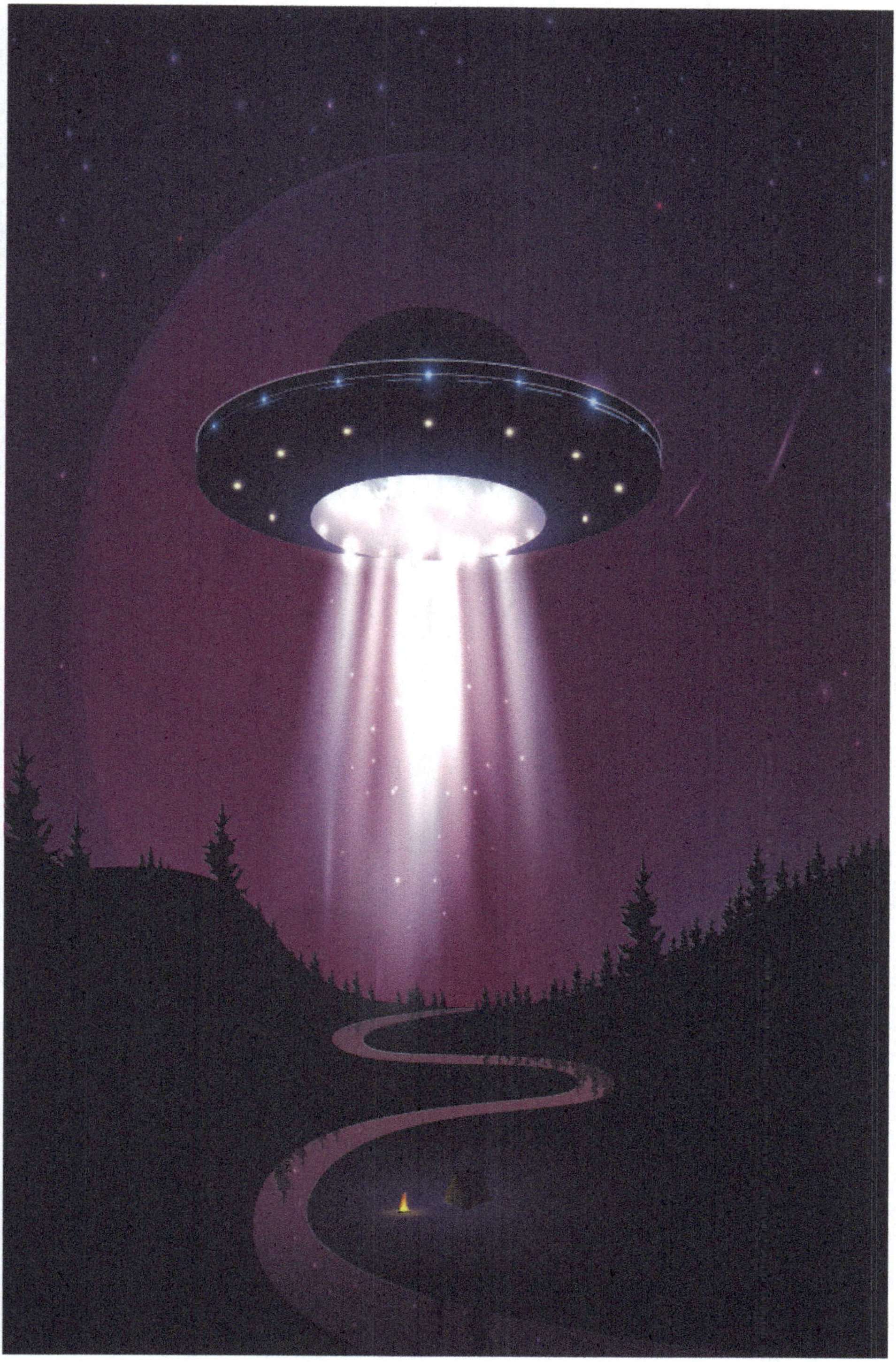

CHAPTER 20

TOP PROGRAMS FOR CHEMICAL, PETROLEUM, & NUCLEAR ENGINEERING

School	Notes
Bucknell University	
California Institute of Technology (CalTech)	
Carnegie Mellon University	
Colorado School of Mines	
Columbia University	
Cornell University	
Georgia Institute of Technology	
Johns Hopkins University	
Lafayette College	
Louisiana State University (LSU)	
Marietta College	
Massachusetts Institute of Technology (MIT)	
Missouri University of Science and Technology	
New Mexico Institute of Mining and Technology	
North Carolina State University	
Northeastern University	
Northwestern University	
Pennsylvania State University	
Princeton University	
Purdue University	
Rensselaer Polytechnic Institute (RPI)	
Rice University	
Rose-Hulman Institute of Technology	
South Dakota School of Mines & Technology	
Stanford University	
Texas A&M University	
Texas A&M University, Kingsville	
Texas Tech University	
The Ohio State University	
The University of Houston	
The University of Oklahoma, Norman	
The University of Texas at Austin (UT Austin)	
Tufts University	
University of Alaska, Fairbanks	
University of California, Berkeley	
University of California, Santa Barbara	
University of Colorado, Boulder	

School	Notes
University of Delaware	
University of Florida, Gainesville	
University of Illinois, Urbana-Champaign	
University of Kansas	
University of Louisiana, Lafayette	
University of Michigan	
University of Minnesota, Twin Cities	
University of Montana/Montana State University	
University of North Dakota	
University of Notre Dame	
University of Pennsylvania	

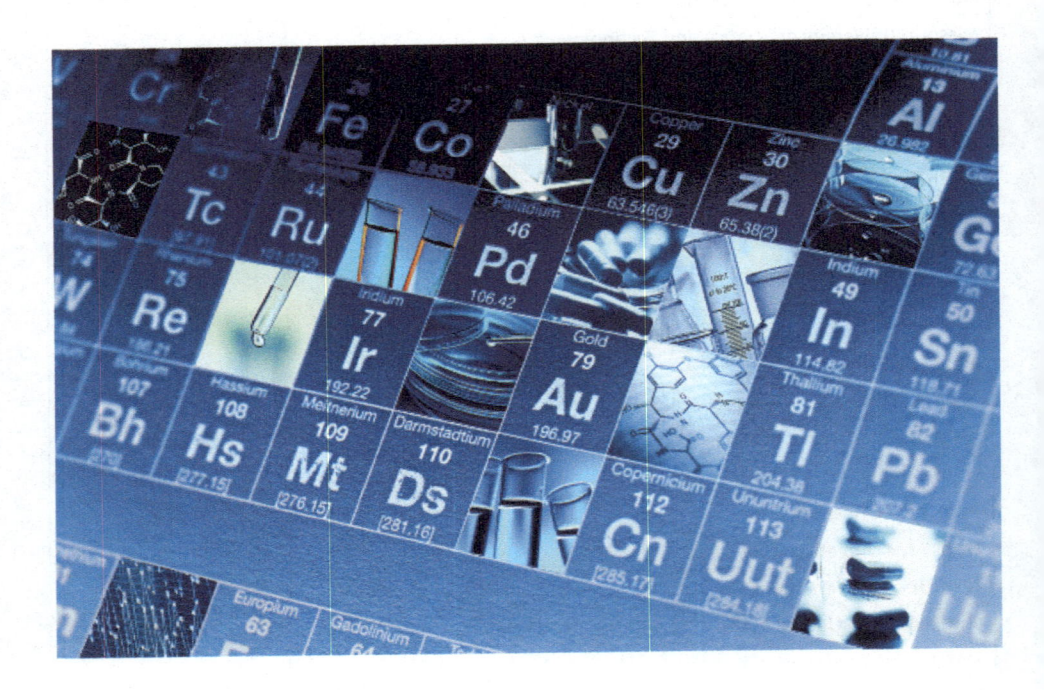

255

JOURNEY TO ART, DANCE, MUSIC, THEATRE, FILM, AND FASHION SERIES

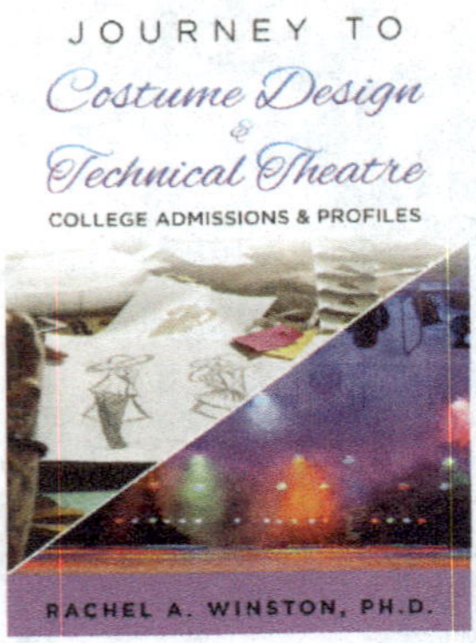

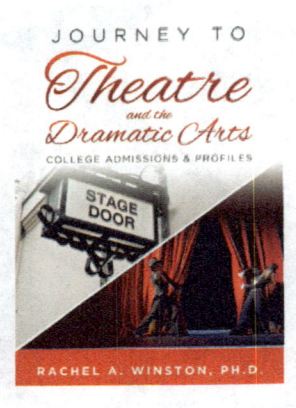

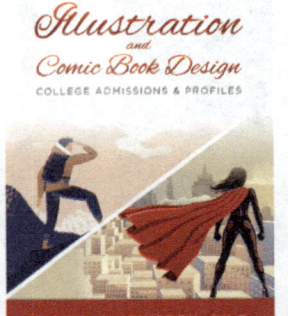

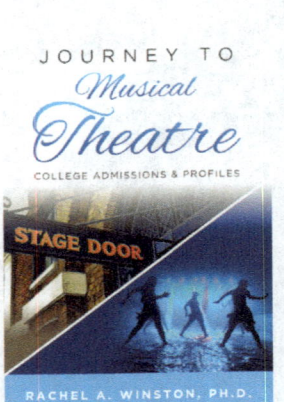

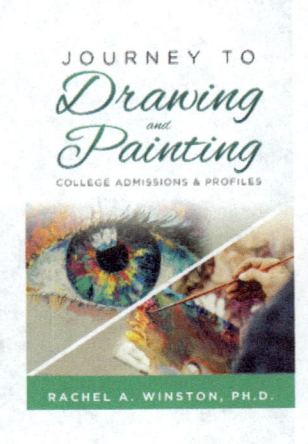

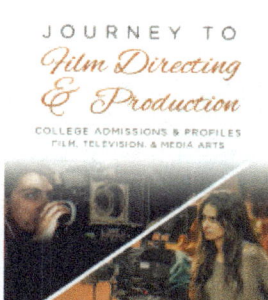

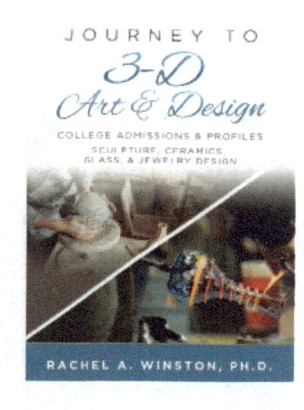

Live your dreams today remembering that discipline is the bridge between dreams and achievement!

"We believe in the American Dream that all people rich or poor can go as far in life as their talents and persistence will take them."
– Lizard Publishing Vision

At Lizard, we help you make your dreams come true.

CONTACT INFORMATION

Phone: 949-833-7706

E-mail: collegeguide@yahoo.com

Website: collegelizard.com and Lizard-publishing.com

COMPREHENSIVE HEALTH CARE SERIES

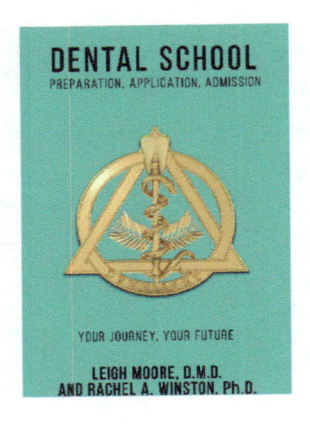

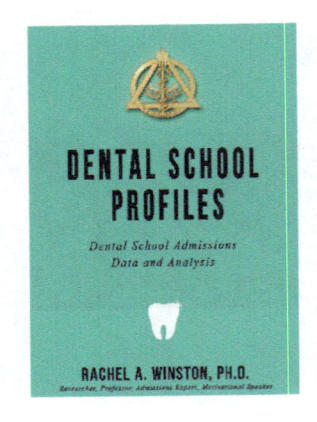

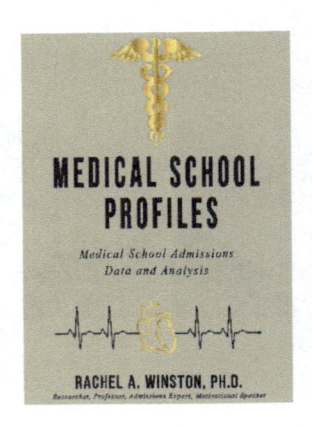

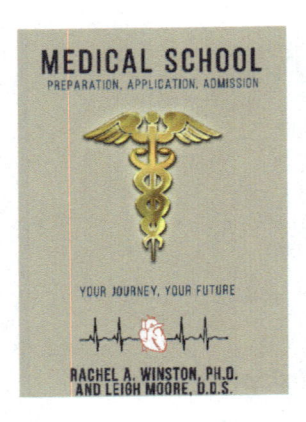

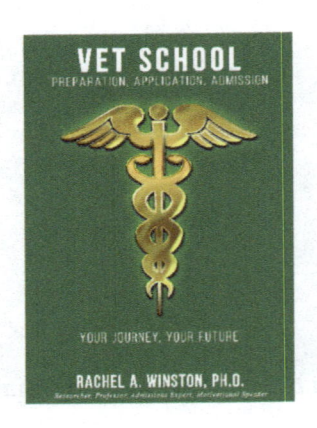

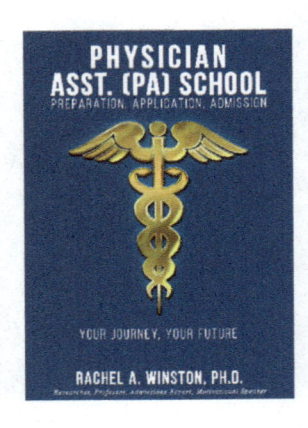

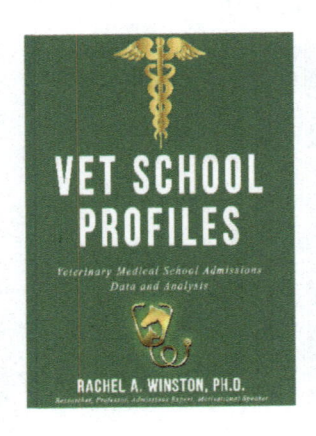

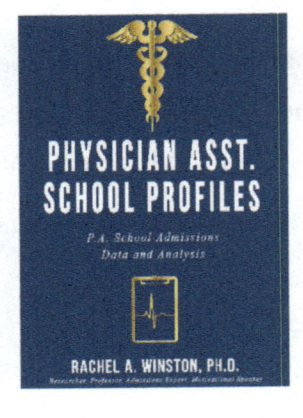

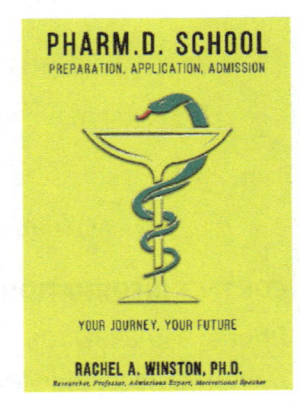

PHARM.D.
SCHOOL PROFILES
Pharmacy School Admissions
Data and Analysis
RACHEL A. WINSTON, PH.D.
Researcher, Professor, Admissions Expert, Motivational Speaker

OSTEO SCHOOL
PROFILES
Osteopathic Medical School Admissions
Data and Analysis
RACHEL A. WINSTON, PH.D.

Is Medical School Your Goal?
FROM
HIGH SCHOOL
TO
MEDICAL SCHOOL
The Ultimate Guide to
BS/MD Programs
Rachel A. Winston, Ph.D.

OSTEOPATHIC
MEDICAL SCHOOL
PREPARATION, APPLICATION, ADMISSION
YOUR JOURNEY, YOUR FUTURE
RACHEL A. WINSTON, PH.D.

COMPREHENSIVE ENGINEERING SERIES

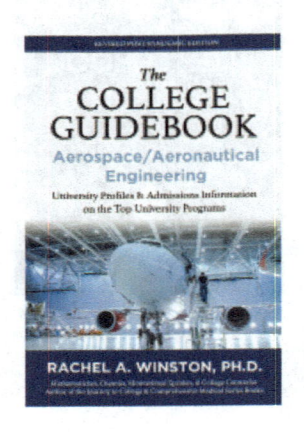

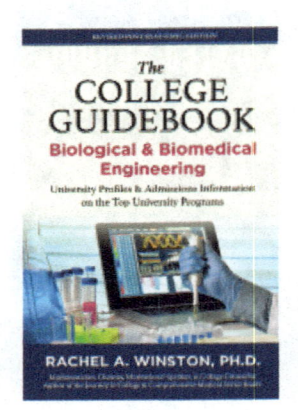

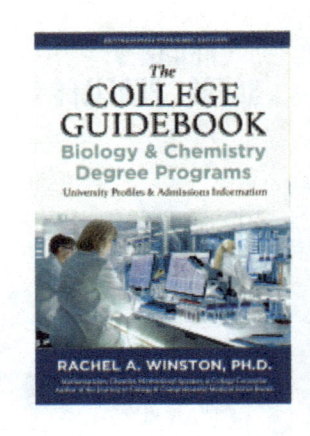

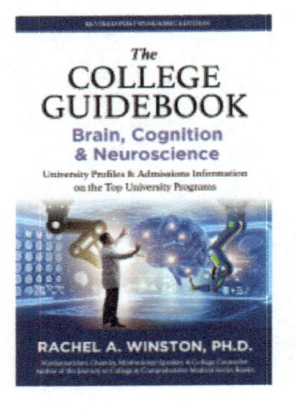

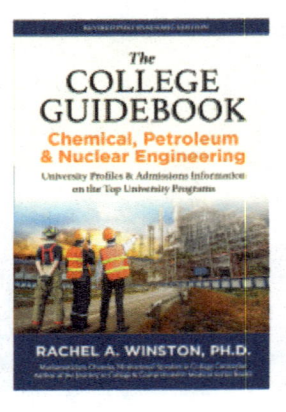

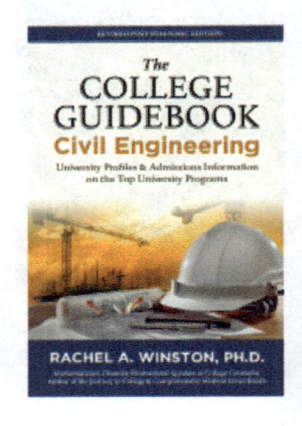

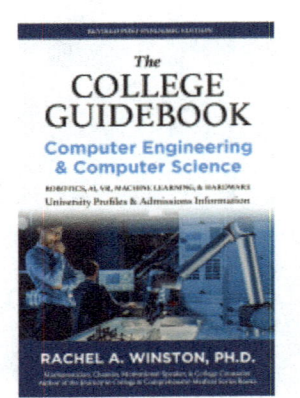

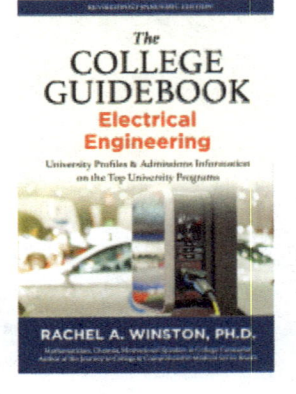

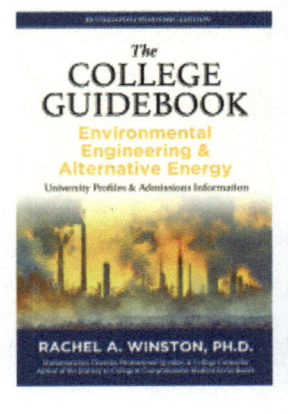

261

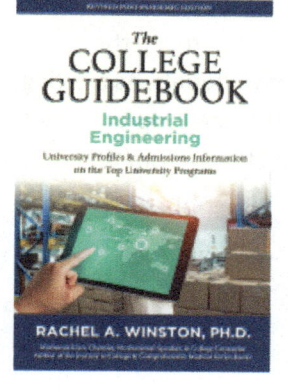

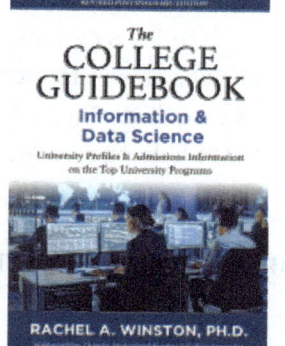

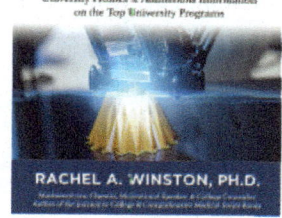

This comprehensive healthcare series is designed in full color to aid the growing number of applicants seeking clear, comprehensive materials. As a college admissions expert and former UCLA College Counseling Certificate Program faculty member, Dr. Winston is dedicated to helping students obtain the information they need.

FOR MORE INFORMATION

bsmdguide.com

medschoolexpert.com

Purchase books at Lizard-publishing.com

SERVICES OFFERED BY LIZARD EDUCATION:

- College Counseling
- Admissions News/Resources
- Essay Support and Editing
- Interview Preparation
- Road Trips to Visit Colleges
- Career Planning/Majors/Resumes
- BS/MD, BS/DO, BS/JD, BS/DDS
- Medical School
- Graduate School (Masters & Doctorate)
- Film Studio and Editing
- Portfolio Assistance/SlideRoom
- Athletics Recruiting/Highlight Films
- International Admissions/Visa/TOEFL
- Financial Aid and Scholarships
- UCs, Ivy Leagues, and Colleges Nationwide
- Book Publishing
- Engineering, Robotics, STEM
- Art Portfolios

Email: collegeguide@yahoo.com

Website: collegelizard.com

LIZARD

INDEX

A

ABET 6, 56, 111, 234

Accreditation 56

ACT 74, 82, 84, 87, 132, 133, 134, 135, 136, 137, 164, 165, 166, 184, 185, 186, 204, 205, 206

Admit Rate 59, 74, 132, 133, 134, 135, 136, 137, 164, 165, 166, 184, 185, 186, 204, 205, 206, 228, 229, 230

Alabama A&M University 235

Alfred University 235

American Society of Mechanical Engineers 6, 58, 102, 111, 147, 152, 155, 156, 158, 174, 175, 189, 191, 193, 212

American University 237

Anderson University 235

Andrews University 45

Angelo State University 235

Application vii, 25, 28, 74, 75, 82, 85, 86, 87, 88, 89, 90, 91, 92, 102, 153, 157, 160, 174, 201, 210, 213, 215, 216, 219

AP tests 87, 90

Architecture 35, 37, 41, 50, 52, 53, 108, 112, 129

Arcosanti 35

Arizona State 203, 204, 225, 230, 232, 235

Arkansas State 235

Arkansas Tech University 235

Articulation 74

Artificial Intelligence 20, 138, 140, 146, 147, 148, 171, 179, 193, 216

ASME 6, 58, 102, 103, 111, 148, 171, 172, 177, 199, 212

Associate of Arts 64, 65, 67, 68

Associate of Science 64, 67, 68

Auburn University 35, 235
Augmented reality 7, 25, 28

B

Bachelor of Arts 64
Bachelor of Engineering 64, 148
Bachelor of Fine Arts 64
Bachelor of Science 64
Baylor University 235
Beaver Works 44
Benedictine College 235
Boeing 36, 50, 58, 178, 220
Boise State University 235
Boston College 43, 59
Boston University 43, 131, 132, 138, 225, 229, 232, 235
Bradley University 235
Bridges 201
Brigham Young University 235
Brown University 50, 131, 137, 161, 226, 229, 235, 237
Bucknell University 131, 135, 153, 226, 229, 231, 235
Bureau of Labor Statistics 108, 112

C

CAD 7, 28, 40, 44, 155, 177
California Baptist University 235
California Institute of Technology 203, 204, 209, 223, 225, 229, 230, 235
California Polytechnic State University 203, 204, 210, 225, 232, 235
California State Polytechnic University, Pomona 235
California State University 235
Cal Poly SLO 204, 210, 229, 232
Candidate Reply Date 74, 89
Canon 36, 46
Carbon-neutral 119
Career ii, v, vi, 12, 27, 43, 53, 58, 67, 87, 92, 94, 102, 112, 113, 118, 119, 121, 122, 123, 142, 151, 211, 220
Carnegie Mellon University 49, 56, 131, 135, 223, 226, 229, 231, 235

Case Western Reserve 163, 166, 179, 226, 229, 231, 235
Catholic University 38, 235
Cedarville University 235
Central Connecticut State 235
Central Michigan University 235
Checklist 74
Chico 235
China 57, 157, 201
Christian Brothers University 235
Citadel 235
City University of New York 236
Clarkson University 236
Class Rank 74
Clemson University 50, 236
CLEP 68, 74
Cleveland State University 236
Coalition Application 74, 85, 86
Code Breakers 43
College credit 41, 43, 74
College Fair 87
College of New Jersey 236
Colorado School of Mines 203, 206, 225, 230, 231, 236
Colorado State University 236
Columbia University 46, 131, 134, 147, 226, 229, 231, 236
Common Application 75, 85
Computer Aided Design 177
Consumer Electronics Show 27
Cooper Union 47, 131, 134, 148, 226, 229, 230, 236
Cornell University 47, 56, 57, 131, 134, 149, 223, 226, 229, 231, 236
Corning 47, 48, 50
COSMOS 36
COVID-19 113
Creative Writing Institute 46
CSS Profile 87, 88, 98, 138

CSSSA 36
CWRU 179

D

Deferred Admission 75
Deferred Enrollment 75
Delft Univ. of Tech 57
Diesel 6, 119
DigiPen 53
Digital Storytelling 38, 50
Doctor of Philosophy 65
Domestic Student 75
Drexel University 49, 131, 135, 155, 226, 230, 231, 236
Drones 144, 177
Duke University 183, 185, 193, 226, 229, 231, 236
Dunwoody College of Technology 236

E

Early Action 75, 84, 88, 133
Early Decision 75, 84, 88, 132, 133, 164, 165, 184, 185, 204, 205
Eastern Michigan University 236
Eastern Washington University 236
Edwards 36, 52, 219
Embry-Riddle 236
Emory University 40
EMPLOYMENT OUTLOOK 107
England 5, 6, 157, 244
environment 7, 13, 14, 18, 27, 40, 50, 53, 114, 118
Environmental Protection Agency 8
EPFL 57
Essay 85, 86, 197
ETH Zurich 57
Euclid 30, 166, 179

F

FAFSA 88, 98, 99, 102, 138, 153, 158, 215, 216
Fairfield University 236

Fee 87
Financial Aid 76, 138, 139, 140, 141, 142, 143, 144, 145, 146, 147, 148, 149, 150, 151, 152, 153, 154, 155, 156, 157, 158, 159, 160, 161, 168, 169, 170, 171, 172, 173, 174, 175, 176, 177, 178, 179, 180, 181, 188, 189, 190, 191, 192, 193, 194, 195, 196, 197, 198, 199, 200, 201, 208, 209, 210, 211, 212, 213, 214, 215, 216, 217, 218, 219, 220, 257
First-Generation 76, 104
Florida A&M 236
Florida Atlantic University 39, 236
Florida Institute of Technology 183, 184, 188, 225, 230, 231, 236
Florida International University 236
Florida Polytechnic University 236
Florida State 236
France 6, 57, 157, 190, 197, 214
Franklin W. Olin College of Engineering 236
Fresno 235
Fullerene 17
Fullerton vi, 235

G

Galileo 31
Gannon University 236
George Mason University 236
Georgetown University 38
George Washington University 38, 236
Georgia Institute of Technology 40, 56, 183, 184, 223, 225, 229, 231, 236
Georgia Southern University 236
Georgia Tech 57, 59, 74, 100, 183, 184, 190, 223
Getty Museum 37
Goddard Space Flight Center 42
Gonzaga University 236
GPA 74, 76, 132, 133, 134, 135, 136, 137, 164, 165, 166, 184, 185, 186, 188, 204, 205, 206
Grace College 236
Grand Canyon University 236
Grand Valley State University 236
Graphene 16, 17

Grove City College 236
GWU vi, 59

H

Harding University 236
Harvard University 43, 57, 131, 132, 139, 225, 229, 231, 236
Hofstra University 237
Hong Kong Univ. 57
Howard University 237

I

Idaho State University 237
Illinois Institute of Technology 41, 237
Imperial College London 57
India 220
Indiana Institute of Technology 237
Indiana University 237
Indus Valley 4
In-State 76
Inter American University 237
Interlochen 45
International 60, 61, 76, 139, 141, 145, 148, 152, 156, 158, 160, 171, 176, 193, 201, 211, 213, 236, 257
Internet of Things 184, 188, 192
Iowa State University 42, 237
Italy 57, 157, 201

J

Jacobs Institute 47
John Brown University 237
Johns Hopkins University 183, 184, 191, 225, 229, 231, 237
Journalism 103, 195

K

Kennesaw State University 237
Kettering University 163, 165, 173, 225, 230, 236
Kevlar 18

King's College 237
Korea Adv. Inst. of Sci. & Tech. 57
KTH Royal Inst. of Tech. 57
KU Leuven 57

L

Lafayette College 131, 136, 156, 226, 229, 231, 237
Laguna College of Art & Design 37
Lake Superior State University 237
Lamar University 237
Lawrence Technological University 237
LEED 16, 181
legacy 3, 76
Lego 30, 144, 172
Lehigh University 131, 136, 157, 226, 230, 231, 237
LeTourneau University 237
Liberty University 237
Licensure 9, 13, 111, 112
LinkedIn 121, 123, 124
Lipscomb University 237
LMU 203, 204, 212, 225, 230, 231
Long Beach 235
Los Angeles 37, 38, 57, 60, 74, 203, 204, 205, 206, 212, 216, 217, 225, 229, 232, 235, 237, 240, 242
Louisiana State 237
Louisiana Tech 237
Lower Division 76
Loyola Marymount 203, 204, 212, 225, 230, 231, 237

M

machine learning 20, 25
Manhattan College 237
Maritime 146, 160, 189, 235, 239
Marquette University 237
Marshall University 237
Maryland Institute College of Art 42
Massachusetts College of Art & Design 43

Massachusetts Institute of Technology 44, 131, 132, 223, 225, 229, 231
Master of Architecture 64
Master of Arts 64
Master of Design 64
Master of Education 64
Master of Engineering 64, 148, 169, 180
Master of Fine Arts 65
McGill University 57
Merit-based 98, 101, 138, 139, 142, 143, 146, 152, 159, 160, 169, 171, 190, 191, 199, 209, 213
Merrimack College 237
Metaverse 3, 26, 118
Mexico 44, 128, 197, 238, 242
Miami University 237
Michigan State 163, 165, 174, 225, 230, 232, 237
Michigan Technological 163, 175, 225, 237
Midwest 128, 169
Midwestern State University 237
Milligan University 237
Milwaukee School of Engineering 237
Minnesota State 237
Mississippi State University 237
MIT 44, 57, 59, 74, 90, 131, 132, 140, 223, 225, 229, 231
MITES 44
Montana State University 238
Montana Technological University 238

N

NAACP 34, 104
Nano 141, 143, 149, 161, 181, 185, 190, 196, 197
Nanyang Technological Univ. 57
NASA 37, 42, 52, 53, 140, 152, 154, 176, 179, 195, 209, 212, 214
National Air and Space Museum 39
National Center for Educational Statistics 30, 68, 69
National College Fair 87
National Institute of Health 35, 42, 44, 45, 48
National Security Agency 38, 40, 42, 51

National Univ. of Singapore 57
Naval Postgraduate School 238
NCES ii, 30, 68, 69
Need-Aware 76
Need-based 37, 69, 98, 99, 139, 141, 142, 146, 154, 156, 169, 191, 192, 200, 209, 216
Need-blind 140, 145
Networking 119, 120, 122, 144, 216
New Jersey Institute of Technology 46, 238
New Mexico Institute 238
New Mexico State University 238
New York Institute of Technology 238
New York University 47, 238
NOAA 8, 9
Nobel Prize 17, 18, 139
North Carolina State 183, 185, 194, 226, 230, 232, 238
North Dakota State 238
Northeast 128, 130
Northeastern University 131, 132, 141, 225, 229, 231, 238
Northern Arizona University 238
Northern Illinois University 238
Northridge 235
Northrop Grumman 52
Northwestern University 41, 57, 163, 164, 168, 225, 229, 231, 238
Norwich University 6, 238

O

Oakland University 238
Ohio Northern University 238
Ohio State University 163, 166, 180, 226, 230, 232, 238
Ohio University 238
Oklahoma Christian University 238
Oklahoma State University 238
Old Dominion University 238
Olin 131, 132, 142, 149, 188, 217, 225, 229, 230, 236
Open Admissions 76
Oregon Institute of Technology 238

Oregon State University 238
Otis College of Art and Design 37

P

PANDEMIC 107
Parker Hannifin 37
Parsons School of Design 47
Pennsylvania State University 49, 131, 136, 158, 226, 230, 232, 238
Placement Tests 76
Point Park University 238
Politecnico de Milano 57
Politecnico de Torino 57
Polytechnic University - San Juan 238
Portal 76, 210
Portland State University 238
Prairie View A&M University 238
President's Volunteer Service Award 77
Princeton University 57, 131, 133, 145, 225, 229, 231, 238
Professional Engineering 13
PROMYS 43
Puerto Rico 237, 238, 240, 242
Purdue University 56, 57, 163, 164, 170, 223, 225, 230, 232, 238

Q

Quinnipiac University 239

R

Regional Representative 88
Registrar 77
Regular Decision 84, 88
REJECTION 91
Rensselaer Polytechnic Institute 131, 134, 150, 226, 230, 231, 239
Research in Science & Engineering 43, 139
Research Science Institute 44
Residency 60, 77
Restricted Early Action 84
Resume 87

Rhode Island School of Design 50
Rice University 183, 185, 196, 226, 229, 231, 239
Ringling College of Art and Design 39
RISE 43
Rochester Institute of Technology 239
Rockhurst University 239
Rolling Admission 77
Rose-Hulman 163, 164, 171, 225, 230, 231, 239
Rowan University 239
RSI 44
Rutgers University 239

S

Sacramento 36, 235
Saginaw Valley State 239
Saint Louis University 239
Saint Martin's University 239
San Diego State University 239
San Francisco State University 239
San Jose State University 239
Santa Clara University 37, 203, 205, 213, 225, 230, 231, 239
SAT 74, 82, 84, 87, 132, 133, 134, 135, 136, 137, 164, 165, 166, 184, 185, 186, 204, 205, 206
Savannah College of Art & Design 40
scholarships 37, 41, 43, 46, 69, 76, 87, 90, 98, 99, 100, 101, 102, 103, 104, 105, 138, 141, 144, 146, 147, 149, 150, 151, 152, 153, 154, 155, 156, 157, 159, 160, 161, 169, 170, 171, 172, 173, 174, 177, 179, 180, 181, 189, 190, 193, 194, 197, 198, 199, 200, 208, 209, 210, 211, 212, 214, 216, 217, 218, 219
School of the Art Institute 41
SCI-Arc 37
Science and Engineering Apprenticeship Program 35, 37, 38, 39, 40, 42, 43, 45, 46, 48, 49, 50, 52, 53
SEAP 35, 37, 38, 39, 40, 42, 43, 45, 46, 48, 49, 52, 53
Seattle Pacific University 239
Seattle University 239
Shanghai Jiao Tong Univ. 57
SOCAPA 37, 47, 52

Sotheby's 47
South Dakota School of Mines 239
South Dakota State University 239
Southern Illinois University 41, 239
Southern Methodist University 183, 185, 197, 226, 230, 231, 239
Southern New Hampshire University 239
Southern University 236, 239
Southern Utah University 239
SpaceX 37, 40, 51, 141, 148, 196
Spider silk 18
Spotify 48
St. Ambrose University 239
Stamps 45, 100, 172, 190
STANDARDIZED TESTING 82
Stanford University 37, 38, 56, 57, 203, 205, 214, 223, 225, 229, 231, 239
St. Cloud State 239
Steam 5, 6
STEM 35, 36, 37, 40, 44, 47, 49, 51, 64, 65, 143, 148, 152, 157, 158, 161, 169, 173, 175, 179, 180, 192, 199, 212, 213, 214, 257
Stevens Institute of Technology 131, 133, 146, 225, 230, 231, 239
Stony Brook University 239
Student Aid Report 88
Summer Melt 77
Summer Programs 53, 87, 145, 147, 209
Summer Science Program 44
SUNY 151, 239, 240
SUNY, Polytechnic Institute 239
Syracuse University 48, 101, 131, 134, 151, 226, 230, 231, 239

T

Tarleton State University 239
Technical Univ. of Denmark 57
Temple University 49, 240
Tennessee State University 240
Tennessee Technological University 240
Tesla 38, 51, 118
Texas A&M University 56, 183, 186, 198, 223, 226, 230, 232, 240, 244

Texas Tech 51, 240
Thomas Jefferson University 240
Tokyo Inst. of Technology 57
Transfer 25, 65, 68, 74, 179
Trine University 240
Tsinghua University 57
Tufts University 45, 131, 133, 143, 225, 229, 231, 240
Tumor 17
Tuskegee University 35, 240

U

UCLA v, vi, 38, 81, 205, 216, 257
UIUC 164, 169, 223
Union College 240
Universidad Ana. G. Mendez 240
University at Buffalo 240
University of Akron 240
University of Alabama 240
University of Alaska 240
University of Arizona 240
University of Arkansas 35, 240
University of Bridgeport 240
University of California 56, 57, 60, 76, 85, 86, 88, 203, 205, 215, 216, 223, 225, 229, 232, 240
University of California, Berkeley 57, 203, 205, 215, 223, 225, 229, 232, 240
University of California, Davis 240
University of California, Irvine 240
University of California, Los Angeles 203, 205, 216, 225, 229, 232, 240
University of California, Merced 240
University of California, Riverside 240
University of California, San Diego 240
University of California, Santa Barbara 240
University of Cambridge 57
University of Central Florida 240
University of Central Oklahoma 241
University of Chicago vi, 42
University of Cincinnati 241

University of Colorado 203, 206, 225, 230, 232, 241
University of Connecticut 241
University of Dayton 241
University of Delaware 241
University of Denver 241
University of Detroit 241
University of Evansville 241
University of Florida 40, 183, 184, 189, 225, 229, 232, 241
University of Georgia 241
University of Hartford 241
University of Hawaii at Manoa 241
University of Houston 52, 241
University of Idaho 241
University of Illinois 41, 56, 74, 163, 164, 169, 223, 225, 230, 232, 241
University of Indianapolis 241
University of Iowa 241
University of Jamestown 241
University of Kansas 241
University of Kentucky 241
University of Louisiana 241
University of Louisville 241
University of Maine 241
University of Maryland 43, 183, 184, 192, 225, 230, 232, 241
University of Massachusetts 45, 241
University of Memphis 50, 241
University of Miami 40, 242
University of Michigan 45, 56, 74, 163, 165, 176, 223, 225, 229, 232, 242
University of Minnesota 163, 165, 177, 225, 230, 232, 242
University of Mississippi 242
University of Missouri 46, 242
University of Mount Union 242
University of Nebraska 46, 242
University of Nevada 242
University of New Hampshire 242
University of New Haven 242
University of New Mexico 242
University of New Orleans 242

University of North Carolina 242
University of North Dakota 242
University of North Florida 242
University of Notre Dame 42, 163, 164, 172, 225, 229, 231, 242
University of Oklahoma 49, 242
University of Oxford 57
University of Pittsburgh 242
University of Portland 242
University of Puerto Rico 242
University of Rhode Island 242
University of Rochester 131, 135, 152, 226, 229, 231, 242
University of San Diego 242
University of South Alabama 242
University of South Carolina 242
University of Southern California 203, 206, 217, 225, 229, 232, 242
University of Southern Indiana 242
University of Southern Maine 242
University of South Florida 242
University of St. Thomas 243
University of Tennessee 50, 243
University of Texas vi, 51, 52, 56, 101, 183, 186, 199, 223, 226, 229, 232, 243
University of Texas - Austin 243
University of Texas - El Paso 243
University of Texas, Permian Basin 243
University of Texas Rio Grande Valley 243
University of Texas - San Antonio 243
University of the District of Columbia 241
University of the Pacific 242
University of Tokyo 57
University of Toledo 243
University of Tulsa 243
University of Utah 243
University of Vermont 243
University of Virginia 183, 186, 200, 226, 229, 232, 243
University of Washington 53, 203, 206, 220, 226, 230, 232, 243
University of West Florida 243
University of Wisconsin 53, 163, 166, 181, 226, 230, 232, 243

University of Wyoming 243
Univ. of Manchester 57
Univ. of New South Wales 57
Univ. of Toronto 57
Upper Division 77
Urbanframe 44
US Air Force Academy 240
USC 38, 60, 206, 217
US Coast Guard Academy 240
US Military Academy 240
US Naval Academy 240
US News & World Report 56
Utah State University 243
Utah Valley University 243
UT Austin 101, 102, 183, 186, 226, 229, 232

V

Valparaiso University 243
Vanderbilt University 183, 185, 195, 226, 229, 231, 243
Vaughn College of Aeronautics and Technology 243
Villanova University 131, 137, 160, 226, 229, 231, 243
Virginia Commonwealth University 52, 243
Virginia Military Institute 243
Virginia Tech 52, 186, 201, 226, 230, 232, 243
Virtual Reality 3, 20, 40
Visit 38, 87, 88, 91, 172, 179, 200, 201
Volunteer Service Award 77

W

Waitlist 77
Waivers 87
Washington State University 243
Wayne State University 244
Weber State University 244
Wellesley College 45
Wentworth Institute of Technology 244
Western Illinois University 244

Western Kentucky University 244
Western Michigan University 244
Western New England University 244
West Texas A&M University 244
West Virginia University 244
Wichita State University 244
Widener University 244
Wilkes University 244
Women's Technology Program 44
Worcester Polytechnic Institute 131, 133, 144, 225, 230, 231, 244
Wright State University 244

Y

Yale University 244
Yield 77
Youngstown State University 244
Youth Design Boston 45

Made in the USA
Las Vegas, NV
31 October 2023